W9-CDV-018

Contents

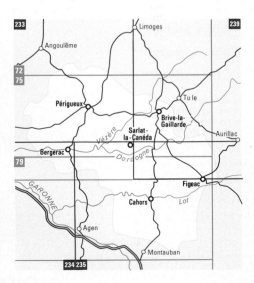

*The **Michelin maps**
you will need
with this Guide
are:*

r. 1

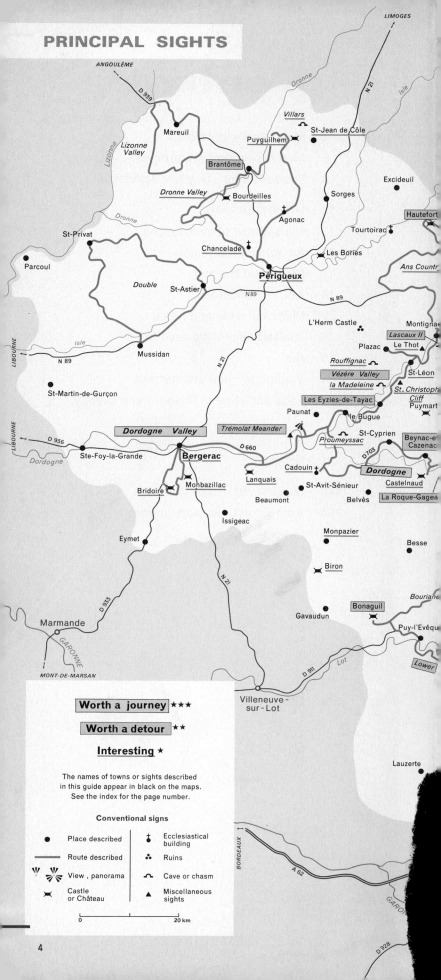

PRINCIPAL SIGHTS

4

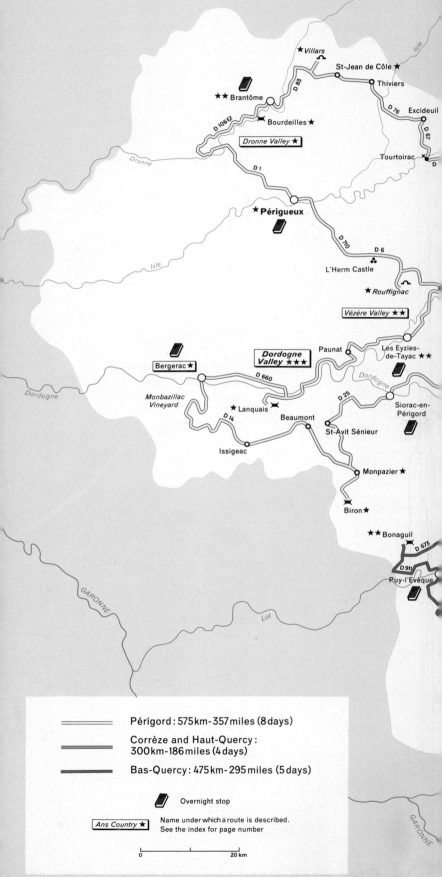

★ Villars

St-Jean de Côle ★

Thiviers

D 83

★★ Brantôme

D 76

Excideuil

D 106 E2

★ Bourdeilles ★

D 67

Dronne Valley ★

Tourtoirac ×

Dronne

D 1

D

★ Périgueux

D 710

D 6

Isle

L'Herm Castle ⚶

Rouffignac

★ Rouffignac

Vézère Valley ★★

Dordogne
Valley ★★★

Paunat

Les Eyzies-
de-Tayac ★★

Bergerac ★

D 660

Dordogne

Monbazillac
Vineyard

D 25

Siorac-en-
Périgord

★ Lanquais

Dordogne

D 14

Beaumont

Issigeac

St-Avit Sénieur

Monpazier ★

Biron ★

★★ Bonaguil

D 673

D 911

Puy-l'Evêque

GARONNE

Lot

GARONNE

Périgord: 575 km - 357 miles (8 days)

Corrèze and Haut-Quercy:
300 km - 186 miles (4 days)

Bas-Quercy: 475 km - 295 miles (5 days)

Overnight stop

Ans Country ★   Name under which a route is described.
See the index for page number

0   20 km

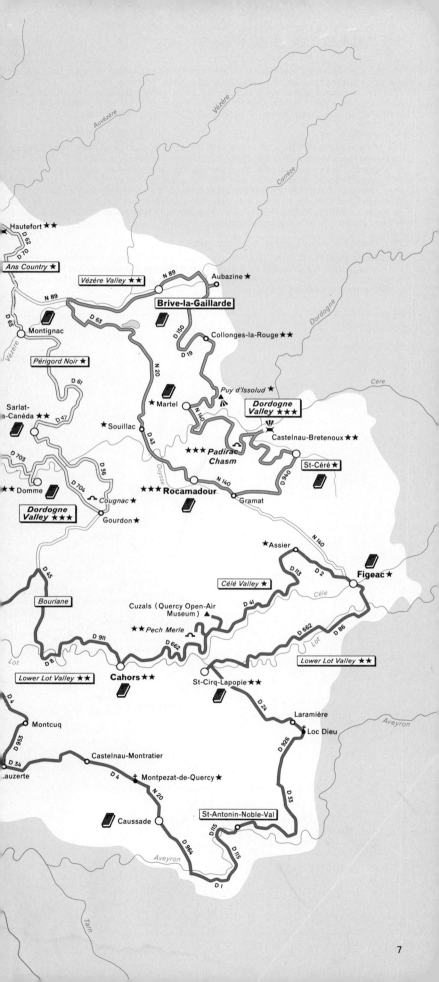

Hautefort ★★

Ans Country ★

Vézère Valley ★★

N 89

Aubazine ★

Brive-la-Gaillarde

Montignac

Collonges-la-Rouge ★★

Périgord Noir ★

★ Martel

Puy d'Issolud ★

Dordogne Valley ★★★

Sarlat-
la-Canéda ★★

★ Souillac

Castelnau-Bretenoux ★★

★★★ *Padirac Chasm*

St-Céré ★

★★ Domme

Dordogne Valley ★★★

Cougnac ★

★★★ **Rocamadour**

Gramat

Gourdon ★

★ Assier

Célé Valley ★

Figeac ★

Bouriane

Cuzals (Quercy Open-Air Museum) ▲

★★ *Pech Merle*

Lower Lot Valley ★★

Lower Lot Valley ★★ **Cahors** ★★

St-Cirq-Lapopie ★★

Laramière

Loc Dieu

Montcuq

Castelnau-Montratier

Lauzerte

Montpezat-de-Quercy ★

St-Antonin-Noble-Val

Caussade

PLACES TO STAY

The mention **Facilities** under the individual headings or after place names in the body of the guide refers to the information given on this page.

The map below indicates towns selected for the accommodation and leisure facilities which they offer to the holidaymaker. To help you plan your route and choose your hotel, restaurant or camping site consult the following Michelin publications.

Accommodation

The **Michelin Red Guide France** of hotels and restaurants and the **Michelin Guide Camping Caravaning France** are annual publications, which present a selection of hotels, restaurants and camping sites. The final choice is based on regular on-the-spot enquiries and visits. Both the hotels and camping sites are classified according to the standard of comfort of their amenities. Establishments which are notable for their fortunate setting, their decor, their quiet and secluded location and their warm welcome are distinguished by special symbols. The Michelin Red Guide France also gives the address and telephone number of local tourist offices and tourist information centres.

Planning your route, sports and recreation

The **Michelin Maps,** at a scale of 1:200 000, cover the whole of France. For those concerning the region see the layout diagram on page 3. In addition to a wealth of road information, these maps indicate beaches, bathing spots, swimming pools, golf courses, racecourses, air fields, panoramas and scenic routes.

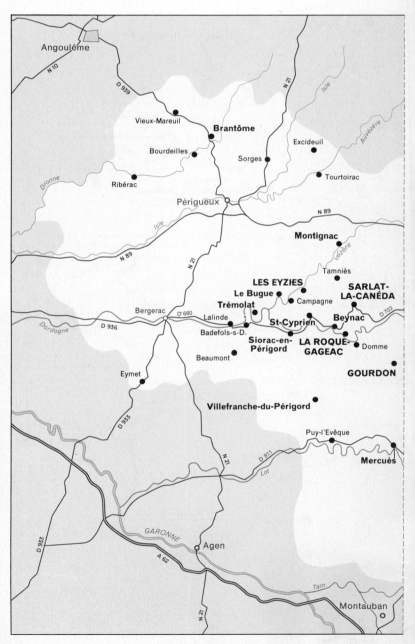

OUTDOOR ACTIVITIES

For addresses and other details see the chapter Practical Information at the end of the guide.

Rambling. – Many long-distance footpaths (Sentiers de Grande Randonnée) enable ramblers to discover the region covered in this guide. Made evident by red and white lines, these footpaths crisscross Périgord and Quercy.

The **GR 6** (Alps-Océan) passes by Figeac, Rudelle, Rocamadour, Souillac, Sarlat, Les Eyzies, Lalinde, Lanquais and Monbazillac.

The **GR 65** (Le Puy-Santiago de Compostela, one of the ways of the famous pilgrimage) follows the Lot Valley to Cahors then branches off southwards to Moissac. One of these trails which branches off, **GR 651**, goes along Célé Valley.

The **GR 36** (Manche-Pyrénées) goes into Périgord northwest via Mareuil, follows the Dronne Valley (Brantôme, Bourdeilles), crosses Chancelade and Périgueux and then goes deeply into Périgord Noir (Rouffignac, Les Eyzies, Beynac). From there the footpath goes on to Cahors via St-Avit-Sénieur, Monpazier, the castles of Biron and Bonaguil, and the Lot Valley.

The **GR 646** links the GR 36 and the GR 6 by following Isle Valley.

The **GR 652** and **64** enable you to discover Bouriane and the Gramat Causse; the **GR 64A** reveals the Périgord Noir.

The **GR 46** (Limousin-Quercy) follows a north-south route crossing Corrèze (Brive-la-Gaillarde, Turenne, Collonges-la-Rouge), then Quercy (Martel, Carennac, Rocamadour, Labastide-Murat, St-Cirq-Lapopie, St-Antonin-Noble-Val).

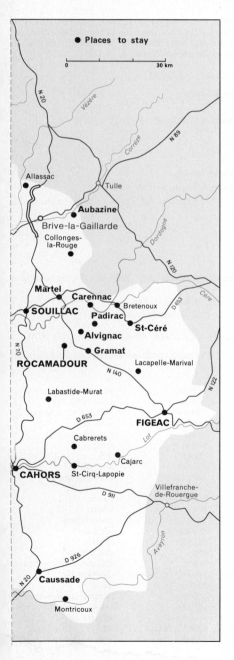

The **GR 461** passes through the prehistoric sites of Lascaux, Régourdou and Le Thot.

Topo Guides give detailed itineraries and useful advice to ramblers. Local short-distance footpaths have also been set up in a number of places in Périgord and Quercy.

Water sports. – The rivers – Dordogne, Vézère, Lot and Célé – play an important role in Périgord and Quercy whether it be geographically, historically, culturally, economically or through sports.

Swimming. – Beaches have been set up along the rivers – but watch out for the current which can be very strong.

Canoe and kayak. – The fast-flowing rivers coming down from Massif Central are perfect for this sport. It is also a pleasant way to discover the numerous castles, châteaux and other sites which are spread along the Périgord and Quercy Valleys.

Sailing and windsurfing. – Several bodies of water allow sailing and especially windsurfing. The most important ones are: Jemaye Lake in Double, Causse Lake near Brive, the reservoirs of Tauriac, Trémolat and Mauzac on the Dordogne and Cajarc and Luzech on the Lot.

Crusing on inland waterways. – Between Luzech and St-Cirq-Lapopie, small houseboats (capacity 4 people), cruise on the Lot River.

Riding holidays. – Several possibilities are offered to lovers of horse-riding.
Trekking through the *causses* is organised by riding centres. For those more daring it is possible to rent horses and set up your own trekking tour following the signposted paths.

Horse-drawn caravan (Roulotte). – This original idea permits you to discover the region slowly, ambling at the slow pace of 15-20km – 9-12 miles a day. The caravans are set up with beds and a kitchen.

Carriage rides (Calèches). – For the lovers of nostalgia and days passed, carriage rides from castle to castle are offered throughout Périgord and Quercy.

Cycling holidays. – Bicycling centres in each *département* have selected thousands of miles of tarred roads and paths which they propose for your cycling holiday through the Lot and Dordogne *départements*. The Dordogne Valley, offering a wealth of tourist sites, is an itinerary particularly appreciated by cyclists.

Speleology. – Périgord and Quercy with their limestone relief are particularly rich in caves and chasms.

Fishing. – Fine stretches of river of first and second categories are offered to fishermen. The Museum-Aquarium at Sarlat *(p 141)* which presents fishing in fresh water, especially on the Dordogne River, will fascinate the fisherman.

Foie-gras weekends. – During the winter a number of Périgord and Quercy farms receive tourists who want to learn to prepare *foie gras* and *confit* the traditional way.

A traditional festival: the Félibrée

Each year in July, a different town of Périgord celebrates the *Félibrée*. The elected town is decorated with thousands of multicoloured paper flowers decorating windows, doors, trees and shrubs forming triumphal arches. The people of Périgord flock from all over the *département* wearing the traditional costume: lace head-dresses, embroidered shawls and long skirts for the women and large black felt hats, full white shirts and black velvet vests for the men.

The queen of the *Félibrée,* surrounded by the *majoral* (a member of the committee) and the keepers of local traditions, receives the keys to the town and makes a speech in *patois* (local dialect).

The crowds then process to mass to the sound of vielles.

They then have a large banquet. Traditionally the meal begins with *chabrol*, a soup of wine and bouillon typical of the southwest, which is served in plates, specially made for the occasion, marked with the name of the *Félibrée* and the date. These plates, which are kept as souvenirs, adorn house interiors and they can also be seen on display in museums of popular arts and traditions as the one in Mussidan *(p 111)*.

LOCAL WORDS AND SPECIAL TERMS

Barri or **barry:** a settlement outside the town walls

Bastide: fortified town of the 13C *(p 32)*

Bolet: porch-staircase characteristic of houses in Quercy *(illustration p 34)*

Cabecou: small goat cheese

Caselle: dry-stone hut

Caveur: truffle hunter

Chabrol: soup with wine added (*see* Félibrée *above*)

Chartreuse: 17 and 18C nobleman or bourgeois house with one storey

Cingle: meander (from the Latin word *cingula* meaning belt), loop or bend found in the Lot and Dordogne Valleys

Cloup: depression in the *causse* (qv)

Cluzeau: shelter dug into the cliff

Cornière or **couvert:** arcaded gallery

Gariotte: dry-stone shelter

Igue: wells or natural chasms in limestone countryside *(p 17)* in Quercy; *edzes* or *eidges* in Périgord

Lauzes: limestone stone slabs used as roofing material *(p 34)*

Segala: a region of poor soil where only rye *(seigle)* would grow

FRENCH WORDS APPEARING ON THE MAPS AND PLANS

For words and expressions used in hotels and restaurants see the annual Michelin Red Guide France.
See also architectural terms pp 28-29.

aéroport	**airport**	grotte	**cave**
ancien (ne)	**former**	halles	**covered market**
barrage	**dam**	hôtel	**mansion, town house**
belvédère	**belvedere**	hôtel de ville	**town hall**
bureau de P.T.T.	**post office**	lycée	**secondary school**
calvaire	**wayside cross**	mont	**mount**
caserne	**barracks**	moulin	**mill**
cathédrale	**cathedral**	musée	**museum**
chapelle	**chapel**	parc des	**exhibition ground**
château	**castle, château**	expositions	
cirque	**amphitheatre**	police	**police**
cité administrative	**municipal or**	pont	**bridge**
	administrative centre	pont tournant	**swing bridge**
donjon	**keep**	remparts	**ramparts**
église	**church**	signal	**beacon**
esplanade	**esplanade**	site	**site, setting**
étang	**pool, pond**	stade	**stadium, sports ground**
foirail	**fair-ground, agricultural**	table d'orientation	**viewing table**
	market place	tour	**tower**
forêt	**forest**	usine	**factory, power station**
gare	**railway station**	vallée	**valley**
gare routière	**bus station**	vers	**towards**
gisement	**deposit**	vieux (vieille)	**old**
gorges	**gorge**	vélodrome	**cycle racing track**

Introduction

APPEARANCE OF THE COUNTRY

FORMATION OF THE LAND

Primary Era. – Beginning about 600 million years ago. It was towards the end of this era that an upheaval of the earth's crust took place: this upheaval or folding movement, known as the "Hercynian fold", the V-shaped appearance of which is shown by dotted lines on the map, resulted in the emergence of a number of high mountains ; notably, the Massif Central, formed by crystalline rocks which were slowly worn down by erosion.

Secondary Era. – Beginning about 200 million years ago. About the middle of this era, there was a slow subsidence of the Hercynian base and the seas then flooded the area. Sedimentary deposits accumulated on the edge of the Massif Central, forming the Quercy *causses* limestone plateaux) during the Jurassic period and then the beds of cretaceous limestone of the Périgord region.

Tertiary Era. – Beginning about 60 million years ago. During this period sideritic deposits (iron carbonate bearing), derived from the Massif Central, covered certain parts of Quercy (Gramat Causse in Bouriane) and argillaceous sands accumulated to the west of Périgord, creating the heathlands dotted with pools (Double and Landais regions).

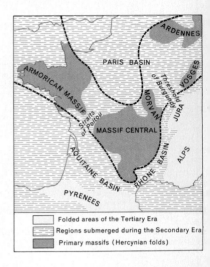

Folded areas of the Tertiary Era
Regions submerged during the Secondary Era
Primary massifs (Hercynian folds)

Quaternary Era. – Beginning about 2 million years ago. It is during this present period that the evolution of man had taken place.
The effects of erosion had by now given the region its present appearance. Rivers emanating from the catchment area of the Massif Central had created the Vézère, Dordogne and Lot Valleys.

COUNTRYSIDE

Périgord

The Périgord is made up of porous and dry cretaceous limestone plateaux deeply cut by valleys which attract the essential economic activity of the region.

Périgord Blanc. – Continuing the Saintonge westwards, the White Périgord (*blanc* = white), aptly named because of its vast chalky, limestone area of white and grey soil, corresponds more or less in area with the Ribéracois.
It is the growing area of Périgord, with cereal crops is added the raising of milking cows and white veals.
Ribérac, the capital of the region, is an important agricultural market centre.

Central Périgord. – Around Périgueux, the countryside of hills and slopes present meadows cut by coppices of oak and chestnut trees. This region is dissected by the rivers of Beauronne, Vern and Dronne, the valley bottoms of which are covered by pastures and arable land; the more important Isle Valley is scattered with small industrial towns like St-Astier with its cement works, Neuvic-sur-Isle with its shoe factories and Mussidan with its factories of textiles and sports clothes.
Périgueux is the chief town and an administrative and commercial centre. Little industry is represented (railway repair workshops, postage stamp printers, construction...).
South of Périgueux around Vergt and Rouffignac, the sideritic deposits which cover the limestone have proven to be a choice soil for the cultivation of strawberries *(p 16)*.
Northeast, Périgord Central lies up against the **Périgord Causse** around Excideuil and Thiviers. This block of Jurassic limestone, carved by the Isle, Auvézère and Loue Valleys, presents the sparse vegetation characteristic of the *causse*.
It is at the foot of the stunted oaks, which are scattered about the countryside, that the most aromatic truffle grows.

Double and Landais. – South of Ribérac, covering the Tertiary deposits coming from the Massif Central, are vast forests made of tall oak and chestnut trees and more and more maritime pines.
The non-porous clay soil of Double is sprinkled with pools. This region, in the past a marshy area, is now a source of timber and known for its good shooting.
The less wild Landais is covered with a forest of maritime pines and at its boundary limits are vineyards and meadows.

Bergeracois. – The region around Bergerac is divided into several sections which all have in common a mild climate favourable to meridional crops.
The Dordogne Valley, very wide at this point, is cut into parcels of land where are harvested tobacco, maize, sunflowers, and cereals, which profit from the fertility of these alluvial deposits.
West of Bergerac, arboriculture dominates. Finally, the slopes are covered with the vineyards of Bergerac and Monbazillac *(p 16)*.
Due to its environment, Bergerac plays an important role in the wine trade and tobacco industry.

Périgord Noir. – Dissected by the Vézère and Dordogne Valleys, this area owes its name, Black Périgord (*noir* = black), to the greater density of trees to be found growing on the sandy soils covering the limestone areas and also to the presence of the holm-oak with its dark, dense foliage, which is prevalent in the Sarladais. The alluvial soil of the valleys, the river courses of which are lined with screens of poplars or willows, supports a variety of crops: wheat, maize, tobacco and walnuts. The lively and prosperous markets sell excellent walnuts, mushrooms, truffles and *foie gras*. Such gastronomic wealth attracts the tourist, he who also appreciates the grottoes with concretions and caves and shelters with sculpted or painted walls. Along the Dordogne and Vézère Rivers, landscapes gentle and harmonious are enhanced by solid golden-coloured limestone buildings roofed with stone slabs *(lauzes)* as seen in Sarlat, capital of Périgord Noir, which has superb examples.

Brive Basin. – The depression of the Brive Basin is a dividing zone between the crystalline escarpments of the Uzerche plateau and the limestone ridges of the Quercy *causses*. It is an area made of sandstone and schists and is drained by the rivers Vézère and Corrèze. In the green valleys cut by screens of poplars, the gentle sloping hills facing the sun specialise in fruit growing. Today Brive is an important centre for the canning of fruit and vegetables. South of Brive, the Corrèze *causse* is covered by large holdings which are used for sheep rearing, renewed exploitation of truffle oak plantations and the fattening of geese for the production of *foie gras*.

Quercy

Formed by a thick layer of Jurassic limestone, with an average height of 300m — 984ft, Quercy is carved by the valleys of the Dordogne, Célé, Lot and Aveyron which delimit the *causses*. The *causses* as a group slope away from the southwestern edges of the Massif Central and down towards the Garonne Valley.

The causses. – This dry land without drainage is dissected by dry valleys (coombs), where fields under grass and a few small holdings of vineyards can be found. The vast area known as the *causses* is covered by juniper, oak and carob trees and sheep graze in pastures divided by stone walls.

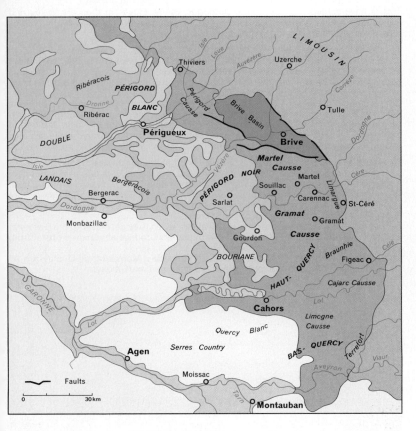

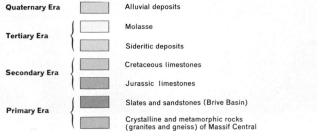

Quaternary Era	Alluvial deposits
Tertiary Era	Molasse
	Sideritic deposits
Secondary Era	Cretaceous limestones
	Jurassic limestones
Primary Era	Slates and sandstones (Brive Basin)
	Crystalline and metamorphic rocks (granites and gneiss) of Massif Central

The Quercy *causses* are an important sheep rearing centre (with some 300 000 head). The plateau sheep or Gramat species is known as the "spectacled" breed, for it has white fleece and black rings round its eyes. It bears high quality wool but it is especially for its fine meat (with very little fat) that this hardy, prolific breed is known. A strict selection is maintained for the ewe-lambs and young rams.

The **Martel Causse**, between the Limousin and the Dordogne Valley, is richer than its neighbours in dry valleys and crops. It bears the name of its main town, Martel, a large agricultural town where sheep skins are sold.

The **Gramat Causse** rising to 350m – 1 148ft offers many natural phenomena (Padirac Chasm) and unusual landscapes. Magnificent canyons break the monotonous but grand horizons of this enormous block of striated limestone 50km – 31 miles wide; in the north lie the Ouysse and Alzou Canyons to the cliff face of which clings Rocamadour; in the south the much longer Célé Canyon. Between the narrow gashes of the Alzou and the Célé lies the arid **Braunhie** (pronounced Brogne – rhyming with Dordogne), a region riddled with caves and ravines. The towns of Gramat and Labastide-Murat have suffered from the rural exodus.

The **Cajarc Causse**, a low-lying plateau, is hemmed in by the banks of the Célé and Lot Rivers, the meanders of which are richly cultivated.

The **Limogne Causse**, with its drier climate, has a very different appearance. Bordered by the valley of the Lot, the plateau is dotted with dolmens and megaliths, which appear amidst the clumps of white truffle oaks, the juniper shrubs and the fields of lavender. Here and there are to be found the curious shepherds' shelters built beside old vineyards, known as *gariottes (qv)*.

There are few big towns, although Limogne-en-Quercy and Lalbenque remain the busiest agricultural centres.

The valleys. – Cutting deeply into the hard limestone, the rivers have carved their valleys, shaping meanders which enlargen as the valley broadens to the point that they become *cingles* – loops in the river – which become wider.

These valleys of the Dordogne, Célé and Lot have been inhabited since prehistoric times. They are laid out with oppidums, châteaux and castles showing the role of these valleys in the region's history. Today, they are covered with rich crops producing maize, vineyards (with the Cahors vineyard in the Lot Valley – *qv*) and orchards.

Towns have settled: Souillac in the Dordogne Valley, Figeac in the Célé Valley and Cahors in a meander of the Lot. Cahors, the *Préfecture* of the Lot *département*, holds mostly an administrative and commercial role.

The limits of Haut-Quercy. – To the east, a fertile area, the **Limargue** and **Terrefort**, divides the *causses* from the crystalline land of the Massif Central. The land spread out in basins and over vast plains favours the production of a variety of crops: greengage plums and strawberries between Carennac and St-Céré, vines, walnut and tobacco plantations growing alongside great meadows.

On the other hand, west of the N 20 as far as Périgord, a layer of sand and clay supports heathlands, coppices, and woodlands. This region, **Bouriane**, resembles more its neighbouring Périgord than Quercy. The tapping of maritime pines for the resin, the timber industry and the sale of livestock, chestnut and walnuts form the basis of the region's economy, the capital of which is Gourdon.

Quercy Blanc. – Southwest of the Lot Valley and Cahors, the Jurassic limestone disappear under the tertiary limestone creating unusual landscapes, *planhès*, vast undulating white areas which have given the region its name White Quercy (*blanc* = white). These plateaux are cut into narrow ridges, *serres*, by the rivers. The crest of the *serres* are levelled off into plains which are covered with sheep grazing pastures and oak forests and when the soil becomes argileous, rich crops.

Between the *serres*, the more or less wide valleys, when they get closer to the Garonne, are fertile corridors where pastures lined with poplars produce abundant crops of fruit, as well as vineyards, cereals and tobacco.

The towns of Montcuq, Lauzerte, Castelnau-Montratier, Montpezat-du-Quercy are all situated on *puechs*, piton-like rocks; they have animated market days.

Quercy Blanc countryside around Lauzerte

AN AGRICULTURAL REGION

Périgord and Quercy are excellent examples of regions which produce varied crops. Four products are identified particularly with this area: truffles, walnuts, tobacco, and *foie gras*, to which can be added strawberries and vineyards.

To know how these products are used in regional cooking, see p 35.

Truffle hunting

Truffles. – The truffle is an edible, subterranean fungus which develops from the mycelium, a network of filaments invisible to the naked eye. They live symbiotically in close association with roots of hazel, holm-oak, lime and especially oak trees. It likes dry limestone soil, a good exposure and clearly marked seasons. Where the truffle grows below ground, above soil the vegetation disappears. Between December and February the truffle hunter *(caveur)*, accompanied by a sow or more often a dog trained especially for truffle hunting, digs into the soil for the harvesting of truffles when they are really ripe and fragrant. There are some thirty types of truffle but the best is the variety known as the Périgord truffle.

The main centres of production and sale in the Dordogne are Brantôme, Thiviers, Excideuil, Périgueux, Thenon, Terrasson, Sarlat, Domme, Sorges; and in the Lot are Cahors, Limogne, Sauzet and especially Lalbenque.

Production, which reached hundreds of tons a century ago, has dropped a great deal and presently Dordogne produces approximately 3 936 long tons.

Today, the planting of truffle oaks has instilled the hope that the production will increase.

Walnuts. – Walnuts are still harvested in large quantities in spite of the fact that their production tends to wane (4 920 to 6 889 long tons a year in Dordogne).

The Marbot nut, an early-ripening variety most common in the Lot, is often sold fresh.

The Grandjean nut, produced in the Sarlat and Gourdon areas, supplies the fruit (green nuts taken out of the husk) of Périgord and Quercy.

The Corne nut grows best in the Hautefort area and the better soils of the *causses*; it is a quality nut but often small in size and has trouble being commercialized.

The Franquette nut is found in the new plantations.

The Dordogne is the second producer of walnuts in France after Isère. Walnuts are cultivated north of the Dordogne, south of the Corrèze and in a large part of the Lot.

Tobacco. – Conditions in Périgord and Quercy and in all parts of southwest France are highly favourable to tobacco growing. It is a vigorous plant which was imported from America in the 16C and was first used for medicinal purposes before becoming the joy of all those who smoke *(for the history of tobacco see Bergerac's Tobacco Museum).*

Tobacco growing. – The traditional varieties of brown tobacco in this area are strictly controlled by the Régie nationale, S.E.I.T.A., whereas light tobacco is treated in the Sarlat factory.

The plant requires assiduous care and a large labour force, but it assures substantial cash income per acre. It is grown particularly on the alluvial soils of the valleys of the Dordogne and the Lot and on the mud terraces of Périgord and Quercy hills; sowing takes place at the end of March; during the end of spring and the summer, work goes on pricking and planting out seedlings, land dressing, topping plants and disbudding. Harvesting is done stem by stem, each stem being covered with 10 to 12 leaves 60 to 90cm – 24 to 32ins long. Curing takes place in ventilated sheds, which can be seen throughout the region, and the air curing lasts about six weeks. Before being sent to the cooperative's warehouses, the leaves are sorted with a great deal of precision. The principal buyer, the S.E.I.T.A., prepares tobacco for smoking. The Lot has the greatest proportion of tobacco grown for snuff.

Tobacco market. – The demand for products with American tobacco taste made from light tobacco increases constantly. This situation has brought about the creation of a research and development program of the different types of American tobacco: Virginia or Burley. The production of the Virginia demands special machines (flue-curing) but these varieties are, nevertheless, in constant growth. For example in Dordogne, it has been recorded that in 1989 800 tonnes of light tobacco were produced.

There are some 10 000 planters in Dordogne, Lot and Lot-et-Garonne *départements*; it is essentially a family business, although mechanization is increasing.

The Dordogne *département* ranks no 1 in France for tobacco production. About 3 500 planters produce approximately 20% of French production.

Foies gras. – This regional speciality *(p 35)* has brought about the full expansion of goose (about 200 000) and duck (about 250 000) raising in Périgord and Quercy. The raising of ducks and geese is primarily for the production of *foie gras* and *confits* (duck or goose cooked in their own fat and preserved in their fat in earthenware pots); however, this is not enough to satisfy local production demands and livers from Hungary and Israel must be imported.

Strawberries. – The Dordogne *département*, thanks to a recent effort, is ranked no 1 for the production of strawberries (equal with Lot-et-Garonne) with about 19 684 long tons. Cultivated first in the Lot and Dordogne Valleys, the strawberries have little by little spread over the plateaux and have become omnipresent in the Vergt and Rouffignac regions in Central Périgord.

In order to protect the strawberry plants from bad weather and enable them to flower and grow in a constant environment, they are placed under plastic sheets which blanket the countryside like long silver ribbons in the spring.

The fruit is left to ripen on these sheets before being picked and sent to large markets in the Paris region or the north of France where the Périgord strawberry is most appreciated.

Wine. – The vineyards of Bergerac and Cahors, already famous in Gallo-Roman times, encountered a number of catastrophes, such as the devastation of the vineyards by phylloxera which totally destroyed the Lot vineyards in the 19C. Today they have found a new expansion and create quality wines which have been granted an *appellation d'origine contrôlée*.

Cahors vineyard. – Quite famous in the Middle Ages, Cahors wine, transported by *gabares* to Bordeaux and then by ships to the various European capitals, was very much sought after.

In 1868, the prosperous vineyards were completely destroyed by phylloxera. The ground was abandoned and the winegrowers emigrated. After the Second World War, it was decided to replant the Cahors vineyards with the Auxerrois variety on the sunny slopes of the Lot Valley and the pebbly terraces of the plateaux. The real expansion of this vineyard was between 1960-70 and continues. Between 1976-83 the surface area of the vineyard had grown from 950ha to 2 400 ha – 2 347 to 5 930 acres and the wine production had more than doubled (about 130 000hl – 2 860 000gal (UK).

The Cahors vineyard produces a wine characterised by its dark red colour and robust full-bodied taste.

Bergerac vineyard. – This vineyard covers 11 000ha – 27 181 acres divided into 93 *communes* and produces an average of 200 000hl – 44 000 000gal (UK) of white wine and 150 000hl – 3 300 000gal (UK) of red wine. Spread over the terraces above the Dordogne Valley, the vineyard is divided into several zones making different varieties: Bergerac, Côtes de Bergerac, Monbazillac, Montravel and Côtes de Montravel, Pécharmant – the name of which comes from Pech Armand – and Côtes de Saussignac.

The Bergerac Regional Wine Council which is located in Bergerac *(p 45)* controls the quality of the wines and grants them an *appellation d'origine contrôlée*.

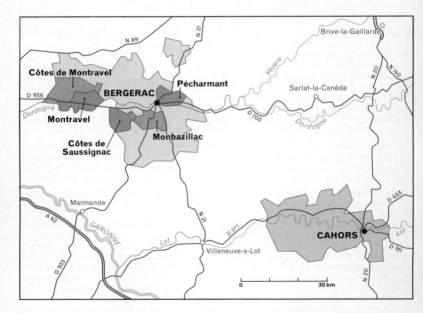

Gourmets...
Each year
*the **Michelin Red Guide France** proposes a revised selection*
of establishments renowned for their cuisine.

CAVES AND CHASMS

Although dispersed in Périgord, the arid *causse* slices through an otherwise luxuriant landscape. The Quercy limestone plateaux roll away to the far horizon, stony, grey and deserted. The dryness of the soil is due to the calcareous nature of the rock which absorbs rain like a sponge.

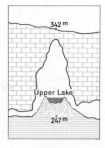

Formation of the Padirac
Great Dome

Water infiltration. – Rainwater, charged with carbonic acid, dissolves the carbonate of lime to be found in the limestone. Depressions, which are usually circular in shape and small in size and are known as **cloups**, are then formed. The dissolution of the limestone rocks containing especially salt or gypsum produces a rich soil particularly suitable for growing crops; when the *cloups* increase in size they form large, closed depressions known as **sotchs**. Where rainwater infiltrates deeply through the countless fissures in the plateau, the hollowing out and dissolution of the calcareous layer produces wells or natural chasms which are called **igues**.

Underground rivers. – The infiltrating waters finally produce underground galleries and collect to form a more or less swift-flowing river. The river widens its course and often changes level, to fall in cascades. Where the rivers run slowly they form lakes, as at Padirac, above natural dams, known as **gours**, which are raised layer by layer by deposits of carbonate of lime. Tourists are able to boat on these lakes. The dissolution of the limestone also continues above the water-level in these subterranean galleries: blocks of stone fall from the roof and domes form, the upper parts pointing towards the surface of the earth. Such is the case with the Great Dome of Padirac which lies only a few feet beneath the surface of the plateau *(see diagram)*. When the roof of the dome wears thin it may cave in, disclosing the cavity from above and opening the **chasm**.

Cave with concretions
① Stalactites – ② Stalagmites
③ Pillar in formation – ④ Completed pillar

Cave formation. – As it circulates below ground, the water deposits the lime with which it has become charged, thus building up concretions of fantastic shapes which defy the laws of gravity and equilibrium. In some caverns, the seeping waters produce calcite (carbonate of lime) deposits which form pendants, pyramids and draperies. The best known formations are stalactites and stalagmites *(see diagram)* and eccentrics.

Stalactites from the cave roof. Every droplet of water seeping through to the ceiling deposits upon it, before falling, some of the calcite with which it is charged. Gradually layer by layer the concretion builds up as the drops are attracted and run down its length, depositing particles before falling.

Stalagmites are formed in the same way but rise from the floor towards the roof. Drops of water, falling always in the same place, deposit their calcite particles which build up to a candle-like shape. This rises towards a stalactite with which it ultimately joins to form a pillar linking the cave floor with the ceiling.

Concretions form very slowly indeed; the rate of growth in a temperate climate is about 1cm – 3/8in every 100 years.

Eccentrics are very fine protuberances which seldom exceed 20cm – 8in in length. They emerge at any angle either as slender spikes or in the shape of small, translucent fans. They are formed by crystallization and seem to disregard the laws of gravity.

Resurgent springs. – Underground rivers form either by the disappearance of a water course into a rift *(igue)* of the *causse*, or by an accumulation of infiltrated water reaching non-porous strata (marl or clay). The water then finds a way through by following the line of the stratum. When the impermeable layer breaks through on the side of a hill, the water emerges once more above ground and is known as a resurgent spring *(see diagram)*. The river at Padirac, for example, flows

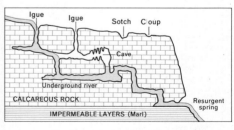

Development of a resurgent spring

underground for some miles, disappearing roughly in the spot where the tour of the Hall of the Great Natural Dams ends and reappearing some 11km – 7 miles away in the Montvalent Amphitheatre.

From prehistory to modern exploration. – The caves and grottoes, providing a natural protection against the cold, were first inhabited by animals and then by man, who left these natural shelters about 10 000 years ago.

At the end of last century, the methodical and scientific exploration of the underground world, with which the name of E.A. Martel is associated, led to the discovery of a certain number of caves and their organisation as a tourist attraction. Knowledge of the underground system is at present very incomplete.

ABC OF PREHISTORY

The Quaternary Era is relatively new since it began only about two million years ago. Nevertheless, it is during this period that the evolution of man has taken place.

There is no definitive evidence of life having existed on the earth in the Pre-Cambrian Age; reptiles, fish and tail-less amphibians appeared in the course of the Primary Era, mammals and birds during the Secondary Era. The primates, the most ancient ancestors of man, appeared at the end of the Tertiary Era and were followed in the Quaternary Era by types ever more advanced.

The slow pace of human progress during the Palaeolithic Age stuns the imagination: it took people nearly two million

QUATERNARY ERA		Years BC
Birth of Christ		
Foundation of Rome		753
IRON		900
BRONZE		2 500
AGE OF METALS		
	Egyptian pyramids	2 800
NEOLITHIC (POLISHED STONE)		7 500
MESOLITHIC		100 000
	UPPER	350 000
PALAEOLITHIC(CHIPPED STONE)	MIDDLE	1 500 000
STONE AGE	LOWER	20 000 000
Appearance of Man		

years to learn to polish stone. In contrast, the few thousand years that followed saw in the Middle and Far East the development of brilliant civilisations, which reached their climax in the construction of the pyramids in Egypt. A few centuries later a new step was accomplished with the discovery of bronze and later still, in approximately 900BC, of iron.

The researchers. – The study of prehistory was a science essentially French in origin and began in the early 19C. Until that time only an occasional allusion by a Greek or Latin author, a study by the Italian scholar Mercati (1541-93) in the 16C and a paper by Jussieu, published in 1723, gave any hint of the existence of ancient civilisations. In spite of the scepticism of most learned men – Cuvier (1769-1832) was their leader – the researchers pursued their investigations in Périgord, Lozère and in the Somme Valley. To Boucher de Perthes (1788-1868), falls the honour of having **prehistory** (the science of man before the invention of writing) recognised. His discoveries at St-Acheul and Abbeville were the starting-point for an important series of studies. Among the eminent pioneers who laid the foundations on which modern archaeology is based are: Edouard Lartet (1801-71), who undertook many excavations in the Vézère Valley and established a preliminary

UPPER PALAEOLITHIC

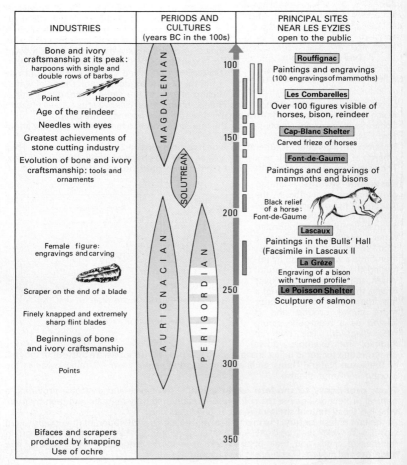

classification for the diverse eras of prehistory; Gabriel de Mortillet (1821-98), who took up and completed the classification adding the names Chellean, Mousterian, Aurignacian, Solutrian and Magdalenian to correspond with the places where the most prolific or most characteristic deposits were found: Chelles in Seine-et-Marne, Le Moustier in Dordogne, Aurignac in Haute-Garonne, Solutré in Saône-et-Loire and La Madeleine near Tursac in Dordogne. Since the end of the 19C the discovery of Palaeolithic tombs,

Woodcarving of a reindeer found at La Madeleine Site

tools, wall paintings and engravings have enabled researches to recount the life and activities of prehistoric man. The names associated with these studies in prehistory are the Abbé A. and J. Bouyssonie, Dr. L. Capitan, D. Peyrony, Rivière, Abbé Lemozi, Cartailhac and R. Lantier; Abbé Breuil (1877-1961), with his detailed accounts and graphic charts, made known the wonders of wall paintings and engravings in France and Spain. More recently André Leroi-Gourhan (1912-86) specialised in the study of Palaeolithic art.

Excavations can only be performed by specialists with knowledge of the geological stratigraphy, the physics and chemistry of rock formations, the nature and form of stones and gravels, the ability to analyse pollen, wood, eventually fossilised, coal and bone fragments.

In the rock shelters and cave mouths, prehistorians uncover hearths (accumulation of charcoal and kitchen middens), tools, weapons, stone and bone furnishings and bone fragments. Vestiges are collected in layers; during excavations each of these different layers is uncovered and the civilisation or period is then reconstructed with the help of the different data unearthed.

Prehistory in Périgord. – Périgord has been inhabited by man since Palaeolithic times. The names Tayacian (Les Eyzies-de-Tayac), Micoquean (La Micoque), Mousterian (Le Moustier), Perigordian and Magdalenian (La Madeleine) are evidence of the importance of these prehistoric sites. Nearly 200 deposits have been discovered of which more than half are in the Vézère Valley near Les Eyzies-de-Tayac *(qv)*.

The evolution of man in the Palaeolithic Age. – Man's most distant ancestors (some 30 000 centuries ago) were the early hominids (i.e. the family of man) of East Africa, who, unlike their instinctive thinking predecessors, were rational thinkers. They evolved into *Homo habilis* followed by *Homo erectus*, characterised by his upright walking (Java man or *Pithecanthropus erectus,* discovered by E. Dubois in 1891, with a cranial capacity halfway in size between the most highly developed ape and the least developed man; and Peking man or *Sinanthropus,* identified by D. Black in 1927), who made rough-hewn tools, chopping tools from split pebbles, and made heavy bifaced implements. Quite similar in appearance to the present *Homo sapiens* is the Cro-Magnon man.

Neanderthal man appeared *c*150 000 years ago. In 1856, in the Düssel Valley (also known as the Neander Valley, east of Düsseldorf, Gemany) were discovered portions of a human skeleton with the following characteristics: cranial capacity approximately 1 500cu cm – 91.5cu in, elongated cranium (dolichocephalus), sharply receding forehead, prominently developed jawbones and small stature (1.60m – 5ft 3in).

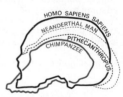

Skeletons with similar characteristics were found in France at La Chapelle-aux-Saints (Corrèze) in 1908, at Le Moustier (Dordogne) in 1909, at La Ferrassie (Dordogne) in 1909 and 1911, and at Le Régourdou (Dordogne) in 1957. Neanderthal man completely disappeared without descendants 350 centuries ago; at the same time the first burial sites were appearing.

Homo sapiens were flourishing in France some 40 000 years ago. Their essential characteristics – perfect upright stance, cranial capacity of about 1 500 to 1 700cu cm – 91.5 to 104cu in, raised forehead, slightly projecting eyebrows – showed him to be highly developed and comparable to present man (*sapiens* = intelligent). Several races have been traced as belonging to this same family.

The **Cro-Magnon man** (skeletons found in the rock shelters of Cro-Magnon in Dordogne and Solutré in Saône-et-Loire) was tall – about 1.80m – 5ft 11in – with long, robust limbs denoting considerable muscular strenght; the skull was dolichocephalic in shape. This people lived from the Upper Palaeolithic to the Neolithic Age.

The **Chancelade man** (skeleton discovered in 1889 at Chancelade, near Périgueux) appeared in the Magdalenian Period; he had a large cranium of dolichocephalic form, a long, wide face, pronounced cheek-bones and a height not more than 1.55m – 5ft 1in.

Scraper on the end of a blade

Point-Harpoon

Necklace

CULTURE AND ART IN THE PALAEOLITHIC AGE

The oldest skeletons, belonging to Neanderthal man, found in Périgord and Quercy date from the Mousterian Period.

Later, during the Ice Age, tribes came, it is believed, from eastern Europe and settled in the Vézère and Beune Valleys. Bordering these valleys were cliffs and slopes pitted with caves and shelters offering many natural advantages, which flat country could not offer: protection from the cold, nearby springs and rivers abundant in fish and narrow ravines used for intercepting game as they passed through. There were, however, several dwelling huts found in the Isle Valley, upstream from Périgueux.

The Palaeolithic Age (*paleos* = ancient, *lithos* = stones) covers the period in which men knew only how to chip flints. An intermediate age, the Mesolithic (*mesos* = middle), separates it from the Neolithic Age (*neos* = new), when man learnt to polish stone. The first group were predators (hunting, fishing and gathering), whereas the last group were farmers and breeders. Skill in flint knapping evolved very slowly and, therefore, the Palaeolithic Age is subdivided into three periods: the Lower, Middle and Upper.

Lower Palaeolithic

Beginning about two million years ago. Men living in this period in Périgord knew how to use fire and hunted big game. The earth suffered three successive ice ages known as the Günz, the Mindel and the Riss Ice Ages (after the tributary valleys of the Danube where they have been studied). Between each ice age, France and Britain had a tropical climate.

Flint knapping began with a cut made by striking two stones violently one against the other, or by striking one against a rock which served as an anvil. These two methods gave rise to the two types of industry shown below.

Abbeville biface	Clacton flints (flakes)
Cleared of its flakes on two sides, the flint kernel is fined down and takes the form of an unevenly peeled fat almond. In the Acheulean Period better finished arrow-heads were obtained.	By using the flakes a relatively smooth or worked face could be obtained. This Clacton industry (it has been pinpointed to Clacton-on-Sea) existed in the Tayacian Period and produced smaller pieces (La Micoque Shelter at Les Eyzies).

Middle Palaeolithic

Beginning about 150 000 years ago. With Neanderthal man there appeared better finished and more specialised tools. Mousterian industry used both bifaced implements and flakes. New methods – the fashioning of flints by a bone or wooden striker – enabled triangular points to be produced, also scrapers, used probably for working skins, and flints adapted to take a wooden handle and serve as hunting clubs.

During the Mousterian Culture some cave entrances were used as dwelling places, others were used as burial places. Man by this time possessed more sophisticated weapons with which to hunt big game and protected himself from the cold with animal skins.

His intelligence was similar to ours.

Scraper-point   Points

Upper Palaeolithic

Beginning about 35 000 years ago. Cro-Magnon man and Chancelade man replaced Neanderthal man. There was a constant improvement in the production of tools; the life style was made easier with the perfection of new hunting methods (their stone industry was no longer based on flakes but rather on blades), enabling man more leisure time and, therefore, time for artistic expression.

Perigordian and Aurignacian Cultures. – These two cultures, following the Mousterian and Levalloisian Cultures and preceding the Solutrean Culture, were contemporary but parallel.

The **Aurignacian** stone industry produced large blades, stone flake tools, burins (a sort of chisel) and points made from antlers (early ones with split base). Cave decoration, applied on blocks of limestone (La Ferrassie near Le Bugue) and at times in tiny caves, consisted of engraved animals, painted or partially carved, or female figures.

At the end of the Perigordian Culture, Gravettians made burins and points; these people decorated their shelter walls (Le Poisson, Laussel) and carved "Venus" figurines, small female statues with exaggerated forms evoking fertility.

| Laussel: Venus with the horn of plenty | Lascaux: horse pierced with lines | Lascaux: charging bison |

The burial places contain some ornaments and jewellery: shells, bead necklaces.
The first examples of wall decoration appear as hands placed flat against the rock and outlined in black or red: these are to be found at Font-de-Gaume and at Le Pech Merle. The animals are only rudimentarily sketched. By the end of this period, man had become a true artist as may be seen by the sculptures at the Le Poisson Shelter and the engravings and paintings found at Font-de-Gaume and Lascaux. La Grève Cave with its engraved bison in "turned profile" (as described by Abbé Breuil: an animal drawn in profile is given certain features as though seen full face) dates from between the late Perigordian and the early Solutrean.

Solutrean Culture. – Very well represented in the Dordogne, this period is distinguished by exquisite low reliefs carved out of limestone slabs (such as the Devil's Oven, found near Bourdeilles and now exhibited in the National Museum of Prehistory at Les Eyzies).
The stone-cutting industry also knew a brilliant period during the Solutrean Culture. Flint blades, following a method of splitting under pressure, became much slimmer, forming blades in the shape of laurel or willow leaves. Shouldered points were used as weapons, after they had been fitted with wooden shafts. It was during this period that the first needles with eyes appeared.

Magdalenian Culture. – It was in this period that bone and ivory craftsmanship reached its peak. The existence of herds of reindeer, which is accounted for by the very cold climate that occurred at the end of the Würm Glacial Period, influenced man towards working bone and antler: perforated batons, sometimes engraved, were used as armatures for points and harpoon heads, projectile tips, sometimes engraved, used as spears and, decorated flattened points.
This is also the period when wall art, depicting essentially animal subjects, reaches its peak. To protect themselves from the cold, the men of the Magdalenian industry lived in the shelter of overhanging rocks or at the mouths of caves; inside these caves were the sanctuaries, placed, at times, quite some distance from the cave entrance.
They used the shelter (as at the Cap-Blanc Shelter) and sanctuary walls to express their artistic or religious emotions by low-relief carving, engraving and painting. This period presents a very sophisticated style contrary to the more rudimentary outline drawings of the Perigordian and Aurignacian Cultures. However, due to the juxtaposition or superimposition of the figures drawn and deterioration (only a few Magdalenian caves are open to the public due to the difficulty in preserving these works of art), the study of these paintings is not easily accessible.

| Pech Merle: horses, outlined hands and black spots | Bara-Bahau: engraving of a horse | Font-de-Gaume: black relief of a horse |

After Lascaux, during the Middle and Upper Magdalenian, the cave-sanctuaries are numerous. Portable art, manifested through smaller objects, is another form of expression developed in the shelters. Animals are much less stylised and more and more realistic whether it be in the details of their anatomy or their movements or faithful rendering of their physical aspects: coat, tail, eyes, ears, hoofs, antlers, tusks.
The style is more ornamental. The perspective of the animals in profile, non-existent in the beginning, is sought after and even distorted during Lascaux's last period. New graphic techniques appear: stencilling, areas left intentionally without colour, polychrome colours... Towards the end of the Magdalenian Culture, art becomes more schematic and human figures made their appearance. This great animal art disappeared from France and Spain; and the herds of reindeer migrated northwards in search of the lichen which was disappearing during the warming up at the end of the Würm Glacial Period.

| Rouffignac: engraving of a mammoth and lines drawn with fingers | Font-de-Gaume: multicoloured bison | Les Combarelles: engraving of a reindeer |

HISTORICAL TABLE AND NOTES

Events in italics indicate milestones for the local history.

Prehistory	As early as the Middle Palaeolithic Age, Périgord and Quercy are inhabited by man *(pp 18-21)*.

Gauls and Romans

BC	The actual Périgord area is inhabited by Petrocorii *(p 117)* and Quercy area by Caduici.
59-51	Conquest of Gaul by Caesar. The last Gaulish resistance to Caesar is at Uxellodunum.
55	*Julius Caesar lands in Britain.*
16	Emperor Augustus creates the province of Aquitaine. The land of the Petrocorii has a capital, Vesunna (Périgueux) and that of the Caduici, Divona Cadurcorum (Cahors).
AD	
1-3C	**Pax Romana.** For three centuries the towns develop: a number of public buildings are built. In the country, near the towns, new crops are introduced by the Romans: walnut, chestnut and cherry trees and especially vineyards.
235-284	Alemans and Franks invade the region. In 276 several towns are razed. Vesunna defends itself behind fortifications built in haste with the stones taken from Roman public buildings.
313	*Edict of Milan. Emperor Constantine grants Christians the freedom of worship.*
476	*End of the Roman Empire.*

Merovingians and Carolingians

486-507	Clovis, king of Franks, conquers Gaul. This campaign ends at the Battle of Vouillé (near Poitiers) in 507 where Clovis kills Alaric II, king of Visigoths. Aquitaine falls into the hands of the Franks.
8C	Quercy and Périgord become counties under the kingdom of Aquitaine.
9C	Dordogne and Isle Valleys and Périgueux are laid waste by Vikings.
10C	The four baronies of Périgord – Mareuil, Bourdeilles, Beynac and Biron – are formed as well as the overlordships of Ans, Auberoche, Gurson, etc. The Périgord County passes into the house of Talleyrand. Powerful families rule Quercy: the Gourdons, Cardaillacs, Castelnaus, Turennes and St-Sulpices.
c950	Beginning of the Pilgrimage to St James's shrine in Santiago de Compostela.
1066	*William the Conqueror lands in England.*
12C	Abbeys founded in Périgord: Cadouin, Dalon, Sarlat, Boschaud, Chancelade... and in Quercy: Rocamadour, Figeac, Souillac and Carennac.

Wars between England and France

1152	When Eleanor of Aquitaine marries Henry Plantagenet she brings as dowry all southwest France *(p 24)*. In 1154 Henry Plantagenet becomes King Henry II. Later on their sons Henry Short Coat and Richard Lionheart occupy and pillage the region.
1190	An agreement between Philippe Auguste and Richard Lionheart: Quercy is ceded to the English with the exception of the abbeys of Figeac and Souillac.
1191	Richard Lionheart dies at Châlus.
early 13C	Albigensian Crusade. Simon de Montfort raids Quercy and Périgord.
1229	The *Treaty of Meaux* (also called *Treaty of Paris*) between the king of France and Raymond VII, Count of Toulouse. It is recognised that Quercy belongs to Raymond VII.
1259	By the **Treaty of Paris**, Saint Louis cedes Périgord and Quercy to the English. The treaty puts an end to the constant fighting and enables the people of the region to live in peace until the Hundred Years' War.
1337	French king Philip VI declares the English-held duchy of Guyenne confiscate.
1340	Edward III of England proclaims himself king of France.
1345	Beginning of the Hundred Years' War in Aquitaine; French king Jean II seeks to win back Aquitaine. The region becomes the battlefield of the war with the taking of Tulle (1346) and Domme (1347).

Lands held by the Plantagenets in 1253

Lands held by the Plantagenets in the beginning of the Hundred Years' War

Lands ceded to the English after the Treaty of Brètigny in 1360

1355	Edward the Black Prince lands in Bordeaux. In 1356 at the Battle of Poitiers King Jean II is vanquished by Edward and taken prisoner.
1360	The **Treaty of Brétigny** cedes Aquitaine to the English as part of the ransom for Jean II's liberty.
1369	Quercy and Périgord are won back by the king of France (Charles V). Du Guesclin, Constable of France, at the liberation of Périgord. During the period that follows the lords of the north of Périgord owe allegiance to the king of France; the lords of south of Périgord to the English.
1405	French take towns in Saintonge and Périgord. Assasination of Duke of Orléans, which results in the civil war between the Burgundians and Armagnacs. Both factions seek English aid.
1420	Henry V of England recognised as king of France under the *Treaty of Troyes.* France divided into three parts controlled by Henry V (Normandy, Guyenne, Paris area), Philip the Good, Duke of Burgundy (Paris area, as well, Burgundy) and the Dauphin (Central France and Languedoc).
1429-1439	Road bandits working equally for the warring factions devastate the region.
1444	Truce of Tours (Charles VII and Henry V); the English retain Maine, Bordelais, parts of Artois and Picardy and most of Normandy.
1449	French take advantage of political situation in England and began a campaign in Guyenne; the people of the region are hostile to the French due to the long tradition of loyalty to the English crown; Bergerac falls in 1450 and Bordeaux in 1451.
1453	Defeat of John Talbot, Earl of Shrewsbury at the **Battle of Castillon,** which marks the end of the Hundred Years' War.
1492	*Christopher Columbus discovers America.*
2nd half of 15-early 16C	During this period of peace, towns are rebuilt and castles are either built or old ones remodelled. Literary life *(p 25)* blossoms: Clément Marot, La Boétie, Brantôme and Montaigne.
1509-47	*Henry VIII's reign.*
1535	*Jacques Cartier sails up the St. Lawrence River.*
1558-1603	*Elizabeth's reign.*

Wars of Religion

1562	Massacre of Protestants at Cahors.
1565	*St Augustine, Florida founded.*
1572	Massacre of St Bartholomew.
1570-90	War is declared: Bergerac and Ste-Foy-la-Grande are Huguenot bastions while Périgueux and Cahors stay Catholic, upholding the Holy League. Vivans, the Huguenot leader, scours Périgord; Périgueux falls in 1575 and Domme in 1588.
1577	Peace of Bergerac *(p 43)* announces the *Edict of Nantes.*
1580	Cahors taken by Henri de Navarre.
1588	*Defeat of the Spanish Armada.*
1589	Henri IV accedes to the throne; converts to Catholicism in 1593; crowned in 1594. Under Henri IV, the County of Périgord becomes part of the royal domain.
1594-95	*Croquant* revolt *(qv).*
1598	**Edict of Nantes** grants Huguenots freedom of worship and places of refuge.
1609	*Hudson sails up the Hudson River.*
1620	*Pilgrim Fathers land at Plymouth, Ma.*
1637	*Croquants* again revolt, this time against Louis XIII's government and Richelieu, who is continually raising taxes.
1664	*British capture New Amsterdam, which they rename New York.*
1685	**Revocation of Edict of Nantes.** Huguenots flee France.

18 to 20C

1714-27	*George I's reign.*
1743-57	Tourny, administrator of the Treasury of Bordeaux, instigates a number of town planning projects in the southwest (Allées de Tourny in Périgueux).
1763	*Peace of Paris ends French and Indian War (1754-63); it marks the end of France's colonial empire in America.*
1775-83	*American Revolution.*
1789	*George Washington chosen as first President of the United States.*
1790	Creation of Dordogne *département.*
1805	*Battle of Trafalgar.*
1812-14	Périgord is a Bonapartist fief; several of Napoleon's generals and marshals are native of the region: Murat, Fournier-Sariovèze, Daumesnil.
1814	*British capture Washington D.C. and burn the Capitol and White House.*
1815	*Battle of Waterloo.*
1837-1901	*Victoria's reign.*
1838	Birth of Léon Gambetta at Cahors.
1853	*Crimean War.*
1861-65	*American Civil War.*
1868	Phylloxera destroys the vineyards of Cahors and Bergerac, causing a rural exodus.
1886	*Statue of Liberty erected.*
1899	*Second Boer War.*
20C	The rural exodus has continued and these depopulated regions live essentially from agriculture and tourism.

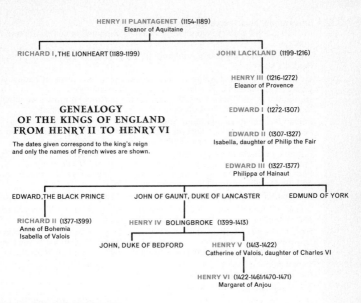

HENRY II PLANTAGENET (1154-1189)
Eleanor of Aquitaine

RICHARD I, THE LIONHEART (1189-1199)   JOHN LACKLAND (1199-1216)

HENRY III (1216-1272)
Eleanor of Provence

**GENEALOGY
OF THE KINGS OF ENGLAND
FROM HENRY II TO HENRY VI**

The dates given correspond to the king's reign
and only the names of French wives are shown.

EDWARD I (1272-1307)

EDWARD II (1307-1327)
Isabella, daughter of Philip the Fair

EDWARD III (1327-1377)
Philippa of Hainaut

EDWARD, THE BLACK PRINCE   JOHN OF GAUNT, DUKE OF LANCASTER   EDMUND OF YORK

RICHARD II (1377-1399)
Anne of Bohemia
Isabella of Valois

HENRY IV BOLINGBROKE (1399-1413)

JOHN, DUKE OF BEDFORD   HENRY V (1413-1422)
Catherine of Valois, daughter of Charles VI

HENRY VI (1422-1461/1470-1471)
Margaret of Anjou

HISTORICAL NOTES

Eleanor's dowry. – In 1137, Prince Louis, son of the king of France, married Eleanor, only daughter of Duke William of Aquitaine. She brought as her dowry the Duchy of Guyenne, Périgord, Limousin, Poitou, Angoumois, Saintonge, Gascony and the suzerainty of Auvergne and the County of Toulouse. But it was an ill-assorted marriage; Louis, who had become king as Louis VII, might be said to be a monk crowned, while his wife was frivolous in character. After 15 years of conjugal misunderstanding, the king on his return from a crusade, had the Council of Beaugency (1152) pronounce his divorce. Eleanor recovered not only her liberty but also her dowry.

Her marriage two months later with **Henry Plantagenet**, count of Anjou and lord of Maine, Touraine and Normandy, was a political disaster for the royal house of France, the Capetians. Eleanor's and Henry's joint domains were already as great as were those of the king of France. Two years later Henry Plantagenet inherited the throne of England which he ruled as Henry II. The balance of power was destroyed and the Hundred Years' War broke out *(p 22)*.

By the building of *bastides (p 32)* in the 13C, the kings of France and England hoped to consolidate their positions and justify their territorial claims. The Capetians and Plantagenets each tried to get a foothold in the other's territories but the Dordogne acted as a dividing line between them *(see map p 22)*. The *Treaty of Paris* in 1259, between St Louis and Henry III of England, was in reality only a truce. Guyenne remained English until the end of the Hundred Years' War in 1453.

Wars of Religion. – As early as 1540 a first centre of Protestantism developed in Ste-Foy-la-Grande; 1544 in Bergerac. Protestantism was upheld in Périgord by the princes of Bourbon-Albret (Jeanne d'Albret, mother of Henri de Navarre) and Caumont-Laforce and in Quercy by Jeanne de Genouillac, the Gourdons, and Cardaillacs. 1570-90 skirmishes and massacres occurred.

The Huguenots, led by **Armand de Clermont**, lord of Piles, fought against **Marshal de Montluc** and his army. After Clermont de Pile's death (a victim of the massacre of St Bartholomew), **Geffroi de Vivans** became leader and devastated the region; his best arm was craftiness; he entered and captured Sarlat during Carnival celebrations and his strategy for the fall of Domme was famous *(p 72)*. The Protestant towns of western Périgord were opposed by the Catholic towns of Périgueux and Cahors (the latter seized by Henri de Navarre in 1580). The Catholic, Pierre de Bourdeille (Brantôme), denounced these religious wars in his writings. He was particularly shocked by the massacre at La Chapelle-Faucher, when the vengeful Huguenot leader Admiral Coligny rounded up 300 peasants in the castle and set it on fire.

Henri IV promulgated the Edict of Nantes; Protestantism was strengthened but with Louis XIII and Richelieu, the fighting reoccurred. Louis XIV declared the Revocation of the Edict of Nantes and as a result many of the people of Périgord emigrated.

Peasant revolts. – The peasant uprisings troubled the rural areas intermittently for some 200 years. Poverty, famine and heavier taxes caused the uprisings. In 1594, the *Croquants* (a peasant movement against the nobles and all forms of oppression) revolted. The peasants united, formed an army and refused to work for their lords. The nobles joined forces and the skirmishes at St-Crépin-d'Auberoche (1595) and St-Condat-sur-Vézère quashed the *Croquant* army.

Forty years later, in 1637, the peasants again revolted, their grievances were the same – nothing had changed. A gentleman, **La Mothe la Forêt**, led an army of several thousand peasants. They attempted to seize Périgueux, succeeded at Bergerac but were stopped at Ste-Foy-la-Grande. They were defeated at La Sauvetat. In spite of La Mothe's surrender and the dissolution of his army, the *Croquants* continued forays in the area and pushed back the royal troops. In 1642, the *Croquants* were once again quashed.

In 1707 a new tax created a new uprising, *Tard-Avisés* (name already given to rebels in 1594). It broke out in Périgord and Quercy but was very rapidly put down. Peasant revolts continued throughout the Revolution.

INTELLECTUAL AND LITERARY LIFE

The courts of love. – There appeared in 12C Périgord a type of lyric poetry, the source of which did not derive from an earlier form: it was the poetry of the **troubadours.** This poetic form, which soon spread to Quercy, developed and flowered in the feudal courts where idle but educated nobles and their ladies enjoyed singing, music and poetry. Troubadors were inventors (*trobar*=to find) of musical airs – both melodies and words in the Oc language. Under the protection and encouragement of their lords, they created new poetic forms: love poems (songs and romances) in which lyrical homage to the lady of the castle illustrated the theme of courtly love; songs of war and satirical ballads. The courts of love each counted several troubadours who would vie in wit with one another on a set subject.

Bertrand de Born (*c*1140-*c*1215), author of *Sirventès*, a play of political and moralistic thought, Bertrand de Gourdon, Aimeric de Sarlat, Giraut de Borneil, native of Excideuil, and Arnaud Daniel de Ribérac were the most famous of these troubadours. This formal poetry had disappeared by the end of the 12C as the conditions under which it flourished were changed by wars and the crusades.

The humanists. – After the Hundred Years' War, during the 15C, intellectual life continued, centering on its new universities – Cahors was founded in 1331 by Jean Duèze, who had become Pope John XXII. In the early 16C printing houses were established in Périgueux, Cahors and Bergerac. But it was the Renaissance, which was marked by an important intellectual movement known as humanism, which restored respect for classical languages and poetic forms. Also a native of Cahors, **Clément Marot** (1496-1544), one of the great poets of the French Renaissance, excelled at composing epigrams and sonnets. He was *valet de chambre* to Marguerite d'Alençon, future Queen of Navarre, and to François I before being named official court poet. His brilliant life at court was cut by several prison sentences due to his penchant for the Reformation. During one of his detentions, he wrote an epistle to the king begging for his freedom and was released. Also of Cahors, **Olivier de Magny** (1529-65), influenced by the Pléiade, after becoming friends with the poet Du Bellay (who wrote of

Magny in one of his sonnets compiled in *Regrets*), wrote verse of considerable lyric quality.

At the same time **Etienne de la Boétie** (1530-63) was born in Sarlat. A humanist and friend of Montaigne, he denounced tyranny in his *Discourse on Voluntary Subjection* and *Contre' un (Against One)*.

In addition there was Pierre de Bourdeille (1535-1614), who wrote under the pseudonym of **Brantôme** (name of the abbey of which he was abbot), was a talented chronicler, who described the lives of great captains and soldiers as well as accounts of the French court.

Jean Tarde (1561-1636) born at La Roque-Gageac was one of the most learned men of his time. This canon of Sarlat was a historian, cartographer, astronomer and mathematician.

17C. – Born in Toulouse, **François Maynard** (1582-1646) spent the greater part of his life at St-Ceré in Quercy. He was a follower of Malherbe and the odes, letters, sonnets and epigrams he left are not without charm.

Fénelon who was born at Fénelon Castle near

Portrait of Pierre de Bourdeille pseudonym Brantôme

Ste-Mondane in 1631 (d 1715) was no less a man of letters than he was a man of the church. He was famous for his *Télémaque*, a tract for the edification of his student duke of Burgundy, dauphin of France. He wrote it at Carennac, on the banks of the Dordogne, where he was senior prior for 15 years.

Age of Enlightenment. – Both from Périgord, **Joseph Joubert** (1754-1824) from Montignac and **Maine de Biran** (1766-1824) from Bergerac were philosophers and moralists of considerable sensitivity: Joubert's *Pensées* are so precise and delicate in style as to make them near perfect; Maine de Biran's work presents metaphysical thought directed to the psychological aspect of experience.

Regional writers. – **Eugène Le Roy** (1836-1907) is Périgord's own novelist. In *Jacquou le Croquant*, which is set at L'Herm Castle, Le Roy describes, in a very vivid style, the peasant uprisings *(Croquants)* which ravaged the region *(p 24)*.

Among the more contemporary authors is **Claude Michelet**, who describes peasant life in Corrèze in his novels.

Make up your own itineraries

– The map on pages 6 to 7 gives a general view of tourist regions, the main towns, individual sights and recommended routes in the Guide.

– The above are described under their own name in alphabetical order (p 37) or are incorporated in the excursions radiating from a nearby town or tourist centre.

*– In addition the layout diagram on page 3 shows the **Michelin Maps** covering the region.*

ART

ABC OF ARCHITECTURE

To assist readers unfamiliar with the terminology employed in architecture, we describe below the most commonly used terms, which we hope will make their visits to ecclesiastical, military and civil buildings more interesting.

Ecclesiastical architecture

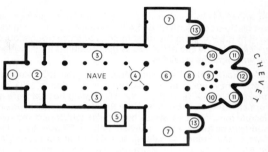

illustration I

Ground plan. – The more usual Catholic form is based on the outline of a cross with the two arms of the cross forming the transept: ① Porch – ② Narthex – ③ Side aisles (sometimes double) – ④ Bay (transverse section of the nave between 2 pillars) – ⑤ Side chapel (often predates the church) – ⑥ Transept crossing – ⑦ Arms of the transept, sometimes with a side doorway – ⑧ Chancel, nearly always facing east towards Jerusalem; the chancel often vast in size was reserved for the monks in abbatial churches – ⑨ High altar – ⑩ Ambulatory: in pilgrimage churches the aisles were extended round the chancel, forming the ambulatory, to allow the faithful to file past the relics – ⑪ Radiating or apsidal chapel – ⑫ Axial chapel. In churches which are not dedicated to the Virgin this chapel, in the main axis of the building is often consecrated to the Virgin (Lady Chapel) – ⑬ Transept chapel.

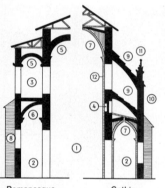

Romanesque   Gothic

◀ illustration II

Cross-section: ① Nave – ② Aisle – ③ Tribune or Gallery – ④ Triforium – ⑤ Barrel vault – ⑥ Half-barrel vault – ⑦ Pointed vault – ⑧ Buttress – ⑨ Flying buttress – ⑩ Pier of a flying buttress – ⑪ Pinnacle – ⑫ Clerestory window.

illustration III ▶

Gothic cathedral: ① Porch – ② Gallery – ③ Rose window – ④ Belfry (sometimes with a spire) – ⑤ Gargoyle acting as a waterspout for the roof gutter – ⑥ Buttress – ⑦ Pier of a flying buttress (abutment) – ⑧ Flight or span of flying buttress – ⑨ Double-course flying buttress – ⑩ Pinnacle – ⑪ Side chapel – ⑫ Radiating or apsidal chapel – ⑬ Clerestory windows – ⑭ Side doorway – ⑮ Gable – ⑯ Pinnacle – ⑰ Spire over the transept crossing.

illustration IV

Groined vaulting:
① Main arch – ② Groin
③ Transverse arch

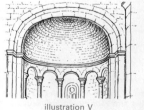

illustration V

Oven vault:
termination of a barrel
vaulted nave

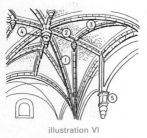

illustration VI

Lierne and tierceron vaulting:
① Diagonal – ② Lierne
③ Tierceron – ④ Pendant
⑤ Corbel

illustration VI

Quadripartite vaulting:
① Diagonal – ② Transverse
③ Stringer – ④ Flying buttress
⑤ Keystone

▼ illustration VIII

Doorway: ① Archivolt. Depending on the architectural style of the building this can be rounded, pointed, basket-handled, ogee or even adorned by a gable – ② Arching, covings (with string courses, mouldings, carvings or adorned with statues). Recessed arches or orders form the archivolt – ③ Tympanum – ④ Lintel – ⑤ Archshafts – ⑥ Embrasures. Arch shafts, splaying sometimes adorned with statues or columns – ⑦ Pier (often adorned by a statue) – ⑧ Hinges and other ironwork.

illustration IX ▶

Arches and pillars: ① Ribs or ribbed vaulting – ② Abacus – ③ Capital – ④ Shaft – ⑤ Base – ⑥ Engaged column – ⑦ Pier of arch wall – ⑧ Lintel – ⑨ Discharging or relieving arch – ⑩ Frieze.

Military architecture

illustration X

Fortified enclosure: ① Hoarding (projecting timber gallery) – ② Machicolations (corbelled crenellations) – ③ Barbican – ④ Keep or donjon – ⑤ Covered watchpath – ⑥ Curtain wall – ⑦ Outer curtain wall – ⑧ Postern.

illustration XI

Towers and curtain walls: ① Hoarding – ② Crenellations – ③ Merlon – ④ Loophole or arrow slit – ⑤ Curtain wall – ⑥ Bridge or drawbridge.

◀ illustration XII

Fortified gatehouse: ① Machicolations – ② Watch turrets or bartizan – ③ Slots for the arms of the drawbridge – ④ Postern.

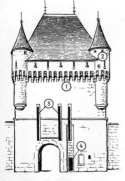

illustration XIII ▶

Star fortress: ① Entrance – ② Drawbridge – ③ Glacis – ④ Ravelin or half-moon – ⑤ Moat – ⑥ Bastion – ⑦ Watch turret – ⑧ Town – ⑨ Assembly area.

ARCHITECTURAL TERMS USED IN THE GUIDE

Aisle: illustration I.
Altarpiece: see retable.
Ambulatory: illustration I.
Apse: illustration I.
Apsidal chapel: illustration I.
Arcade: a range of arches within a larger arch.
Archivolt: illustration VIII.
Atlantes: supports in the form of carved male figures.
Axial or Lady Chapel: illustration I.
Bailey: open space or court of stone built castle.
Barrel vaulting: illustration XVIII.
Bartizan: illustration XII.
Basket-handled arch: depressed arch.
Bastion: illustration XIII.
Bay: illustration I.
Billet: a moulding made up of several bands of raised short cylinders or square pieces set at intervals and used as decoration (such as around an archivolt).
Bracket: small supporting piece of stone or timber to carry a beam or cornice.
Buttress: illustration II.
Capital: illustration IX.
Caryatids: supports in the form of carved female figures.
Cenotaph: a monument to a person buried elsewhere.
Chevet: French term for the east end of a church: illustration I.
Chicane: zig-zag passageway.
Coffered ceiling: vault or ceiling decorated with sunken panels.
Corbel: see bracket: illustration VI.
Credence: side table, shelf or niche for eucharistic elements.
Crypt: underground chamber or chapel.
Curtain wall: illustration X.
Depressed arch: three-centred arch sometimes called a basket-handled arch.
Diagonal ribs: illustrations VI and VII.
Dome: illustrations XVI and XVII.
Engaged column: illustration IX.
Flamboyant: last phase (15C) of French Gothic architecture; name taken from the undulating (flame-like) lines of the window tracery.
Fresco: mural painting executed on wet plaster.
Frieze: decorated band either in relief or painted.
Gable: triangular part of an end wall carrying a sloping roof; the term is also applied to the steeply pitched ornamental pediments of Gothic architecture: illustration III
Gallery: illustration II.
Gargoyle: illustration III.
Glacis: illustration XIII.
Groined vaulting: illustration IV.
Half-timbered: timber-framed construction.
High relief: haut-relief.
Horseshoe arch: can either be pointed or rounded.
Hood-mould: a projected moulding above a window or decorative unit to protect it from the rain.
Impost: a member in wall formed of a bracket-like moulding on which the end of an arch rests.
Jetty: overhanging upper storey.
Keel vaulting: resembling an inverted ship's hull.
Keep or donjon: illustration X.
Keystone: middle and topmost stone in an arch or vault.
Lintel: illustration VIII.
Loophole or **arrow slit:** illustration XI.
Low relief: bas-relief.
Machicolations: illustration X.
Maze: a complex geometric design of tiles, which the faithful followed crawling on their hands and knees; and where the master craftsman signed his name.
Merlon: illustration XI.
Misericord: illustration XIX.
Moat: generally water-filled.
Modillion: small console supporting a cornice.
Mullion: a vertical post dividing a window.
Oculus: round window.
Organ case: illustration XIV.
Oven vaulting: illustration V.
Overhang: jetty or overhanging upper storey.
Parapet wall: see watchpath: illustration X
Parclose screen: screen separating a chapel or the choir from the rest of the church.
Pendant: illustration VI.
Peristyle: a range of columns surrounding or on the façade of a building.
Pier: illustration VIII.
Pietà: Italian term designating the Virgin Mary with the dead Christ on her knees.

Pilaster: engaged rectangular column.
Pinnacle: illustrations II and III.
Piscina: basin for washing the sacred vessels.
Polyptych: a painted or carved work consisting of more than 3 leaves or panels folded together.
Porch: covered area before the entrance to a building.
Postern: illustrations X and XII.
Putti: naked cupids or cherubims represented in painting or sculpture.
Quadripartite vaulting: illustration VII.
Ravelin: illustration XIII.
Recessed arches: illustration VIII.
Recessed tomb: funerary niche.
Retable: illustration XV.
Rose window: illustration III.
Semicircular arch: round-headed arch.
Spire: illustration III.
Stalls: illustration XIX.
Torus: large convex moulding semicircular in shape at the base of a column or pedestal.
Tracery: intersecting stone ribwork in the upper part of a window.
Transept: illustration I.
Transverse arch: illustration XVIII.
Triforium: illustration II.
Triptych: three panels hinged together, chiefly used as an altarpiece.
Tunnel vaulting: see barrel vaulting.
Twinned: columns, pilasters, windows, arches... grouped in twos.
Voussoir: one of the stones forming an arch.
Wall walk: see watchpath.
Watchpath: illustration X.
Watch turrets: see bartizan.
Wheel window: see rose window.

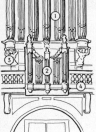

◄ Illustration XIV

Organ:
① Great organ case –
② Little organ case –
③ Caryatids – ④ Loft

Illustration XV ►

Altar with retable or altarpiece:
① Retable or altarpiece –
② Predella – ③ Crowning piece – ④ Altar table –
⑤ Altar front

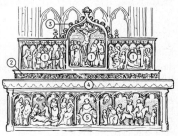

◄ Illustration XVI

Dome on squinches:
① Octagonal dome –
② Squinch – ③ Arches of transept crossing

Illustration XVII ►

Dome on pendentives:
① Circular dome – ② Pendentive
③ Arches of transept crossing

Illustration XIX ►

Stalls:
① High back – ② Elbow rest –
③ Cheek-piece – ④ Misericord

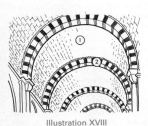

Illustration XVIII

Semicircular or barrel vaulting:
① Vault – ② Transverse arch

ART IN PÉRIGORD AND QUERCY
For the definitions of art terms see pp 28-29

The Vézère Valley, prehistoric sites of Les Eyzies and the caves of Quercy contain the finest examples of the artistic endeavors of prehistoric man, the first known manifestations of art in France *(p 20)*.

The large periods of construction correspond with periods of calm: Pax Romana, 12C, which was a time when a number of monasteries were built, as well as the period which spans the end of the 14 to 16C. During times of war – Hundred Years' War and Wars of Religion... – the peoples' main concern was their protection thus the fortification of their towns, castles and churches.

Bonaguil Castle

Gallo-Roman Art

Of all the buildings constructed by the Gauls and the Romans only a few have withstood the test of time. Souvenirs of the period of the Gauls do survive in several sites in Quercy – Capdenac-le-Vieux, Murcens, Impernal and Puy d'Issolud – which dispute the honour of being the site of the battle of **Uxellodunum,** last site of Gaulish resistance to Caesar.

During the Roman occupation, Vesunna (Périgueux), the capital of the Petrocorii, and Divona Cadurcorum (Cahors) capital of the Caduici, were important towns and numerous public buildings were erected.

In Périgueux, Roman remains uncovered suggest the magnificence of the ancient city of Vesunna: Vesunna's Tower, the excavations of a large 1 and 2C villa, the arena ruins as well as the mosaics, steles and altars exhibited in the Périgord Museum.

In Cahors, the grid-like town plan shows Gallo-Roman influence: the arch of Diana, all that is left of the baths, is the only Gallo-Roman architectural still standing. The Cahors Museum of Henri Martin houses a 3C sarcophagus and a carved lintel.

Romanesque Art

After the troubled times of the early Middle Ages, marked by the Viking invasions, the decadence of the Carolingian dynasty and the struggles between the great feudal barons, the year 1000 marks the beginning of a new era in the art of building.

Simultaneously, with the affirmation of the royal power, came a vast surge of faith throughout France: Carolingian buildings, which were too cramped and no longer suited to the needs of the times, were replaced by churches of much greater size built with bolder methods.

Religious architecture

In Périgord. – Périgord is rich in Romanesque churches. Their plain, severe appearance was enhanced by the use of a fine golden limestone with warm overtones. The exteriors were startling for the extreme simplicity of their decoration: the doorways without tympana were adorned with recessed orders carved with tori and saw-tooth, festoon-like decoration... The church's inside plan was simple as well; apsidal chapels opened off the chancel (St-Jean-de-Côle, Tourtoirac, Montagrier) and most of the east ends were flat. The predominance of just a nave is a custom in this area; only four churches have been built with side aisles.

The originality of the Périgord Romanesque style is in its vaulting – the **dome.** Brought back from the Orient, according to some specialists, a French invention according to others, the dome offers several advantages over cradle vaulting, which necessitates powerful buttresses. The dome on pendentives allows the support of the weight of the vault to be divided between the side walls and the transverse arches of the nave. Often used over the transept crossing, the domes also vault the nave when they follow one right after another as shown in Périgueux at St-Étienne-de-la-Cité, where this type of "doming" was first employed (followed by Trémolat, Agonac, Grand-Brassac, Cherval...). The nave is thus divided into several square bays vaulted with a dome on pendentives; the role of the pendentives is to serve as transition from a square to a circular base. St-Front in Périgueux with its Greek-cross plan covered with five domes is unique *(photograph p 118)*.

If these characteristics are to be found in many Romanesque buildings in Périgord, some churches have a different design: the nave is lined on either side by aisles (St-Privat, Cadouin) and the vaulting is rounded and pointed barrel. A number of façades are adorned with rows of arcades showing the relation with the art styles of the Saintonge and Angoumois regions.

Tympanum of St-Pierre at Carennac

In Quercy. – Quercy Romanesque style presents a number of similarities with that of Périgord Romanesque: same simple plan, same use of the dome (St-Stephen in Cahors, Souillac) same material – limestone. And yet the Quercy churches are much richer in sculptural decoration showing the influence of Moissac and the Languedoc School, the centre of which was at Toulouse. The school's workshops took inspiration from Byzantine art, illuminations and Antiquity and created carved doorways which were among the most beautiful in France at that time: remains of Souillac doorway with its admirable Prophet Isaiah, tympana of Cahors, Carennac, Martel and Collonges-La-Rouge, on the boundary between Quercy and Limousin.

Civil and military architecture. – There are few traces left of civil architecture of the Romanesque period. The former town hall of St-Antonin-Noble-Val in Quercy, although it has been considerably restored, is an interesting example of municipal Romanesque architecture of the 12C, with its sculptured gallery, arcaded portico and tall square belfry. The feudal fortresses erected in the 10 and 11C were greatly altered in later centuries and can scarcely be said to have resisted the warfare and destruction of the times. The only remaining buildings of this period are the keeps, last refuge of the defence systems, which were usually square in shape. Castelnau-Bretenoux Castle in Quercy, with its strongly fortified keep, is a good example of a feudal construction built on a hilltop site. In Périgord, parts of the castles of Biron and Beynac, Bourdeilles, Mareuil, Commarque and Castelnaud..., date back to the Romanesque period.

Gothic Art

Gothic art was born in the first half of the 12C, apparently in the Ile-de-France and very gradually superseded the Romanesque style. It arrived quite late in Périgord and Quercy.

Religious art

Architecture. – The essential elements of Gothic art – quadripartite vaulting, based on diagonal ribs, and the systematic use of the pointed arch – were to undergo changes according to the different geographical regions.
The south did not adopt the Gothic elements of the north and this new art style – Gothic – stayed closely linked to Romanesque traditions. Therefore, Gothic art, specifically southern, the said Languedoc School, is characterized by the construction of wide naves, without side aisles, many-sided apses and the use of massive buttresses, between which have been erected chapels, to assure the thrust of the vaulting (in the north, flying buttresses play this role).
Due to their geographical position, Périgord and Quercy were influenced by the north and south, shown at times in the same building. Sarlat cathedral, for example, presents a nave and side-aisles and soaring flying buttresses typical of northern Gothic, whereas the side chapels are evidence of the southern Gothic. In Quercy, the Languedoc School influenced the church plans – a nave almost as wide as it is high, without side aisles, but with side chapels – at Gourdon, Martel, Montpezat-du-Quercy and St-Cirq-Lapopie.

Monasteries. – Monastic architecture produced some remarkable groups of buildings which have not always been able to withstand the ravages of time: of the former Cistercian Abbey of Beaulieu-en-Rouergue only the abbey church (13C), remarkable for its pointed vaulting and its elegant heptagonal apse, remains. On the other hand there remain at Cadouin and Cahors, cloisters built in the Flamboyant style and at Périgueux, the cloisters which date from the 12 to the 16C to build.

Fortified churches. – During the 13 and 14C, while Gothic churches were being built in other regions, the insecurity that reigned throughout southwest France was the reason why churches were fortified and veritable fortresses with crenellated towers, watchpaths... were used as sanctuaries (churches at Rudelle and St-Pierre-Toirac). These churches constituted the surest refuge against the violence of marauding armed bands.

Sculpture and painting. – From the second half of the 13 to the 15C were carved several remarkable works of art: the tomb of St Stephen at Aubazine, Entombment (15C) at Carennac, tomb of the Cardaillacs at Espagnac-Ste-Eulalie and the recumbent figures of Cardinal Pierre des Prés and his nephew Jean des Prés in the collegiate church at Montpezat-du-Quercy.
Frescoes are mural painting done with water-based pigments on fresh plaster, which allows the colours to sink; this technique was used to decorate numerous chapels and churches. The west dome in Cahors cathedral is entirely covered with 14C frescoes.
In Rocamadour the chapels are painted with frescoes inside and on the exterior façades. In the chapels of St-André-des-Arques, Martignac, Soulomès (Quercy), Cheylard at St-Geniès and the Montferrand-du-Périgord churchyard, naive 14 and 15C frescoes recounting the Holy Scriptures are a fine example of how both peasants and lords were clothed.

Civil and military architecture. – A number of **castles** in Périgord and Quercy were constructed during the Gothic period as can be seen in the architectural details found at Bourdeilles, Château-l'Évêque, Beynac-et-Cazenac, Castelnaud, Castelnau-Bretenoux and Cabrerets. Bonaguil is in a class of its own, for although it was built at the end of the 15C and early part of the 16C it has all the features of a medieval fortress *(photograph p 30).* In the **towns** an important burst of construction occurred after the Hundred Years' War. This building boom hit Sarlat, Périgueux and Bergerac as well as Cahors, Figeac, Gourdon, Martel... The façades of the town houses are opened by large pointed arches on the ground floor – where the small shop was set up – depressed arched or rose windows on the upper floors and the whole ornamented with turrets. Among the finest examples of this period note Hôtel de la Raymondie in Martel, the Mint in Figeac, Hôtel Plamon in Sarlat and the famous Valentré Bridge in Cahors.

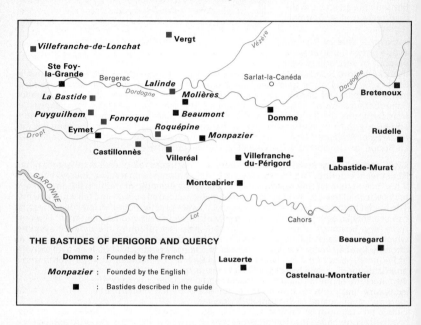

THE BASTIDES OF PERIGORD AND QUERCY

Domme : Founded by the French

Monpazier : Founded by the English

■ : Bastides described in the guide

The bastides. – These new, more or less fortified towns (from the Oc language word: *bastidas),* appeared in the 13C; and in the 14C their fortified aspect was developed.

The founders. – The principal founders were Alphonse de Poitiers (1249-71) – Count of Toulouse and brother to Saint Louis; and from 1272 on, the lords acting upon the orders of Philip the Bold, Philip the Fair and King Edward I, also Duke of Aquitaine.

Development. – Their construction satisfied economic, military and political needs. The founders took advantage of the growth of the population and encouraged people to settle on their land, which had been previously divided up in equal parcels. They in return for the land (land to live on and land to cultivate) were granted a charter, guaranteed protection, had no military service and had the right to inherit.

The bailie represented the king, dispensed justice and collected taxes, however, the consuls, elected by the people, administered the town; the town had recorded gains. After the Albigensian Crusade, the Count of Toulouse, Raymond VII built about 40 *bastides*; with the outbreak of hostilities between the French and English over the Périgord, Quercy and Agenais borders, the political and military advantages of the *bastide* were confirmed. Alphonse de Poitiers had built Eymet, Castillonès and Villeréal along the Dropt River as well as Villefranche-du-Périgord and Ste-Foy-la-Grande. The king of England responded with the construction of Beaumont (1272), Molières, Lalinde and Monpazier (1285); while in 1281 Philip the Bold founded Domme.

Urbanism. – All the *bastides,* whether French or English, were built to an identical plan: a chequered square or rectangular plan (Ste-Foy-la-Grande, Monpazier) and yet they differed either because of the terrain and type of site needed or because of the possibilities of population growth and defence purposes. In addition, the *bastide* was at times built around a pre-existing building – a fortified church as in Beaumont or a castle.

The plan of Monpazier is the most characteristic; it is on a quadrilateral plan with straight streets which crossed alleys known as **carreyrous** at right angles; while narrow spaces or **andromes** divided the house and served as fire breaks, drains or even latrines; in the centre of town the "square" was surrounded with covered arcades or **couverts** also known as **cornières** and contained a wooden covered market *(halle).* The church and cemetery stood either near the main square or its periphery; the outer walls were punctuated with towers and gateways and surrounded the *bastides.* The new towns sometimes enjoyed a name that was evidence of their founder (Villeréal = royal town), their privileges (Villefranche) or their link to a castle (Castelnau). Most of the *bastides,* built some 500 years ago, no longer look as they once did; the best preserved are Monpazier, Domme and Eymet.

*Each year the **Michelin Red Guide France***
revises its selection of hotels and restaurants in the following categories
- pleasant, quiet, secluded
- with an exceptionally interesting or extensive view
- with gardens, tennis courts, swimming pool or equipped beach.

Renaissance Art

At the beginning of the 16C, the artistic movement in France was revitalized by the influence of Italy. Artistic treasures in Italy awoke in the king, François I, and the noblemen, the desire to copy the architecture and sculpture and introduce it to their native land, which they did by employing Italian artists.

Architecture. – In Périgord and Quercy, the new style flowered at Assier where the château and church were built at the beginning of the 16C by Galiot de Genouillac, Grand Master of the Artillery under François I, who had participated in the campaign in Italy. This château, a remarkable realization, comparable to the finest châteaux of the Loire Valley, was unfortunately three-quarters destroyed. The châteaux of Montal and Puyguilhem, by their grace and style, link themselves also to the Loire Valley châteaux. Most of the other châteaux built in the 16C show an important defensive side in spite of the windows, dormers, chimneys and other pure Renaissance architectural elements. This is the case in the châteaux of Monbazillac, Losse and Bannes while the châteaux of Cénevières, Bourdeilles, Lanquais and Les Bories and the church at Rouffignac were partially transformed by the Renaissance; Biron Castle graced itself with a fine Renaissance chapel.

Civil architecture was also influenced by the graceful Italian style: Roaldès Mansion in Cahors, Consul's House (or Cayla House) in Périgueux, Hôtel de Maleville in Sarlat, and Hôtel de Labenche in Brive.

Sculpture. – In Quercy, at Assier, the remarkable friezes carved with militaristic attributes, which decorate the outside of the church and the interior façade of the château, are among the most original works of the Renaissance. Inside the church, the tomb of Galiot de Genouillac completes this unit.

The inner court of Montal Castle is an outstanding example of the Italian style with its busts in high relief, works of art of realism and excellent taste; inside, the remarkable staircase rivals those of the châteaux of the Loire. In the chapel at Biron Castle, the recumbent figures of the Gontaut-Birons are decorated with carvings influenced by the Italian Quattrocento (15C).

Classical Art

The classical period (17-18C) did not produce much in the region. The Château de Hautefort and its hospital with its central plan, on the borders of Limousin and Périgord, are very good examples of classical architecture, while the Château de Rastignac, built in the early 19C, is an almost exact copy of the White House in Washington, D.C.

Architectural elements such as staircases and door frames are more frequent. The wood sculpture that remains is interesting: for example, the monumental altarpiece in the baroque style located in St-Front in Périgueux.

A window of La Boétie's House in Sarlat

TRADITIONAL RURAL ARCHITECTURE

The solid and elegant rural architecture of Périgord and Quercy are among the finest in France. Many houses doomed to ruin, due to the rural exodus, have been saved by lovers of old stones who have restored these houses and established them as their holiday homes (more than half of the houses in Lot are holiday homes).

The chartreuse. – This house, quite preponderant in the southwest of France – in Périgord alone some 200 have been accounted for – is a manor-house reflecting more a way of life than social rank or pretention. It began appearing in the 17C, spread in the 18C and was popular until the late 19C (most were built 1650-1850).
This one-storey rural manor-house is often a wine-grower's residence. The architectural details either exterior (symmetry, moulding, balustraded terrace...) or interior (a series of rooms are built off a north-oriented corridor) distinguish it from the farmhouse. It is not a château, although at times because of its size, it could be considered one.

Périgord houses. – The most typical house of **Périgord Noir** is a sturdy block-like construction in golden limestone topped with a steeply pitched roof covered with flat brown tiles or *lauzes*; Périgord *lauzes* are neither slate nor layered schist-like tiles but small limestone slabs. Set horizontally, their weight is such (500kg/m²) that they require a strong, steeply pitched timberwork roof to distribute the weight. In the wealthier houses, small towers or dovecots frame the house.

In Périgord Blanc or the **Ribéracois**, the low houses in grey or white limestone are opened by windows topped by *œils-de-bœuf*. The flat roof covered with Roman-style terracotta tiles already announces a more meridional style.
In **Double**, a land of woods, traditionally the houses were in clay and half-timbered.

Périgord house

Quercy houses. – Built in blocks of white limestone mortared in lime, the solid Quercy houses present an ensemble of volumes, additions, towers and openings which makes for a fine rural building.
Traditionally, the ground floor, slightly below ground level, called the *cave*, shelters the stable, sheds and store rooms. The first floor was used as the living quarters; access is via an outside staircase which gives onto a terrace protected by a porch or *bolet* held up by stone or wood columns.

Quercy house

Two types of roofing are found: the steeply pitched roof with flat tiles or sometimes *lauzes* and the slightly pitched roof covered with Roman-style terracotta tiles.

Dovecots. – There are many dovecots in the area: either as small towers attached to the main building, or isolated, sometimes topped by a porch. These elegant dovecots of very varied architecture were nearly all built between 1750-1850; they were intended less for the keeping of pigeons than for their droppings, an excellent manure for the small holdings. So important was this manure that when the property was divided on the death of the owner, the pigeon droppings were divided among the heirs in the same way as the land and poultry.
In Quercy, the dovecots belonged to the peasant and not the lord as in Périgord and other regions, where a privilege had to be paid in proportion to the number of columns supporting the dovecot.

Dry-stone huts. – Here and there are to be found, isolated in a field, the curious shepherds' shelters built of flat stones with strange conical roofs, known as **gariottes** or **caselles**. Peasants use them as shelters, tool sheds or barns.

A dovecot

FOOD AND WINE IN PÉRIGORD AND QUERCY

Geese from Périgord

Périgord and Quercy are a kingdom of gastro-nomic delights. Their names spring to mind truffles, *foies gras* and *confits*, specialities which rank high among the culinary glories of France. Since the 15C, Périgueux restaurant owners and their *pâtés* have been famous. Louis XV ennobled the Périgord cook, Villereynier, who by royal favour, was styled "Villereynier de la Gâtine, Pastrycook to the king". During the Revolution, the master-cooks Lafon and Courtois continued to supply both France and England with their part-ridge *pâtés*. Until then Périgord *pâté* was made from partridges stuffed with chicken livers and chopped truffles. Later, the *pâté* was made with truffled goose liver after a precept found in 1726 by Close of Strasbourg. Talleyrand, on the strengh of his Périgord connections, won his toughest diplomatic battles around a sumptuous table: truf-fled *pâté* and Monbazillac were his surest allies. This rich food uses local products *(see pp 15-16)*: truffles, *cèpes* (a mushroom), walnuts, and of course geese, duck and pork, which are the pride of the Périgord and Quercy farm.

Menu. – The meal always begins with a *tourain*, a white garlic soup made with goose fat and eggs, followed by *foie gras* or *pâté de foie* (general term meaning liver *pâté*) and then *cèpe* or truffle omlette. The main course then arrives, a *confit d'oie aux pommes sarladaises* (goose preserved in its own fat, browned and served with potatoes also cooked in the goose fat); a refreshing salad seasoned with walnut oil and walnuts, fol-lowed by a *cabecou*, a Quercy goat cheese and finally, if you have any room left, a delicious walnut cake, again a speciality of the region.

Truffles. – *See more on truffles pp 15 and 142*. This underground mushroom, which when fully grown weighs about 100g – 3 1/2oz, is considered by the reputed gastro-nomer, Curnonsky, to epitomize the perfumed soul of Périgord. The epicure's black diamond, the truffle, speckles all food with its large, dark patches and can be seen and tasted in all *foies gras, pâtés*, poultry, *ballottines* (a mixture of white turkey meat and *foie gras* moulded in aspic) and *galantines*. It enhances every food it touches with its per-meating aroma.
It can also be eaten alone wrapped and cooked in the fire, but because of its rarity and price, this is the supreme luxury.

Foies gras. – The liver of considerable weight is obtained by the forced feeding of geese or ducks. After three months loose in the fields they have a transitory diet which consists of flour, meat and corn and then the three weeks of forced feeding begin, during which, with the help of a funnel, three times a day at set hours they ingurgitate 30-40k – 66-88lbs of a maize mash. After this diet, their liver reaches the weight of 600 to 1 500g – 21-53oz. These livers can be served different ways: *foie d'oie* (goose liver) can be preserved and is found as a block *(bloc)*, as a *pâté* or as a *terrine*. It is also presented as *mousse de foie gras* (75% minimum of liver) or as *mousse de foie d'oie* (50% minimum of liver) or included in the *ballottine*.
The duck liver, a more subtle taste, is often eaten as it is.

Confits. – Traditional basis of Périgord and Quercy cookery, the *confit* was a method which enabled the peasant, before the freezer arrived on the scene, to preserve the dif-ferent pieces of the goose after having taken out the liver. Today a speciality, *confits* are still prepared in the traditional method. The cut pieces are cooked in their fat for three hours and then preserved in large earthenware pots. This procedure is used for goose, duck, turkey and pork (pork *confit* is called *enchauds*). Pure goose fat takes the place of butter in Périgord cooking and is used for example, to cook *pommes de terres sarladaises*.

Stuffings and sauces. – Stuffing is also frequently used: moist and tasty, flavoured with liver and truffles, stuffing garnishes poultry, game, suckling pig and the famous *cou d'oie farci* (stuffed goose neck).
The sauces most commonly used are the *rouilleuse* which goes with and gives colour to poultry *fricassée*, and Périgueux sauce, a Madeira sauce made with fresh truffles.

Wine. – *See map of vineyards p 16*. The wine of **Cahors** is dark red in colour and full-bodied in flavour. The wine improves if left to mature 2 to 3 years in the cask and 10 years in the bottle; it then acquires a body and nose and may be drunk with poultry, game, roasts and cheese.
The **Bergerac** region, where a large area is planted with Sauvignon grape, produces both red and white wine. Among the white wines **Monbazillac** stands alone. Golden, clinging and fragrant, this heavy wine can be served as an *apéritif* or with *foie gras* or dessert. It owes its special fragance to the *pourriture noble* – noble rot – which reduces the acidity of the raisin; this procedure dates from the Renaissance. Monbazillac acquires its full flavour after 2 to 3 years and will keep for 30 years.
The white wines (Montravel and Bergerac), fragrant and fruity, can be served with seafood and fish; the soft, sweet white wines (Côtes de Bergerac, Côtes de Montravel, Haut Montravel, Saussignac), are served as an *apéritif* or with white meats.
The red wines (Bergerac, Côtes de Bergerac), fruity and well-rounded, can be drunk while young, whereas **Pécharmant**, an excellent full-bodied, generous wine, takes a long time to mature.

Sights

★★★ **Worth a journey**
★★ **Worth a detour**
★ **Interesting**

Sightseeing route with departure point indicated

Ecclesiastical building: Catholic - Protestant		Castle, Château - Ruins	
Building (with main entrance)		Wayside cross or calvary - Fountain	
Ramparts - Tower		Panorama - View	
Gateway		Lighthouse - Windmill	
Gardens, parks, woods		Dam - Factory or power station	
Statue - Viewing table		Fort - Cave	
Miscellaneous sights		Megalithic monument	

Other symbols

Motorway (unclassified)	Hospital - Covered market
Interchange complete, limited, number	Main post office (with poste restante)
Major through road	Tourist information centre
Dual carriageway	Car park
Stepped street - Footpath	Police station (Gendarmerie)
Pedestrian street	Barracks
Unsuitable for traffic	Cemetery - Synagogue
Pass - Altitude	Stadium
Station - Coach station	Racecourse - Golf course
Metro station - Cable-car	Outdoor or indoor swimming pool
Ferry (river and lake crossings)	Skating rink - Mountain refuge hut
Swing bridge	Pleasure boat harbour
Ferry services: Passengers and cars Passengers only	Telecommunications tower or mast
Airport	Water tower - Quarry
	Reference number common to town plans and MICHELIN maps

MICHELIN maps and town plans are north orientated.

Main shopping streets are printed in a different colour in the list of streets.

Town plans: roads most used by traffic and those on which guide listed sights stand are fully drawn; the beginning only of lesser roads is indicated.

Local maps: only the primary and sightseeing routes are indicated.

Abbreviations

A	Local agricultural office (Chambre d'Agriculture)	**J**	Law Courts (Palais de Justice)	**POL.**	Police station
C	Chamber of Commerce (Chambre de Commerce)	**M**	Museum	**T**	Theatre
H	Town Hall (Hôtel de ville)	**P**	Préfecture Sous-préfecture	**U**	University

⊘ Times and charges for admission are listed at the end of the guide

The practical information chapter, at the end of the Guide, regroups:
– a list of the local or national organisations supplying additional information
– a section on admission times and charges.

Sights

AGONAC

Michelin map **75** fold 5 or **233** fold 42 – Local map p 81

This Périgord Blanc (White Périgord) town lies in a pleasant setting in a hilly region abounding in walnut trees and truffle-oaks.

🕐 **St-Martin**. – The stunted outline of the church stands erect in the Beauronne Valley, beside the D 3ᴱ, south of the town.

The great square bell tower and the buttresses (16C) were added after the destruction caused by the Protestants during the Wars of Religion.

The interior has all the characteristics of a Romanesque style, often seen in Périgord: an arched nave, domes above the pre-chancel and the sanctuary and a flat chevet. The nave has three late-11C bays; the main dome, which is on pendentives and supports the bell tower, was built in the 12C; the system of two-storey high defence chambers, encircling the dome recalls the troubled times when churches were turned into fortresses.

The chancel is decorated with archaic style capitals of monsters spewing leaves.

ALLASSAC

Michelin map **75** fold 8 or **239** fold 26 – Facilities

Situated in an undulating countryside near the Vézère, Allassac has a certain charm with its old houses roofed with slate.

The Gothic **church**, built of black schist set off in places with red sandstone, is preceded by a machicolated belfry-porch.

Near the church stand the only remains of the old fortifications, Caesar Tower, built in drystone in the 9 and 12 C.

EXCURSIONS

Donzenac. – Pop 1 947. *6km – 4 miles to the southeast by the D 25.*
This small town is built near the rich Brive Basin *(qv)*. It held a strategic position during the feudal wars; several houses remain around the church and its 13C bell tower.

St-Bonnet-la-Rivière. – *17km – 11 miles. Leave Allassac to the northwest by the D 134.*
Le Saillant. – This hamlet is in a pleasant setting at the mouth of the Vézère Gorges *(p 146)*. From the beautiful old bridge with pointed cutwaters spanning the Vézère, can be seen, on the right bank, surrounded by a moat, a 12C manor-house (restored), where Mirabeau (1749-91) the orator resided.

Leave Le Saillant to the west by the D 134 then bear left to Objat then take the D 901 towards Juillac.

St-Bonnet-la-Rivière. – Pop 334. Standing in this small village is a Romanesque church, which is circular in shape and is flanked by a belfry-porch. Legend has it that a knight on his return from the Holy Land built a church to resemble the Holy Sepulchre.

★ ANS COUNTRY

Michelin map **75** fold 7 or **233** folds 43 and 44 and **239** fold 25

The Ans Country, limited by Limousin and Périgord was the most important overlordship of the Limoges viscounty. Many of the villages in the area still have as part of their name the word "d'Ans": Badefols-d'Ans, Ste-Eulalie-d'Ans, Granges-d'Ans... In 1607 the overlordship was united with the crown under the reign of Henri IV. The countryside is lovely; the rolling hills are covered with a patchwork of woods, fields planted with crops and walnut trees. One of the major agricultural activities is the raising of sucking calves.

ROUND TOUR STARTING FROM MONTIGNAC
101km – 62 1/2 miles – about 3 hours

The itinerary described below extends beyond the limits of the Ans Country but does go from one end of it to the other.

Montignac. – *Description p 110.*

Take the D 704 northwards and bear left into the D 67.

Auriac-du-Périgord. – This charming village has a Romanesque church, which is transformed in the 15C. It is linked to the presbytery by a balustrade.

Turn around and bear left on the D 65; at La Bachellerie bear left to the Château de Rastignac.

Château de Rastignac. – Designed by a native of Périgord, the architect Mathurin Blanchard, the château was built between 1811 and 1817 by the Marquis de Rastignac. This handsome neo-classical building bears a striking resemblance to the White House in Washington DC *(see Michelin Green Guide to Washington DC)*. It comprises a rectangular main building surmounted by a terrace adorned with a pillared balustrade. A semicircular peristyle with eight Ionic columns forms the façade on the garden side. Burnt down by the Germans in 1944, the château has since been restored.

Once on the N 89, drive westwards beyond Thenon, bear right on the D 68.

Ajat. – Pop 297. In this village, the Romanesque church, which has an oven-vaulted apse roofed with stone slabs, and the machicolated castle walls, make a picturesque group.

Take the road to Bauzens.

Bauzens. – The Romanesque church's main doorway has an unornamented tympanum resting on a saddle roof and small columns with carved capitals. A relieving arch supports a triple arcade.

From Bauzens go north on the D 67ᴱ; bear right towards Ste-Orse.

Once at Ste-Orse, the road follows the crest line and offers lovely views of the impressive silhouette of the Château de Hautefort, perched on its promontory and the wooded countryside of the Auvézère.

Bear left onto the D 71.

This road goes down into Hautefort (fine wiews of the château) and skirts Coucou Lake (Étang du Coucou; swimming).

★★Château de Hautefort. – *Description p 92.*

Take the D 62 towards Badefols-d'Ans.

Badefols-d'Ans. – Pop 511. The lordship of Badefols was the property of the Born family. One of the members of the family, Bertrand de Born *(qv)*, a soldier and poet, was mentioned in Dante's *Divine Comedy.*
A sturdy square keep, the oldest part of the castle, was once linked to a 15C main building. The 18C wing, on a right angle, serves as living quarters. Burned by the Germans in 1944, the Castle has since been restored.

Continue along the D 71.

The road offers views of the Auvézère to the north and the Vézère to the south. The landscape shows both the features of a Périgord countryside – gentle fertile slopes where crops grow, fields cut by quickset hedges, walnut plantations and lines of poplars – and that of a Limousin countryside – farmlands divided by trees, dense woods and sandstone houses roofed no longer with the pink tile of Périgord but with grey slate.

St-Robert. – *Description p 137.*

The D 51 and the D 64 descend into the Vézère Valley. The road crosses the red sandstone village of Villac.

After Beauregard-de-Terrasson **Peyraux Castle** appears on the left, clinging to its wooded hill. The main building is flanked by two round feudal towers.

At Le Lardin-St-Lazare pick up the D 704 which takes you back to Montignac.

★ LES ARQUES
Pop 173

Michelin map **79** fold 7 or **235** fold 10 – 6km – 3 1/2 miles south of Cazals – Local map p 52

In this tranquil Bouriane *(qv)* village are two interesting churches both of which have undergone extensive restoration.

Ossip Zadkine. – Russian by birth and French by adoption, the sculptor Zadkine (1890-1967) arrived in Paris in 1909. He was first influenced by cubism, a style which he subsequently abandoned.
In 1934 he bought the house at Les Arques where he realised his most important works (*Diana, Pietà, Christ*); they prevail by their monumental expression and well-constructed forms.

Zadkine Museum. – Three rooms display examples of the artist's work: lithographs, tapestries, bronzes (*Musical Trio*, 1928) and monumental wood sculptures *(Diana)*. An audio-visual presentation shows an interview of Zadkine.

★St-Laurent. – Located in the centre of the village, this church is all that is left of a priory-deanery founded in the 11C by Marcilhac Abbey *(p 103)*. When the nave was restored in the 19C, it was narrowed and shortened; yet the apse and apsidal chapels have kept the purity of the Romanesque style. Certain archaisms have been preserved such as the oculus in the south arm of the transept, a characteristic of the Carolingean style, and the tori at the base of the columns supporting the transverse arches. The most original part of the vessel is the form of the arches: round horseshoe-shaped arches onto which open the apsidal chapels and rampant arches which adorn the passageway between the apse and apsidal chapels.
Two moving works by Zadkine enhance the church's interior: the monumental **Christ★** (on the back of the façade) and the **Pietà★** (in the crypt).

St-André-des-Arques. – *Go down towards the Masse River, cross the D 45.*
Set in a clearing, this church presents a remarkable series of **frescoes★** of the late 15C, discovered in 1954 by Zadkine.
The chancel window is framed by the Annunciation and on either side by the apostles with either the instruments of their punishment – St Andrew and the x-shaped cross and Matthias and the halberd – or the instruments with which they are symbolised in art: St Peter with his keys, St James with his pilgrim's staff and St Thomas with his architect's set square. On the vault, spangled with red stars, is Christ in Majesty seated on a rainbow-shaped throne with one hand blessing and the other holding the globe. He is surrounded by the symbols of the four Evangelists. On the pillars of the apse, which are holding up a triumphal arch, are St Christopher and on the other side the Infant Jesus waiting for Christopher to help him cross the river.

*The layout diagram on p 3 shows the **Michelin Maps** covering the region. In the text, reference is made to the map which is the most suitable from a point of view of scale and practicality.*

Michelin map **75** southeast of fold 19 or **235** fold 11 or **239** fold 39

This Quercy village, due to the generosity of Galiot de Genouillac, possesses two remarkable Renaissance monuments.

Galiot de Genouillac (1465-1545). – Page under Charles VIII, then first gentleman of the bedchamber under Louis XII and finally Grand Master of the Artillery under François I, Jacques Galiot de Genouillac enjoyed announcing that he had served under three kings. This captain – a military man and a brilliant tactician – was covered with titles: Master of the Horse, knight in the Order of St Michael, Seneschal of Quercy, Superintendent of Finances and Grand Master of the Artillery. He also organised the camp of the Field of Cloth of Gold near Calais in 1520 when François I met Henry VIII. Proud of his accomplishments, the flashy Galiot de Genouillac had them recounted on a frieze on both the castle and church. His motto, with is double meaning – *J'aime Fortune* (I love fortune!) or *J'aime Fort Une* (I love one greatly) – can also be found on both buildings.

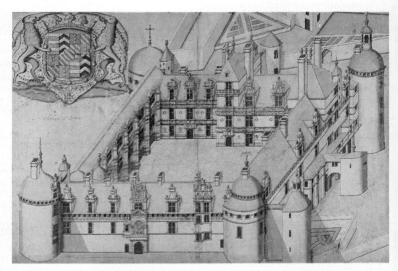

Gaignières's ink and watercolour rendering of the castle in 1680

⊘ **Castle**. – "Although built in a very ugly setting, in rough, ugly and mountainous country, the Castle of Assier," Brantôme (historian and biographer, 1540-1614) maintained, "equals in splendour the palaces of the Loire Valley," and he went on: "the best furnished house in France with its quantities of silver, tapestries and silks." Galiot de Genouillac wanted a sumptuous residence displaying his wealth and glory, a wish which was fulfilled to judge by Gaignières's ink and watercolour rendering of the castle in 1680 *(see above)*. Unfortunately as early as 1766, the castle was sold by his descendants and broken up. Only the guards' wing was saved; it is much plainer than the other three wings which were decorated in the more grand Renaissance style. The castle was saved from total abandonment when Prosper Mérimée, in 1841, had the castle classed as a historical monument.
The exterior façade has preserved its machicolations between two round towers. In the centre above the monumental entrance, framed by two Doric columns, is a niche which held the equestrian statue of Galiot de Genouillac. The roof once in the form of an upturned ship's keel and covered with stone slabs was pierced by several dormer windows, like those which can still be seen.
The **interior façade★** has none of the severity of its counterpart. On the contrary, it shows a classical purity. It is decorated with friezes divided into sections running above each storey. The many scenes from the legend of Hercules symbolise the captain's omnipotence; cannons spurting flames recall his office of Grand Master of the Artillery. Between each window medallions with busts were placed – only the bust of a Roman emperor remains.
Inside, in the lower rooms with pointed arched vaulting, architectural elements of the castle can be seen as well as a remarkable 17C recumbent figure of Anne de Genouillac, who was a Maltese prioress, and a small exhibit on Galiot de Genouillac (including a hologram of his armour which was bought by the Metropolitan Museum of Art in New York City – *see Michelin Green Guide to New York City*).
A fine staircase in the transitional Gothic-Renaissance style leads to the 1st floor. On the landing is a finely carved limestone **pillar★**. It depicts on one side Fortune, on the second side Galiot de Genouillac's trophies and on the third side Hercules fighting the Nemean Lion. Also on the 1st floor a room displays 17C grisailles.

★**Church** (**Église**). – This was built between 1540 and 1549 and is the original structure. The decoration on the outside is a long panegyric of Galiot de Genouillac's exploits and titles to fame.
A **frieze** goes right round the church. The subjects depicted include: sieges, battles, knights, foot-soldiers and artillerymen, and will surprise the visitor who will hardly expect to see such warlike motifs ornamenting a religious building. The frieze is a useful document on 16C arms and costume.

The **doorway** has a classical air: on the tympanum two cherubim proffer to the Virgin the captain's insignia, his sword as the Master of the Horse and St Michael's chain. The portico, formed by two columns surmounted by a triangular pediment, supports a domed niche.

Inside, the first chapel on the north side contains the great captain's **tomb**: the recumbent figure in court dress lies on a marble sarcophagus; above in high relief, Galiot de Genouillac is shown surrounded by his military emblems and two gunners who would appear to be waiting for his orders to fire.

The **stellar vaulting** of this chapel, which forms a dome supported on squinches, is an outstanding and very unusual feature.

★ AUBAZINE   Pop 673

Michelin map **75** fold 9 or **239** fold 26 – Local map p 56 – Facilities

Aubazine is in a pleasant setting of wooded hills between the Corrèze and Coiroux. The grey houses, roofed in slate and set on a crest facing the Coiroux Gorges, are dominated by the imposing church which recalls the great Cistercian abbey that once stood there and of which only a few buildings remain.

The founder. – St Stephen, who was born in a hamlet in Corrèze in 1085, founded the Abbey of Aubazine as a hermitage in 1125. In 1142 the community adopted the rule of St Benedict and was dependent of the Abbey of Dalon. St Stephen was installed as abbot by the Bishop of Limoges and during his abbacy the community expanded rapidly. In 1147 the monks adopted the Cistercian Law, becoming a sister house of Cîteaux. A larger church had to be built; it was started in 1156.

In the nearby Coiroux Gorges once stood a convent for nuns founded by St Stephen in 1142. Only a 13C chapel in ruins remains.

A local saying stated that one with a daughter at Coiroux gains a son-in-law at Aubazine.

★**Church (Église).** – The abbey church was built during the second half of the 12C on the Cistercian plan. The octagonal bell tower, one storey high and adorned with arcades and twinned bays, looks refined on an otherwise austere monument. The Limousin influence is noticeable.

The size of the church is easily imagined upon learning that when the church was truncated in the 18C, it lost six bays. The main façade was built during that time.

Inside, the nave has three bays with barrel vaulting and aisles with groined vaulting. The transept crossing is topped by an elegant dome on pendentives which is the base of the bell tower. Transept chapels with flat east walls open each arm of the chancel, which is ended by a five-sides apse. The building, as a whole, has a certain harmony and grandeur.

The 12C stained-glass windows are executed in grisaille.

★★**Tomb of St Stephen.** – *In the south arm of the transept.* This remarkable memorial takes the form of a stone shrine and was placed over the tomb of the founder in the 13C. The recumbent figure's face has been disfigured by his faithful flock, who scraped at the stone in the hope of collecting dust, which they believed to be miraculous.

The canopy above the recumbent figure has two sloping sides and rests on arcades supported by small columns; the sloping sides are decorated with high reliefs. On one side, the Virgin with the Child Jesus on her knees is shown greeting St Stephen and his religious orders of monks and nuns on earth; on the other side (not visible) the same characters reappear before the Virgin and Jesus on the day of their resurrection as the dead. The richness of the decoration, the delicacy and truth of the facial expressions make this one of the most precious architectural specimens of Gothic times.

Furnishings. – In the south aisle is a splendid oak cupboard (12C) embellished with blind arcades. It is one of the oldest pieces of religious furniture in France.

The 18C stalls are quite archaic. Men and women, animals and monsters cover the misericords in picturesque and caricatural detail.

In the first chapel, in the north arm of the transept, a 15C polychrome stone *Pietà* is notable for the immense spiritual expression it exudes. Although primitive and plain, the detail is admirable – look at the Virgin's hands tightly clutching her son's falling body.

⊙**Former abbey (Ancienne Abbaye).** – The conventual buildings are now occupied by a community of nuns, Catholics following the Oriental rite. The visitor sees the chapter house with its groined vaulting resting on two huge round columns, the former common room also with groined vaulting but resting on square pillars, the monolithic fountain or *lavabo* and the fish-breeding pool, fed by a canal 1.5km – 1 mile long dug by the Cistercians to supply the abbey with water.

EXCURSION

★**Puy de Pauliac.** – *Take the D 48 along the Coiroux Gorges and bear left onto a smaller road to the summit.*

A path (*1/4 hour on foot Rtn*) through heather and chestnut trees leads up to the top (520m – 1 760ft) from where there is a wide **view**★ (viewing table) southeast onto Vic Rock and northwards onto Monédières Massif.

Continue along the D 48 to the **Coiroux Tourist Centre** (Centre Touristique du Coiroux) where facilities (swimming, sailing, windsurfing and golf) have been set up around a lake.

★ BEAULIEU-EN-ROUERGUE ABBEY

Michelin map **79** fold 19 or **235** fold 19 – 10km – 6 miles southeast of Caylus – Local map p 130

⊙ On the border of Quercy and Rouergue, the charming Seye Valley was the place where, in 1144, several monks sent by St Bernard founded an abbey which was called Beaulieu (*Belloc* in Occitanian).

After the Revolution, the abbey was partly dismantled and became a farm. It was not until 1960 that restoration was started by the abbey's new owners and pursued when it was donated to the Caisse des Monuments Historiques (Historic Buildings Commission) in 1973. The result is remarkable, especially the church, which is an excellent example of Cistercian architecture.

Several of the abbey buildings house the **Contemporary Art Centre** (Centre d'Art Contemporain) which holds exhibits and a festival of contemporary music in the summer.

★**Church (Église)**. – This fine building erected in the mid-13C is a good example of the pure Gothic style: pointed vaulted nave lit by rose and lancet windows.

The elegant heptagonal apse ends the transept which has, above its crossing, an octagonal **dome** on squinches. A square chapel opens off each transept.

Abbey buildings (Bâtiments abbatiaux). – The **chapter house**, the oldest part of the abbey, opened onto the cloisters (no longer standing) with three pointed arches. It is made up of two bays each covered with three pointed vaults supported by two mighty columns.

The **cellar**, on the ground floor of the Laymen's Building (Bâtiment des Convers), has ten cross-ribbed vaults resting on four columns, the capitals of which are adorned with leaves with little relief. The beauty of the room, the refinement in the detail used, as shown in the unadorned pendants, demonstrates the careful attention that the Cistercians paid in the construction of each building, even an annexe.

BEAUMONT   Pop 1 302

Michelin map **75** fold 15 or **235** fold 5 – Facilities

Beaumont was built as a *bastide* in 1272 by the Seneschal of Guyenne in the name of Edward I, king of England, and today retains only traces of the fortifications but presents many arcaded houses.

St-Front. – This church, built by the English in 1272, has four strong towers flanking the façade and east end, and a parapet walk. It was the last outpost of defence in the town in time of war. Last century restoration was carried out on a considerable scale greatly modifying the military character of the building. On the west face, capitals decorated with carved foliage carry the recessed arches of a fine doorway, which is surmounted by a gallery with a delicately ornate balustrade.

Rampart ruins. – A good view of the curtain walls, the 13C fortified Luzier Gate (Porte de Luzier) and the impressive outline of St-Front can be seen by going westwards, beyond the line of ramparts.

EXCURSION

Château de Bannes. – *5km – 3 miles northwest by the D 660 and then a road on the left*. Perched on a rocky spur, the château was built at the end of the 15C by the bishop of Sarlat, Armand de Gontaud-Biron. What is so incongruous in this château is that the military features – machicolated towers – are tempered by the carved doorway and richly decorated dormer windows surmounted by finials and pinnacles in the Early Renaissance style.

BELVÈS   Pop 1 652

Michelin map **75** fold 16 or **235** fold 5 – Local map pp 76-77

Belvès is built in a picturesque hilltop setting overlooking the Nauze Valley. Arrive from the southeast by the D 52 or from the south by the D 710 to get a complete picture of the whole town: the old houses with their turrets and pinnacles and the terraces arranged as gardens or covered with foliage.

Place d'Armes. – Still to be seen in the square in the centre of the town, are the old belfry and the **covered market** (halle) with its round tiled roof: note the pillory chain attached to one of the pillars.

The former Dominican monastery surmounted by an octagonal bell tower is in Place de la Croix-des-Frères. There are some fine Gothic and Renaissance houses between the two squares. Rue des Filhols also starts from Place d'Armes. Note on the left the restored Hôtel Bontemps, a fine Renaissance mansion.

Each year
*the **Michelin Red Guide France***
revises its selection of stars for cuisine (good cooking)
accompanied by a mention of the culinary specialities and local wines;
and proposes a choice of simpler restaurants offering
a well-prepared meal, often with regional specialities for a moderate price.

Michelin map **75** folds 14 and 15 or **234** folds 4 and 8 or **235** fold 5 – Local maps pp 46 and 78

Spread out on both banks of the Dordogne where the river tends to be calmer and the valley widens and forms an alluvial plain, Bergerac is surrounded by prestigeous vineyards and fields of tobacco, cereals and maize.

In the heart of this town, which evokes the charm of the southern towns, the restoration of the old quarter brought about the renovation of 15 and 16C houses.

An intellectual and commercial crossroad. – The town's expansion began as early as the 12C. Benefiting from its situation as a port and bridging point, the town's middle class developed rapidly, due to their successful trade between the central provinces of Auvergne and Limousin and Bordeaux.

In the 16C, this Navarre fief became one of the bastions of Protestantism. The city knew a brilliant period. The town's printing presses published pamphlets which circulated throughout the Protestant world. In August 1577 the *Peace of Bergerac* was signed between the king of Navarre and the representatives of King Henri III; this was a preliminary to the *Edict of Nantes* (1598). But in 1620, Louis XIII's army took over the town and destroyed the ramparts. After the *Revocation of the Edict of Nantes* (1685), the Jesuits and Recollects tried to win back their Protestant disciples. A certain number of Bergerac citizens, faithful to their Calvinist beliefs, emigrated to Holland, a country where they had maintained commercial contacts.

Bergerac was the capital of Périgord until the Revolution, when the capital was transferred to Périgueux, which also became Préfecture of the département...

In the 19C, wine growing and river boating prospered until the onslaught of phylloxera and the arrival of the railway.

Bergerac today. – Essentially an agricultural centre, Bergerac is the capital of tobacco in France and as a result the Experimental Institute of Tobacco and the Tobacco Planters Centre of Learning and Perfection are located here.

In addition the 11 000ha – 27 170 acres of vineyards surrounding the town produce wine with an *appellation d'origine contrôlée* (literally controlled place of origin) which includes: Bergerac, Côtes de Bergerac, Monbazillac, Montravel and Pécharmant *(qv)*. The Regional Wine Council, which establishes the *appellation* of the wines, is located in the Recollects' Cloisters *(p 45)*.

The main industrial enterprise of the town is the powder factory producing nitro-cellulose for use in such industries as film-making, paint, varnish and plastics.

Famous citizens. – Oddly enough the "Cyrano" of Edmond Rostand's play was inspired by the 17C philosopher Cyrano de Bergerac whose name was in no way linked to this fair town. Not discouraged in the least bit, the town took it upon themselves to "adopt" this wayward son and erect a statue in his honour Place de la Myrpe. Whereas the philosopher Maine de Biran was a native son of Bergerac; he was born here in 1766.

★OLD BERGERAC *time: 1/2 hour (4 hours including the museums)*

A pleasant stroll through this maze of streets and shaded squares can be enhanced by a visit to the various museums.

Start at the car park which is located at the old port.

Old port (Ancien port) (C). – Try to imagine the *gabares (qv)* mooring here to drop off the products and wood, which came from the upper valley, and load on the barrels of wine for England and Holland via Bordeaux.

Leaning against the house, at the bottom of Rue du Port, is an amusing metre bar, which gauges the Dordogne's floods.

Rue du Château (C 5). – Overlooking this street, which makes a sharp turn, is an unusual balustraded balcony hanging over the street.

★★Tobacco Museum (Musée du Tabac) (C). – The museum is located in the **Peyrarède Mansion★** (Maison Peyrarède), also known as the French Kings' House, an elegant building (built in 1603) and ornamented with a corbelled turret. This remarkable and beautifully presented collection traces the history and evolution of tobacco through the centuries.

On the **first floor** the origin and evolution of the plant is described. Until the 15C tobacco was used only by the American Indians, who believed it possessed medicinal properties. On display are tobacco pouches, **calumets** or peace pipes and Indian pipes.

After the discovery of the New World, tobacco was introduced to Europe. Jean Nicot brought it into France in *c* 1560; he sent snuff to Catherine de' Medici to cure her migraines.

Smoking became such a craze that Pope Urbain VIII went so far as to excommunicate the smokers and Louis XIII forbade the sale of tobacco before proceeding to levy a tax. At this time tobacco was presented in the form of a carrot which then had to be grated to form powder. The **graters** exhibited are amazing works of art carved in wood or ivory.

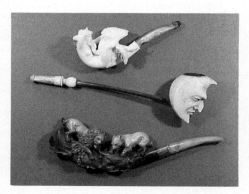

Two cigarette holders and a pipe in the Tobacco Museum

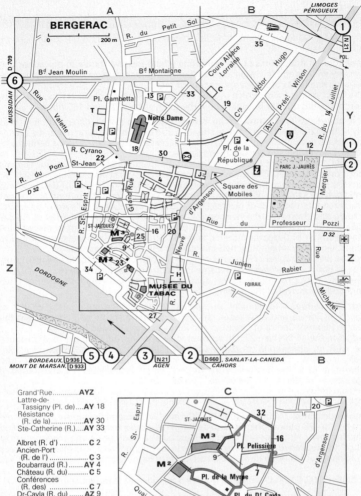

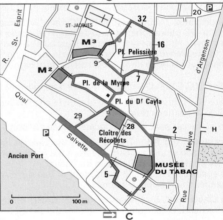

At the end of the 18C snuff is sold directly in powder form, which is preserved in large handpainted **porcelain jars.** Each smoker carries his own snuffbox. Exhibited alongside the jars are a number of these **snuffboxes,** some of which were decorated with portraits of Louis XVIII, Napoleon or Charles X. This was a way for the smoker to express his political views.

The next step in the art of smoking was the pipe. The pipe had been in use in Holland since the early 17C, but its use was considered vulgar and common. Officers of the First Empire started the fashion and were quickly followed by the Romantics, including George Sand. There are 19C **satirical engravings** depicting the art of consuming tobacco. In the display cabinets, **pipes** in porcelain, meerschaum and wood have been decorated with comic subject matters and portraits of famous people.

Finally in the mid-19C, the cigarette arrives on the scene and with it, its accessories, including the elegant ivory **cigarette holders.**

On the **second floor** works of art are displayed depicting tobacco and smokers. *Two Smokers* from the 17C northern French School, *Three Smokers* by Meissonier and the charming *Interior of the Tobacconist's Shop* by David II Teniers, known as Teniers the Younger.

Nearby is the pedestal table made by the Mexican Indians. It is fascinating to see how the table's marquetry has been made with cigar bands.

A section is devoted to the cultivation of tobacco (planting, harvesting, drying, etc...) especially in the Bergerac region.

⊙**Museum of Urban History** (Musée d'Histoire Urbaine). – In a house adjoining the Peyrarède Mansion are displayed objects – maps, documents, architectural remains, furnishings – evoking Bergerac's history.

Also worth noting are glazed earthenware, which had been made in 18C Bergerac, and old town plans.

After leaving Peyrarède Mansion towards the left, walk to Place du Feu and then the crossroads of Rue d'Albret.

Rue d'Albret (C 2). – At the end of this street to the right is the town hall, the former convent of the Sisters of Faith.

On the left, on the corner of Place du Feu, is a vast edifice with pointed arched doorways.

Place du Docteur-Cayla and Place de la Myrpe (C). – This large, charming shaded square is lined with half-timbered houses. In the middle of Place de la Myrpe stands the statue of Cyrano de Bergerac enveloped in his cape.

Recollects' Cloisters (Cloître des récollets) (C). – Located between Place du Docteur-Cayla and the quays, the old Recollects monastery houses the Regional Wine Council. The brick and stone building was built between 12 and 17C. The interior courtyard has a 16C Renaissance gallery beside an 18C gallery. In the southeast corner is the monks' small oven.

Go down the steps into the vaulted wine cellar where the meetings of the Bergerac wine society, Conférence des Consuls de la Vinée, are held. There is an audio-visual presentation on the Bergerac vineyards.

The sumptuously decorated great hall on the first floor affords a fine view of the Monbazillac vineyards.

The wine-testing laboratory is in the eastern part of the building. The wine-tasting room can be visited; it is here that annually all the Bergerac wines are tasted to determine whether they can have the *appellation d'origine contrôlée*.

The tour ends at the **Wine Centre** (Maison du Vin) at the corner of Place de la Myrpe. The chapel attached to the Recollects monastery is now a Protestant church.

★Museum of Wine, River Boating and Cooperage (Musée du Vin, de la Batellerie et de la Tonnellerie) (C M²). – Located in a lovely brick and half-timbered house at the end of Place de la Myrpe, this museum is divided into three sections.

On the first floor, the importance of barrel-making in the Bergerac economy is explained. The coopers had to undergo severe controls concerning barrel capacity, the type of wood used, etc...

The section on wine shows the evolution of the Bergerac vineyards through the centuries and the type of houses the winegrowers lived in.

The second floor concerns the river boats. Models of the various kinds of river boats, *gabare,* flat-bottomed boats with sails, which transported the different kinds of goods on the Dordogne River. They did not go above Bergerac, which was the port where the transshipment of the goods occurred. Photos show the bustling port of Bergerac in the 19C, as well as fishing scenes, such as the netting of fish, especially during the return of the salmon or shad to spawn.

Place Pélissière (C). – This large square was opened up after the demolition of some run-down houses. Spread on different levels around a fountain it is overlooked by St-Jacques, a former pilgrimage centre on the Way of St James; near it is the Museum of Sacred Art.

Museum of Sacred Art (Musée d'Art Sacré) (C M³). – Displayed in the small mission station are objects of religious connotation: paintings, sculptures and sacred vases of different styles. Note the Lauzerte stone, an unusual archaic statue discovered in a chapel in Lauzerte (in Tarn-et-Garonne *département*).

Rue St-James (C 32). – The street is lined with 15, 16 and 17C half-timbered houses with mullioned windows.

Rue des Fontaines (C 16). – The Vieille Auberge at the corner of Rue Gaudra has preserved its moulded arcades, 14C capitals, and pointed arched windows.

Rue des Conférences (C 7). – The name of this street (*conférences* means conferences) calls to mind the meetings held before the *Peace of Bergerac (qv)*. It is bordered by half-timbered houses.

Cross the Place de la Myrpe and Place du Docteur-Cayla and take Rue des Récollets to the old port (and car park).

ADDITIONAL SIGHT

Notre-Dame (AY). – Built in the Gothic style this 19C church has a slender bell tower. There are two fine paintings in the east chapel: an *Adoration of the Magi* attributed to Pordenone, a Venetian painter, student of Giorgione, and especially an *Adoration of the Shepherds* attributed to the Milanese, Ferrari, student of Leonardo da Vinci. In the west chapel is an immense Aubusson tapestry portraying the Bergerac coat of arms.

EXCURSIONS

Monbazillac Vineyard. – *Round tour of 27km – 16 1/2 miles – about 1 1/2 hours. Leave Bergerac southwards on the D 13.*

This road crosses a market-garden area and then the meadowlands of the Dordogne alluvial plain before reaching the first slopes and vineyards *(the vineyard area is marked in green on the local map).*

The famous vineyard of Monbazillac has a reputation that goes back hundreds of years. There is a story that in the Middle Ages, when pilgrims from Bergerac were visiting Rome, the pope asked, "And where is Bergerac?" "Near Monbazillac", replied the chamberlain.

The white wine of Monbazillac is a sweet wine and is served with *foie gras* as well as dessert. The bunches are picked when the «noble rot» mold attacks them (drying up the water) – a guarantee of quality.

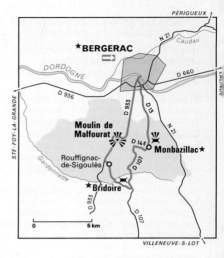

★**Château de Monbazillac.** – *Description p 107.*

> *Beyond the castle take, in the village, the D 14ᴱ to the right and soon after the D 107 to the left.*

The road winds its way through carefully cultivated vineyards.

★**Bridoire Castle** (Château de Bridoire). – This Protestant fortress was partly destroyed by Montluc in 1568 and rebuilt under Henri IV. It was restored in the 19 and 20C. The castle is made up of two large main buildings set at right angles flanked by round towers facing an inside courtyard which is closed by a crescent-shaped curtain wall. It recalls Château de Monbazillac by its grey stone, its roof of brown tiles and massive round machicolated towers.

The road crosses **Rouffignac-de-Sigoulès,** a wine growers' village, where the houses have often been roofed with round tiles.

> *Take the D 933 to the right which runs alongside the vineyards. A road climbs up to Malfourat Mill.*

Malfourat Mill (Moulin de Malfourat). – Viewing table. The mill, now lacking sails, stands on top of a hillock. From the bar terrace there is a **panorama★** of the Monbazillac vineyard and to the north of Bergerac and the Dordogne Plain.

The D 933 is picturesque as it drops down through the vineyards to Bergerac.

Caudau Valley. – *38km – 23 1/2 miles. About 1 hour. Leave Bergerac by ① on the N 21 then take a right on the D 21 which follows the Caudau Valley.*

Lamonzie-Montastruc. – Pop 407. Perched on a rock to the left of the road is Château de Montastruc, a handsome building in the classical style. Its main building is 16C and flanked by 15C circular corner towers while another façade is 18C.

> *Continue along the D 21 then at Clermont-de-Beauregard take a path to the left.*

La Gaubertie Castle (Château de la Gaubertie). – Built in the 15C, this castle was completely restored in the early 20C. The large main building, the façade of which overlooks Caudau Valley, is flanked by a square tower on one side and a round corbelled tower on the other side. A machicolated watchpath rides right around the castle. The 17C chapel stands not far from the castle.

> *At Clermont-de-Beauregard, take a small road towards St-Laurent-des-Bâtons, which follows Caudau Valley.*

St-Maurice Castle (Château de St-Maurice). – In this cool valley and hidden by trees stands St-Maurice Castle with its 14 and 15C buildings crowned with machicolations.

> *After the castle turn letf on another small road.*

Go through St-Armand-de-Vergt, which has an attractive Romanesque church.

> *Turn left on the D 42 then right.*

The road skirts **Neuf Font Lake** (Lac de Neuf Font) where there are swimming and pedal boats.

> *From the lake take the D 8 to Vergt.*

Vergt. – Pop 1 419. This large agricultural district has become one of the main strawberry centres. The soil (ferrugineous sand) of the region adapts perfectly to the cultivation of this fruit. This explains why at certain times during the year great plastic sheets can be seen protecting the strawberries.

Admission times and charges to the sights described are listed at the end of the Guide.

Every sight for which there are times and charges is indicated by the symbol ⊙ in the margin in the main part of the Guide.

BESSE · Pop 183

Michelin map 75 southwest of fold 17 or 235 fold 10

Standing in the centre of the forest that covers much of Quercy between the Lot and the Dordogne, is the little village of Besse with its interesting Romanesque church roofed with *lauzes (qv)*, which forms an attractive picture with the 16 and 17C château.

Church (Église). – The east end ends in an oven-vaulted apse. The belfry porch, which has an asymmetrical roof, protects a remarkable carved **doorway**★. On either side of the door two capitals in archaic style and ornamented with simple figures support the recessed arches. Among the subjects depicted are the Seven Deadly Sins, scenes in the Garden of Eden, an angel with the Paschal lamb, and hunting scenes.

Doorway

EXCURSION

Villefranche-du-Périgord. – Pop 800. Facilities. *8km – 5 miles to the south by the D 57.* This *bastide (qv)*, commanding the valley of the Lémance, still has a vast covered market and some of the arcades surrounding its main square.

★★ BEYNAC-ET-CAZENAC · Pop 460

Michelin map 75 fold 17 or 235 fold 6 – Local map pp 76-77 – Facilities

Beynac Castle *(photograph p 67)* stands on a remarkable **site**★★, rising from the top of a rock; it commands the beautiful Dordogne Valley as it winds between hills crowned with castles.

A redoutable stronghold. – In the Middle Ages Beynac, Biron, Bourdeilles and Mareuil were the four baronies of Périgord. When the Capetians and the Plantagenets were rivals, the castle, captured by Richard Lionheart, was used as a base by the sinister **Mercadier**, master-at-arms, who banded his men to pillage the countryside on behalf of the king of England. In 1214 during the Albigensian Crusade, Simon de Montfort seized the castle and dismantled it. The castle was later rebuilt, as we see it today, by a lord of Beynac.

During the Hundred Years' War, when the Dordogne marked the front between the English and the French – Beynac under the English in 1360, captured by the French in 1368 and Castelnaud under the English – there were constant skirmishes and raids between the French, based at Beynac, and the English at Castelnaud *(p 66)*. Once peace had returned, the castle was left once more to watching over the village.

★★**Castle** (Château). – *Access by car take the D 703 on leaving the village to the west (3km – 2 miles) or on foot by the village.*

The castle is in the form of an irregular quadrilateral extended on the south side to form a bastion. The austere crenellated keep dates from the 13C. A double curtain wall protected the castle from attack from the plateau; on all the other sides there is a sheer drop of 150m – 492ft to the Dordogne. The main building, dating from the 13 and 14C, is prolonged by the 15C seignorial manor-house to which a bartizan was added in the 16C.

Interior. – The great Hall of State, where once the nobles of Périgord used to assemble, has fine broken barrel vaulting; the oratory is decorated with Gothic frescoes, naïve in style, with lively draughtsmanship depicting the Last Supper, a Christ of Pity at the foot of His Cross, such as He appeared to St Gregory according to the medieval legend, and members of the Beynac family.

From the watchpath and the south bastion, which overlook the Dordogne and are reached by the main staircase (17C), there is a wonderful **panorama**★★ of the valley and from left to right, of the Domme Barre and the castles of Marqueyssac, Castelnaud and Fayrac.

Wayside cross (Calvaire). – This stands on the cliff edge 150m – 492ft to the east of the castle. A **panorama**★★ as wide as the one from the castle watchpath can be seen from this point.

Village. – A steep footpath lined with 15, 16 and 17C houses goes from the village to the castle. It passes at the foot of a 14C tower. When visiting the Museum of Proto-History, the visitor can better grasp the tower's interior; at its summit, the terrace offers an interesting view of the valley.

Museum of Proto-History. – Objects (originals and facsimiles) assembled by theme introduce the civilisation (2000/1000BC) and techniques of the region's first farmers and iron workers.

Once through the pointed-arched gateway part of the village's curtain wall, the footpath continues to the **church**, the former castle chapel, remodelled in the 15C.

Archaeological Park. – Gaulish fortifications, dwellings, workshops, and sepulchers from the Neolithic Period to the Iron Age have been reconstructed.

Cazenac. – *3km – 2 miles west.* This hamlet possesses a 15C Gothic church from which there is a lovely view of the valley.

★ BIRON CASTLE

Michelin map **75** south of fold 16 or **235** fold 9

Biron Castle, perched at the top of a *puy*, rears up the great mass of its towers and walls on the borders of Périgord and Agenais and commands a wide horizon.

From the Capitol to the Tarpeian Rock. – Among the many celebrated men of the Biron family, the fate of **Charles de Gontaut** should not be forgotten.
Friend of Henri IV, he was one of his first lieutenants then he was appointed first Admiral and then Marshal of France. In 1598 the Barony of Biron was created and conferred as a dukedom on Charles de Gontaut who was next promoted to Lieutenant-General of the French Army and then Governor of Burgundy. Even these honours did not satisfy him and in league with the Duke of Savoy and the Spanish Governor of the state of Milan, he laid a plot which would have led to the breaking up of the kingdom of France. Biron, his treason exposed, was pardoned. But the mercy of Henri IV did nothing to halt his ambitions. Once more he plotted against his lord. Once again he was exposed and was taken before the king, who agreed to pardon him if he would confess his crime. The proud Biron refused. He was beheaded in the Bastille on 31 July 1602.

From medieval fortress to the present. – This castle is made up of buildings of very different styles, the work of fourteen generations of Gontaut-Biron, who owned the castle from the 12 to 20C.
Already in the 11C a medieval fortress existed here, razed by Simon de Montfort in the 13C, the castle was reconstructed. During the Hundred Years' War, the castle exchanged between English and French hands incessantly and was badly damaged. In the late 15C and during the 16C, Pons de Gontaut-Biron, former Chamberlain of Charles VIII, decided to transform his castle into a lovely Renaissance château like those he had seen in the Loire Valley. He altered the buildings east of the court of honour and had built the Renaissance chapel and colonnaded arcade. It was planned that by the arcade, a great staircase would lead down the slope. Work was interrupted and only resumed in the 18C.
This mass of buildings and 10 000sq m – 107 600sq ft of roof have made it exceedingly difficult for individual owners to maintain the castle. The Dordogne *département* bought it in 1970 and began a massive restoration program and set up an art centre, which organises exhibits every summer, as well.

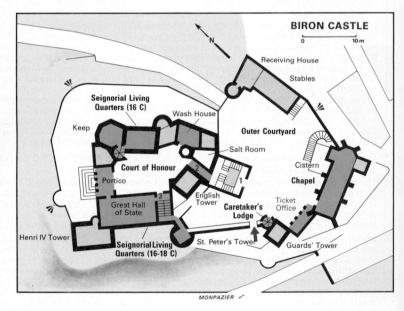

⊙TOUR

Outer courtyard. – Surrounding the castle's living quarters on three sides, the outer courtyard includes the caretaker's lodge, chapel, the receiving house and the salt room. The guards' tower, now the **caretaker's lodge,** is an elegant building in which are happily juxtaposed crenellations, a watchpath and Renaissance decoration.
The **chapel** was built in the Renaissance style in the 16C. A pierced balustrade runs round the base of the roof. The lower chamber once served as a parish church for the village; the upper chamber or seignorial chapel, which opens directly onto the courtyard has remarkable pointed vaulting. It shelters **two recumbent figures,** the sculpture of which shows the influence of the Italian Quattrocento (15C) period. The recumbent figure of Armand de Gontaut-Biron, bishop of Sarlat, is decorated by three seated figures of the virtues, while the recumbent figure of his brother Pons (d 1524) is carved in low relief and recounts the life of Christ underlined by a macabre frieze. Both figures were damaged during the Wars of Religion. The chapel also contained a *Pietà* and an *Entombment,* two remarkable works of art, which were sold to the Metropolitan Museum of Art in New York City *(see Michelin Green Guide to New York City).*
From the terrace between the chapel and the receiving house, a large turretted building, there is a bird's-eye view of the town.
The salt room is a larder where salt provisions were stored.

Court of honour. – Access is by a staircase (1) and a pointed vaulted corridor (2). Opening onto this inner courtyard or court of honour is a portico. On the right, the 16C seignorial living quarters, with Renaissance windows, contain elegant restored galleries now used for art exhibitions. On the left, the 16 to 18C main building has an elegant remodelled staircase (3), which goes up to the Great Hall of State, the timberwork roof of which is in the form of a ship's keel and has just been rebuilt.

In the basement, the kitchen, the former garrison's refectory, is a vast room (22 x 9m – 72 x 30ft) with pointed-barrel vaulting. The large 13C polygonal keep was remodelled in the 15C and became part of the other buildings.

From the castle terraces, the **view**★ extends over the rolling countryside and the Biron's other fief, the *bastide* of Monpazier *(qv)*.

★★ BONAGUIL CASTLE

Michelin map ⁷⁹ fold 6 or ²³⁵ southeast of fold 9 – Local maps pp 52 and 102

This majestic fortress *(photograph p 30)*, which stands on the borders of Périgord Noir and Quercy, is one of the most perfect examples of military architecture from the late 15 and 16C. Its uniqueness is that, although it appears to be the traditional defensive stronghold able to hold off any attack, its conception was also adapted to the use of firearms: loopholes, arquebus...

In addition, Bonaguil, which was built neither as a lookout post nor as a fortress but as a sure place of refuge, able to withstand attack of any kind, presented the novelty in 1480-1520 of using firearms essentially for defensive purposes: this is already the theory of what a fort is.

A strange character. – It was a strange quirk of character that made **Bérenger de Roquefeuil** enjoy proclaiming himself the "noble, magnificent and most powerful lord of the baronies of Roquefeuil, Blanquefort, Castelnau, Combret, Roquefère, Count of Naut". Belonging to one of the oldest families of Languedoc, he was a brutal and vindictive man, and, in his determination to be obeyed, did not hesitate to use force. But extortion and outrage brought revolt; the better to crush this, Bérenger transformed Bonaguil Castel, which had been built in the 13C, into an impregnable fortress. It took him nearly 40 years to build his fortified eagle's aerie, which looked an anachronism when compared with the châteaux being erected by his contemporaries for a life of ease at Montal, Assier and along the Loire. However, his castle was never attacked and was intact on the eve of the Revolution. Although, dismantled during the Revolution, this colossus, in spite of its mutilations, still stands today as a challenge hurdled by the last of the feudal barons at the Renaissance.

This masterpiece of military architecture, while still keeping the traditional defences against attack by escalade or sapping, was also designed to make use of artillery.

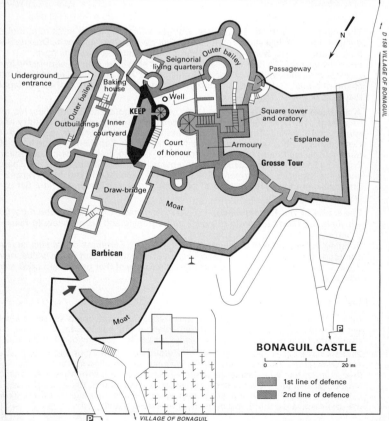

BONAGUIL CASTLE

0 ————— 20 m

1st line of defence
2nd line of defence

⊙ Castle. – *Time: 1 1/2 hours.* After passing through the outer wall, the visitor comes to the barbican. This was an enormous bastion on its own with its own garrison, powder store, armouries and way of escape. The barbican formed part of the 350m – 380yds long first line of defence ; its bastions, thanks to the embrasures, permitted cross-firing.

The second line of defence consisted of five towers of which one, known as the Grosse Tour, is among the strongest round towers ever to have been built in France. The tower is 35m – 115ft high and is crowned with corbels; the upper storeys served as living quarters, the lower held the muskets, culverins and harquebuses, etc.

The keep overlooked both lines of defences; it served, with its cant walls, not only as a watch tower but also as a command-post. Shaped like a vessel with its prow, the most vulnerable point, turned towards the north, it was the last bastion of the defence. Inside, a room houses arms and objects (pottery, stained-glass windows) found during the excavation of the moats.

With a well sunk through the rock, outbuildings (baking house), where provisions could be stored, monumental chimneys and drainage systems, dry internal ditches, and vaulted tunnels which enabled the troops to move about quickly, the castle garrison of about a hundred men could easily withstand a siege provided they were not betrayed or starved out.

Travel with the **Michelin Sectional Map Series** *(1:200 000).*
They are revised regularly.

LES BORIES CASTLE

Michelin map 🔢 fold 6 or 🔢 fold 43 – 12km 7 1/2 miles northeast of Périgueux

⊙ The castle, built in the 16C by the St-Astier family, stands in a pleasant site on the bank of the Isle River.

The castle comprises the main building, flanked by two round towers and a massive, square battlemented tower.

The **interior architecture★** is outstanding. A monumental staircase rises inside the square tower with a small room occupying the space in the centre on each floor; there was a Gothic chapel on the ground floor. The kitchen has groined vaulting and is very ornate; it has two huge chimneypieces with basket-handled arches.

In the guard room there is an unusual vault on squinches resting on pointed ribs starting from a central column.

The great hall contains Louis XIII furnishings, a fine Renaissance chimney and a Flemish *verdure* (tapestry in shades of green).

★ BOURDEILLES   Pop 728

Michelin map 🔢 fold 5 or 🔢 north of fold 42 – Local map p 81 – Facilities

The impressive castle of Bourdeilles, with the village clustered at its foot, makes a delightful picture as it stands on the rocks that rise up sheer above the Dronne River. It was here, in 1540, that the famous chronicler, Brantôme *(qv),* was born.

From the vast terrace (terrasse, *east of the plan)* above the church, admire the lovely **view★** of the castle and its setting: a Gothic bridge with cutwaters, an old mill in the shape of a boat and roofed in round tiles and the green waters of the river lapping the rocks below.

A coveted spot. – In 1259 Saint Louis ceded Périgord and Bourdeilles, his most important barony, to the English. This incredible desertion made the country rise in revolt and divided the Bourdeille family: the elder branch supported the Plantagenets, the younger branch, the Maumonts, the Capetians. A little later, after plots and lawsuits and urged on by the king, Géraud de Maumont, Counsellor to Philip the Fair, seized the castle of his forebears. He turned it into a fortress. Then, to show his strength in Périgord, Philip the Fair exchanged land in Auvergne for Bourdeilles and installed in time of peace, a strong garrison within the fief of his enemies, the English.

The smile of the Renaissance. – Credit for the plans for the 16C castle must go to Jacquette de Montbron, wife of André de Bourdeille and sister-in-law to Pierre de Brantôme.

Building started in haste at the promise of a visit by Catherine de' Medici, and was abandoned when the visit was cancelled. The Renaissance part of the castle, nevertheless, is an interesting example of the architecture of that period and adds a light note to the 13C group of buildings.

★CASTLE *time: 1 1/2 hours*

⊙ Cross the first fortified curtain wall, pass under the watchpath to penetrate the second wall and enter the outer courtyard, planted with a fine cedar. Continue to the esplanade, on which were built two castles, one in the 13C, the other in the 16C.

Medieval castle. – The 13C castle, built by Géraud de Maumont on older foundations and hence given the name New Castle, is an austere building surrounded by a quadrangular curtain wall. Inside the main building, a great hall holds exhibitions; it is surmounted by an octagonal keep topped by machicolations, the walls of which are 2.40m – 7ft thick. From the upper platform of the keep there is a good overall view of the castle and a plunging **view** of the river and the old mill.

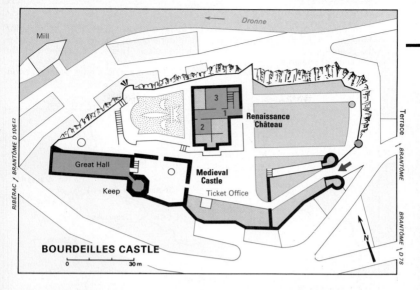

BOURDEILLES CASTLE

Renaissance château. – Sober and elegant in appearance, the château consists of a rectangular main building and a wing at right angles to it. It houses remarkable **furnishings**★★ collected by two patrons who donated their collection to the Dordogne *département*.

On the ground floor a gallery (1) contains a series of 15 and 16C wooden chests and a splendid 16C carved panel from the Burgundy School portraying the Teaching of the Infant Jesus. In an adjoining room (2) note the recumbent figure of Jean de Chabannes and a replica of the Holy Sepulchre, which came from Montgé Priory. The hall of armour (3) with its fine old tiling, contains corsairs' sea chests and a magnificent Renaissance table.

On the 1st floor visit the dining hall with its 16C carved **chimneypiece**★★ decorated with palm leaves and the Gothic room preceding the **gold salon.** This sumptuously decorated room has a painted ceiling, woodwork and monumental chimneypieces by Ambroise Le Noble of the Fontainebleau School. Note the magnificent tapestry, after a cartoon by Laurent Guyot, showing François I and his falconers.

In three rooms on the 2nd floor there are 15 and 16C Spanish paintings, cabinets with secret drawers, a 16C canopied bed, armchairs in Cordova leather, a fine 17C octagonal table and especially the heavily carved and gilded **bed of Emperor Charles V.**

EXCURSION

Boulou Valley. – *Round tour of 22km-14 miles-about 1 1/4 hours. Leave Bourdeilles northwards on the C 301.*

St-Julien-de-Bourdeilles. – In this modest hamlet is a small Gothic church with two lovely statues in polychrome wood and parts of a 17C altarpiece.

Take the C 5 towards La Gonterie-Boulouneix; at the intersection, bear left.

Boulouneix. – A Romanesque chapel with a domed bell tower stands in the middle of a cemetery. In the chancel 17C mural paintings represent Mary Magdalene and St Jerome. The façade with two storeys of arcades is of Saintonge (historic Aquitaine) influence.

About 100yds after the church, bear left towards Au Bernard.

The road descends through the woods (hornbeam and filbert) to the marshy Boulou Valley. Several prehistoric sites were uncovered in the region.

Bear right on the C 2.

Paussac-et-St-Vivien. – Pop 399. Several 16C houses and an interesting fortified **church** are part of this village.

The church's defensive areas, built above the three domes covering the nave and chancel, are visible. The south wall is decorated with arcades. Inside note the capitals decorated in slight relief with naive carvings, a large Christ in polychrome wood and a Louis XV-style pulpit.

Take the C 2 towards Brantôme; at Les Guichards bear right towards Les Chauses, leaving the road to Puy-Fromage on the left.

From the road you will soon see Bourdeilles and its tall keep.

Make up your own itineraries
 - *The map on pp 6-7 gives a general view of tourist regions,
   the main towns, individual sights and recommended routes in the Guide.*
 - *The above are described under their own name in alphabetical order
   (p 37) or are incorporated in the excursions radiating from a nearby town
   or tourist centre.*
 - *In addition the layout diagram on page 3 shows the **Michelin Maps** covering
   the region.*

BOURIANE

Michelin map **79** folds 6 and 7 or **235** folds 9, 10 and 14

Bouriane extends from Gourdon to the Lot Valley and west of the N 20. It is a region where the limestone formation disappears under a bed of sideritic sand (iron carbonate bearing), which is a lovely red and ochre colour. This soil is excellent for the cultivation of chestnut, pine and rye.
A great number of rivers carve through the plateau creating a hilly, wooded countryside scattered with farms.

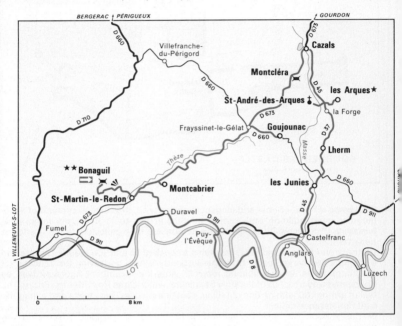

ROUND TOUR FROM BONAGUIL

97km – 60 miles – about 3 hours – local map above

★★**Bonaguil Castle.** – *Description p 48.*

> *Take the road to St-Martin-le-Redon.*

There is a lovely **view**★ of the fantastic outline of Bonaguil Castle *(qv)*, surrounded by woods.

St-Martin-le-Redon. – Pop 249. This charming village is known for the St-Martial source water, which had the reputation of curing skin ailments.

> *Take the D 673 and turn right to Montcabrier.*

Montcabrier. – Pop 352. The *bastide (qv)* was founded in 1297 by Guy de Cabrier, who gave it his name. It was granted a charter of franchises by Philip the Fair. Overlooking the square, several old houses (including the 16C house of the king's court) are laid out as dictated on the original plan. The church, partly rebuilt in the 14C, has a Flamboyant doorway (restored) surrounded by a fine open-bayed bell tower. Inside a plain 14C statue of St Louis, the parish's patron saint, is surrounded by ex-votos. This statue was the purpose of a local pilgrimage.

> *Return to the D 673 and continue on it to Frayssinet-le-Gélat, then turn right onto the D 660.*

Goujounac. – Pop 184. Around the church there had been a Romanesque priory (ruins can be seen). On the south wall, the Romanesque tympanum represents Christ in Majesty, blessing, and surrounded by the symbols of the four Evangelists. This is the work of a Quercy sculptor, most likely influenced by the tympanum of Beaulieu-sur-Dordogne.

> *Return to Frayssinet-le-Gélat and turn right onto the D 673.*

Montcléra Castle (Château de Montcléra). – This late-15C castle is made up of a fortified gatehouse, square keep and main building, flanked by round machicolated towers.

Cazals. – Pop 472. This former *bastide (qv)* of the kings of England is built around its main square.
A stretch of water with amenities has been set up along the banks of the Masse River.

> *Take the D 45 which follows the Masse Valley and after 6km – 3 1/2 miles, turn right to St-André-des-Arques.*

St-André-des-Arques. – *Description p 39.*

> *Return to the D 45 and continue straight on to Les Arques.*

★**Les Arques.** – *Description p 39.*

> *Return to the D 45 and at La Forge take the D 37.*

Lherm. – Pop 228. This little village of white limestone houses with steeply-pitched roofs covered with small brown tiles is dominated by a bell tower, a turret and several dovecots. In an isolated, small wooded valley, the church, the former seat of a priory, has a Romanesque apse and a plain barrel-vaulted nave of ashlar-stone. The chancel holds a profusely decorated altarpiece of gold and carvings against a blue background, a rather grandiose, local interpretation of the baroque style. The building was altered in the 16C; fine Renaissance-style door.

Continue along the D 37.

Les Junies. – Pop 250. The 15C castle flanked by round towers is ornamented with elegant Renaissance windows.

Set apart from the village, the 14C church, an austere building, has massive proportions. It was part of a priory, attached to the Dominican order in 1345 and which had been founded by one of the local lords, Gaucelin des Junies, Cardinal of Albano.

Follow the D 45 to Castelfranc in the Lot Valley. Cross the river and at Anglars pick up the itinerary of the Lot Valley (p 99) which takes you back to Bonaguil Castle.

★★ BRANTÔME   Pop 2 101

Michelin map **75** fold 5 or **233** south of fold 31 – Local map p 81 – Facilities

Brantôme lies in the smiling valley of the Dronne. Its old abbey and picturesque **setting★** make it one of the pleasantest places in Périgord.

HISTORICAL NOTES

The chronicler Brantôme. – The literary fame of **Pierre de Bourdeille** *(illustration p 25),* better known as Brantôme, brought renown to the abbey of which he was commendatory abbot.

Born in 1540 the third son of the Baron of Bourdeilles, Brantôme spent the first years of his life at the court of Marguerite of Valois, queen of Navarre, as both his mother and maternal grandmother were members of the royal household. In 1549 he went to Paris to continue his education, which he completed in 1555 at the university of Poitiers. He began life as a soldier of fortune and courtier, went with Mary Stuart to Scotland, travelled in Spain, Portugal, Italy and the British Isles and even to Africa. Wild ventures brought him into contact with the great in an era rich in scandal.

After fighting at Jarnac in 1569, he withdrew to his abbey and began his famous chronicles. The Huguenots twice threatened to destroy the abbey during the Wars of Religion and he had to use all his diplomatic skill with Coligny, one of the leaders of the Protestants, to save it from being pillaged. He left the abbey to return to court as chamberlain to Charles IX. In 1584 a fall from his horse crippled him and he left the restless and impetuous Valois court to retreat to the peace of his monastery and finish his chronicles.

Brantôme, whose posthumous fame lies in his *Les vies des hommes illustres et grands capitaines* ("Lives of Illustrious Men and the Great Leaders") and *Les vies des dames galantes* ("Lives of Gallant Ladies") in which moral and historical facts are sometimes confused, was a lively, witty and sometimes cynical historian. He knew Ronsard, the poet, and other great writers of his time personally; he told a good tale well with piquant detail; his style was simple and has served as a model to many writers.

SIGHTS

★★**Banks of the Dronne River.** – To get a complete picture of this romantic spot amble along the banks of the Dronne; the old houses with their flower-covered balconies and trellises and the lovely gardens near the abbey reflect into the tranquil mirror of water. The charm lies in the harmony, serenity and calm of the scene and the softness of the light.

A 16C elbow bridge with asymmetrical arches, a Renaissance house with mullioned windows and the abbey, clinging to the limestone cliffs, make an attractive picture.

Former Abbey (Ancienne abbaye). – Brantôme Abbey, founded by Charlemagne in 769 to house the relics of St Sicaire, which attracted a multitude of pilgrims, was under the Benedictine rule. Sacked by the Normans, it was rebuilt in the 11C by Abbé Guillaume. In the 16C, it became in commemdam with Pierre de Mareuil as commendatory abbot (he had constructed the most interesting of the buildings) followed by his nephew, Pierre de Bourdeille.

The buildings which you see before you are those built in the 18C by Bertin, administrator of Périgord.

Abbey church (Église abbatiale). – Angevin vaulting, a compromise between crossribbed vaulting and the dome, replaced the two original domes in the 15C. The nave is plain and elegant; a bay in the form of a cross with below it three depressed-arched windows, illuminate the flat east end.

The baptistry is adorned with a 14C low relief in stone of the Baptism of Christ. Another low relief, this time dating from the 13C and showing the Massacre of the Innocents, may be seen underneath the porch above the font, which rests on a fine Romanesque capital decorated with strapwork.

Near the main doorway go into one of the cloistral galleries from where you can get a glimpse of the former chapterhouse can be had, the palm tree vaulting of which rests on a central column.

★★Bell tower (Clocher). – The bell tower was built apart from the church upon a sharp rock towering 12m – 39ft high beneath which open vast caves. It was erected in the 11C and is the oldest gabled Romanesque bell tower in Limousin. It was made up of four storeys, each stepped back and slightly smaller than the one below and topped by a stone pyramid. The ground floor storey is roofed with an archaic dome where the evolution from the square to the elipse is obtained by triangular ribs held up by marble columns, an architectural element recovered most likely from a Merovingian construction. The three other storeys are opened with round arched bays supported by columns with plainly decorated capitals.

Conventual buildings (Bâtiments conventuels). – These buildings, today, are occupied by the town hall and museum. The two pavilions located in each wing are in the pure 18C style as is the central part of the main building. Inside, a beautiful monumental staircase dating from the 17C, when the building was an abbey, leads to the monks' dormitory, which has a fine timber ceiling. The Renaissance style staircase to the town hall was built in the 19C.

Caves (Grottes). – In the caves, behind the abbey, the monks had installed outbuildings: bakeries and wine cellars.
In the largest of the caves immense sculptural groups were carved into the living rock. One represents the Triumph of Death and the other a Crucifixion of Italian influence dating from the second half of the 15C.
Nearby, the fountain of St Sicaire spouts.

Fernand Desmoulin Museum (Musée Fernand-Desmoulin). – The museum (completely renovated), which is in the former abbey, contains a **collection of prehistoric art** consisting of items found during local excavations including bone and silex tools. Note the fine series of engravings on bone excavated from the Rochereil Site, on the banks of the Dronne.
Works by local artists are exhibited in other rooms. The end room is devoted to the haunting pictures of the painter, Fernand Desmoulin (born in 1835 near Nontron), which were produced while he was under the influence of a medium.

EXCURSIONS

★Dronne-Valley. – *Description p 80.*

Château de Richemont. – *7 km – 4 miles to the northwest. Leave Brantôme by the D 939 and take to the right the road leading to St-Crépin-de-Richemont. After 1km – 1/2 mile an avenue on the right leads to the château.*
This ungainly château composed of two buildings at right angles was built in the late 16C by the chronicler Brantôme. On his death in 1614 he was interred in the chapel, situated on the ground floor of the great square corner tower, where he had written his epitaph. On the entrance building's first floor is Brantôme's room, with fine woodwork.

Michelin Guides

The Red Guides (hotels and restaurants)
Benelux - Deutschland - España Portugal - main cities EUROPE - France - Great Britain and Ireland - Italia

The Green Guides (picturesque scenery, beautiful buildings and scenic routes)
Austria - Canada - England: The West Country - France - Germany - Great Britain - Greece - Italy - London - Mexico - Netherlands - New England - New York City - Portugal - Rome - Scotland - Spain - Switzerland - Washington DC and 10 Guides on France

---

BRIVE-LA-GAILLARDE   Pop 54 032
Michelin map **75** fold 8 or **239** fold 26 – Local map p 56

Brive which owes its nickname *La Gaillarde* – the bold – to the courage displayed by its citizens on the many occasions when it was besieged, is an active town in the Corrèze alluvial plain. It is in the middle of the rich Brive Basin, where market gardening and orchards prosper.
Located at the crossroads of Bas-Limousin (Lower Limousin), Périgord and Quercy *causses* (limestone plateaux), Brive is an important railway junction and is seeking to become the economic capital of the region.
Its main industries are canning of food, especially fruit and vegetables picked in the area.
The plan of Brive is an excellent example of how a town can expand concentrically, with as its centre the old quarter and St Martin's Collegiate Church.

A brilliant career. – Guillaume Dubois (1656-1723), the son of an apothecary from Brive, took the Orders and became tutor to Philip of Orléans; he became Prime Minister, when Philip was appointed regent during the minority of Louis XV. Offices and honours were heaped upon him; he became Archbishop of Cambrai and then a cardinal. He made an alliance with England, which thus ensured a long period of peace in France.

A glorious soldier. – Brune enlisted in the army 1791 and rose to become a general commanding the army in Italy in 1798. Following victories in Holland and Italy he was appointed ambassador at Constantinople. He became the symbol of the Revolution and died, a victim of a Royalist mob, in 1815 at Avignon.

BRIVE LA GAILLARDE

Faro (R. du Lt-Col.) .... BZ 7
Gambetta (R.) .... BZ
Gaulle (Pl. Ch.-de-) .... BYZ 8
Hôtel-de-Ville (R.) .... AZ 12
Paris (Av. de) .... ABY
République (R. de la) .... AZ
Toulzac (R.) .... BY

Anatole-France (Bd) .... BY 2
Dalton (R. Gén.) .... BY 4
Dauzier (Pl. J.-M.-) .... BY 5
Delessert (R. B.-) .... BY 6
Halle (Pl. de la) .... BY 10
Hôtel-de-Ville (Pl. de l') ... BY 13
Lyautey (Bd Mar.-) .... AZ 14
Salan (R. du) .... BZ 16
Teyssier (R.) .... BY 19

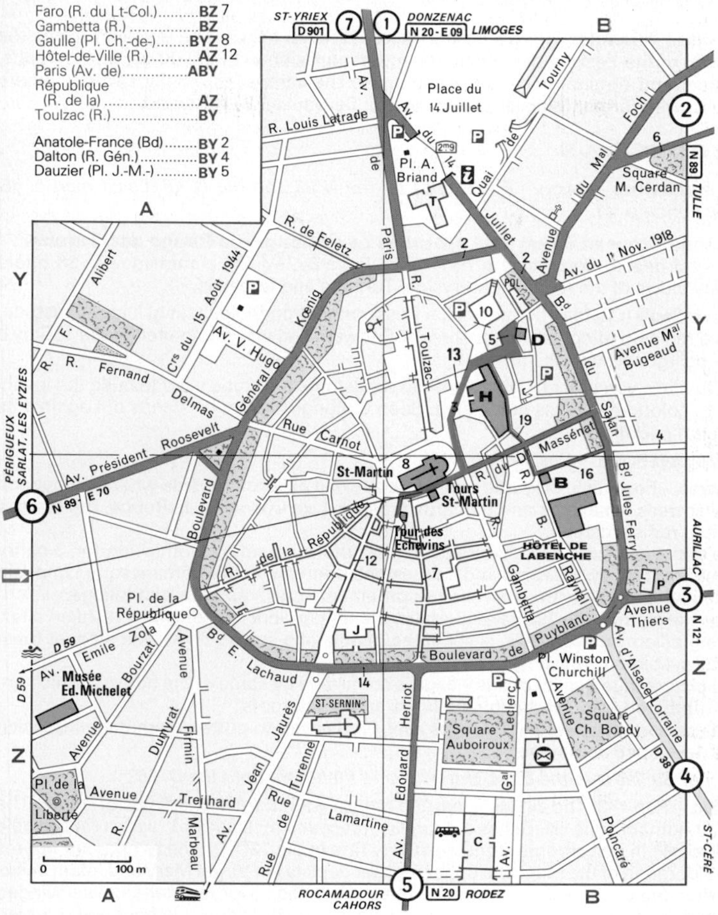

OLD TOWN *time: 1 1/2 hours*

The old town located in the heart of the city, bounded by a first ring of boulevards, has been successfully restored. The buildings, old and new, create a harmonious ensemble of warm sandstone.

St Martin Collegiate Church (Collégiale St-Martin) (ABZ). – Only the transept, apse and a few of the capitals are Romanesque, traces left of a 12C monastic community. Inside, over the transept crossing, is an octagonal dome on flat pendentives, characteristic of the Limousin style. The nave and aisles are 14C and the chancel was faithfully rebuilt by Cardinal Dubois in the 18C; note the 13C baptismal font. From the exterior admire the historiated capitals and modillioned cornice of the apsidal chapels.

Échevins Tower (Tour des Échevins) (BZ). – In the narrow Rue des Échevins stands a *hôtel* with a fine corbelled Renaissance tower pierced by mullioned windows.

St Martin's Towers (Tour St-Martin) (BZ). – The two towers, of the 15 and 16C, overlook Place Krüger.
Positioned at the corner of Rue Raynal and Rue du Salan is the 18C Hôtel des Bruslys (**BZ B**).

Turn right into Boulevard Jules-Ferry.

★**Hôtel de Labenche** (BZ). – Built in 1540 by Jean II de Calvimont, lord of Labenche and the king's keeper of the seals for the Bas-Limousin, the *hôtel* is a magnificent example of Renaissance architecture in Toulouse style and is the most remarkable secular building in town. From the inside courtyard can be seen the two main buildings set at right angles above which are large arches. The golden hue of the stone enhances the beauty of the building's decorative elements: mullioned windows adorned with festoons and slender columns and surmounted by busts of men and women set in niches.
The *hôtel* has been set up as a museum, housing the town's collections, which include archaeology, decorative arts and popular arts and traditions.

Former College of the Doctrinaires (Ancien collège des doctrinaires) (**BY H**). – Today these 17C buildings house the town hall. The façade on Rue Teyssier is of fine classical arrangement and the wall decorated with a colonnade overlooks an inner courtyard.

Place de l'Hôtel de Ville (BY 13). – On this large square, modern buildings (Crédit Agricole) and old turreted mansions form a harmonious architectural unit.
The 16C **Treilhard Town House (D)** presents two main buildings joined by a round tower, decorated by a turret.

ADDITIONAL SIGHT

ⓥ **Edmond Michelet Centre** (Centre Edmond-Michelet) **(AZ).** – The museum traces the history of the Resistance movement and deportation with paintings, photographs, posters and original documents relating to the camps, especially Dachau, where E. Michelet, former Minister under General De Gaulle, was interned.

EXCURSIONS

★**1 Aubazine.** – *14km – 8 1/2 miles by the N 89 and the D 48. Local map p 56. Description p 41.*

★**2 Round tour of 54km – 33 1/2 miles by Collonges-la-Rouge and Turenne.** – *About 3 hours – local map p 56 – leave Brive by ④.* The picturesque D 38 offers lovely views of the rolling countryside, Turenne and its castle.

Lacoste Castle (Château de Lacoste). – This former stronghold, built of local sandstone, has a main building flanked by three 13C towers and was completed in the 15C by a fine polygonal staircase turret.

At Noailhac you enter the region of red sandstone, the stone used to build the lovely warm-coloured villages of the area. Soon Collonges-la-Rouge stands out against its verdant backdrop.

★★**Collonges-la-Rouge.** – *Description p 71.*

Meyssac. – Pop 1 255. Meyssac is in the centre of a hilly countryside where walnut and poplar trees, vineyards and orchards prosper. Like Collonges-la-Rouge, the town is built in red sandstone.

The **church** is an unusual mixture of architectural elements: a Gothic interior, a belfry porch fortified by hoarding and a limestone doorway in the Romanesque Limousin style and adorned with small capitals ornamented with animals and foliage.

Near the church, the 18C **covered market,** the timberwork roof of which rests on alternating pillars and columns, is set in the middle of a square lined with elegant town houses, some of which have towers.

The picturesque quality of this village is confirmed by some of the houses, which are half-timbered with overhanging storeys and porch roofs.

The red earth, known as Collonges clay, lends itself to pottery manufacture, which has developed in Meyssac.

For Saillac take the D 14, the D 28 and then right onto the D 28ᵉ.

Saillac. – Pop 143. The village is nestled amidst walnut trees and fields of maize. The small Romanesque **church** has a doorway, preceded by a narthex, with a remarkable **tympanum★** in polychrome stone, relatively rare in the 12C. On the tympanum figures the Adoration of the Magi; the upper register depicts the Virgin Mary and Infant Jesus surrounded by Saint Joseph and the three kings; the lower register shows a winged leopard and an angel wrestling the Leviathan. The tympanum is held up by a pier, composed of twisted columns adorned with foliage and hunting scenes, which probably came from a pagan monument.

In the chancel, topped by a dome on pendentives, are elegant historiated capitals.

Once on the D 19, turn left, then right on the D 8.

★**Turenne.** – *Description p 144.*

Continue along the D 8, and turn left towards La Gleyjolle.

★**La Fage Chasm.** – *Description p 145.*

Turn around, turn left to the D 73, then turn right.

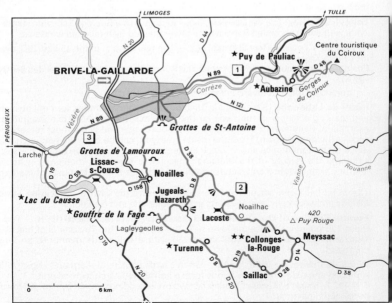

Jugeals-Nazareth. – Pop 502. This village was founded by Raymond I de Turenne on his return from the First Crusade. He set up a leper-house which he entrusted to the Knights Templar. Admire the 14, 15 and 16C houses.

The D 8 and the D 38 go back to Brive-la-Gaillarde.

★③ **Causse Lake.** – *Round tour of 33km – 20 1/2 miles – about 2 hours – local map above. Leave Brive by* ⑤ *on the N 20.* The road rises immediately above the Brive Bassin.

St Antony Caves (Grottes de St-Antoine). – These caves, hollowed out of sandstone, were used as a retreat by St Antony of Padua while he was living at Brive. They form an open-air sanctuary. Franciscans still provide hospitality for today's pilgrims. Follow the Stations of the Cross to the top of a hill from where there is a good view of Brive.

Take the small signposted road to the left.

Lamouroux Caves (Grottes de Lamouroux). – This picturesque group of caves arranged in five tiers was used by man in times of danger.

Noailles. – Pop 515. Noailles, lying in a pleasant setting of verdant hills, is dominated by its castle and church perched on a hill.

⊘The **church**, topped by a bell gable of the Limousin style, has a Romanesque apse and chancel with slender columns adorned with realistic historiated capitals (cripples with crutches). In the pointed-vaulted nave there are memorial plates of the De Noailles family. There is a painting by Watteau's teacher Claude Gillot (*The Preparations of the Crucifixion*).

The Renaissance **château**, seat of the De Noailles family, is decorated with pinnacled windows, the pediment of which is ornamented with angels bearing the De Noailles coat of arms.

From Noailles, go west on the D 158.

The road climbs towards the lake and Corrèze Causse, an area of white limestone and yellow clay, where juniper and oak grow.

★**Causse Lake** (Lac du Causse). – Also called Chasteaux Lake (Lac de Chasteaux), this superb body of water (90ha – 222 acres), set in a very verdant countryside in the lovely Couze Valley, is a marine leisure centre (swimming, sailing, water-skiing, windsurfing, sculling...).

The D 158 goes to Lissac-sur-Couze.

Lissac-sur-Couze. – Set apart from the lake, this elegant manor, flanked by battlemented turrets, was a military tower in the 13 and 14C. The church beside it has a bell gable.

The D 59 overlooks the lake and meets up with the D 19 which goes to Larche. From Larche take the N 89 to Brive-la-Gaillarde.

★ # BRUNIQUEL   Pop 446

Michelin map 🔢 fold 19 or 🔢🔢🔢 east of fold 22 – Local map p 130

Bruniquel, the bold outline of its castle set like a crown above the town, lies in a picturesque **setting**★ at the mouth of the great gorges that the Aveyron has cut through the Limogne Causse (limestone plateau).

According to Gregory of Tours (bishop, theologian and historian, 538-594), Bruniquel originated from the founding of a fortress on this spot by **Brunhilda**. The memory of this princess, who was the daughter of the king of the Visigoths and the wife of Sigebert, king of Austrasia, is kept alive by the castle tower that bears her name. Cruelties perpetrated on account of her rivalry with Fredegund, her sister-in-law, caused war between Austrasia and Neustria in the 6C. The death of the princess herself was so macabre that it has become famous: she was bound by her hair, an arm and a leg to the tail of an unbroken horse and smashed to pieces.

★**Old Town.** – Bruniquel is a pleasant place its remaining fortifications, town gateways, old belfry and its sloping alleys lined with old houses roofed with round tiles.

⊘**Castle.** – The castle, built in lovely yellow stone on foundations going back, it is said, to the 6C, has parts still standing that date from the 12 to 18C. The barbican, which defended the approaches to the castle from the village side, stands on the esplanade before the main building. If one is to believe the legend, Queen Brunhilda owned the castle, the massive square tower of which bears her name.

The Knight's Hall was built in the 12 and 13C and is decorated inside with small pillars and capitals.

There is a good view of the valley from a terrace near the chapel. Stairs lead to the first floor where a beautiful 17C chimneypiece with baroque decoration may be seen in the Guard Room.

In the seignorial part of the castle, a Renaissance gallery looks straight down over the cliff hollowed out with rock shelters, to give a wide **view**★ of the river flowing below.

EXCURSION

Montricoux. – Pop 754. Facilities. *6km – 3 1/2 miles to the northwest.*
Montricoux was built up on terraces above the right bank of the Aveyron River where it broadens out in a wide plain. The old curtain walls are still standing, as is the square keep that formed part of a 13C castle that is no more. Place Marcel-Lenoir and certain alleys contain picturesque half-timbered houses with medieval overhanging storeys of the 13, 14, 15 and 16C.

LE BUGUE

Michelin map 75 fold 16 or 235 fold 1 – Local map p 146

At the entrance to Périgord Noir *(qv)*, this active, local commercial centre, where local products are marketed, is positioned on the north bank of the Vézère, near its confluence with the Dordogne.

Aquarium. – Via large windows, a circular gallery allows you to observe the many European fresh water fish (trout, gudgeon, perch, tench...).

Fossil Site (**Le Gîte à fossiles**). – The palaeontology collection of 3 000 items comes, for the most part, from deposits in the region.

Bara-Bahau Cave (**Caverne de Bara-Bahau**). – The cave which is about 300ft long, ends in a chamber blocked by a rock fall. On the roof of the chamber, amid the protrusions in the rock face, may be seen drawings made with sharpened flints and fingers (Magdalenian Culture) and bear claw scratches (Mousterian Culture). The finger drawings were discovered in 1951 by the Casterets and depict horses, aurochs, bison, bears and deer.

EXCURSION

★Proumeyssac Chasm (**Gouffre de Proumeyssac**). – *3km-2 miles to the south.* A tunnel drilled into a hill, overlooking the Vézère, leads to a platform built half-way up the chasm. This platform offers a view of this underground dome which is decorated, particularly at the base of the walls, with fine yellow and white concretions. Water seeps through abundantly, adding to the stalactites which, in some places, are very numerous and form draperies, pure coloured stalagmites and fantastic shapes such as the eccentrics and triangular crystallisations that are building up from the floor of the caves. Also to be seen are different objects undergoing petrification.

★ CADOUIN

Michelin map 75 fold 16 or 235 fold 5 – Local map pp 76-77

The Abbey of Cadouin, founded in a narrow valley near the Bessède Forest in 1115 by Robert d'Arbrissel, was soon after taken over by the Cistercians and was extremely prosperous during the Middle Ages.
The church and cloisters, restored after the Revolution, constitue an interesting architectural group around which has grown a small village, with its old covered market. Louis Delluc, the film director, was born here in 1890 (d 1924).

The Holy Shroud of Cadouin. – The first written mention of the Holy Shroud appeared in 1214 in an act decreed by Simon de Montfort. This linen cloth adorned with bands of embroidery had been brought from Antioch by a priest from Périgord and was believed to be the cloth that had been wrapped around Christ's head.
The shroud became an object of deep veneration and attracted large pilgrimages, bringing great renown to Cadouin. It is said that Richard Lionheart, St Louis and Charles V came to kneel before it in reverence. Charles VII had it brought to Paris and Louis XI to Poitiers. When the abbey was threatened by the English during the Hundred Years' War – the Romanesque cloisters and many of the outbuildings were destroyed – the Holy Shroud was first entrusted to the care of the monks at Toulouse and then later to those at Aubazine. It was only returned to Cadouin, at the end of the 15C, after endless lawsuits and the intervention of the pope and Louis XI. An important restoration was launched and new buildings were built, but they were damaged during the Wars of Religion.

Tradition v.s. science. – In 1934 two experts attributed the Holy Shroud of Cadouin to the 11C, as the embroidered bands bore kufic inscriptions citing an emir and caliph having ruled in Egypt in 1094 and 1101. The bishop of Périgueux, thus, had the pilgrimage to Cadouin discontinued.
In 1982 two researchers from the C.N.R.S. went over the study from the beginning and added certain facts to the 1934 conclusions: only the embroidered bands, characteristic of the art work produced during the Fatimid dynasty, date from the late 11C; also, it was quite unlikely that an Egyptian craftsman in the late 11C, would have embroidered a cloth that was said to have been wrapped around Christ's head 1 000 years before.

★Church (**Église**). – The building, completed in 1154, presents a powerful and massive façade divided horizontally into three sections, where the influence of the Saintonge style is evident: the middle section opened by three round-arched bays and lighting the church's interior, divides the upper and lower arcaded sections. Tall buttresses running vertically cut the façade into three, showing the church's very rigorous interior plan: one nave and side aisles.
This austere architectural plan, where decoration is virtually limited to the play of light on the stone, emphasies the ornamental effect brought about by the gold colour of the Molières stone.
The finely proportioned building broke away from Cistercian architecture with its interior plan: a chancel with an apse between two apsidal chapels, a dome at the transept crossing capped by a pyramidal bell tower, roofed with chestnut shingles and a more elaborate interior decoration (windows surrounded by mouldings, capitals with foliage and stylised animals; and in the two arms of the transept the elegant capitals are decorated with interlacing and palm fronds). And yet the harmonious proportions and the grandeur of the construction emanate a spirituality proper to Cistercian sanctuaries.

★★Cloisters (Cloître). – The generosity ⊙ of Louis XI enabled the cloisters to be built at the end of the 15C in the Flamboyant Gothic style. The work, in fact, continued to the middle of the 16C as the Renaissance capitals of some of the columns bear witness. Despite the damage suffered during the Wars of Religion and the Revolution, the cloisters were saved and restored in the 19C, thanks to the particular attention they were given by historians and archaeologists alike.

At each corner there is a fine door: the royal door is adorned with the arms of France and Brittany as both Charles VIII and Louis XII had been married to Anne of Brittany, the benefactress of Cadouin. The pendants are carved into people and amusing little scenes. In the north gallery, facing the reader's lectern, may be seen the abbot's throne emblazoned with the abbey arms: the many scenes illustrated on either side end in a large fresco of the Annunciation. The east gallery, commonly known as the Royal

Cloisters

Gallery, contains pillars cast in the form of towers and decorated with themes from the Old and New Testaments (Samson and Delilah, Job, etc).

The recently restored chapter house and two other rooms have been set up as a ⊙ **Pilgrimage Museum** (pilgrims' banners, sacred vases, reliquaries).

EXCURSION

Round tour of 31km – 18 1/2 miles. – *Allow 2 hours. Leave Cadouin to the west on the D 25 and take the D 27 to the right.*

Molières. – Pop 294. This unfinished English *bastide (qv)* has a Gothic church with a façade flanked by a tall two-storey square defensive tower.

St-Avit-Sénieur. – *Description p 131.*

   Follow the D 25 towards Beaumont, bear left on the D 26 and then right.

Ste-Croix. – Pop 84. This small village contains a charming Romanesque church and, nearby, the partly ruined buildings of an old priory. The 12C church has pure lines. Contrasting with the small round tiles that roof the nave are the larger stone slabs *(lauzes)* which cover the east end and the apsidal chapels. Above the façade stands a gabled bell tower.

Montferrand-du-Périgord. – Pop 185. This charming terraced village rising above the Couze Valley is dominated by its partly ruined castle and 12C keep. The covered market with its fine old pillars, the old houses and dovecots make a picturesque scene.

Above the village, in the cemetery, stands a Romanesque chapel, which is decorated inside with an attractive group of 12 to 15C frescoes.

★★ CAHORS   Pop 20 774

Michelin map **79** fold 8 or **235** fold 14 – Local maps pp 91, 100-101 and 102 – Facilities

Cahors, enclosed by a meander in the Lot River and overlooked by rocky hills, was a flourishing commercial and university city in the Middle Ages and still retains precious items from its past. The city, which for centuries occupied only the eastern section of the peninsula, has slowly spread covering the entire tongue of land and has now extended beyond to the neighbouring hills. **Boulevard Gambetta** (BYZ), a typical southern town promenade lined with plane trees, cafés and shops, is the great north-south thoroughfare of the city; its busy, bustling atmosphere recalls that Cahors is an important commercial centre. As *Préfecture* of the Lot *département,* the city has increased its administrative and public services.

As a tourist centre, the former capital of Quercy is an excellent starting point for tours of the Célé and Lot Valleys.

The sacred spring. – A spring, discovered by Carthusian monks, led to the founding of Divona Cadurcorum, later known as Cadurca and later still as Cahors. First the Gauls and then the Romans worshipped the source. The town grew rapidly in size: a forum, a theatre, temples, baths and ramparts were built. This spring still supplies the town with drinking water.

The golden age. – In the 13C Cahors became one of the great towns of France and knew a period of considerable economic prosperity due in no small part to the arrival of Lombard merchants and bankers. The Lombards were brilliant businessmen and bankers but also operated less reputedly as usurers.

The Templars, in turn, came to Cahors; gold fever spread to the townspeople and Cahors became the first banking city of Europe. Money was lent to the pope and to kings, and Cahors counting houses were everywhere. The word *cahorsin*, which was what the people of Cahors were called, was synonymous with the word usurer.

The loyal city and the ungrateful king. – At the beginning of the Hundred Years' War, the English seized all the towns in Quercy: Cahors alone remained impregnable, in spite of the Black Death which killed half the population.

In 1360, under the *Treaty of Brétigny (qv)*, Cahors was ceded to the English, but the town, still unconquered, refused to be handed over. The king of France then ordered the keys of the city to be delivered up although the consuls protested: "It is not we who are abandoning the king, but the king who is abandoning us to a foreign master." By 1450, when the English left Quercy, Cahors was a ruined city.

Cahors and the Reformation. – After several decades of peace, Cahors was able to regain some of its past prosperity; unfortunately in 1540 the Reformation reached the city and rapidly caused dissension among the population. 1560 saw the massacre of the Protestants. Twenty years later the town was besieged by the Huguenots, led by Henri de Navarre. The assault lasted three days. Once fallen, the city was plundered.

Gambetta's childhood. – Léon Gambetta has a special place even among the famous men of Cahors, who included Pope John XXII (1316-34), who founded the university in Cahors in 1332 (more successful than the one in Toulouse and it functioned until the 18C) and the poets Clément Marot (1496-1544) and Olivier de Magny (1529-61) *(qv)*.

Born in 1838, the son of a grocer – his father was of Genoese extraction and his mother the daughter of a chemist from Molières – young Gambetta played truant from school, dreamed of wild adventures and hoped to sail the seven seas. However, after a short spell at boarding school, he suddenly developed a passion for learning and began reading Greek and Latin on sight.

One day the young student went to watch a case at the Assize Court and became fascinated with the drama of the courtroom: the die had been cast, Léon Gambetta gave up all idea of going to sea to become a barrister.

In 1856 Léon Gambetta left Cahors for Paris to enrol in the Faculty of Law. His outstanding career as lawyer and statesman had begun. This ardent patriot, member of the Legislative Assembly, took an active part in the downfall of Napoleon III, in the proclamation of the Third Republic on 4 September 1870, and in the forming of a provisional government (he became Minister of the Interior).

Paris besieged by the enemy, Gambetta left the city in October 1870 in a balloon, floated over the German lines and landed in Tours where he was able (he also became War Minister) to organise the country's defence against the Prussian Army; an armistice was signed in 1871.

He became head of the Republican Union, President of the Chamber of Deputies in 1879 and Prime Minister from November 1881 until January 1882. He died at the age of 44 on December 31, 1882.

There is not a town or city in France which has not paid hommage to this republican statesman by naming a street or square after him.

⋆⋆VALENTRÉ BRIDGE (PONT VALENTRÉ) (AZ) *time: 1/2 hour*

The Valentré Bridge is a remarkable example of French medieval military architecture. The three towers, with machicolations and crenellated parapets, and the pointed cutwaters breaking the line of the seven pointed arches, give it a proud bearing.

The best view of the Valentré Bridge and its towers, which rise 40m – 130ft above the river, is from a little way upstream on the north bank of the Lot.

A legend in which the Devil plays an important part, although he loses in the end, is linked to the construction work which began in 1308 and went on for more than fifty years. The architect was in despair at the slow progress of the bridge and agreed to sign a pact with the Devil by which the Devil would bring all the materials necessary to the site and the architect, in his turn, would hand over his soul. The bridge rose

Valentré Bridge

quickly and work neared completion. The architect did not relish the idea of eternal torment and suddenly thought of commanding the Devil to bring him water in a sieve. After a few vain attempts the Devil admitted himself beaten but in revenge, he broke off the topmost stone of the central tower, which has been known ever since as Devil's Tower. Every time the stone was replaced, it fell off. When the bridge was restored last century, the architect had the stone firmly fixed and on the corner he had carved the little figure of a devil trying to dislodge it.

The original appearance of Valentré Bridge was considerably modified in 1879 when the bridge was restored: the barbican, which reinforced the defences from the town side, was replaced by the present-day gate.

The bridge was originally an isolated fortress commanding the river; the central tower served as observation post, the outer towers were closed by gates and port-cullises. A guard house and outwork on the south bank of the Lot provided additional protection. The fortress defied the English during the Hundred Years' War and Henri de Navarre at the time of the siege of Cahors (1580), as well; it was never even attacked.

★ ST STEPHEN'S CATHEDRAL AND ITS PRECINCTS
time: 1 hour

★St Stephen's Cathedral (Cathédrale St-Etienne) (BY). – The clergy built this church as a fortress for reasons of safety in troubled times as well as of prestige. At the end of the 11C, Bishop Géraud of Cardaillac began to build a church on the site of a former 6C church. Much of Bishop Géraud's church remains standing to this day. The tri-lobed south door dates from 1119. The north door is 12C, the restoration work on the original east end dates from the 13C. The west face was built early in the 14C and the paintings within the domes and in the chancel were executed at the same time. The Flamboyant-style cloisters and some of the outbuildings were commissioned at the beginning of the 16C by Bishop Antoine de Luzech.

Exterior. – The west face is made up of three adjoining towers. The central one is topped by a belfry and opens with double doors. Above, on the first storey, the rose window is surrounded by blind arcades. In spite of windows with twin bays comple-ting the decoration, the austere, military appearance of the façade remains.

★★North Door (Portail Nord). – This Roman-esque door was once part of the main façade; it was transferred to the north side of the cathedral before the present wall was built. The **tympanum** depicts the Ascension. It was carved in about 1135 and from its style and technique belongs to the Languedoc School.

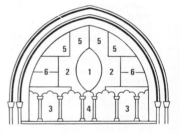

A mandorla or almond-shaped glory is the centrepiece of the composition: the haloed figure of Christ (1) stands with the right hand upraised and the left clasping a closed book. On either side an angel (2) explains the miracle to the Apostles who are seen below in the trefoiled blind arcades (3); beneath the central arch is the Virgin Mary (4) raising her hand to point to her Son. Above Christ four cherubim (5) fly out from the clouds to greet Him and take away His halo. On either side of Christ and the angels the sculptor has depicted scenes from the life of St Stephen (6): his prediction, his arrest by the Jews, his stoning, and the hand of God protecting the martyr.

The cathedral apse, with its two balustrades on the upper register, appears massive and yet it does not interrupt the building's harmony.

Interior. – Enter by the west door and cross the narthex which is slightly raised; the nave is roofed with two huge domes on pendentives. There is a striking contrast between the pale stone of the nave and the chancel adorned with stained glass and paintings. The frescoes of the first dome were uncovered in 1872; these show the stoning of St Stephen in the central medallion, the saint's executioners around the frieze and eight giant-sized figures of prophets in the niches.

The chancel and the apse have Gothic vaulting. Among the radiating chapels, which were added in the 15C is the Chapel of St Anthony, which opens on to the chancel through a beautiful Flamboyant door.

★Cloisters (Cloître) (BY E). – Dating from 1509, these Renaissance cloisters were built after those of Carennac *(p 65)* and Cadouin *(p 58)* with which they have a number of stylistic similarities. Access to the cloisters is through a door on the right of the chancel. They are still rich in carved ornament in spite of considerable damage. The galleries are roofed with stellar vaulting; of the decorated pendants, only one remains above the northwest door showing Jesus surrounded by angels. The jambs are decorated with niches which formerly contained statues. Near the chancel door is a spiral staircase and on the northwest corner pillar a graceful carving of the Virgin of the Annunciation, wrapped in a fine cloak, her hair falling to her shoulders.

In the **Chapel of St-Gausbert** a fresco of the Last Judgment and 16C paintings on the ceiling have been uncovered.

The chapel also contains ecclesiastical objects: church vestments, statues and por-traits of 93 Bishops of Cahors from the 3 to the 19C.

Enter the inner court of the former arch-deaconry of St-Jean through the door in the northeast corner of the cloisters. Note the lovely Renaissance decoration.

Pass in front of the covered market and take Rue Nationale.

Rue Nationale (BZ). – This was the main thoroughfare of the active Badernes Quarter. At no 16, the panels of a lovely 17C **door** are decorated with fruit and foliage.

Across the way, the narrow Rue St-Priest (BZ 28) has kept its medieval appearance.

Rue du Docteur-Bergounioux (BZ 13). – At no 40 a 16C townhouse has an interesting Renaissance façade opened by windows influenced by the Italian Renaissance style.

Turn around, walk back and cross Rue Nationale.

Rue Lastié (BZ 20). – At no 35 note the Radiant-style windows.

On Place St-Priest a wooden staircase (Louis XIII style) can be seen; it served two buildings. At no 117, a 16C house has kept its small shop on the ground floor which supports a first floor opened with twin bays.
At no 156 half-timbered brick houses have been restored.

Rue St-Urcisse (BZ 30). – The late 12C St-Urcisse Church opens by a 14C doorway. Inside, the two chancel pillars are decorated with elegant historiated capitals.
The street is lined by several half-timbered houses with a *soleilho,* an open attic *(see Figeac's secular architecture).*

Ⓥ **Roaldès Mansion** (Maison de Roaldès) (BY L). – The mansion is also known as Henri IV's Mansion because it is said that the king of Navarre lived there during the siege of Cahors in 1580.

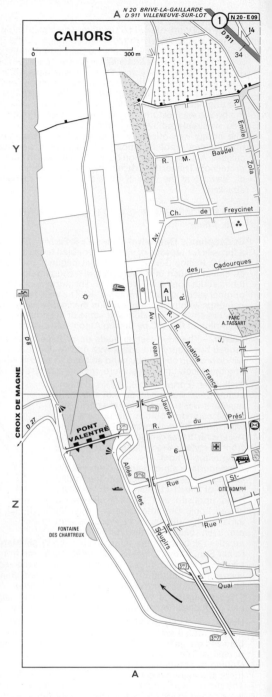

The house dates from the end of the 15C and was restored in 1912. In the 17C it became the property of the Roaldès', a well-known Quercy family.
The half-timbered south side is surmounted by a balcony and topped by a massive round tower.
The north side, overlooking the square, presents mullioned doors and windows and different ornamental motifs – Quercy rose, flamboyant sun, lopped off tree – used by the Quercy School of the early 16C.
Inside, the rooms, access via a spiral staircase, are furnished with interesting pieces and especially, lovely carved chimneys where the decorative motifs – Quercy rose, lopped off tree – of the Quercy School have been used.

Go along Quai Champollion to the Cabessut Bridge.

Cabessut Bridge (**Pont Cabessut**) (BY). – From the bridge there is a good **view★** of the upper part of the city, the Soubirous Quarter. The towers bristling in the distance are: Tower of the Hanged Men or St John's Tower, the bell tower of St-Barthélemy, John XXII's Tower, Royal Castle Tower and the Pélegry College Tower.

Rue Clément-Marot skirts Square Olivier-de-Magny.

Square Olivier-de-Magny (BY). – It is bordered by several old houses.

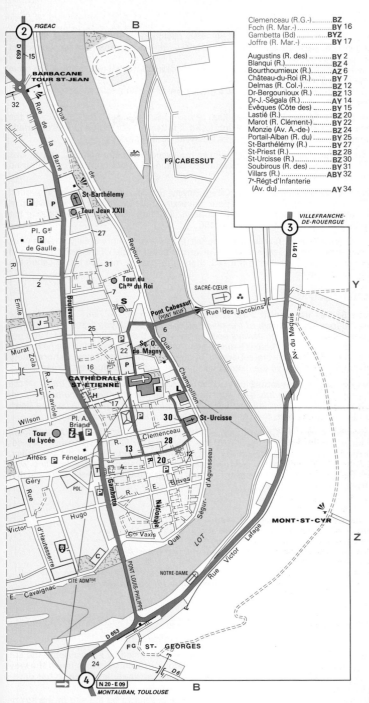

ADDITIONAL SIGHTS

★Barbican and St John's Tower (Barbacane et Tour St-Jean) (BY). – The ramparts, constructed in the 14C, completely cut off from the adjoining countryside the isthmus formed by the meander of the Lot River. Remains of these fortifications can still be seen and include a massive tower at the west end, which sheltered the powder magazine, and the old doorway of St-Michel, which now serves as entrance to the cemetery. It is on the east side, however, where the N 20 enters the town, that the two most impressive fortified buildings remain: the barbican and St John's Tower.

The barbican is an elegant guard house which defended the Barre Gateway; St John's Tower or the Tower of the Hanged Men (Tour des Pendus), was built on a rock overlooking the Lot River.

St-Barthélemy (BY). – This church was built in the highest part of the old town, and was known until the 13C as St-Etienne de Soubiroux, "*Sancti Stephani de superioribus*" (St Stephen of the Upper Quarter) in contrast to the cathedral built in the lower part of the town. The church was rebuilt to its present design over the centuries. It now contains a rectangular belfry-porch with three lines of bays of depressed arches one above the other; the belfry, the base of which dates from the 14C, has no spire; it is built almost entirely of brick.

63

The nave, with its pointed vaulting, was designed in the Languedoc style. In the chapel, nearest the entrance, on the left, a marble slab and bust recalls us that John XXII was baptised in this church.

The *cloisonné* enamels on the cover of the modern baptismal font recount the main events in the life of this famous Cahors citizen.

The terrace near the church affords a good view of the Cabessut suburb and the Lot Valley.

John XXII's Tower (Tour de Jean XXII) (BY). – This tower is all that remains of the palace of Pierre Duèze, brother of John XXII. It is 34m – 112ft high and was originally covered in tiles; twin windows pierce the walls on five storeys.

Lycée Tower (Tour du Lycée) (BZ). – From the Lycée Gambetta building, which was once a Jesuit college, rises a graceful 17C octagonal tower built of rose-coloured brick.

Pélegry College Tower (Tour du Collège Pélegry) (BY S). – The College was founded in 1368 and at first took in thirteen poor university students; until the 18C, it was one of the town's most important establishments. The fine hexagonal tower above the main building was constructed in the 15C.

Royal Castle Tower (Tour du Château du Roi) (BY). – Near Pélegry College stands what is today the prison and was once the governor's residence. Of the two towers and two main buildings erected in the 14C, there remains the massive tower called the Royal Castle Tower.

EXCURSIONS

★**Mount St-Cyr Viewpoint** (Point de vue du Mont-St-Cyr) (BZ). – *7km – 4 miles by the Louis-Philippe Bridge south of the plan and the D 6 which you leave after 1.5km – 1 mile to reach the mount, always bearing left.* From the top (viewing table) you get a good **view★** of Cahors: there is a marked contrast between the old and the new quarters of the town, which are separated by the Boulevard Gambetta, Cahors' main artery. In the background the distinctive shape of Valentré Bridge can be seen.

★**Croix de Magne Viewpoint** (Point de vue de la Croix de Magne). – *5km – 3 miles. At the exit west of Valentré Bridge, bear right and then left; just after the agricultural school (école d'agriculture) bear left and left again at the top.* From near the cross a **view★** extends over the *causse,* the Lot meander, Cahors and Valentré Bridge.

★**Viewpoint north of Cahors** (AY). – *5km – 3 miles. Take Rue du Dr. J.-Ségala* (AY 14) *which branches off the N 20 to the right just after St John's Tower.* This pleasant road runs along the tops of the hills and affords good views of the Lot Valley, and Cahors in its setting: the old town stepped like an amphitheatre, bristling with belfries and battlemented towers and lines of fortifications and bridges, the most distinctive being Valentré Bridge.

The current **Michelin Red Guide France**
offers a selection of pleasant, quiet and well-situated hotels.
Each entry includes the facilities provided
(gardens, tennis courts, swimming pool and equipped beach)
and annual closure dates.
Also included is a selection of establishments recommended for their cuisine:
well-prepared meals at a moderate price, stars for good cooking.

CAPDENAC   Pop 1 033

Michelin map **79** fold 10 or **235** fold 11 – Local map pp 100-101

Capdenac-le-Haut, perched on a promontory and encircled by a meander in the Lot River, occupies a remarkable **site★**. This small town, which still looks much the way it did in the past, overlooks Capdenac-Gare, a busy railway junction which has developed in the valley.

Uxellodunum. – Some historians claim Capdenac-le-Haut to be the site of the stronghold of Uxellodunum, the last site of Gaulish resistance to Caesar (others claim it to be at Puy d'Issolud *(qv),* near Martel). Important excavations, especially those in 1815 headed by the Champollion *(qv)* brothers (including the famous Egyptologist), uncovered the necessary data which proved that the stronghold was a Gallo-Roman town.

The besieged town. – When was Capdenac not under siege? It was besieged at least eleven times! This can be explained for two reasons: it played a major role during the Middle Ages and it held a key position in Quercy.

In the beginning of the 8C King Pepin the Short seized a fortress built on this spot. Later, at the time of the Albigensian Crusade, Simon de Montfort *(qv)* occupied Capdenac in 1209 and in 1214. During the Hundred Years' War, the English besieged the town, settled in it and were dislodged by the future King Louis XI. At the beginning of the 16C, Galiot de Genouillac *(qv),* Grand Master of the Artillery under François I, acquired the castle. During the Wars of Religion it became one of the main Protestant strongholds. After the death of Henri IV, Sully came to live in it and stayed several years.

Ramparts (Remparts). – Remaining of the 13 and 14C are vestiges of the outer walls and the citadel as well as the Northern Gate (Comtale), the village entrance and the Southern Gate (Vijane).

Keep (Donjon). – This powerful square tower, flanked by battlemented turrets (13-14C) ⏱ houses the tourist information centre and a small **museum** which recounts Capdenac's history.

From the square, overlooked by the keep, branch off Rue de la Peyrolie and Rue de la Commanderie; both streets are lined with half-timbered houses with overhanging storeys and pointed arches.

⏱ **Roman Fountain (Fontaine Romaine).** – Known also as the **English Fountain** (Fontaine des Anglais), the steep staircase of 135 steps carved into the cliff face above Capdenac-Gare leads to two pools set in a cave. Champollion, inspired by the site, wrote that it seemed like the revered spot of an oracle, where one goes to seek one's destiny.

Viewpoints. – Around the promontory there are several viewpoints. From a terrace near the church, the **view★** extends over to the loop in the Lot River and its valley, a patchwork of cultivated fields. On the eastern side a terrace looks down on Capdenac-Gare.

★ CARENNAC
Pop 376

Michelin map **75** fold 19 or **239** northeast of fold 38 – Local map p 75 – Facilities

One of the most attractive sights to be found along the Dordogne is at Carennac, where the picturesque houses of the Quercy, with their brown tile roofs and the manor-houses, flanked with turrets, cluster round the old priory in which Fénelon once lived.

Fénelon at Carennac. – The priory-deanery at Carennac, which was founded in the 10C and attached to the famous abbey at Cluny in the following century, owes its fame to the long stay made there by François de Salignac de la Mothe-Fénelon before he became Archbishop of Cambrai.

While he was still a student at Cahors, Fénelon used to enjoy spending his holidays at his uncle's house, senior prior of Carennac. In 1681 Fénelon's uncle died and the young abbot succeeded him, remaining at the priory for fifteen years. Fénelon was greatly revered at Carennac; he enjoyed describing the ceremonies and popular rejoicing that greeted his arrival by boat and his installation as commendatory prior. Tradition has it that Fénelon wrote *Télémaque* while living at Carennac. The description of the adventures of Ulysses' son was at first only a literary exercice, but was subsequently turned into a tract for the edification of the Duke of Burgundy, Louis XIV's grandson, when Fénelon was appointed his tutor.

The Ile Barrade, in the Dordogne, was renamed Calypso's Island and the visitor will still be shown a tower in the village which is called Télémaque's Tower in which, it is maintained, Fénelon wrote his masterpiece.

THE VILLAGE *time: 1/2 hour*

The charming village, where some of the houses still standing date from the 16C, has barely changed since Fénelon's day, although the deanery and its outbuildings suffered considerable damage at the time of the Revolution. The deanery was suppressed by order of the Royal Council in 1788 and put up for auction and sold in 1791.

Of the old ramparts there remain only a fortified gateway, and of the buildings, the castle and the priory tower. Go through the fortified gateway.

St-Pierre. – In front of this Romanesque church, which is dedicated to St Peter, stands a porch with a beautiful 12C carved **doorway★**. It is well preserved and from its style would appear to belong to the same school as the tympana of Beaulieu, Moissac, Collonges and Cahors. In a mandorla (almond-shaped glory) in the centre of the composition *(photograph p 31)*, Christ is seen in Majesty. His right hand is raised in blessing. He is surrounded by the symbols of the four Evangelists. On either side are the Apostles on two superimposed registers and there are two bowing angels on the upper register. The tympanum is framed with a foliated scroll in the Oriental style. Its base is decorated with a frieze of Greeks and small animals. The continuation of the animals was pursued on a protruding band which doubled the doorway arch, of which a dog and bear can still be seen on the left.

Inside, the archaic capitals in the nave are interesting for their ornamentation consisting of fantastic animals, foliage and historiated scenes.

⏱ **Cloisters (Cloître).** – The restored cloisters consist of a Romanesque gallery adjoining the church and three Flamboyant galleries. Stairs lead to the terrace.

The chapter house, which opens onto the cloisters, shelters a remarkable **Entombment★** (15C). Christ lies on a shroud carried by two disciples: Joseph of Arimathaea and Nicodemus; behind these figures, two holy women surround the Virgin and the Apostle John; on the right Mary Magdalene wipes away a tear. The faces show a certain rustic quality.

Castle (Château). – Temporary exhibitions are held in the castle which stands next to the church. A room on the first floor has a fine wooden ceiling, painted in the Renaissance style.

*The **Michelin Sectional Map Series** (1:200 000) covers the whole of France.*
They show
 - difficult or dangerous stretches of road,
 - gradients, ferries, weight and height restrictions.
These maps are a must for your car.

★★ CASTELNAU-BRETENOUX CASTLE

Michelin map 75 fold 19 or 239 fold 39 – Local maps pp 75 and 133

On the northern border of Quercy stands Castelnau-Bretenoux Castle with the village of Prudhomat lying at its foot. The great mass of the castle's red stone ramparts and the towers rise up from a spur commanding the confluence of the Cère and the Dordogne. The scale on which the castle defence system was built makes it one of the finest examples of medieval military architecture.

More than three miles round, the castle, as Pierre Loti wrote, "is the beacon... the thing you cannot help looking at all the time from all angles: this cock's comb of blood-red stone rising from a tangle of trees, this ruin poised like a crown on a pedestal dressed with a beautiful greenery of chesnut and oak trees."

Turenne's egg. – From the 11C onwards the barons of Castelnau were the strongest in Quercy; they paid homage only to the counts of Toulouse and styled themselves the Second Barons of Christendom. In 1184 Raymond de Toulouse gave the suzerainty of Castelnau to the viscount of Turenne. The baron of Castelnau refused to accept the insult and paid homage instead to Philip Augustus, king of France. Bitter warfare broke out between Turenne and Castelnau; King Louis VIII intervened and decided in favour of Turenne. Whether he liked it or not the baron had to accept the verdict. The fief, however, was only symbolic: Castelnau had to present his overlord with... an egg. Every year, with great pomp and ceremony a yoke of four oxen bore a freshly laid egg to Turenne.

Castle. – Round the strong keep built in the 11C, there grew up during the Hundred Years' War a huge fortress with a fortified curtain wall. The castle was abandoned in the 18C and suffered depredations at the time of Revolution. It caught fire in 1851 but was cleverly restored between 1896 and 1932. The ground plan is that of an irregular triangle flanked by three round towers and three other towers partially projecting from each side. Three parallel curtain walls still defend the approaches, but the former ramparts have been replaced by an avenue of trees.

In following the ramparts a view★ develops of the Cère and Dordogne Valleys to the north; northwest of Turenne Castle set against the horizon; west the Montvalent Amphitheatre; southwest of Loubressac Castle and due south of Autoire Valley.

The court of honour, where stand the round keep and an impressive square tower 62m – 203ft high, known as the Saracen's Tower, gives one an idea of the vast scale of this fortress, the garrison of which numbered 1 500 men and 100 horses.

Interior. – In addition to the lapidary museum, containing the Romanesque capitals of Ste-Croix-du-Mont in Gironde, many other rooms should be visited on account of their decoration and furnishings done by the former proprietor, a singer of comic opera, Jean Moulierat, who bought the castle in 1896. The former Chamber of the Quercy Estates General is lit by large Romanesque windows; the pewter hall and the grand salon contain Aubusson and Beauvais tapestries; the oratory has stained glass windows dating from the 15C and a 14C triptych of the Crucifixion and the life and martyrdom of St Bartholomew.

St Louis Collegiate Church (Collégiale St-Louis). – Built by the lords of Castelnau in red ferruginous stone, the collegiate church stands at the foot of the castle. Visible nearby are a few canons' residences.

Enter the church. The lords' chapel has lovely quadripartite vaulting, the pendant of which is emblazoned with the Castelnau coat of arms. The furnishings include 15C stalls, a 17C retable and 18C altars; one of which is surmounted by a multicoloured wood Virgin with bird (15C), quite naive in style.

★ CASTELNAUD CASTLE

Michelin map 75 fold 17 or 235 west of fold 6 – Local map pp 76-77

The impressive ruins of Castelnaud Castle stand erect on a wonderful **site★★** commanding the valleys of the Céou and the Dordogne. Right opposite stands Beynac Castle (qv), Castelnaud's implacable rival throughout the conflicts of the Middle Ages.

An eventful history. – In 1214 Simon de Montfort (c1165-1218, father of the English statesman and soldier) took possesion of the castle belonging to the Castelnaud family. In 1259 Saint Louis ceded the castle to the king of England who held it for several years.

During the Hundred Years' War the castle constantly changed French and English hands. Once peace was declared the castle was in terrible condition. During the whole of the second half of the 15C the castle was being rebuilt. Only the keep and curtain wall have kept their 13C appearance. In the 16C the castle was once again transformed: the artillery tower was added.

After the Revolution it was abandoned and partially destroyed.

In 1969 a major restoration program was undertaken which has enabled the buildings to be rebuilt.

Castle. – The castle is an example of a medieval fortress with its powerful machicolated keep, curtain wall, living quarters, inner bailey... And yet certain parts of the castle – artillery tower, loopholes – were added when the transformations occurred and reflect the evolution of weapons in siege warfare. In the artillery tower, recreated scenes demonstrate artillerymen in action. Primitive cannons, stone balls, and a number of other weapons complete the display. The main part of the building contains the Middle Ages Siege Warfare Museum.

There are two audio-visual presentations: one explains the history of the castle and the other a history of fortifications and siege warfare tactics in the Middle Ages.

Castelnaud Castle with Beynac Castle in the background

The castle grounds include a barbican, inner bailey and the reconstitution of a 12C catapult and a 15C bombard.
From the ward the view extends southwards onto Céou Valley. At the east end of the terrace is an exceptional **panorama**★★★ of one of the most lovely views of the Dordogne Valley: in the foreground the patchwork of fields with screens of poplars hemmed by a wide loop in the river; further on, lie Beynac with its castle, Marqueyssac Castle and, at the foot of the cliffs, La Roque-Gageac and, in the far distance, a line of wooded and rocky hills skirting the Dordogne Valley.

CASTELNAU-MONTRATIER   Pop 1 914

Michelin map **79** folds 17 and 18 or **235** fold 18

This hilltop *bastide (qv)* was founded in the 13C by Ratier, lord of Castelnau, who gave it his name. It replaced a small village, Castelnau-de-Vaux, built at the foot of the hill, which was destroyed by Simon de Montfort *(qv)* in 1214 at the time of the Albigensian Crusade.

Square (Place). – Triangular in shape, this shaded square has preserved some covered arcades and old houses.

Windmills (Moulins). – North of the promontory stand three windmills, one of which is still in working order.
In the past these tower mills with rotating caps were numerous in Quercy.

CAUSSADE   Pop 6 132

Michelin map **79** fold 18 or **235** fold 18 – Facilities

Caussade, at the southern edge of the Limogne Causse, was a Protestant stronghold during the Wars of Religion.
At the beginning of the 20C, it was a centre of the straw-hat making industry, but fashions change, and today the factories turn out canvas hats and miscellaneous items for seaside resorts.

Church (Église). – The original church belfry, built in rose-coloured bricks, can still be seen, graceful and eight-sided, rising three storeys high and topped by a crocketed spire; the remainder of the building was rebuilt in 1882 in the Gothic style.
The old quarter near the church contains a few old houses.

EXCURSIONS

Notre-Dame-des-Misères. – *13km – 8 miles to the southwest by the N 20 and from Réalville bear right on the D 40.* The chapel, founded in 1150 in a plesant setting, is crowned by an octagonal Romanesque belfry, two storeys high and with double arcades.

Puylaroque. – Pop 614. *14km – 8 1/2 miles to the northeast by the D 17.*
Puylaroque was once a *bastide* of Bas-Quercy; its flat-roofed houses are grouped on the top of a hill overlooking the valleys of the Cande and the Lère. A few corbelled houses with half-timbered walls can still be seen in the narrow streets near the church, which has a massive square belfry adjoining the main doorway. Views far over the rolling Quercy countryside and the plains of Caussade and Montauban can be obtained from several of the town's esplanades and especially from the one near the church.

Michelin map 🄻🄽 fold 19 or 🄻🄽🄴 west of fold 19

This little village of Bas-Quercy is set in a picturesque spot above the right bank of the Bonnette, a tributary of the Aveyron. The best view of the old town, closely grouped round the church with its tall bell tower and overlooked by the ruins of the 14C fortress, is from the southwest along the D 926.
At the foot of the old town lies a small artificial lake.

Covered Market (Halle). – The great size of the market is evidence of Caylus's long-standing commercial importance. The old grain measures may still be seen cut into the stone.

Church (Église). – This was once a fortified church as may be seen from the buttresses topped by machicolations.
Inside, near the chancel, on the north side of the 14C nave, stands a gigantic figure of **Christ*** carved in wood in 1954 by Zadkine (qv). The work is very striking and at the same time deeply moving. The 15C stained-glass windows (restored) in the chancel are noteworthy.

Rue Droite. – In Rue Droite, starting from the church, there are several medieval houses, in particular the 13C gable-fronted house known as the **Wolves' Lair** (Maison des Loups) adorned with corbels and gargoyles in the form of wolves, from which the house derives its name.

EXCURSIONS

Lacapelle-Livron. – *Round tour of 10km – 6 miles – about 1 hour. Leave Caylus to the north.* The road affords good views of the Bonnette River and soon passes, on the left, a path that leads to the pilgrimage chapel of Notre-Dame-de-Livron, and becomes a picturesque corniche-style road overlooking the valley.

Notre-Dame-des-Grâces. – Built at the end of a promontory, this little pilgrimage chapel with its *lauze* roof is Gothic in style with a finely sculptured doorway.
From nearby, at the tip of the promontory, there is a wide view of the Bonnette Valley in its setting of hills dotted with woods and meadows.

Lacapelle-Livron. – Pop 157. This old village with its *lauze*-roofed houses has a group of buildings, mostly in ruins, which was formerly a commandery of the Order of Knights Templars; after 1307 it passed to the Order of St John with the Knights of Malta until the Revolution. There remains a fortified manor-house, overlooking the Bonnette, with a central courtyard, preserving the original layout of the commandery. To the south, beside the small Romanesque fortified church is a powerful bell tower-keep, whose watchpath has a few remaining brackets. The church is opposite the former refectory, which is now the guard room.

Cornusson Castle. – *8km – 5 miles east on the road to Cornusson.* This castle, for the most part rebuilt in the 16C and flanked by numerous towers, stands well placed on a wooded hill comanding the Seye.

★ CÉLÉ VALLEY

Michelin map 🄻🄽 folds 9 and 10 or 🄻🄽🄴 folds 10, 11 and 14

The Célé (*celer* = rapid), which owes its name to its swiftness, is a delightful Quercy river which has cut a steep-sided valley through the *causse (qv)*. The Célé Valley, in addition to passing through beautiful country, contains important prehistoric sites and archaeological remains.

Valley of Paradise (Le Val Paradis). – The Célé rises in the chestnut woods that grow on the granite soil of Cantal; it enters Quercy and makes directly for the Lot River, but within 5km – 3 miles its course is blocked by Capdenac Hill. The Célé gets around this obstacle by turning westwards and cutting through 40km – 25 miles of limestone. This has resulted in a series of picturesque defiles, where the river can be seen winding along, still undermining the bases of the steep and many-hued rock walls. Adding to the beauty of the valley are the old mills built beside the river, and the archaic villages that stand perched on cliff ledges or half-hidden in the greenery: it is not surprising that the former priory at Espagnac (p 82) was called the Valley of Paradise.

The "Hébrardie". – Throughout the Middle Ages the greater part of the Célé Valley was under the control of the Hébrard family of St-Sulpice, so that it virtually constituted a feudal benefice. The period, when the influence of the Hébrards was so great, was known locally as the "Hébrardie". The family, which lived at St-Sulpice (p 69), enlarged or rebuilt the priories of Espagnac and Marcilhac and protected the local inhabitants, particularly at the time of the Hundred Years' War. This great family numbered not only soldiers among its members – one was appointed seneschal of Quercy – but also eminent ecclesiastics such as Aymeric, Bishop of Coïmbra of Portugal and Anthony, Bishop of Cahors.

FROM CONDUCHÉ TO FIGEAC
65km – 40 miles – about 1/2 day – local map p 69

The D 41 starts at Conduché, where the Célé flows into the Lot, and goes up the valley. The road is squeezed between the river bed and the cliff face, which rises at one side like a wall and at times even overhangs the route below. Many crops grow in the valley, with maize tending to replace tobacco: the characteristic line of poplars marks the course of the river.

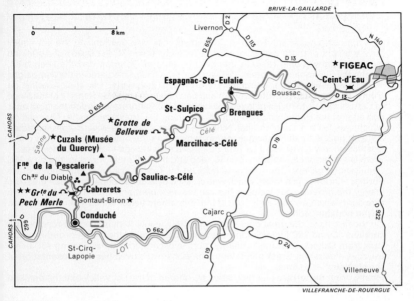

Cabrerets. – Pop 213. Facilities. Cabrerets, set in a rocky amphitheatre, occupies a commanding position at the confluence of the Sagne and Célé Rivers.

A good overall **view**★ of Cabrerets and its setting may be obtained from the left bank of the Célé, which is reached by crossing the bridge. Opposite stand the ruins of the **Devil's Castle** (Château du Diable), or Castle of the English, which cling to the formidable Rochecourbe cliff. This eagle's aerie served as a base from which the English could pillage the countryside during the Hundred Years' War.

On the far left is the impressive outline of the 14 and 15C **Gontaut-Biron Castle**★ overlooking the valley. A big corner tower flanks the buildings that surround an inner courtyard. One of the facade's mullioned windows opens onto the terrace, with its ornamental balustrades, which hangs up over the road 25m – 82ft.

The D 13 then the D 198 lead up the valley of the Sagne to Pech Merle Cave.

★★**Pech Merle Cave.** – *Description p 114.*

Return to Cabrerets.

Shortly after Cabrerets the *corniche* road crosses the face of high stone cliffs.

Pescalerie Fountain (Fontaine de la Pescalerie). – This is one of the most attractive sights of Célé Valley: a beautiful waterfall pours out of the rock wall quite near the road. It marks the surfacing of an underground river that has cut its way through the Gramat Causse; beside the waterfall an ivy-covered mill stands, half-hidden by trees.

As the road emerges from a tunnel, the cliffs are seen to overhang the south bank of the river. At this point the valley widens out.

Take the small road left to Cuzals.

Cuzals. – Also known as the **Quercy Open-Air Museum,** the museum illustrating Quercy peasant life exhibits two traditional rural habitations (reconstructed): one from the end from the Ancien Régime (c1786) and the other from the early 20C (c1910).

The **Museum of Water** explains the different functions and uses of water.

Finally, in the castle, there are exhibits of Quercy history as well as the history of the Cuzals estate; a dentist's office has been reconstructed.

Sauliac-sur-Célé. – Pop 106. This old village clings to an awe-inspiring cliff of coloured rock. In the cliff face can be seen the openings to the fortified caves used in time of war as refuges, by the local inhabitants : the most agile climbed up by way of ladders; invalids and animals were hoisted up in great baskets.

Beyond Sauliac the valley widens; the valley bottom covered with alluvial soil produces crops and pasture land and several round dry-stone shelters can be seen.

Marcilhac-sur-Célé. – *Description p 103.*

★**Bellevue Cave.** – *Description p 104.*

Between Marcilhac-sur-Célé and Brengues the contrast intensifies between the rocks, with their sparse vegetation, and the valley, which is densely cultivated with maize, sunflowers, vineyards and tobacco plantations.

St-Sulpice. – Pop 116. The houses and gardens of this old village lie within the shadow of an overhanging cliff. The approach is guarded by a 12C castle which was rebuilt in the 14 and 15C. It is still the property of the Hébrard family of St-Sulpice.

Brengues. – Pop 150. This small village is in a pleasant setting, perched on a ledge overlooked by a vertiginous bluff.

As far as Boussac the valley sometimes widens and sometimes narrows; rich farmhouses stand solidly, their dovecots *(qv)* beside them.

Espagnac-Ste-Eulalie. – *Description p 82.*

Above Boussac the cliffs finally disappear and the countryside becomes one of wooded hills where the Célé spreads out into a wide alluvial bed.

Ceint d'Eau. – This 15 and 16C castle, flanked by massive machicolated towers, rises above the D 13 and overlooks the Célé Valley, which widens out at this spot.

★**Figeac.** – *Description p 86.*

★ CÉNEVIÈRES CASTLE

Michelin map 🟨🟨 fold 9 or 🟦🟦🟦 west of fold 15 – 7km – 4 miles east of St-Cirq-Lapopie – Local map pp 100-101

This imposing castle climbs up to the vertical rock face overlooking the Lot Valley from a height of more than 70m – 230ft. As early as the 7C the Dukes of Aquitaine had a stronghold built here. In the 13C the lords of Gourdon had the keep built. During the Renaissance, Flottard de Gourdon, who had participated in the campaigns in Italy with François I, completely rearranged the castle. His son, Antoine de Gourdon, converted to Protestantism and participated alongside Henri IV at the siege of Cahors (qv) in 1580. He pillaged the cathedral of Cahors and loaded the high altar and altar of the Holy Shroud onto boats returning to Cénevières Castle. The boat on which was loaded the high altar sank in a chasm along the way. Before his death Antoine built a small Protestant church, which is in the outer bailey. He died childless; his widow remarried a La Tour du Pin – a new lineage took over Cénevières.

From the exterior can be seen the 13C keep and the 15C main wings joined by a 16C Renaissance gallery. The gallery is held up by Tuscan columns and above it are dormer windows. The moat, which was crossed by a drawbridge, has been filled up. Inside, the ground floor includes the vaulted salt room and kitchen; the keep has a trap door, which permits a glimpse of the three floors below which include the cellar, prison and dungeons.

On the first floor, the great drawing room with a lovely Renaissance painted ceiling contains 15 and 16C Flemish tapestries and the shrine of the Holy Shroud brought back from Cahors. The small alchemy room is decorated with fascinating 16C naive frescoes illustrating Greek mythology. The alchemist's oven has a representation of the philosopher's stone.

Finally, from the terrace plunging **views** are offered of the Lot Valley and the perched village of Calvignac.

★ CHANCELADE ABBEY

Michelin map 🟨🟨 fold 5 or 🟦🟦🟦 fold 42 – 7km – 4 miles northwest of Périgueux – Local map p 81

The abbey appears as a peaceful haven overlooking the Beauronne. Founded in the 12C by a monk, who adopted the rule of St Augustine, the abbey was protected by the bishops of Périgueux and later answered directly to the Holy See. It, therefore, prospered and was accorded considerable privileges: asylum, safety and franchises. In the 14C the abbey was compromised; the English captured it, sent the monks away and installed a garrison. Du Guesclin freed it, but not for long, as the English took it over again and held onto it until the mid-15C. During the Wars of Religion, the abbeys buildings were partly destroyed by Protestants from Périgueux.

In 1623 Alain de Solminihac, the new abbot, undertook the reformation and restoration of Chancelade. He was so successful that he was named Bishop of Cahors by Louis XIII. The abbey was able to function calmly until the Revolution, when it became national property.

Church (Église). – The Romanesque doorway, the recessed orders of which have nailhead moulding, is surmounted by an elegant arcade showing Saintonge influence, underlined by a modillioned cornice. The square, Romanesque bell tower is made up of three tiers of arcades, some of which are rounded and others of which are pointed. Inside, few elements are left of the original 12C church: the nave was re-vaulted with pointed vaulting and the east end was razed. 13 and 14C frescoes decorate the church walls. In the earliest part of the chancel are depicted two important scenes, one representing St Christopher and the other probably of Thomas Becket, to whom the monks of Chancelade had consecrated an altar after he was canonised (1173). The 17C stalls, in walnut, have preserved their misericords carved with motifs of palm leaves, roses, shells, etc...

Conventual Buildings (Bâtiments conventuels). – They include the abbot's lodgings and the outbuildings around the courtyard and garden, which are made up of the 15C pointed barrel-vaulted laundry room (now an exhibition hall), stables, workshops and a fortified mill. Adjoining the courtyard is the garden. The abbot's lodgings' (also called Bourdeilles's lodgings) north façade is flanked by two turrets, one of which is opened by a finely decorated door (late 15C).

St-Jean Chapel (Chapelle St-Jean). – This charming, small parish church was consecrated in 1147. Its façade is opened by a semicircular doorway with three barely perceptible pointed-recessed arches, surmounted by a bay framed by slender columns, and above that, a low relief of a lamb carrying a cross. There is a fine rounded apse with buttresses.

EXCURSION

Merlande Priory (Prieuré de Merlande). – 8km – 5 miles northwest on the D 1. The road between Chancelade and Merlande rises through a wood of chestnut and oak trees. In a deserted clearing in Feytaud Forest stand a small fortified chapel and a prior's house, both restored, solitary reminders of the Merlande Priory founded here in the 12C by the monks of Chancelade. The chapel appears to be a fortress-like structure due to its 4-sided plan. It is a Romanesque building with two bays: the first has a transverse arch and pointed-barrel vaulting replacing the original dome, the second is roofed with an attractive dome on pendentives. The chancel, the oldest part, slightly above the level of the nave and preceded by a rounded triumphal arch, has barrel vaulting and a flat east end. It is bordered by a series of blind arcades adorned with finely carved archaic **capitals**★: tangled up monsters and lions devouring palm-leaf scrolls make up a bizarre but striking fauna.

Michelin map **75** south of fold 9 or **239** south of fold 26 – Local map p 56 – Facilities

Collonges "the red", built of red sandstone, has set its small manor-houses, old houses and Romanesque church in a green countryside where vines and walnuts grow. A historic atmosphere pervades the streets of this lovely old town.

The village developed in the 8C around its church and priory, a dependency of the powerful Charroux Abbey in the Poitou region. In the 13C, Collonges was a part of the viscounty of Turenne *(qv)* and, thus, received franchises and liberties. Much later on, in the 16C, Collonges was the place chosen by the leaders of the viscounty for their holidays. To accommodate themselves, they constructed charming manors and mansions flanked with towers and turrets, which is what makes this town so unique.

TOUR *time: 1 hour*

Start near the old station (ancienne gare).

Mermaid's House (Maison de la Sirène). – This 16C corbelled house, with a porch and beautiful stone slab *(lauzes)* roof is adorned with a mermaid holding a comb in one hand and a mirror in the other.

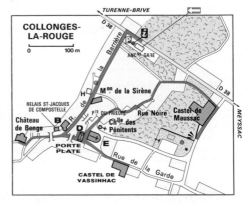

Farther along may be seen the pointed gateway arch (Porte du Prieuré) of the former Benedictine priory, which was destroyed during the Revolution.

Hôtel des Ramade de Friac (B). – The *hôtel*, crowned by two turrets, was the former town house of the powerful Ramade de Friac family.

Go past the Relais de St-Jacques-de-Compostelle – the name recalls that Collonges was a pilgrims' stopping place along the famous way of St James – and through a covered passageway; soon afterwards, in an alley on the right, stands an old turreted house.

Château de Benge. – Set with a backdrop of poplars and walnuts is this proud towered and turreted manor-house with its lovely Renaissance window.

Flattened Gateway (Porte Plate). – This gateway, called thus because it has lost its towers, was part of the town walls protecting the church, cloisters and priory buildings.

Covered market (Halle) (D). – The grain market, with its timberwork supported by thick pillars, contains a village oven.

Church (Église) (E). – The church, which dates from the 11 and 12C, was fortified during the Wars of Religion in the 16C. It was at this time that the great square keep was strengthened by a defence chamber communicating with the watchpath and that the tympanum was placed in the new gable out of harm's way.

★**Tympanum.** – Having been carved in the white limestone of Turenne, the 12C tympanum stands out among all the red sandstone. It depicts the Ascension (or perhaps the second coming of Christ) and was apparently carved by sculptors of the Toulouse School. The upper register shows the figure of Christ surrounded by angels, holding the Gospels in one hand, the other raised in benediction. The lower register shows the saddened Virgin surrounded by the eleven Apostles. The whole tympanum is outlined by a pointed arch ornamented with a fine border of carved animals.

Church

★**Bell tower**. – The 12C bell tower is in the Limousin style: two lower square storeys pierced with round-arched bays are surmounted by two octagonal storeys flanked by gables. The belfry comes out of the transept crossing.

Interior. – In the 12C, the church presented a cruciform plan around the transept crossing. The dome above the transept crossing rests on 11C pillars. Modifications occurred in the 14 and 15C, when side chapels were added as well as a second nave in the Flamboyant style.

★**Vassinhac Manor-house** (Castel de Vassinhac). – This elegant house was owned by Gédéor de Vassinhac, lord of Collonges, captain-governor of the viscounty of Turenne. Built as a manor-house in 1583, it bristles with large towers and pepper-pot-roofed turrets; although it has many mullioned windows, its defensive role is obvious from its many loopholes and battlemented turrets.

Former Penitents' Chapel (Ancienne Chapelle des Pénitents). – The chapel was built in the 13C and rearranged by the Maussac family at the time of the Counter-Reformation.

Rue Noire. – This street cuts through the oldest part of Collonges, where old houses can be seen set back one from the other, ornamented with turrets and towers and adorned with wisteria and climbing vines.

Maussac Manor-House (Castel de Maussac). – This building is embellished with a turret and a porch roof above the main door. A battlemented turret projects from the square tower, which is overlooked by a dormer window.

This manor-house was the refuge, before the Revolution, of the last member of the Maussac family, who then left for Italy and was to become the chaplain to Napoleon's sister, Princess Pauline Borghese.

Continue further south along the street to enjoy a pretty **view**★ of Collonges, Vassinhac Manor-house and the bell tower.

★ **COUGNAC CAVES** (Grottes de COUGNAC)

Michelin map **75** fold 18 or **235** fold 6 – 3km – 2 miles north of Gourdon

These caves are fascinating for two reasons: their natural concretions and their Palaeolithic paintings similar to those of Pech-Merle (qv).

⊙**Tour**. – The caves, consisting of two chasms about 200m – 300yds apart, spread their network of galleries beneath a limestone plateau.

The first cave consists of three small chambers with roofs raining closely packed and sometimes slender stalactites.

The second cave is bigger and has two remarkable chambers: the **Pillar Chamber**★ (Salle des Colonnes) is particularly striking for the perspective provided by its columns reaching from the ceiling to the floor and the **Hall of Prehistoric Paintings** (Salle des Peintures Préhistoriques) contains designs in ochre and black including deer, mammoths and human figures.

★★ **DOMME**   Pop 910

Michelin map **75** fold 17 or **235** fold 6 – Local map pp 76-77 – Facilities

Domme is remarkably situated on a rocky crag overlooking the Dordogne Valley.

Captain Vivans's exploit. – While the struggles of the Reformation were inflaming France, Domme was resisting the Huguenots who were overrunning Périgord. Yet, in 1588, the famous Protestant Captain **Geoffroi de Vivans** (qv) captured the town.

One night he and thirty of his men climbed along the Barre Rocks (Rochers de la Barre), a place so precipitous that it had not been thought necessary to fortify it, and entered the sleeping town. Vivans and his men created an infernal row and opened the tower doors to their waiting army. The inhabitants were not sufficiently wide awake to resist. Vivans became master of the town (for four years), installed a garrison, burnt down the church and the Cénac Priory (p 77) and established the Protestant faith.

Having joined the Catholics, Vivans sold them the *bastide*, without a fight, but was careful to leave the place in ruins at the appointed hour (10 January 1592). His name was carved on the inside of one of the rampart towers.

★★★**PANORAMA**

From the promontory, the view embraces the Dordogne Valley from the Montfort Meander to the east, to Beynac to the west.

Flowing east to west from the undulating countryside of Périgord Noir, the Dordogne River widens at the foot of Domme, in a fertile valley scattered with villages and farms, and continues its way below the cliffs of La Roque-Gageac and Beynac.

Changing with the time of day – hazy in the early morning fog, bright blue between lines of green poplars in the noonday sun, a silver ribbon in the evening light – the Dordogne winds its way through the carefully cultivated fields (maize, tobacco, cereals) against a backdrop of wooded hills.

Barre Belvedere (Belvédère de la Barre). – The esplanade at the end of the Grand'Rue offers a panorama of the valley below. The bust represents **Jacques de Maleville** (1741-1824) one of the authors of the *Code Civil* (Common Law).

Cliff Walk (Promenade des Falaises). – Continue along the promontory eastwards and below the gardens. The view is more expansive than at the Barre Belvedere.

Gardens (Jardin Public). – In the middle of these pleasant gardens, at the tip of the promontory, is a **viewing table**. As you leave the gardens bear right towards the old mill.

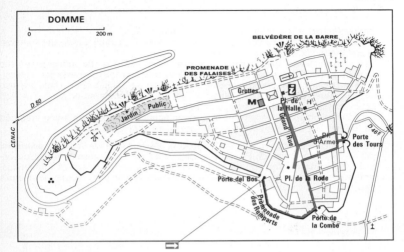

★THE BASTIDE

Founded by Philip the Bold in 1283, this *bastide* is far from presenting the perfect rectangular plan of the *bastide* as such – it is more in the form of a trapezium. The surrounding fortifications have been adapted to the terrain; inside the fortified town, the streets follow a geometric plan when at all possible, considering the terrain. The houses built in a fine gold stone are ornamented with flower-covered balconies and outside staircases.

Rampart Walk (Promenade des Remparts). – When you come to the **Del Bos Gateway** (Porte del Bos), which has a pointed arch and was once closed with a portcullis, bear left to walk inside the ramparts.

Opposite the **La Combe Gateway** (Porte de la Combe), turn left towards the town where there are many fine houses to be seen. The beauty of the gold stone and the flat brown tiles is often enhanced by the addition of elegant wrought-iron balconies and brightened by climbing vines and flower-decked terraces.

Go through the late 13C **Towers' Gateway** (Porte des Tours), the most impressive and best preserved of the town's gateways. On Place des Armes' side the wall is rectilinear but on the exterior side the gateway is flanked by two massive semicircular rusticated towers, which were defended by a battlemented turret, of which one can still see the machicolations. The towers were built by Philip the Fair and originally served as guard rooms. They later held the Templars, imprisoned between 1307 and 1318, who left their mark with graffiti.

Place de la Rode. – This is the place where the condemned were broken on the wheel. The **House of the Money Minter** is decorated with fine Gothic apertures.

Grand'Rue. – This shopping street is lined with shops displaying specialities of Périgord *(p 35)*. At the corner of the first street on the right is a lovely Renaissance window.

Place de la Halle. – In this large square *(photograph below)* stands an elegant 17C **covered market** (halle). Facing it is the 16C **Governors' House** (Maison des Gouverneurs) flanked by an elegant turret; it houses the tourist information centre.

Covered market and Governors' House

ADDITIONAL SIGHTS

⊘**Caves (Grottes).** – The entrance is in the covered market.
These caves served as refuge for the townspeople of Domme during the Hundred Years' War and the Wars of Religion.
So far about 450m – 490yds of galleries have been cleared for the public to visit; the chambers are usually small and are sometimes separated by low passages. The ceilings in certain chambers are enriched with slender white stalactites. There are also places where stalactites and stalagmites join to form columns or piles. The Red Chamber (Salle Rouge) contains eccentrics *(qv)*.
Bones of bison and rhinoceroses, discovered when the caves were being prepared for tourists, are displayed at the exact place where they were found.

⊘**Museum of Popular Arts and Traditions (Musée d'Art et de Traditions populaires) (M).** – In an old house on Place de la Halle, this museum presents a restrospective of Domme life through reconstructed interiors and displays of furnishings, clothing and husbandry. Archives and photographs also help to recount the village's past.

★★★ DORDOGNE VALLEY

Michelin map 🎟 folds 15 to 19 or 🎟 folds 5 and 6 and 🎟 folds 37 to 39

The Dordogne is one of the longest rivers in France and is said to be the most beautiful. The variety and beauty of the countryside through which the river flows and the architectural glories that mark its banks make the valley a first-class tourist attraction.

Château de la Treyne

A lovely journey. – The Dordogne begins where the Dore and the Dogne meet at the foot of the Sancy, the highest peak in the Massif Central. Swift-flowing and speckled with foam, it crosses the Mont-Dore and Bourboule Basins and soon leaves the volcanic rocks of Auvergne for the granite of Limousin. Between Bort and Argentat, where once the river flowed between narrow ravines, there are now a series of reservoirs and great dams. The river quietens for a short time after Beaulieu, as it crosses the rich plain where it is joined by the Cère River, which rises in Cantal. From this point the Dordogne is a great river, though it remains swift and temperamental; the *causses* (limestone plateaux) of Quercy bar its way and so with a pioneering spirit it pierces a passage through the Montvalent Amphitheatre. Once beyond Souillac and on the Perigord plateaux, the river begins to flow past great castles, washing the bases of the rocks on which they perch. Starting at Limeuil, where the river is joined by the Vézère, the valley widens out and after crossing rapids reaches Bergerac and then the Guyenne Plains with their vineyards. At the Ambès Spit, the Dordogne completes its 500km – 310 mile journey; it joins the Garonne, which it nearly equals in size, and the two flow on together as the Gironde.

The capricious Dordogne. – The Dordogne flows swiftly in the mountains and the plains, but its volume varies: winter and spring rain storms and the melting of the snows on the Millevaches Plateau and in the mountains of Auvergne bring floods almost every year which are sudden, violent and sometimes disastrous. Dam construction and other civil engineering projects – Bort, Marèges, L'Aigle, Le Chastang, Argentat – in the upper valley have enabled the flow to be controlled.

The days of the gabares. – For a long time there was river traffic on the Dordogne. A world of sailors and craft lived on the river in spite of the dangers and the river's uneven flow. The boatmen used flat-bottomed boats knows as *gabares* or *argentats*, after the town with the largest boat-building yards. These big barges, sailing downstream, carried passengers and cargo, especially oak for cooperage to Bordeaux; sailing upstream they loaded salt at Libourne and continued their journey up to Souillac *(qv)* where it was sold. The journey was full of the unexpected and the *gabariers* had to be skilled to get their boats through. When they arrived, the boats were broken up and sold for timber. Today river traffic plies solely on the lower Dordogne; upstream the only boats to be seen are those of anglers or canoeists.

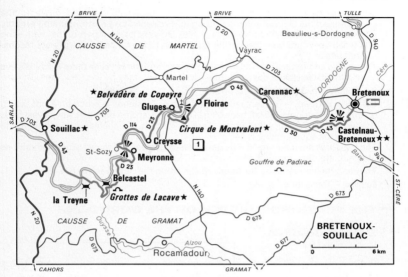

**THE QUERCY STRETCH OF THE DORDOGNE

☐ From Bretenoux to Souillac

56km – 35 miles – about 3 hours – local map above

Bretenoux. – Pop 1 213. Facilities. In its leafy river setting, this former *bastide*, founded in 1277 by a powerful lord of Castelnau, has conserved its grid plan, its central square, covered arcades and parts of the ramparts.

After the picturesque **Place des Consuls** with its 15C turreted town house, go through a covered alley to the old manor at the corner of the pretty Rue du Manoir de Cère. Turn right and right again returning via the pleasant quay along the Cère.

The river receives the waters of the Cère, before passing within sight of the impressive mass of Castelnau-Bretenoux Castle.

Castelnau-Bretenoux Castle. – *Description p 66.*

Downstream from Castelnau, the Bave Tributary *(p 133)* joins the Dordogne, which divides into several streams flowing in a wide valley bounded to the south by the cliffs of the *causses*.

Carennac. – *Description p 65.*

Beyond Carennac, the Dordogne cuts a channel between the Martel and Gramat *causses* before entering the beautiful area of the Montvalent Amphitheatre.

Floirac. – Pop 296. A 14C keep is all that remains of the old fortifications.

Montvalent Amphitheatre (Cirque de Montvalent). – The road is very picturesque, running for the most part beside the river, though sometimes rising in a corniche above it. Each bend affords attractive views of the valley and the *causse* cliffs.

> *Cross the Dordogne, take the D 140 towards Martel and then right on the D 32 to the Copeyre Belvedere.*

Copeyre Belvedere (Belvédère de Copeyre). – There is a good **view** of the Dordogne and the Montvalent Amphitheatre from a rock on which stands a wayside cross beside the D 32. The Dordogne can be seen at the foot of the cliffs creating a wide arc through pastures divided by lines of poplars; on the left, to one side of the river, is the Puy d'Issolud and on the right, on the other side, the village of Floirac.

> *Turn round and follow the right bank of the Dordogne.*

Gluges. – This village (old houses) lies along the river in a beautiful **setting** at the foot of the cliffs.

The road then rises winding around a tall, overhanging, ochre-coloured cliff, sometimes hidden by a thick carpet of ivy; it continues its run, at times carved into the cliff.

Creysse. – Pop 248. The charming village of Creysse with pleasant, narrow streets, brown-tiled roofs, houses approached by flights of steps and bedecked with climbing vines, lies at the foot of the rocky spur, on which stands a pre-Romanesque church, the former castle chapel, with its curious twin apses. The church and the remains of the nearby castle are reached by a stony alleyway, which climbs sharply to a terrace. It is from a little square shaded by plane trees, near the war memorial, that you get the best general view of the village.

Beyond Creysse the road follows the willow-bordered bank as far as St-Sozy and then crosses the river on the bridge at Meyronne.

Meyronne. – Pop 201. From the bridge over the Dordogne, there is a pretty **view** of the river and the village – former home of the bishops of Tulle – with its charming Quercy houses picturesquely built into the cliffs.

The road, subsequently, follows the course of the Dordogne through a beautiful countryside of rocks and cliffs, then crosses the Ouysse River near Lacave.

Lacave Caves. – *Description p 95.*

Ⓥ **Belcastel Castle** (Château de Belcastel). – A vertical cliff dropping down to the confluence of the Ouysse and the Dordogne is crowned by a castle standing proudly in a remarkable **setting★** *(photograph p 148)*. Only the eastern part of the main wing and the chapel date from the Middle Ages; most of the other buildings were reconstructed later.

The chapel and terraces are open to the public. From the terraces there is a bird's eye view of the Ouysse and the Dordogne.

Follow the D 43 to the next bridge.

Ⓥ **Château de la Treyne**. – The château *(photograph p 74)* stands perched on a cliff, which on one side overlooks the left bank of the Dordogne, and on the other side, a vast park. Burned by the Catholics during the Wars of Religion, the château was rebuilt in the 17C; only the square tower is 14C.

The buildings are now a hotel. The park (French gardens and chapel (where exhibitions are held) are open to the public.

The road then crosses the Dordogne to run along the right bank to Souillac.

★Souillac. – *Description p 142.*

★★★ THE PÉRIGORD STRETCH OF THE DORDOGNE

② From Souillac to Sarlat

32km – 20 miles – about 1 1/2 hours – local map above

★Souillac. – *Description p 142.*

Leave Souillac to the west by the D 703.

Only subtle differences distinguish the countryside of Quercy from that of Périgord Noir, through which the Dordogne flows below Souillac.

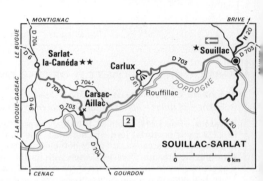

SOUILLAC-SARLAT

The river is calmer and its meanders, separated only by narrow rock channels, form a series of rich basins. Peaks crowned with dark trees ring the horizon.

The road crosses the nicely cultivated alluvial plains surrounded by wooded hills, and follows the river bordered with poplars – a typical Périgord Valley scene.

A couple of miles after Viviers, leave the D 703 and turn right towards Carlux.

Carlux. – Pop 565. Overlooking the valley from its dominating position, the village has kept some old houses and a small covered market. Two towers and an imposing curtain wall are all that remains of the large castle, once belonging to the viscounty of Turenne. From the castle terrace there is a lovely view of the valley and its cliffs, which were used as the castle foundations.

Return to the D 703.

Carsac-Aillac. – Pop 950. The modest but delightful church of Carsac, built in a lovely golden stone, stands in a country setting not far from the Dordogne. The porch in the façade has five recessed arches resting on small columns. The massive Romanesque bell tower and the apse are roofed with stone slabs.

The nave and the aisles have elegant pendants; the bay of the chancel has rounded-barrel vaulting. A small dome on pendentives rises above the transept crossing; the chancel ends in a Romanesque apse with oven vaulting and is adorned with interesting, archaic, oriental-style capitals. Gothic chapels are situated on either side of the nave and at the entrance to the chancel.

There are strikingly modern **stained-glass windows** and a **Stations of the Cross** by Zack. The Stations are arresting for their primitive style and philosophical austerity; the texts are taken from the writings of Paul Claudel (diplomat and author: 1868-1955).

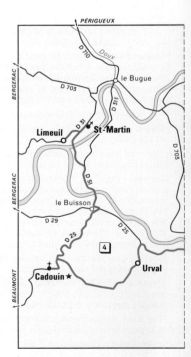

At Carsac-Aillac, join the D 704, which runs along the valley bottom to Sarlat.

★★Sarlat. – *Description p 138.*

③ From Sarlat to St-Cyprien
60km – 37 miles – about 4 hours – local map below

This trip is the most attractive in Périgord. Great rocks rise up at every step, golden in colour and crowned with old castles and picturesque villages.

★★Sarlat. – *Description p 138.*

Carsac-Aillac. – *Description p 76.*

From Carsac-Aillac onwards the road, which follows the right bank of the Dordogne, overlooks the fine bend of the river known as the Montfort Meander.

Montfort. – *Description p 109.*

Soon after Vitrac, Domme, on its rocky promontory, comes into view on the left.

Cénac. – Pop 900. The only remaining evidence of the large priory built in Cénac in the 11C is the small Romanesque **church**, which stands outside the village. Even the church did not escape the Wars of Religion, and only the east end escaped the depredations of the Protestants serving under Captain Vivans *(qv)* in 1589. The short nave and transept were rebuilt in the 19C.

Go into the churchyard to get an overall view of the east end with its fine stone roof and its column-buttresses topped by foliated capitals. A cornice, decorated with modillions bearing small carved figures, runs round the base of the roof of the apsidal chapels.

Inside, in the chancel and the apse, there is a series of interesting **historiated capitals**, which date from 1130. A very varied and realistic animal art enlivens these capitals; the scenes depicted include Daniel in the Lions' Den and Jonah and the Whale.

★★Domme. – *Description p 72.*

Here is the most beautiful part of the whole valley: the Dordogne, lined with poplars, widens out considerably and flows through a mosaic of farmland and meadows. Then follows the most extraordinary settings in which towns and castles could be built.

★★La Roque-Gageac. – *Description p 128.*

★Castelnaud Castle. – *Description p 66.*

A short stretch of road between Castelnaud and Les Milandes Castle passes below Fayrac Castle.

Fayrac Castle. – A double curtain wall surrounds the interior courtyard, which is reached by two drawbridges. The 16C buildings bristling with pepperpot roofs form a complex yet harmonious unit in spite of the 19C restorations (note the pseudo-keep). The castle is positioned in a verdant setting on the south bank of the Dordogne facing Beynac-et-Cazenac.

Les Milandes. – Built in 1489 by François de Caumont, the **castle** remained the property of this family until the Revolution. In the past the castle was associated with the well-known American singer, Josephine Baker, or *La Perle Noire* as she was known in her Paris cabaret heyday in the 20's and 30's. It was here that she achieved her dream of a "village of the world": gathering children of different races, religions and nationalities, bringing them up together to promote mutual understanding.

A spiral staircase gives access to the various floors. In addition to the possessions of the De Caumont family are furniture and effects belonging to Josephine Baker. The castle is surrounded by an attractively arranged garden. From the terrace there is a view of the park.

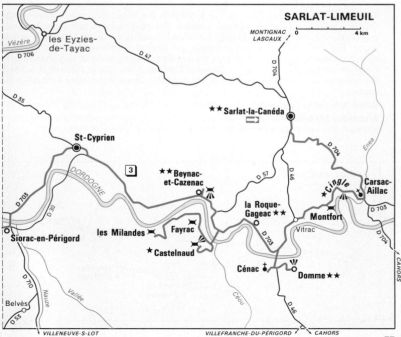

Return by the same road and cross the river by the Castelnaud Bridge to take the D 703 on the north bank of the Dordogne.

★★Beynac-et-Cazenac. – *Description p 47.*

Beyond Beynac, the valley does not widen out much before St-Cyprien.

St-Cyprien. – *Description p 135.*

④ From St-Cyprien to Limeuil
34km – 21 miles – about 1 1/2 hours – local map pp 76-77

St-Cyprien. – *Description p 135.*

Below St-Cyprien, the Dordogne runs through an area where meadows and arable fields spread out to the cliffs and wooded slopes, marking the edge of the valley.

Siorac-en-Périgord. – Pop 871. Facilities. This small village, sought out for its beach, has a 17C castle and a small Romanesque church.

From Siorac take the D 25, then bear left to Urval.

Urval. – This charming village set in a small valley is dominated by its massive 12C church. The walls of the rectangular chancel are covered with blind arcading held up by archaic capitals. The two black marble columns have been taken from a former construction.

Near the church is the medieval communal oven.

Take the small road, southwest of Urval, to Cadouin.

★Cadouin. – *Description p 58.*

From Cadouin the D 25 continues to Le Buisson through rolling hills covered with underbrush and chestnut trees.

Cross over the Dordogne in the direction of Périgueux (D 51). Continue along the D 51 towards Limeuil, after crossing the Vézère turn right into the D 31.

St Martin's Chapel (Chapelle St-Martin). – Encircled by cypresses, this plain, 12C chapel presents a pre-chancel roofed with a dome on pendentives. Built by the English, the chapel was consecrated in 1194. A carved inscription evokes the patronage of the Archbishop of Canterbury, Thomas Becket, murdered by King Henry II's knights in Canterbury Cathedral in 1170 (canonised in 1173). Richard Lionheart *(qv)*, son of Henry II, is cited as being one of the chapel's founders.

Limeuil. – Pop 362. *Walk up the main street.* Built on a steep promontory, this old village, set in tiers overlooking the confluence of the Dordogne and Vézère Rivers, offers a picturesque **site★**. Its two bridges set at right angles spanning each of the rivers marks the confluence. Traces of its past as a fortress town are recalled in climbing up the ancient narrow streets to the site of the old castle and church. A tiny medieval gateway, above the church, marks the limits of the old fortified town.

As the Dordogne flows past Limeuil, the town's historic past as an active river and fishing port is brought to mind.

⑤ From Limeuil to Bergerac
53km – 33 miles – about 2 1/2 hours – local map below

Limeuil. – *Description above.*

Take the D 31 on the right bank of the Dordogne.

Soon after the confluence of the Dordogne and the Vézère, the very picturesque road overlooks the Dordogne at Roches Blanches (viewpoint) across from Sors Plain.

Trémolat. – Pop 543. Facilities. Set in a bend in the river, this picturesque village contains an unusual 12C Romanesque **church**. Behind a massive belfry porch stands a veritable fortress with its high bare walls brightened by the warm ochre and yellow stone. The Périgord-Romanesque interior consists of a nave roofed by a series of domes on pendentives. The dome on the transept crossing rests on egg-shaped pendentives. In the churchyard, the **Chapel of St-Hilaire** (Chapelle St-Hilaire) is a small Romanesque building reached by a lovely doorway, above which runs a modillioned cornice.

When you get to Trémolat follow northwards the "Route du Cingle de Trémolat".

Racamadou Belvedere (Belvédère de Racamadou). – From the water-tower platform appears an outstanding **panorama★★** of the well-known Trémolat Meander.

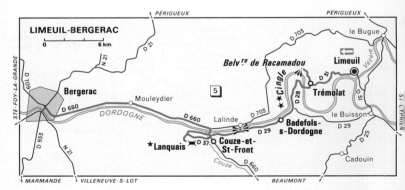

★★Tremolat Meander (Cingle de Trémolat). – At the foot of a semicircle of high, bare, white cliffs cut by greenery, coils the river, spanned by bridges of golden stone and reflecting lines of poplars. Beyond the wonderful stretch of water, which is often used for rowing regattas, lies a vast mosaic of arable fields and meadows; far away on the horizon, one can see the hills of Bergerac, Issigeac and Monpazier.

Return to Trémolat and cross the south bank of the Dordogne.

The valley is dotted with tobacco-drying sheds.

Badefols-sur-Dordogne. – Pop 150. Facilities. The village occupies a pleasant site beside the Dordogne. The country church stands close to the foot of the castle ruins perched on the cliff. This fortress served as the hide-out for the local thieves and robbers who used to ransack the *gabares (qv)* as they sailed downstream.

From the bridge leading to Lalinde (Facilities), there is a fine **view** of the Dordogne.

Couze-et-St-Front. – Pop 831. Located at the mouth of the small Couze Valley, this active little town has specialised since the 16C in papermaking. It was the most important papermaking centre of Aquitaine, and, at its peak, thirteen mills were functioning. Only two mills remain from those prosperous times: at the **Larroque Mill** (Moulin de Larroque) one can see the making of filigreed paper using traditional methods.

From the D 660, south of the village, is a charming Romanesque church (now used for offices). It has a fine bell tower and its east end is roofed with roundtiles.

From Couze-et-St-Front continue to the village and Château de Lanquais.

★Château de Lanquais. – *Description p 95.*

Turn back, take the D 37 on the left and cross the Dordogne once again.

The D 660 follows the wide alluvial valley down to Bergerac.

★Bergerac. – *Description p 43.*

DOUBLE

Michelin map 🖽 folds 3, 4 and 5 or 🎟🎟 folds 41 and 42

During the Tertiary Era waterways came down from Massif Central, spreading deposits of argillaceous sands which formed, notably, Sologne, Brenne and Double.

This area of Double, positioned west of Périgord between the rivers Dronne to the north and Isle to the south, presents wild landscapes of forest, sprinkled with pools and dotted with half-timbered and clay houses.

It was a poor, desolate region: feaver-ridden stagnant waters, a robbers lair and wolves den. Under the Second Empire (1852-70) the area underwent improvements: roads were built, pools drained, soils improved and maritime pines planted. These pines with oak and chestnut makeup, today, the major part of the forest cover. The people of the Double have been fishbreeding, emptying the pools every two years. Today 60% of the area is overrun by forest, the wood is used for timber and is a paradise for hunters. The remaining 40% is for medium-sized farms which concentrate on dairying and fattening of livestock.

ROUND TOUR STARTING FROM ST-ASTIER

102km – 63 miles – 4 hours – local map p 80

St-Astier. – Pop 4 736. Lying on the Isle River bank, the old city centre, where a few Renaissance houses may still be seen, is overlooked by its church supported by massive buttresses and a magnificent **bell tower** adorned with two tiers of blind arcades.

The cement works built near the Isle River make St-Astier look like an industrial town.

The D 43, always winding and sometimes hilly, crosses a picturesque countryside of hills.

St-Aquilin. – Pop 388. The church built in a transitional Romanesque Gothic style ends in a chancel with a flat east end.

Le Bellet Castle (Château du Bellet). – The fine tiled roofs and massive round towers of this castle, built on the side of a hill, come into view on the right.

Bear right towards Segonzac.

Château de la Martinie. – This elegant 15C and Renaissance building adorned with a balustrade above the carriage gateway has been converted into a farm.

Segonzac. – The Romanesque church (11-12C) was altered and enlarged in the 16C.

Return to the D 43.

The road along the crest offers fine views onto the Dronne Valley and Ribéracois; its hilly cereal-growing countryside is dotted with clumps of trees.

Siorac-de-Ribérac. – Pop 228. Overlooking a small valley, the fortified Romanesque **church** has a single nave roofed at the end with a dome.

St-Martin-de-Ribérac. – Pop 594. Born and buried in this village is Guy de Larigaudie (1908-40), one of the leaders of the French Boy Scout movement during the period between the two wars.

Ribérac. – Pop 4 291. Facilities. Located north of Double, Ribérac is the capital of Ribéracois, which is also called Périgord Blanc (White Périgord), a rich agricultural region where especially cultivation of cereals and rearing of cattle and white veal are practised.

Take the D 708 southwestwards.

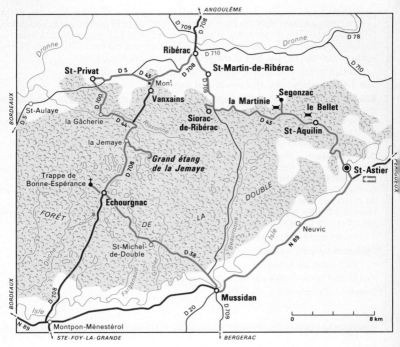

Vanxains. – Pop 667. The town has kept several lovely houses (16-18C) and a Romanesque fortified **church**.

Inside, the vast rectangular chancel, lit by a triple bay, decorated with blind arcading and a richly carved stringcourse, and the pre-chancel, beneath a dome with elegant capitals, are evidence of the Romanesque origin of this otherwise very altered church. In the Gothic part of the church's 15C north aisle is a 17C carved wood altarpiece. The heavy belfry-porch dates back to the 16C.

> *Return to the D 708 in the opposite direction and at a monument turn left into the D 43 then into the D 5 westwards.*

St-Privat. – *Description p 137.*

> *From St-Privat, the D 100 goes to La Gâcherie, turn left into the D 44 and then turn right into the D 708. At La Jemaye bear left onto the lake road.*

Jemaye Lake (Grand Étang de la Jemaye). – In the middle of Jemaye Forest, the lake has been set up as a water sports centre with a beach and activities such as fishing, windsurfing ...

The D 708 going south crosses great maritime pine plantations.

Echourgnac. – Pop 443. Not far from the village on the D 38 stands the **Trappist Monastery of Bonne-Espérance** (Trappe de Bonne-Espérance). The monastery was founded in 1868 by the Trappist monks from Port-du-Salut in Mayenne, who wanted to help the local population in this particularly underprivileged area. They set up a model cheese-making farm, collecting milk from the neighbouring farms. Their cheese, Trappe, is very similar to Port Salut. The monks had to leave the monastery in 1910 and were replaced in 1923 by sisters who continued the cheese-making industry.

The road to the south (D 38) crosses Double Forest and skirts several pools of water.

Mussidan. – *Description p 111.*

> *From Mussidan, the N 89 along the Isle, returns to St-Astier.*

★ DRONNE VALLEY

Michelin map 🔢 fold 5 or 🔢 folds 31 and 42

A tributary of the Isle, the Dronne River runs north of Périgord, carving cliffs between Brantôme and Bourdeilles. Its valley is carpeted with meadows, ploughed land and poplars, as soon as it widens, while the slopes and plateaux are covered with juniper and forested with oak and chestnut.

ROUND TOUR FROM PÉRIGUEUX
110km – 68 miles – allow 1 day – local map p 81

★**Périgueux**. – *Description p 117. Time: 3 hours.*

> *Leave Périgueux by ⑤ on the D 939 and the D 710.*

★**Chancelade Abbey**. – *Description p 70.*

> *Take the D 1 and after La Chapelle-Gonaguet turn into a narrow road on the right and follow the signposts.*

Merlande Priory. – *Description p 70.*

> *Return to La Chapelle-Gonaguet and continue on the D 1 to Lisle. From there cross the Dronne River and turn left to Montagrier.*

Montagrier. – Pop 385. From the end of a terrace near which stands the church of Montagrier ringed by cypress trees, there is a wide view of the verdant Dronne Valley. The church, once the chapel of a priory (long since disappeared) which was a dependency of Brantôme Abbey, was poorly restored in the 19C. The only parts of the 12C building still standing are the transept crossing surmounted by a dome on pendentives and the five apsidal chapels.

The D 103 and the D 1, between Montagrier and Grand-Brassac, afford fine views of the Dronne and its smiling valley.

⊘**Grand-Brassac**. – Pop 528. This small village has an interesting **fortified church**. From the 13C onwards, fortified devices were added to the church so that it might serve as a refuge. The crenellations, defensive galleries, and narrow openings, more resembling loopholes than bays, give the building a severe appearance.

The north doorway's decoration brings together sculpture of different periods: an arch adorned with fine foliated scrolls and containing statuettes, which formed part of a group depicting the Adoration of the Magi, is surmounted by five 16C statues, sheltered by an overhanging porch roof. Among the figures are Christ between St John and the Virgin, and lower down, St Peter and another saint. Inside the church, the narrowness of the nave increases the feeling of immense height.

From Grand-Brassac take the D 1 in the opposite direction and turn left towards Creyssac. This lovely road winds above the valley to Bourdeilles.

★**Bourdeilles**. – *Description p 50.*

Cross back over the Dronne and follow the D 106ᴱ² to Brantôme.

★★**Brantôme**. – *Description p 53.*

From Brantôme take the D 78 and then turn left onto the D 83. At Quinsac turn right into the D 98 and follow the signposts to Boschaud Abbey.

Boschaud Abbey (Abbaye de Boschaud). — This Cistercian abbey was founded in 1163 in the wooded valley of *Bosco Cavo* (meaning hollow wood), which was the origin of the name of Boschaud.

Destroyed during the Hundred Years' War and the Wars of Religion, the abbey was partially rebuilt in the late 17C. Beginning in 1950, the Historic Buildings Commission and another association (Club du Vieux Manoir) began the restoration.

Traces of monastical buildings permit to reconstitute the abbey plan with its gatehouse, monks' living quarters, cellar, etc. The chapter house has preserved its five openings which gave onto the cloisters.

The exceedingly plain church is the only church known of the Cistercian order whose nave, today almost entirely destroyed, was vaulted by a series of domes.

Note the interesting and unusual architectural cross-section made up of the partially destroyed pendentives and calotte of the nave's first dome.

★**Château de Puyguilhem**. – *Description p 123.*

Go south on the D 3.

⊘ **La Chapelle-Faucher**. – Dominating the Côle River, this **castle** has kept its entrance postern and curtain wall.

The 15C main part of the building is crowned by a crenellated watchpath; the 18C living quarters adjoin the castle; the lovely vaulted stables lining the courtyard were added in the 17C.

In 1569, during the Wars of Religion, the Huguenot leader Admiral de Coligny, with an army of 3 000, laid siege to the castle. If the chronicler Brantôme can be believed, 260 peasants were brutally killed here.

Agonac. – *Description p 38.*

The D 3ᵉ goes to Château-l'Évêque.

Château-l'Évêque. – The episcopal castle gave its name to the town. Since the 14C the castle has been altered several times. It is made up of an asymmetrical main building. Its façades on the Beauronne Valley are opened with mullioned windows and running round the roof line is a machicolated watchpath.

The parish church was where St Vincent de Paul was ordained by Monsignor François de Bourdeille in September 1600 at the early age of 20.

The D 939 returns to Périgueux.

ESPAGNAC-STE-EULALIE
Pop 77

Michelin map **79** fold 9 or **235** west of fold 11 – Local map p 69

In this delightful village built in the picturesque setting of a series of cliffs, the houses with their turrets and pointed roofs are grouped round the former priory known as Notre-Dame du "Val-Paradis" (Our Lady of the Valley of Paradise, *p 66*).

Former Priory of Notre-Dame (Ancien Prieuré Notre-Dame). – Founded in the 12C by the monk Bertrand de Griffeuille of the Augustinian Order, it was attached to the Abbey of La Couronne (near Angoulême). In 1212 the priory became a convent for the Augustinian canonesses and expanded considerably under the ægis of Aymeric Hébrard *(see below)*, Bishop of Coïmbra. In 1283 the convent was moved to avoid flooding from the Célé River. During the Hundred Years' War the convent suffered considerably; the cloisters were destroyed and the church was partly demolished. It was rebuilt in the 15C, however, and the community continued till the

Priory's bell tower

Revolution. The conventual buildings are occupied by the rural centre and flats *(gîtes communaux)*, which are let for the holidays by the *commune*.

⊘ **Church** (Église). – The present Flamboyant-style church has replaced a 13C building of which there still remain the walls of the nave, a doorway and jutting out beyond the walls, the ruins of bays which were destroyed during fires in the 15C. The exterior is peculiar for several reasons: the pentagonal chevet is higher than the nave and, on the south side, the bell tower is surmounted by a square brick and timber chamber, topped by an octagonal roof of limestone slabs. Inside, the three tombs with recumbent figures placed in funerary niches are those of Aymeric Hébrard de St-Sulpice (d 1295) and of a knight, Hugues de Cardaillac-Brengues (buried here in 1342) and his wife, Bernarde de Trian. On the high altar, with a 17C gilded wood predella, stands an 18C retable framing a picture of the Assumption, after the painting by Simon Vouet.

EXCIDEUIL
Pop 1 584

Michelin map **75** folds 6 and 7 or **233** northwest of fold 44 – Facilities

The last ruins of Excideuil Castle, recalling times when there were viscounts of Limoges and counts of Périgord, crown a hill overlooking the Loue Valley.

Castle. – A curtain wall, one-time façade of the feudal castle, links the two dismantled keeps, built respectively in the late 11 and 12C. Beside the medieval fortress stands a Renaissance mansion with recently added turrets and mullioned windows. It once belonged to the Talleyrand family, for whom Louis XIII raised Excideuil to the title of marquisate in 1613.

A pleasant walk around the castle *(time: 1/2 hour)* is possible and a good view of the building can be enjoyed from the banks of the river.

⊘ **Church** (Église). – The former 12C Benedictine priory was very much altered in the 15C, which explains why the church has a fine Flamboyant doorway on its south side. Inside are a 17C gilded altarpiece (from the neighbouring Franciscan church) and a polychrome *Pietà*, Our Lady of Excideuil, which is surrounded by ex-voto.

On the border of Bergeracois and Agenais, Eymet is still a small Périgord village famous because of its gourmet food factories canning goose and duck liver *(foie gras)*, and *galantine ballotine (p 35)*.

The bastide. – *Time: 3/4 hour*. Founded in 1271 by Alphonse de Poitiers, the *bastide* – even though it was granted a charter guaranteeing privileges and liberties – was ruled by several seignorial families who were either in allegiance with the king of France or the king of England. In consequence, it had an eventful history during the Hundred Years' War and the Wars of Religion. The ramparts were razed under Louis XIII.

Place Centrale. – The arcaded square is lined with old half-timbered or stone houses, some of which are opened with mullioned windows. In its centre is a 17C fountain.

Keep (Donjon). — This 14C tower is all that remains of the castle.

⊙ A small **museum** has been set up inside displaying regional art and folklore (clothes, tools etc.) as well as prehistoric objects.

*The **Michelin Motoring Atlas France** does not replace the yellow sheet maps, which slip conveniently into a pocket or handbag with the local Green Guide. The atlas, the guides and the sheet maps are invaluable to travellers in France.*

★★ LES EYZIES-DE-TAYAC   Pop 858

The village of Les Eyzies stands attractively in a grandiose setting of steep cliffs crowned with evergreen oaks and junipers, at the confluence of the Vézère and Beune Rivers. The Vézère River, lined on either side by poplars, now winds between meadows and farmland, now narrows to flow beside walls of rock 50 to 80m — 164 to 262ft high. Shelters cut out of the bases of these limestone piles served as dwelling places for prehistoric man while the caves, which generally appear half-way up the cliffs, were used as sanctuaries. The discovery within the last hundred years of these dwellings all within a limited radius of Les Eyzies has made the village the capital of prehistory.

On the outskirts of town, on the road to Tursac, stand the old ironworks bringing to mind the town and region's industrial past (from the Middle Ages to the Second Empire — 1852-70). Although the present buildings (warehouse and worker's accommodations) date from the 18C, the forge's origin goes back to the 16C, when its main livelihood was supplying iron to the merchants of Bordeaux.

THE CAPITAL OF PREHISTORY *local map p 84*

The lower Vézère during the cavemen era. – During the Second Ice Age and at the time when the volcanoes of Auvergne were active, prehistoric man, in the wake of the animals he hunted for food, abandoned the northern plains, where the Acheulean and Abbevillian civilisations had already evolved, for warmer areas to the south. The lower Vézère, the bed of which was then some ninety feet above its present level, attracted the migrants because of its forested massifs, its natural caves, which were easily accessible, and overhanging rocks which could be hollowed out into shelters more easily than the friable and fissured limestone of the Dordogne Valley.

Men inhabited these cave dwellings for tens of thousands of years and left in them traces of their daily tasks and passage such as bones, ashes from their fires, tools, weapons, utensils and ornaments. Their civilisation evolved simultaneously with the world around them. Animal species evolved into those we know today: after elephants and bears came bisons, aurochs, mammoths and, later still, muskoxen, reindeer, ibex, stags and horses.

When the climate grew warmer and rainfall more abundant at the end of the Magdalenian Period, man abandoned the caves for the hillside slopes facing the sun.

The archaeologist's' paradise. – Methodical study of the deposits in the Les Eyzies region has considerably increased our knowledge of prehistory *(pp 18-21)*. The Dordogne *département* has greatly contributed to the science of prehistory with more than 200 deposits discovered, of which more than half are in the lower Vézère Valley. In 1863 work began at the Laugerie and Madeleine Deposits; the discovery of objects such as flints, carved bones and ivory, tombs (in which the skeletons had been coloured with ochre) greatly encouraged the early research workers. In 1868 workmen levelling soil unearthed the Cro-Magnon shelters' skeletons. Soon afterwards more thorough research in the Le Moustier and La Madeleine Caves enabled two great periods of the Palaeolithic Age to be defined: the periods were called after the cave deposits — Mousterian and Magdalenian *(see pp 18-21)*. Discoveries proceeded apace in prehistoric site and **deposits**: La Micoque, Upper Laugerie, Lower Laugerie, La Ferrassie (south of Savignac-de-Miremont), Laussel and Pataud Shelter; in **shelters and caves** containing hidden carvings and drawings: Le Cap Blanc, Le Poisson, La Mouthe, Les Combarelles, Bernifal and Commarque; and in caves containing polychrome **wall paintings**: Font-de-Gaume and Lascaux. The study of the engravings on bone, ivory and stone, as well as of low reliefs, wall engravings and paintings has permitted to establish the beliefs, rituals, way of life and artistic evolution of Palaeolithic man.

Associated with the excavations and research are: L. Capitan, D. Peyrony, Abbé H. Breuil, H. Bordes, A. Leroi-Gourhan, H.L. Movius and H. de Lumley.

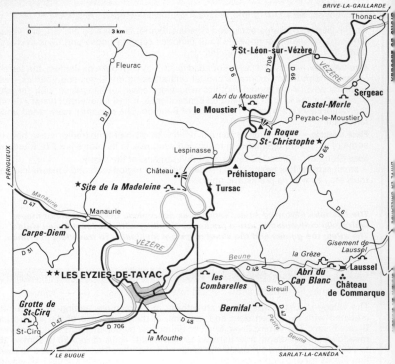

SIGHTS

Les Eyzies

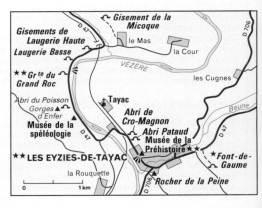

★★National Museum of ⊘ Prehistory (Musée National de la Préhistoire). – The museum is in the former castle of the barons of Beynac. The 13C fortress, restored in the 16C, hangs half-way up the cliff, beneath a rock overhang, overlooking the village. From the terrace, on which stands a Neanderthal man interpreted by the sculptor Dardé, there is a good view of Les Eyzies and the valleys of Vézère and Beune. The rich display of prehistoric objects and works of art discovered locally over the last eighty years is exhibited in two buildings. To complete the collection are diagrams showing the chronology of prehistoric eras, sections through the earth's strata and photographs.

A gallery on the 1st floor is devoted to different stone-chipping techniques and a synthesis of prehistory. Prehistoric art is represented by wall paintings and carvings as well as domestic objects.

The 2nd floor contains objects from all the prehistoric periods combined. The Breuil Gallery presents castings of prehistoric works of art from other museums. One gallery has assembled an extraordinary collection of carved limestone slabs dated between 30 000 and 15 000 years representing animals, female silhouettes... Nearby, ornaments made of stone, teeth or bone and weapons (spears, pierced bone implements, harpoons...) are exhibited alongside castings of the principal female figurines of Europe. On the top floor in a large gallery is a fascinating display, explaining the evolution of flint knapping as long ago as 2.5 million years.

In the other building the Magdalenian tomb of a woman from St-Germain-la-Rivière, complete with its skeleton and a skeleton from Roc de Marsal has been reconstructed.

Cro-Magnon Shelter (Abri de Cro-Magnon). – This cave was discovered in 1868 and revealed, in addition to flints and carved bones of the Aurignacian and Gravettian Cultures, three adult skeletons which were studied by Paul Broca *(qv)*, the surgeon and anthropologist who founded the School of Anthropology in France. The discoveries made in this cave were of prime importance in prehistoric studies, since they enabled the characteristics of the Cro-Magnon race *(qv)* to be defined.

★Font-de-Gaume Cave (Grotte de Font-de-Gaume). – *Leave the car on the road to ⊘ St-Cyprien opposite a cliff-spur. A path takes you up 440yds to the cave entrance.* The cave runs back in the form of a passage 130yds long with chambers and other ramifications leading off it. The cave has been known for a considerable time, with the result that since the 18C, visitors have left their mark, not recognising the importance of the wall paintings. Detailed examination and study of the paintings date them as belonging to the Magdalenian Period. Beyond a narrow passage, known as the Rubicon, are many multi-coloured paintings, often superimposed on one another: all the drawings of horses, bison, mammoths, reindeer and other deer indicate great artistic skill, which, after Lascaux, forms the finest group of polychrome paintings in France. The frieze of bison, painted in brown on a white calcite background, is remarkable.

Pataud Shelter (Abri Pataud). – An excavated shelter is shown as it was when it was discovered.

La Peine Rock (Rocher de la Peine). – This great rock, worn jagged by erosion, partially overhangs the road. A Magdalenian deposit was discovered within it.

⊙ **Tayac Church (Église de Tayac).** – The warm, gold-coloured stone enhances this 12C fortified church. Two crenellated towers, arranged as keep-like structures and roofed with *lauzes*, frame the main body of the church. The tower above the doorway serves as the bell tower.
The doorway is intriguing with the first recessed arch, polylobbed, giving an oriental air while the two reused blue marble columns, with Corinthian capitals, show Gallo-Roman influence.
Inside, the three naves, divided by large arcades resting on piers and the timberwork ceiling, are rarely found in the Périgord.

Along the D 47

⊙ **Museum of Speleology (Musée de la Spéléologie).** – The museum is installed in the rock fortress of Tayac, which commands the Vézère Valley. The four chambers, cut out of the living rock, contain a selection of items pertaining to speleology: pot holing equipment, exhibits describing the geological formation and natural life of the pot holes and various models.

⊙ **Lower Laugerie Deposit (Gisement de Laugerie Basse).** – An important find under a pile of loose rocks, at a place called Les Marseilles, has brought to light a large collection of tools dating as far back as the reindeer age.
A section shows the strata of human remains which accumulated between the middle of the Magdalenian Period to the Iron Age. A small building displays some of the items discovered.

⊙ **Upper Laugerie Deposit (Gisement de Laugerie Haute).** – Scientific excavations going on for over a century in a picturesque spot at the foot of high cliffs have revealed examples of the work and art of the cavemen at different degrees of civilisation.
The excavations begun in 1863 have since been conducted by stages: 1911, 1921, 1936-39 and again over the past couple of years. The work has enabled several sections to be made, which demonstrate the importance of this area, inhabited continuously by man from the middle of the Perigordian to the middle of the Magdalenian Period; that is to say, during the some 300 centuries of the Upper Palaeolithic Age.
The sections confound the imagination as they make one movingly aware of how slowly man has progressed through the millennia. Two human skeletons have been discovered beneath masses of fallen earth in the western part of the deposits. Note the drip stones or channels cut in the rock in the Middle Ages to prevent water from running along the walls and entering the dwellings.

★★**Grand Roc Cave (Grotte du Grand Roc).** – There is a good **view**★ of Vézère Valley
⊙ from the stairs leading up to the cave and the platform at its mouth. The 40 to 50yds of tunnel enables one to see, within chambers that are generally small in size, an extraordinary display of stalactites, stalagmites and eccentrics resembling coral formations, as well as a wonderful variety of pendants and crystallisations.

La Micoque Deposit (Gisement de la Micoque). – This deposit revealed many items belonging to periods known as the Tayacian and Micoquian Ages, which fall between the end of the Acheulean and the beginning of the Mousterian Ages. The finds are exhibited at Les Eyzies National Museum of Prehistory.

⊙ **Carpe-Diem Cave (Grotte de Carpe-Diem).** – Here and there in this 200yds long passage, as it winds through the rock, stalagmites and different coloured stalactites can be seen.

⊙ **St-Cirq Cave (Grotte de St-Cirq).** – *Access via the road into which falls the D 47 southwards.* In a small cave underneath an overhanging rock were discovered engravings from the Magdalenian Period, representing horses, bison and ibex. However, the cave is best known for the painting of the **Man of St-Cirq** (at times inappropriately called the Sorcerer of St-Cirq, one of the most remarkable representations of a human figure found in a prehistoric cave.
A small museum exhibits fossils and prehistoric tools.

Along the Vézère River

The sights are described from north to south so that they could appear on the itinerary of the Vézère Valley *(p 146)*.

Castel-Merle. – *Description p 147.*

⊙ **Le Moustier.** – This village, at the foot of a hill, contains a famous **prehistoric shelter** (Abri du Moustier). The prehistoric finds excavated here include a human skeleton and many flint implements. After the finds a culture in the Middle Palaeolithic Age was named Mousterian. An interesting 17C carved confessional may be seen in the village church.

★St-Christophe Cliff (La Roque St-Christophe). – For half a mile this long and ☉ majestic cliff rises vertically (80m — 262ft) above the Vézère Valley. It is like a huge hive with about a hundred caves hollowed out of the rock on five tiers. Excavations are underway at its feet (traces of the Bronze Age), but man lived here from the Upper Palaeolithic Age. In the 10C the cliff terraces served as the foundation for a fortress used against the Normans and during the Hundred Years' War, being subsequently destroyed during the Wars of Religion at the end of 16C. From the **Pas du Miroir**, it was once possible to see one's reflection in the Vézère, for the river at one time flowed at the foot (30m — 99ft) of the cliff.
The terrace affords a good bird's-eye **view★** of the valley.

☉ **Prehistory Park (Préhistoparc)**. – In a small cliff-lined valley, carpeted with undergrowth, a discovery trail reveals reconstituted scenes of Neanderthal and Cro Magnon man's daily life: mammoth hunting, cutting-up of reindeer, cave painting, burial customs...

Tursac. – The church is dominated by a huge, stark bell tower; a series of domes, characteristic of the Romanesque Périgord style *(p 30)* covers the church.

★La Madeleine Site. – *Description p 103*.

Beune Valley

☉ **Les Combarelles Cave (Grotte des Combarelles)**. – A winding passage 275yds long has many markings, on its walls for the last 130yds of its length some superimposed one upon another. The drawings include nearly 300 animals: horses, bison, bears, reindeer and mammoths can be seen at rest or in full gallop. This cave was discovered in 1901 at about the same time as Font-de-Gaume Cave *(p 84)* and demonstrated the importance of Magdalenian art at a time when the learned were still sceptical about the worth of prehistoric studies.
A second passage with similar cave drawings was the stage on which prehistoric man acted out his life, as can be seen from the traces of domestic middens and the tools of Magdalenian men which have been discovered.

☉ **Bernifal Cave (Grotte de Bernifal)**. – *On foot*. Cave paintings and graceful carvings illustrate Magdalenian art.

☉ **Cap-Blanc Shelter (Abri du Cap-Blanc)**. – Excavation of a small Magdalenian deposit in 1909 led to the discovery of **carvings★** in high relief on the walls of the rock shelter. Two bisons and particularly a frieze of horses were carved in such a way as to use to full advantage the relief and contour of the rock itself. At the foot of the frieze a human grave was discovered.

☉ **La Grèze Cave (Grotte de la Grèze)**. – This small cave is famous for its engraved bison (between late Upper Perigordian and early Solutrean); there is also a mammoth and a *megaloceros* (Irish Elk).

Commarque Castle (Château de Commarque). – The impressive castle ruins on the south bank of the Beune River stand facing Château de Laussel. Commarque was built as a stronghold in the 12 and 13C and for a long time it belonged to the Beynac family. Betrayed, it was occupied by the English and retaken by the lord of Périgord, who then returned it to the baron of Beynac. Considerable parts of the fortifications are still standing. The keep with its machicolations, the chapel and the various living quarters emerge from a mass of greenery to form a romantic setting.

Château de Laussel. – This 15 to 16C château (rearranged in the 19C) is perched on a cliff dropping straight down to the Beune Valley. The building is small but elegant. A few hundred yards farther along the valley a large prehistoric deposit (Gisement de Laussel) was discovered, which contained several human-like forms in low relief and the famous Venus with the horn of plenty *(illustration p 21)* from the Gravettian Culture; it is now exhibited in the Aquitaine Museum in Bordeaux.

★ FIGEAC   Pop 10 511

Michelin map **79** fold 10 or **235** fold 11 – Local maps pp 69 and 100-101 – Facilities

Sprawled out along the north bank of the Célé and hemmed in by large avenues lined with plane trees, Figeac began at the point where the Auvergne meets the Haut-Quercy. A commercial town, it had a prestigious past as is shown in the architecture of its tall sandstone town houses.
The small city's main industry is the Entreprise Ratier, which specialises in aeronautical construction.

From abbots to king. – Figeac began developing in the 9C around a monastery, which itself began expanding in the 11 and 12C.
The abbot was the town's lord and governed it with the aid of seven consuls. All administrative services were located inside the monastery. Because Figeac was on the pilgrimage route running from Le Puy and Conques and on to Santiago de Compostela *(see Michelin Green Guide to Spain)*, crowds of pilgrims and travellers flocked in.
Benefiting from its geographical situation between Auvergne, Quercy and Rouergue, the town's craftsmen and shopkeepers were prosperous.
In 1302, an abbot gave up the rights over the town to Philip the Fair. The town was then governed by consuls, elected by its citizens, and a provost, who represented the king; a royal mint was established.
The Hundred Years' War and the Wars of Religion – the Calvinists occupied the town from 1598-1622 – took its toll on this otherwise successful town.

Jean-François Champollion. – Champollion, the outstanding Orientalist, whose brilliance enabled Egyptology to make such great strides, was born at Figeac in December 1790. By the time he was 14, he had a command of Greek, Latin, Hebrew, Arabic, Chaldean and Syrian. After his studies in Paris, he lectured in history, at the young age of 19, at Grenoble University.

Rosetta Stone. – In 1799 a polished basalt tablet, showing three different inscriptions (Egyptian hieroglyphics, cursive script and Greek), was discovered by members of Napoleon's expedition to Egypt. In 1814 the English physicist **Thomas Young** (1773-1829) began studying the riddle of the Rosetta Stone *(in the British Museum, see Michelin Green Guide to London)*. A wrong turn in his investigations prevented him from fully deciphering the riddle. The task of complete decipherment was first accomplished by Champollion, who established that the texts were identical. He then discovered that the hieroglyphics denoted not only syllabic sounds but also ideas. Eager to prove his theory he went to Egypt and deciphered many texts. His discoveries were halted by his untimely death at the early age of forty-two.

★OLD FIGEAC *time: 1 1/2 hours*

The old quarter, surrounded by boulevards which trace the location of the former moats, has preserved its medieval town plan with its narrow and tortuous alleys.
The buildings, built in elegant beige sandstone, exemplify the architecture of the 13, 14 and 15C. Generally the ground floor was opened by large pointed arches and the first floor had a gallery of arcaded bays. Underneath the flat tiled roof was the *soleilho*, an open attic, which was used to dry laundry, store wood, grow plants etc...; it was separated by columns or pillars in wood or stone, sometimes even brick, which held up the roof. Other noticeable period characteristics discovered during the tour of the old quarter are: corbelled towers, doorways, spiral staircases and top floors, some of which are half-timbered and in brick.

★**Mint (Hôtel de la Monnaie) (M¹)**. – *Tourist information centre.* This late 13C building, restored in the early 20C, exemplifies Figeac's secular architecture with its *soleilho*, pointed arches on the ground floor and the depressed arched windows placed either singly, paired or in groups, opening up the façade. It is interesting to compare the façade overlooking the square, which was rebuilt with the elements of the former consul's house of the same period, and the other plainer façades. The octagonal stone chimney was characteristic of Figeac construction at the time, but very few examples remain.
The word *Oustal dé lo Mounédo* owes its name to the Royal Mint created in Figeac by Philip the Fair. It has since been established that the stamping workshop was located in another building and that this handsome edifice was the place where money was exchanged.
The Mint contains a **museum** which includes sculpture from religious and secular buildings (including the door of the Hôtel de Sully), sarcophagi, grain measurements, old coins and town seals originating from the period when the town had its seven consuls.

Take Rue Orthabadial and turn right into Rue Balène.

Rue Balène (2). – At no 7 stands the 14C **Balène Castle** (Château de Balène), which houses the Lotois Centre of Contemporary Art. Its medieval fortress-like façade is lightened by a pointed-arched doorway and the chapel windows with decorated tracery. Exhibitions are held in pointed-vaulted rooms.
At no 1, the 15C **Hôtel d'Auglanat,** which housed one of the king's provosts, is decorated with a lovely basket-arched doorway and battlemented turret.

Via Rue Gambetta and Place aux Herbes continue to Place Edmond-Michelet.

St-Sauveur. – This former abbey church, the oldest parts of which date from the 11C, has kept its original cross plan: a high nave with 14C chapels off the aisles. The nave is unusual due to the lack of symmetry between its north and south sides. The south side includes: in the lowest section, rounded arcades; in the middle section, a tribune with twinned bays within a larger arch; and in the upper section, 14C clerestory windows.
On the north side, rebuilt in the 17C (as was the vaulting), the tribune disappeared during the Wars or Religion.
The chancel, surrounded by the ambulatory, was rebuilt in the 18C. Two Romanesque capitals, remnants of the earlier doorway, support the baptismal font.

Notre-Dame-de-Pitié. – The former chapter house (13C) prolonging the southern arm of the transept, is interesting for its proportions and decoration: large carved wooden panels, painted and gilded in the 17C.
Between St-Sauveur and the Célé River on Place de la Raison, the site of the former cloisters and abbey gardens, is the obelisk dedicated to Champollion.

Take Rue Tomfort, passing in front of Rue Roquefort from where you can see Galiot de Genouillac's (qv) turreted house. Turn left into Rue Clermont.

Rue Gambetta (20). – This is the old town's main street. At nos 31 and 43, note the Gothic windows and carvings.

Place Carnot (7). – Formerly Place Basse. This, the heart of the old town, was where a 16C stone-covered market once stood. Note the lovely old mansions around the square, especially Cisteron Mansion (now a Crédit Agricole) with its corner turret.

Place Champollion (12). – Also called Place Haute. The commandery of the Knights Templars is identified by its Gothic windows. In Impasse Champollion stands the birthplace of the famous French Egyptologist, now the **Champollion Museum (M²)**. Documents recount Champollion's life. Items, originals (Royal Stela) and copies, evoke the uses of Egyptian writing and the history of its decipherment.
Admire one of the few castings of the Rosetta Stone *(see above)*.
Also on display are burial customs and objects.

Bear right into Rue Émile-Zola and left into Rue Delzhens.

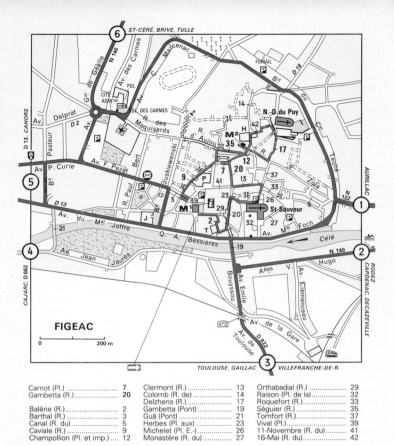

FIGEAC

0 _____ 200 m

Rue Delzhens (17). – Known also as Rue de la Viguerie, this narrow, tortuous, uphill street has preserved its medieval atmosphere.
At no 3, the 14C **Hôtel du Viguier** (*viguier* means provost), has kept its square keep and watch turret.

Notre-Dame-du-Puy. – The church is located on a height, offering a good view of the city and its surrounding countryside.
This Romanesque edifice, greatly altered in the 14 and 17C, contains a large altar-piece (late 17C) carved in walnut, framing a painting celebrating the Assumption; on the upper register is a Coronation of the Virgin. Go around it and note on the chancel capitals a Virgin in Majesty and a Crucifixion.

Go back down via Rue Pavée.

Rue Pavée ends up in front of the town hall, located in the former 17C Hôtel de Colomb.

From Place Champollion take Rue Séguier.

Rue Séguier (35). – The atmosphere of the Middles Ages pervades this narrow street, lined with houses with overhanging storeys, mullioned windows, niches, pointed arches, turrets...

Rue Caviale (9). – Across from no 35 is a town house, with mullioned windows, which is known as Louis XI's House because the king may have stayed there in 1463.

At Place Barthal turn left and return to the Mint (Hôtel de la Monnaie).

EXCURSIONS

Needles of Figeac (Aiguilles de Figeac). – These two octagonal-shaped obelisks, standing south and west of town, measure (with their base) respectively 14.50m – 47ft and 11.50m – 38ft. It is believed that there were four "needles" marking the boundaries of land over which the Benedictine abbey had jurisdiction.
From the D 922, south of Figeac, one of the needles – **Meander Needle** (Aiguille du Cingle), also known as Aiguille du Pressoir (Press Needle) – can be seen.

Cardaillac. – *Pop 453. 11km – 7 miles northwest of town. Leave Figeac by* ⑥ *on the N 140 and then take the D 15 to the right;*
This town is the home territory of the Cardaillacs, one of the most powerful Quercy families.
The old quarter of the fort stands on a rocky spur above the town. Of this triangular-shaped fortification, dating from the 12C, there remain two square towers: the Clock or Baron's Tower and Sagnes Tower. Only the latter is open. The two tall rooms with their vaulted ceilings are reached by a spiral staircase. From the platform admire the fine view of the Drauzou Valley and the surrounding countryside.

The main throughroutes are clearly indicated on all town plans.

★ FOISSAC CAVES (Grottes de FOISSAC)

Michelin map 79 fold 10 or 235 folds 11 and 15 – 10km – 6 miles north of Villeneuve

⏱ Discovered in 1959, Foissac Caves total 8km – 5 miles of galleries. An underground stream, which drains the caves, is a tributary of the Lot into which it flows near Balaguier. During the visit note the gleaming white stalactites and the lovely formations in the Obelisk Chamber (Salle de l'Obélisque); the stalagmites and ivory tower-like formations in the Michel Roques Gallery. In one gallery, Cave-in Gallery (Salle de l'Éboulement), there is a roof covered with round mushroom-like formations, thus proving that the stalactites were in the gallery well before earthquakes changed the aspect of the cave. These bulbous stalactites, known as "the onions" (Oignons), are also worth noting.

These caves were occupied by man during the Bronze Age and evidence of his daily existence is apparent throughout: the "hearth", bronze utensils and large curve-shaped pottery. Also visible are skeletons of a man and woman and the imprint of a child's foot, fixed here in the clay 4 000 years ago...

The Michelin Sectional Map Series (1:200 000) covers the whole of France.
When choosing your lunchtime or overnight stop
use the above maps as all towns listed in the Red Guide are underlined in red.
When driving into or through a town
use the map as it also indicates all places with a town plan in the Red Guide.
Common reference numbers make the transfer from map to plan easier.

GAVAUDUN Pop 269

Michelin map 79 fold 6 or 235 fold 9 – 12km – 7 1/2 miles northwest of Fumel

Gavaudun lies in a picturesque **setting**★ in the narrow, winding valley of the Lède.

⏱ **Keep (Donjon).** – A massive 12-14C crenellated keep rises (6 storeys) from the top of a rock spur overlooking the river and the village. The keep is reached by a staircase cut into the rock.

EXCURSIONS

St-Sardos-de-Laurenque. – *2km – 1 mile to the north.*
⏱ The 12C **church** has an interesting carved doorway, capitals adorned with animals and human figures and a frieze decorated with fish. Note the outstanding capitals in the Romanesque nave.

St-Avit. – *5km – 3 miles to the north.* The pleasant road winds along Lède Valley to the hamlet of St-Avit. Its church, its round east end roofed with *lauzes*, and several old houses lie in a pastoral setting overlooking the valley.
Bernard Palissy was born here (1510-90). He is remembered as a glass-blower and potter. He sought to rediscover the formula of a certain glaze and invented a ware halfway between Italian and glazed earthenware. He produced rustic-wares, which were dishes made to resemble little ponds with the appropriate animals – lizards, snakes, fish – and colours – greens, greys, browns.

Sauveterre-la-Lémance. – Pop 743. *19km – 11 1/2 miles northeast.* Edward I of
⏱ England (regnal dates 1272-1307), also Duke of Aquitaine, had this **fortress** built in the late 13C to defend his land from Philip III the Hardy. A massive keep, two towers and a curtain wall *(no railings)* are all that remains.

★ GOURDON Pop 5 076

Michelin map 75 fold 18 or 235 fold 6 – Facilities

Gourdon is the capital of a green undulating countryside called Bouriane *(qv)*. The town, situated on the borders of Quercy and Périgord, rises in tiers up the flank of a rocky hillock, upon which once stood the local lord's castle.
By following the circular route of avenues which have replaced the old ramparts, pleasant views of the hills and valleys of Bouriane can be obtained.

GOURDON

Briand (Bd A.) 2
Cardinal-Farinié (R. du) 4
Cavaignac (Av.) 5
Dr-Cabanès (Bd) 7
Gaulle (Pl. Ch.-de-) 8
Hôtel-de-Ville (Pl. de l') 9
Libération (Pl. de la) 12
Mainiol (Bd) 14
République (Allées de la) 17
Zig-Zag (R.) 18

Book well in advance
as you may have difficulty
in finding a room
for the night during
the summer season.

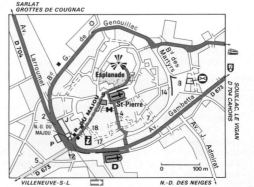

SIGHTS

★Rue du Majou. – The fortified gateway, Porte du Majou and, on the left, the chapel of Notre-Dame-du-Majou (which had been backed up against the ramparts) are at the beginning of the street of the same name.

This picturesque and narrow street was the main street; it is lined by old houses with overhanging storeys and ground floors with large pointed arches. Just after no 24, there is a good view, to the right, of the old fashioned Rue Zig-Zag. No 17, the former Anglars Mansion, has pretty mullioned windows.

Town Hall (Hôtel de Ville) (H). – This former 13C consulate, enlarged in the 17C, has covered arcades, which are used as a covered market.

⊘ **St-Pierre.** – The church was begun in the early 14C and was formerly a dependency of Le Vigan Abbey *(p 89)*. The chancel is supported by massive buttresses. The door in the west face is decorated with elegant archivolts and is framed by two tall asymmetrical towers. The large rose window is protected by a line of machicolations, a reminder of former fortifications.

The vast nave has pointed vaulting; wood panels of the 17C, carved, painted and gilded, decorate the chancel and the south transept.

Go round the outside of the church from the left and go up the staircase and the ramp, which leads to the esplanade where the castle once stood.

Esplanade. – There is a **panorama★** to be seen from the terrace (viewing table): beyond the town, the roofs of which can be seen in tiers below the massive roof of St-Pierre's in the foreground, one can see the churchyard, a forest of cypress trees, then the plateaux stretching out from the valleys of the Dordogne and the Céou.

Return to Place de l'Hôtel de Ville and go round the outside of the church starting from the right.

There are some old houses opposite the east end, including one with a fine early-17C doorway.

Opposite the south door of the church take the Rue Cardinal-Farinié which goes downhill and contains old houses with mullioned windows and flanking turrets. This will bring you back to the Place de la Libération.

⊘ **Franciscan Church (Église des Cordeliers) (D)**. – The church of the former Franciscan monastery is worth a visit. It has a massive belfry porch added in the 19C. The slender and pure lines of the nave, restored in 1971, are characteristic of early Gothic; the fine septilateral apse is lit by 19C stained-glass windows.

At the entrance, in the middle of the nave, stands a remarkable **font★**, on the outside of which Christ the King with the twelve Apostles (14C) are depicted on the thirteen trefoiled blind arcades.

EXCURSIONS

★Cougnac Caves. – *3km – 2 miles north on the D 70. Description p 72.*

⊘ **Notre-Dame-des-Neiges Chapel (Chapelle de N.-D.-des-Neiges)**. – *1.5km – 1 mile to the southeast.* Set in the small valley of the Bléou, this 14C chapel, a pilgrimage centre, was restored in the 17C. It has a 17C altarpiece.

⊘ **Le Vigan.** – Pop 836. *5 km – 3 miles east on the D 673.* A Gothic **church**, which is the remains of an abbey founded in the 11C, became a chapter for canons regular in the 14C. The church's east end is overlooked by a tower rising from the transept crossing. There is fine pointed vaulting over the nave and chancel with its five radiating chapels.

★ GRAMAT CAUSSE

Michelin map **75** folds 18 and 19 **79** folds 8 and 9 or **235** folds 6, 7, 10 and 14 – Facilities

The Gramat Causse, which extends between the Dordogne Valley in the north and the Lot and Célé Valleys in the south, is the largest *causse (qv)* in Quercy. It is a vast limestone plateau lying at an average altitude of 350m – 1 148ft, containing many natural phenomena and unusual landscapes.

Autumn is the time to cross the *causse*, when the trees are turning and shed a golden light on the grey stones and rocks and the maples add a splash of deep red.

★THE PLATEAU

① From Cahors to Souillac

101km – 62 1/2 miles – about 1 day – local map p 91

★★Cahors. – *Description p 59.*

Leave Cahors by ②

The D 653 runs beside the north bank of the Lot, passes by **Laroque-des-Arcs** and **Notre-Dame-de-Vêles Chapel** *(p 101)* and then goes up the charming Vers Valley, which, at times, widens out into meadowland and at times narrows between tall grey cliffs.

St-Martin-de-Vers. – Pop 112. In this small village the houses with brown-tiled roofs, cluster round the church of a former priory and its asymmetrical bell tower.

The road climbs up to the *causse* where dry-stone walls and sparse vegetation stretch away as far as the eye can see.

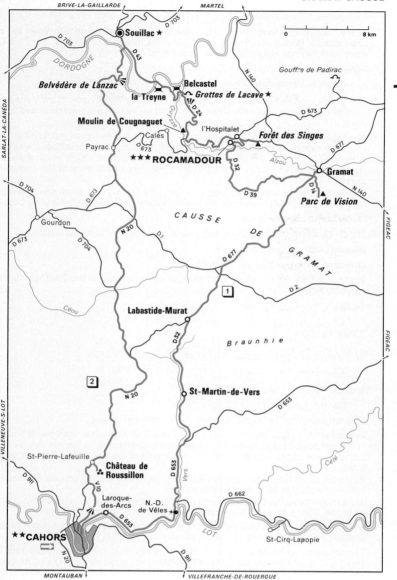

Labastide-Murat. – *Description p 94.*

Beyond Labastide-Murat, the D 677 crosses the east side of the *causse* and then wends down to Gramat.

> *Just before the Gramat railway station turn right and take the D 14 for 1km – 1/2 mile.*

Gramat Safari Park (Parc de Vision de Gramat). – This park extending over 38ha – 94 acres was acquired by the local authorities in view of showing animals and plants in their natural environment.

A botanical park, containing trees and shrubs from the *causse* (durmast oak, dogwood, ash...) is being created.

The animal park includes mainly European species living in semi-captivity in their natural habitat. Some of these animals – wild ox, Przewalskis' horses, ibexes, bison – are species which existed during prehistoric times.

A collection of farmyard animals shows a variety of domestic fowl, pigs, etc.

Follow the signposted itinerary over 3km – 2 miles for a pleasant tour.

> *Make for the D 677 which leads to Gramat.*

Gramat. – Pop 3 838. Facilities. Capital of the *causse* that bears the same name, Gramat is also a great fair town (sheep).

It is a good starting point for visits to Padirac, Rocamadour and the area that lies between the Lot and the Dordogne.

It was here that the **French Police Training Centre for Handlers and Dogs** (Centre de formation des maîtres de chien de la Gendarmerie) was established in 1945.

> *Return to the D 677 and immediately after, take the D 39 to the right to the point where it joins the D 32, turn right.*

The D 32 goes to the edge of the plateau, with fine **views** of Rocamadour crossing Alzou Canyon. Enter Rocamadour by the narrow pointed-arched gateways.

***Rocamadour. – *Description p 124.*

Leave Rocamadour to the northeast by the D 32 and continue to **L'Hospitalet** *(p 127)* **(good views** of Rocamadour); take the D 36 in the direction of Gramat. The Monkey Reserve (Forêt des Singes) is nearby on the right.

Monkey Reserve. – *Description p 127.*

Return to L'Hospitalet where you join the D 673 towards Calès.

This pretty road wends down the Ouysse Valley and affords views of the Valley and the Gramat Causse to the left. After 9km – 5 1/2 miles take a signposted road to the right.

⊙ **Cougnaguet Mill** (Moulin de Cougnaguet). – The rounded arches of this fortified mill span a derivation of the Ouysse in a charming, cool and verdant **setting**. It was built in the 15C, at the foot of a sheer cliff, on the site of a former mill to which the water rights were granted in 1279. There are four millstones, one of which is still in working order.

Continue along the small road which climbs to the D 247, into which you turn left. It affords splendid **views*** of the Dordogne Valley and of Belcastel Castle at its best.

*Lacave Caves. – *Description p 95.*

The D 43, which you join on the left, passes at the foot of Belcastel Castle.

Belcastel Castle. – *Description p 76.*

Château de la Treyne. – *Description p 76.*

Beyond Château de la Treyne the road cuts across a bend in the Dordogne before reaching Souillac.

*Souillac. – *Description p 142.*

THE N 20

② From Souillac to Cahors

68km – 42 miles – about 2 1/2 hours – local map p 91

*Souillac. – *Description p 142.*

Leave Souillac on the N 20 going south.

After crossing the Dordogne, the road rises above the valley.

Lanzac Belvedere (Belvédère de Lanzac). – There is a wide view from the left of the N 20 *(car park)* of the Dordogne Valley, where Château de la Treyne can be seen standing out to the east and that of the dovecot of Le Bastit Castle to the southeast.

Beyond Lanzac Belvedere, the pleasant and picturesque road crosses the *causse*, which stretches as far as the eye can see.

At St-Pierre-Lafeuille, take the little road to the left and follow it for 1km – 1/2 mile so as to see, from a distance, the impressive ruins of the Roussillon Castle.

⊙ **Roussillon Castle.** – This medieval fortress is owned by the Gontaut-Biron family. Massive round towers rise above the valley.

Turn around and return to the N 20. 3km – 2 miles after St-Pierre-Lafeuille turn left into the V 10, which runs along the hilltops and gives good views of the countryside, the hills and Lot Valley before bringing you suddenly upon the **site*** of Cahors.

**Cahors. – *Description p 59.*

** Château de HAUTEFORT

Michelin map 🔢 fold 7 or 🔢🔢 north of fold 44

Dating from the 17C and property of the Bastard family since 1929, Château de Hautefort, the proud form of which dominates the skyline, resembles the royal palaces of the Loire Valley rather than the Périgord fortresses. The château was seriously damaged by fire on the night of 30-31 August 1968. Restoration, begun in 1969, was conducted with care and fidelity, returning the château to its former appearance.

Bertrand the Troubadour. – The first castle of Hautefort was built by the Limousin family of Las Tours and passed by marriage, in the 12C, to the house of De Born of whom Bertrand, mentioned by Dante in the *Divine Comedy*, is the most well-known member. **Bertrand de Born**, the famous troubadour, much appreciated in the courts of love *(qv)*, became a warrior-knight when the need arose to defend the family castle against his brother Constantine. With the support of Henry Short Coat, he succeeded in having Henry II acknowledge his rights in 1185, in spite of Constantine's efforts, supported by Richard Lionheart. However, in 1186 Constantine returned and razed Hautefort. Renouncing everything, Bertrand retired to take the monastic orders.

Marie de Hautefort. – The beautiful and virtuous Marie, also known as Aurore, daughter of the first Marquis of Hautefort, lady-in-waiting to Anne of Austria, has remained famous for the deep admiration and platonic love with which she inspired Louis XIII (1610-43). In 1646 she married the Duke of Halluin and reigned over literary circles and the *Précieuses* drawing rooms. She died in 1691 at 75 years of age.

Château

TOUR *time: about 1 hour*

The site of Hautefort, set on a hill in the middle of an immense amphitheatre, was evidently used very early for its strategic position: in the 9C the viscounts of Limoges had already placed a stronghold here. During the Middle Ages several castles succeeded each other of which there are some traces (the courtyard's west corner tower). The defensive position of the castle was strengthened in the 16C (barbican flanked by two crenellated bartizans and preceded by a drawbridge) during the bellicose times of the Wars of Religion.

Complete reconstruction of the castle was instigated by Jacques-François de Hautefort (c1630). It lasted some forty years; the plans were attributed to the architect Nicolas Rambourgt, who kept the former living quarters but made considerable alterations. The pavilions set at opposite ends were only completed in the 18C.

The harmonious ensemble of buildings – Renaissance and classical – contributes to the elegant originality of the building.

Walk. – Skirt the beautiful park (40ha – 99 acres) to the terraces, planted with flowers and cypress trees, which overlook the village and offer views onto the park.

To reach the entrance to the château go to the end of the esplanade and cross the drawbridge over the moat, which is now decorated with flowers and boxwood. The court of honour is a vast square open on one side to the village, clustering at the foot of the walls, while on the other three sides it is surrounded by the living quarters. To the south are two round towers topped with domes and lantern turrets.

Interior. – The restoration has recreated several rooms and has repaired the great staircase, very badly damaged in the 1968 fire. The gallery is adorned with two marble busts of the 16 and 18C (Seneca and Marcus Aurelius, respectively) and two vases in Toro stone; the doors are exact replicas.

The tapestry gallery includes three 16C Flemish wall-hangings and one from Brussels, depicting scenes from the Old Testament. The dining room contains 17C paintings and the state room's walls are covered with Cordoban leather.

Inside the southeast tower is a 17C chapel containing 16C paintings on leather and the altar from Charles X's coronation.

The southwest tower has beautiful chestnut **timberwork★★**, the work of the Compagnons du Tour de France guild. It also contains the museum of Eugène Le Roy (1836-1907) *(qv)*, who was born at Hautefort, in the château itself, and wrote *Jacquou le Croquant (see L'Herm Castle below)*. Another room contains objects saved from the fire.

Church (Église). – Built on a vast square south of the château, the church was the former chapel of an almshouse founded by the Hautefort family. It has a fine slated dome topped by a lantern turret.

L'HERM CASTLE

Michelin map 75 south of fold 6 or 233 fold 43

In Barade Forest, in the heart of Périgord Noir, stands L'Herm Castle.

The castle was built in 1512 by Jean III of Calvimont, president of the Parliament of Bordeaux and ambassador to Charles V in 1526. A series of violent crimes cast a pall of blood over the castle's history. Jean III was killed here, as was his daughter Marguerite, murdered in 1605 by her husband François d'Aubusson, who married Marie de Hautefort immediately after. This couple commited about ten murders. In 1682 the castle was bought by another Marie de Hautefort *(qv)*, the first Marie's niece; then it was abandoned.

Recollection of these tragic events gave Eugène Le Roy *(qv)* the idea of making the castle the setting of his novel *Jacquou le Croquant (see above)*.

Emerging out of the forest are the castle ruins with its powerful crenellated towers. The hexagonal staircase tower opens by a doorway with the Flamboyant style in mind, yet already under the Renaissance style influence. The second archivolt, decorated with crockets propels its pinnacle upwards. On either side of the door the carved figures of men-at-arms are badly in need of repair. Inside, rising in one sweep without interruption, the remarkable **spiral staircase**★, the centre pillar of which is adorned with rope moulding, is roofed with quadripartite vaulting, with an intricate network of liernes and tiercerons creating a lovely palm tree effect. From the tower's windows plunging views can be had of the monumental chimneys decorating the three floors. They all bear the Calvimont coat of arms; the coat of arms of the third floor chimney is held by two angels.

ISSIGEAC   Pop 686

Michelin map 75 fold 15 or 235 southwest of fold 5

The little town of Issigeac, lying in the Banège Valley, possesses an interesting church and castle and picturesque half-timbered and corbelled houses.

Church (Église). – The church, was built by Armand de Gontaut-Biron, Bishop of Sarlat, at the beginning of the 16C and, a good example of late Gothic architecture. A belfry porch, supported by large buttresses, contains a doorway with a tympanum decorated with twisted recessed arches.

Bishops' Castle (Château des Évêques). – The castle was built by another Bishop of Sarlat, François de Salignac, in the second half of the 17C. It now houses the town hall. The building is vast and is flanked by two square towers, each with a corbelled turret of brick and stone on its north side. Fénelon resided here in 1681.

EXCURSION

Château de Bardou. — *7km — 4 miles to the east by the D 25, after 5.5km — 3 miles turn right.*
This interesting château (15-17C), now restored, stands in a fine parkland setting.

The times indicated in this Guide
when given with the distance allow one to enjoy the scenery
when given for sightseeing are intended to give an idea
of the possible length or brevity of a visit.

LABASTIDE-MURAT   Pop 732

Michelin map 75 south of fold 18 or 235 fold 10 — Local map p 91 — Facilities

Labastide-Murat, which stands at one of the highest points on the Gramat Causse *(qv)* was originally Labastide-Fortunière, but changed its name to Murat in honour of one of its most glorious sons.
The modest house in which Joachim Murat was born, on the southwest side of the town, and the château that he had build for his brother André preserve the memory of one of the French Empire's (1804-14) most valiant soldiers.

The fantastic destiny of Joachim Murat. – Murat was born in 1767, the son of an innkeeper. He was destined for the Church, but at twenty-one decided instead to be a soldier. The campaigns in Italy and Egypt enabled him to gain rapid promotion under Napoleon, whose brother-in-law he became by his marriage to Caroline; he was elevated to Marshal of the Empire, Grand Duke of Berg and of Cleves and King of Naples. The phenomenal bravery he displayed on all the battlefields of Europe, his influence over his troops whom he did not hesitate to lead in battle, made him a legendary hero. His star dimmed like that of his master, whom he abandoned in the dark days of the Empire. His miserable end in 1815 is but one more in a life full of contrasts: after the Bourbons has returned to Naples, he tried to reconquer his kingdom, but was taken prisoner and shot.

⊘ **Murat Museum (Musée Murat).** – The museum is in the house where Murat was born *(alleyway to the left of the church)*. One can see the 18C kitchen, the inn saloon, a large genealogical tree where ten European countries and several royal families are represented and, on the first floor, mementoes of the King of Naples and of his mother.

EXCURSIONS

Soulomès. – Pop 128. *3km – 2 miles to the southeast by the D17.* There is a Gothic
⊘ **church** with a square chevet and a Romanesque belfry porch which once formed part of a commandery of the Order of the Knights Templars in this small village on the Gramat Causse. Interesting 14C frescoes have been uncovered in the chancel. They illustrate scenes from the life of Christ: Jesus and Mary Magdalene, the Doubting of St Thomas, the Entombment and Christ Resurrected before a Knight.

Vaillac. – Pop 105. *5km – 3 miles to the northwest by the D 17.* The outline of a massive feudal castle looks down on this modest little village built on the *causse*. The castle was built in the 14 and 16C and consists of a huge main building flanked by five towers and of a keep. Another building, which formed part of the outbuildings, was used to stable as many as 200 horses.

LACAPELLE-MARIVAL Pop 1 337

Michelin map **75** folds 19 and 20 or **235** fold 7 or **239** fold 39 – Facilities

The town has kept many buildings that bear testimony to its age and importance as the fief of Lacapelle-Marival which was held from the 12 to 18C by the Cardaillac family.

Castle. – The massive, square, machicolated keep with watch towers at each corner, was built in the 13C. The living quarters, abutting on one side and divided by massive round towers, were added in the 15C.
The Gothic church, an old town gateway and the 15C covered market, supported on stone piles and roofed with round tiles, make a charming group with the castle.

EXCURSION

Round tour of 27km – 16 1/2 miles. – *About 1 hour. Leave Lacapelle-Marival by the D 940 to the south.*

Le Bourg. – Pop 222. The church is the only building to remain of a former priory. The transept and chancel are adorned with Romanesque arcades and fine capitals.
  Turn right into the N 140.

Rudelle. – Pop 155. The **church**, founded in the 13C by Bertrand de Cardaillac, the lord of Lacapelle-Marival, looks like a feudal keep crowned by a terrace with a crenellated parapet. From the churchyard *(access by an alleyway to the right of the church)*, there is a view of the east end and the building as a whole.
At ground level a pointed-vaulted hall is used as the parish church. The upper storey is reached by a wooden staircase climbing to the gallery, then by a ladder, a trap-door and finally a stone staircase. This refuge, which now contains the bells, is lit by narrow loopholes. To reach the terrace, which also provided refuge, another ladder and stone staircase have to be climbed. The machicolated watchpath affords a fine view of the village.
  Follow the N 140 to Thémines, then take the D 40 to the right.

Aynac. – Pop 689. Aynac Castle, set amidst woods and meadows, is a riding centre. Its crenellated corner towers, topped by domes, crowd close to the keep.
  The D 940 returns to Lacapelle-Marival.

★ LACAVE CAVES (Grottes de LACAVE)

Michelin map **75** fold 18 or **235** fold 6 – Local maps pp 75 and 91

Near the valley of the Dordogne making a deep cut through the Gramat Causse, a series of caves, at the foot of the cliffs beside the river, was discovered in 1902 by Armand Viré, a student of E.A. Martel.
The galleries visited by tourists are a mile long *(on foot Rtn)* and divide into two groups, visited one after the other. The shapes of the concretions in the caves look like people, animals, buildings and even whole cities; delicate stalactites hang from the ceilings.
The first group contains stalagmites and stalactites. Through the second group, underground rivers run from *gour* to *gour* (natural dams) and flood out into lakes with beautiful reflections. In the Lake Chamber (Salle du Lac) the fluorescent nature of the concretions makes the parts that are still growing, glow in the dark. The Hall of Wonders (Salle des Merveilles) contains beautiful eccentrics.
Flints were discovered as well as prehistoric tools and weapons made of bone and horn, when the caves were being arranged for visitors.

★ Château de LANQUAIS

Michelin map **75** centre of fold 15 or **235** fold 5 — Local map p 78

The 14 and 15C main building, with the defensive characteristics of a fortified castle, was modified when a Renaissance building was added during the Wars of Religion. On the façade facing out, where the impact of cannon-balls (traces of a skirmish in May 1577 during the Wars of Religion) are still visible, the first floor is opened by loopholes only.
On the courtyard side, Renaissance elegance appears on the harmonious **façade★**: divided into vertical registers, underlined horizontally by moulding and stone string courses marking the entablatures and lit by triangular pedimented windows. The dormer windows attract notice because of their rustic work, open gables and carved niches.
Inside, note the two finely carved **chimneys★** and a flint collection.

LARAMIÈRE

Michelin map 🔢 north of fold 19 or 🔢 southwest of fold 15

Set in the Limogne Causse, dotted with dolmens and *caselles (qv)*, Laramière has fine remains of a priory.

⊘ **Laramière Priory (Prieuré de Laramière)**. – The former priory was founded in 1148 by the monk Bertrand de Grifeuille of the Augustinian Order, who had founded the priory at Espagnac-Ste-Eulalie *(qv)*.

The buildings, built in the 12 and 13C, formed a quadrilateral but some of the buildings were destroyed during the Wars of Religion. The Jesuits arrived in the mid-17C and raised the height of the bailiff's house.

Of the restored buildings, which are open, you will see the chapel vaulting, the Romanesque hall, which welcomed the pilgrims of Santiago de Compostela and especially the **chapter house** with

Chapter house

its walls and vaulting painted with geometric motifs and its capitals bearing carved effigies of St Louis and Blanche de Castille. On the church's south wall, funerary niches shelter the donors' tombs: Hugues de la Roche and his wife.

EXCURSION

Beauregard. – *6km – 3 1/2 miles west. Access by a small path left of the road.*

La Borie du Bois Dolmen (Dolmen de la Borie du Bois). – One of Quercy's finest dolmens.
Continue along the D 55.

Beauregard. – Pop 167. This *bastide (qv)* has kept its street plan (streets at right angles). Its 17C **covered market**, roofed in stone slab *(lauzes)*, has grain measures carved into the rock. On the church's parvis is a lovely 15C cross.

LARROQUE-TOIRAC CASTLE

Michelin map 🔢 fold 10 or 🔢 south of fold 11 – 14 km – 8 1/2 miles southwest of Figeac – Local map pp 100-101

⊘ The castle, clinging to a high cliff face, overlooks the village and the Lot Valley. The fortress was built in the 12C and was owned for a long time by the Cardaillac family, who championed Quercy resistance to the English during the Hundred Years' War. The castle, after being taken and retaken by the English, was finally burnt down at the end of the 14C, but was raised again from its ruins during Louis XI's reign.

A path starting from the church parvis *(car park)* leads to a round tower built at the beginning of the Hundred Years' War as defence against artillery attack. It leads to the part of the castle formerly the servants' quarters and then through to the courtyard. The huge keep, which once stood 30m — 98ft high but was razed to only 8m — 26ft in 1793 on the orders of the Commissioners of the Convention, is pentagonal, the better to resist the force of rocks hurled down at it from the cliffs above. A spiral staircase, in a Romanesque tower abutting on the main building, leads to the different storeys. The guard room has a fine Romanesque chimneypiece, the main hall a Gothic one; the upper floors contain furnishings from the time of Louis XIII to the Directoire period (early 17 to late 18C).

LASCAUX CAVE

Michelin map 🔢 south of fold 7 or 🔢 fold 44 – Local map p 146

Lascaux Cave is ranked first of the prehistoric sites of Europe for the number and quality of its paintings.

The cave was discovered 12 September 1940 by four young boys looking for their dog, who had fallen down a hole. With a makeshift lamp, they discovered an extraordinary fresco of polychrome paintings on the walls of the gallery they were in. The teacher at Montignac was immediately told of the discovery, who just as quickly notified Abbé Breuil *(qv)*. The abbot arrived and examined the paintings with meticulous care baptising the cave the "Sistine Chapel of Périgord".

In 1948 the cave was opened to the public which recognised the importance of the cave; in fifteen years more than a million people admired the famous Lascaux paintings. But, unfortunately, in spite of all the precautions taken (weak lighting, air conditioning, airlock), the carbon dioxide and the humidity produced two sicknesses: green (a term used to explain the growth of moss and algae) and white (less visible but much more serious being a deposit of white calcite).

In 1963, in order to preserve this treasure, it was decided to close the cave to the public. Ten years later, the idea of a facsimile of Lascaux was evoked. The project, Lascaux II, opened in 1983.

An exceptional group of paintings. – The cave, carved out of the Périgord Noir *(qv)* limestone, is a relatively small cavity, 150m – 492ft long. It is made up of four galleries, the walls of which are covered with more than 1 500 representations either engraved or painted. These works were created between 17 000 and 12 000 years ago, during the Magdalenian Period *(qv)*. At that time the cave was open to the exterior. Sometime after the cave artists had decorated the cave, the

The Great Black Bull from Lascaux Cave

porch collapsed and a flow of clay tightly closed off the cave.

The airtight entrance and the impermeable ceiling are the reasons for the lack of concretions and the perfect preservation of the paintings fixed and authenticated by a thin layer of natural calcite.

The cave includes the Bulls' Hall, which extends into an axial gallery *(see Lascaux II)*; these two areas hold 90% of the cave paintings.

To the right of the Bulls' Hall a passage leads to the apse, which extends into the nave and the Feline Gallery. To the right of the apse opens the Well Gallery, whose lower section is decorated with a simplified scene of a wounded bison chasing a man, one of the rare representations of a human figure *(a reproduction can be seen at Le Thot Centre of Research and of Prehistoric Art)*. Such narrative paintings are unique in the history of prehistoric art.

A wide range of fauna appears on the cave walls; the cavemen used the wall contours to give relief to the subject matter. Reproduced are the animals hunted during the early Magdalenian Period: aurochs, horses, reindeer, bison, ibexes, bears and woolly rhinoceroses appear side by side or superimposed, creating extraordinary compositions. The seemingly disorganised paintings (drawings superimposed onto previous drawings or figures apparently illustrated with a sense of hierarchy, leave researchers perplexed), the absence of all landscape form (ground, plants, small animals) suggest a more ritual form of expression rather than an narrative sense. The geometric signs and enigmatic drawings, accompanying the fauna (lines, points, grill-like forms, ovals, sticks) bring to mind the possible existence of a sanctuary.

The Lascaux style. – There is a Lascaux style: animals with small, elongated heads, swollen stomachs, short legs, constant movement and fur illustrated by dabs of coloured pigment. The horns, antlers and hoofs are often drawn in 3/4 view – at times even full face – while the animal itself is drawn in profile; this procedure is known as the turned profile.

★★**Lascaux II**. – Located some 200yds from the original cave, the facsimile is a remarkable reconstitution of the upper part of the cave, including the Bulls' Hall and the axial gallery. A detailed description of how the facsimile was made can be found at Le Thot Centre of Research and of Prehistoric Art *(p 143)*, a worthwhile follow-up visit to Lascaux.

As early as 1966, The National Geographic Institute (Institut Géographique National – IGN) had accomplished a photogrammetric survey of Lascaux using three-dimensional scenes of the cave and stereo images. This survey enabled the facsimile's conception in an opencast quarry; a project taken on by the Dordogne *département* in 1980.

Once the cave walls were reproduced, the painter Monique Peytral copied the cave paintings using slides and the numerous surveys she had taken. She used the same materials (pigments, tools...) as the cave artists.

Two small rooms, reproducing the original airlock, present the history of Lascaux Cave, items discovered in the cave's archaeological strata — tallow lamps, coloured powders, flints used by the engravers — a model of the scaffolding used, a copy of a panel of the bisons back to back, the dating methods, and the flint and bone industries. In the Bulls' Hall only the upper part of the wall and the vaulting, covered with calcite, were used. This is a remarkable graphic composition. The second animal, the only imaginary animal figure represented at Lascaux, has been called a unicorn because of its two-odd looking horns protruding from a bear-like muzzle; it has the body of a rhinoceros. The other animals represented include magnificent black bulls, one of which is 5m — 16 1/2ft long, red bison, small horses and deer.

The axial gallery (diverticule axial) presents a vault and walls covered with horses, bovidae, ibex, bison and a large deer. A charming frieze of long-haired ponies, a large black bull and a large red pony, demonstrate a very developed art style.

Régourdou. – *1km – 1/2 mile east*. On this prehistoric site discovered in 1954 numerous objects and bones were discovered (a skeleton of Régourdou man, 70 000 years old and now displayed in the Périgord Museum in Périgueux; *p 122*). All these discoveries are representative of the Mousterian industry. In the cave, now open to the sky, near the burial ground of Régourdou man, was found a pile of bear bones, which some specialists have interpreted as traces of a bear burial ground.

A small museum contains bones (a cast of Régourdou man's jawbone) and tools.

Lauzerte has a picturesque **setting★** and can be seen from afar in the undulating country of Bas-Quercy where the limestone hills are separated by fertile plains. A former *bastide (qv)* built in 1241 by the Count of Toulouse, it was occupied by the English.

Upper Town. – The grey stone houses with their almost flat roofs are clustered round the church of St-Barthélemy and Place des Cornières.

This square (Place des Cornières), with its covered arcades *(cornières)*, has a half-timbered house. There are several old houses in Rue du Château, some half-timbered, some Gothic in style with twin windows and others Renaissance with mullioned windows. All-embracing views can be had of the gentle, rolling countryside of hills and small valleys.

EXCURSIONS

Quercy Blanc (White Quercy). – *Round tour of 24km – 15 miles – about 3/4 hour. Southeast of Lauzerte take the D 81 which branches off the D 953*. The route indicated provides many views of the town of Lauzerte and takes the motorist through this picturesque hilly region *(photograph p 14)*. There is a marked contrast between the somewhat poor plateau, where lines of cypresses and houses with flat roofs covered with pale pink round tiles give a southern aspect to the countryside, and the valleys and hillsides richly covered in crops. The different types of soil enable the peasant farmer to grow a variety of crops and to achieve true economic independence within his own holding. In the valleys there is also a contrast: the valley bottoms contain rich meadows hemmed by lines of poplars, which gradually give way to a land of cereal growing; on the hillsides small parcels of land are diligently cultivated, especially those bearing vines (*Chasselas de Moissac*), fields of melon or fruit trees.

Montcuq. – *Pop 1 082. 13km – 8 miles to the northeast by the D 953*. Chief town of a castellany to which Raymond VI, Count of Toulouse, granted a charter of customary law in the 12C, Montcuq was the centre of many a bloody battle during the Albigensian Crusade, Hundred Years' War and Wars of Religion. All that remains of this once fortified village is a tall castle keep (12C), standing on a hillock overlooking the Barguelonnette River. The view extends over the surrounding hills and valleys.

LIZONNE VALLEY

Michelin map 75 fold 4 or 233 folds 30 and 41

At the limits of Périgord and Angoumois (the region around Angoulême), the Lizonne River has formed a natural boundary, which has had its importance in history. The Petrocorii *(qv)* many, many years ago had already used it to establish the limits of their land; during the early Middle Ages, their descendants defended it by building wooden strongholds perched on large man-made earth **mounds** (Grésignac, Bourzac and as a last defensive post, La Tour-Blanche).

The Lizonne is also the linguistic boundary between the north and south; on the Périgord side the people still speak Oc language *(langue d'oc)*, while on the opposite bank they speak Oïl language *(langue d'oïl)*. Oïl and Oc were the words used for yes in the north and south, respectively.

Bourzac Country. – The old Bourzac castellany was established around a feudal fortress. This undulating countryside spreading north to Fontaine and south to St-Paul-Lizonne, is characterised by the abundance of its crops and the beauty and tranquility of its villages, huddled around often fortified, Romanesque churches.

ROUND TOUR FROM LUSIGNAC

37km — 23 miles - time: 2 1/2 hours

Lusignac. – Pop 192. Built on a height, the village forms a harmonious group with its 15C fortified **church** built on the foundations of a 12C domed nave (17C carved wood altarpiece), old houses and 15-17C manor-house.

Go north (D 97) to Bouteilles-St-Sébastien, then bear right immediately.

St-Martial-Viveyrol. – Pop 264. The austerity of the Romanesque church, with its two domes and belfry-keep, is emphasised by its narrow bays. The defense chamber set above the vaulting is pierced by large openings around each of which are four holes; in time of attack a floor could then be added, held up by the props set in the holes.

Continue northwards.

Cherval. – *Description p 105*.

Champagne-et-Fontaine. — Pop 511. In the village of Champagne stands a church, which was subsequently fortified. Inside the twin nave was covered with pointed vaulting in the 16C; outside the porch has recessed arches.

Several fine houses and the 16C Chaumont Manor-House (restored) complete the picture.

Take the road to Vendoire.

Vendoire. – The village château, enhanced by a semicircular central pediment, was built under Louis XIV. East of the château, the small Romanesque church has a polygonal apse. The west façade, in great need of repair, has kept a first level of arcades, showing Saintonge influence.

A road along the ridge continues to Nanteuil-Auriac.

⊘ **Nanteuil-Auriac**. – Pop 384. The **church** shows visible evidence of several additions. Romanesque in origin, as the apse of fine capitals and the domed chancel indicate; fortified, at a later date, with a belfry porch and a raised apse; then in the 16C the church was provided with side aisles and pointed vaulting, the corbels of which remain. The entrance porch is typically Renaissance.

Bouteilles-St-Sébastien. – The church is a fine example of the trend, which existed in the area during the Hundred Years' War, of fortifying Romanesque churches. Here the apse was raised to form with the bell tower an unusual keep.

Go west on the D 97, then bear left towards St-Paul-Lizonne.

⊘ **St-Paul-Lizonne**. – Pop 337. The fortified **church** contains a **painted ceiling★** and a late 17C altar.

LOC DIEU ABBEY

Michelin map **79** north of fold 20 or **235** fold 15 — 9km — 5 1/2 miles of Villefranche de-Rouergue

⊘ On the borders of Rouergue and Quercy, the former Loc Dieu Abbey *(Locus Dei — divine place)* was built in 1123 by Cistercian monks from the abbeys of Dalon and Pontigny. Restored and renovated in the 19C by Paul Goût, the monastic buildings were transformed into a castle half-feudal, half-Renaissance in appearance.

The cloisters and chapter house, destroyed during the Hundred Years' War, were rebuilt in the 15C. Only three of the 15C cloisters' galleries remain and these were restored in the 19C. The chapter house, also 15C, is supported by two elegant octagonal columns with fine mouldings.

★**Church (Église)**. – The church was built between 1159 and 1189 using sandstone of many shades, but with ochre and yellow predominating; the completed building is a wonderful example of the Cistercian style, simple and unadorned, well-proportioned and pure of line. The nave, which is more than 20m — 66ft high, is flanked by narrow aisles. Most Cistercian churches end in a flat east end, but this one has five radiating chapels. The transept, the crossing of which is roofed over with a square lantern tower, has four transept chapels; one of them *(first chapel in south arm)* contains a precious 15C **triptych★**, in carved and painted wood, framing a Virgin and Child. The church has quadripartie vaulting but its elevation remains Romanesque in character.

★★ LOT VALLEY

Michelin map **79** folds 5 to 10 or **235** folds 9 to 11 and 14 and 15

The Lot River is most beautiful where it cuts across the Quercy *causses (qv)*. The river flows at the foot of rocks covered with chestnut woods and promontories on which perch old villages; elsewhere the waters flow in great loops round picturesque towns and cities.

From the Cévennes Mountains to the Agenais. – The Lot is a tributary of the Garonne. It rises in the Cévennes on the slopes of Le Goulet Mountain at an altitude of 1 400m – 4 600ft and flows right across the southern part of the Massif Central.

The winding course is an uninterrupted series of meanders or loops, *cingles*, circling tongues of land, some only a couple of hundred yards across. As it flows between the tall limestone cliffs of the Quercy *causses*, its thousand curves provide splendid and constantly changing views. The valley is always picturesque, sometimes wild and bare, sometimes smiling and fertile. The Lot leaves Quercy before Libos and, after flowing a further 480km — 300 miles, enters the Garonne in the Agenais Plain.

Scenes from the past. – Before the railway came, the Lot was an important navigational route. The river was first improved by Colbert and was later equipped with dams and even canals to cut across the promontories of the wider bends, as at Luzech *(qv)*.

A fleet of barges, known as *sapines* or *gabares (qv)*, sailed on the Lot, bringing to Bordeaux cheeses from Auvergne, coal from Decazeville and wine from Cahors.

The Lot vineyards. – The slopes of the valley of the Olt – the Oc language name for the Lot, which is still found in such place names as St-Vincent-Rive-d'Olt and Balaguier-d'Olt – have long been famous for their vineyards. Quercy wines, with their high alcoholic content, have played a great part in making Cahors and the Olt Valley famous *(pp 16 and 35)*.

In 1C AD the Roman Emperor Domitian punished Cahors for revolting by destroying its vineyards; after two centuries of teetotalism, Probus revoked the sentence. Despite the boycott on Bordeaux, through which the wine was shipped, wines from the Lot Valley were preferred by the English for many centuries: Eleanor of Aquitaine brought Quercy to the king of England as part of her dowry; in 1287 letters patent were granted by the king in favour of these wines. The wine was exported to Poland, to Russia – where only the wine of Cahors could entice the Tsar Peter the Great from vodka – and even to Italy. Legend has it that popes insisted on serving this wine at mass.

Two men of Quercy, the poet Clément Marot *(qv)*, and Galiot de Genouillac *(qv)*, gave the wine to François I to taste, and the king's palate delighted in its velvet smoothness. Later, vines from the Lot were transported at great cost to Fontainebleau to create the Royal Vine Arbour.

★★CLIFFS AND PROMONTORIES

From Figeac to Cahors
115km – 71 1/2 miles – about 1 day – local map pp 100-101

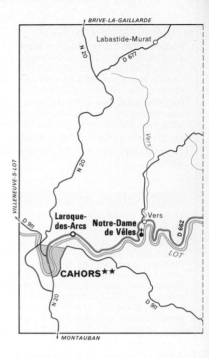

As it crosses Quercy, the Lot flows at the foot of hillside slopes, often sheer cliffs. Leaving Rouergue, the river hurls itself against the spur on which stands the old town of Capdenac, and then pushes its way between the cliff walls of the *causses*. Sometimes the cliffs enclose the river, and from their tops, there are fine views of the valley.

★**Figeac**. – *Description p 86.*

Leave Figeac southeast.

Capdenac. – *Description p 64.*

After Capdenac-Gare, take the D 86, which runs along the south bank of the river and soon provides pretty views of Capdenac. The river makes a wide bend in the centre of an alluvial plain on which crops are grown. Beyond St-Julien-d'Empare, this picturesque road provides a good view of the Capdenac amphitheatre.

After Pont-de-la-Madeleine the road runs beside the Lot through a countryside of rocks and undergrowth. Shortly after Balaguier-d'Olt you reach St-Pierre-Toirac.

St-Pierre-Toirac. – Pop 161. This small village, on the north bank of the Lot, possesses an interesting **church** of the 11 and 14C. The Romanesque apse alone belies the fortified appearance of this building which served as a defence point with its massive crenellated keep and upper floor. The short nave has cradle vaulting and primitive style capitals. The chancel has trefoil arches; saw-toothed arches surround the stained-glass windows of the apse. Recently discovered Merovingian sarcophages have been placed behind the church.

Larroque-Toirac Castle. – *Description p 96.*

Many delightful villages are to be seen on the north bank which is dominated by high rocks and vertical cliffs; as the valley widens, the Lot, lined with poplars, spreads out into a great sheet of water near which grow tobacco and cereals.

Montbrun. – Pop 61. The village of Montbrun rises in tiers on a rocky promontory encircled by steep cliffs. It looks down on the Lot and faces La Mounine's Leap *(see below)*. Towering above the village are the ruins of a fortress that once belonged to one of Pope John XXII' s brothers, then to the powerful Cardaillac family.

Cajarc. – Pop 1 184. Facilities. The town was made famous because the former President Pompidou had a house here.

Near the church, the Hébrardie Mansion, with Gothic windows, is what remains standing of a 13C castle.

A fine reservoir on the Lot has been created.

Cross the river at Cajarc and follow the D 127 up the south bank as far as La Mounine's Leap. The road overhangs the Lot to start with and immediately after Saujac, rises and winds around to overlook a wooded gorge, before reaching the top of the *causse*.

★**La Mounine's Leap** (Saut de la Mounine). – There is a good **view★** of the valley from the top of this cliff and, from the end of the spur, you can see out over a wide bend in the river as it circles a mosaic of arable fields. Over on the left, on the far bank, stands Montbrun Castle.

The curious name, *Saut de la Mounine* – the little monkey's leap – comes from a rather strange legend. The lord of Montbrun was determined to punish his daughter for her love of another lord's son and ordered her to be hurled from the top of the cliff; a hermit, appalled at this cruel idea, disguised a small blind monkey (*mounine* in Oc language) in women's clothes and hurled it into the air. The father saw the object falling and regretted his cruel action; on seeing his daughter alive and well his joy was so great that he forgave her.

Once again on the river's north bank, the road climbs rapidly and passes near a chapel (Chapelle de la Capellette) built in the 12 and 13C, known as the little chapel (thus *capellette*) and of which only the apse remains. From this spot there is a wide view of the valley.

Calvignac. – Pop 203. This old village, where a few traces of its fortress may still be seen, is perched on a spur on the river's south bank.

Staying on the same bank take the D 8 which leads to Cénevières.

★**Cénevières Castle**. – *Description p 70.*

From Tour-de-Faure admire St-Cirq-Lapopie in its remarkable setting on the river's south bank.

★★**St-Cirq-Lapopie**. – *Description p 134.*

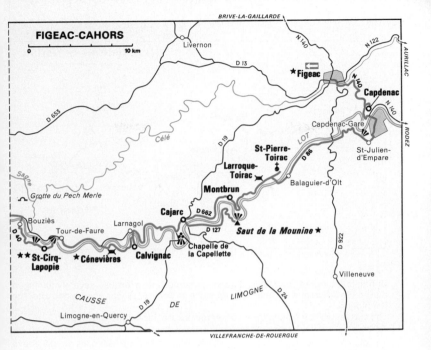

Beyond St-Cirq-Lapopie, the D 40, which is built into the cliff, has been designed as a tourist route. There is a good **view★** of the confluence of the Lot and the Célé from a small belvedere. From the same spot a wide bend of the Lot can be seen curving between white and yellow cliffs; magnificent poplars and fields add to the beauty of the landscape.

Immediately after Bouziès, cross the Lot and again take the D 662. This runs close beside the river in a picturesque, sometimes wooded, cliff setting. In several places the road has been cut out of the living rock. Past Vers the valley broadens out, cliffs are replaced by wooded hills and the alluvial soil is given over to arable farming.

Notre-Dame-de-Vêles. – This small pilgrimage chapel was built in the 12C and has a fine square bell tower and a Romanesque apse.

Laroque-des-Arcs. – Pop 379. Its name is a reminder of the aqueduct which crossed the Francoulès Valley and took water to Cahors. A three-tiered bridge held the aqueduct which transported water over 20km — 12 miles from Vers to Divona (ancient Cahors). The consuls of Cahors had it razed in 1370. An old tower perched on a rock beside the Lot enabled guards to watch the river traffic and exact tolls.

★★Cahors. – *Description p 59.*

THE MEANDERS OF THE LOT'S LOWER REACHES

From Cahors to Bonaguil
85km – 52 1/2 miles – about 5 hours – local map p 102

From Cahors to Puy-l'Évêque, the Lot winds in a series of meanders – *cingles* – through Quercy *causses*; beyond, it goes into a flatter region and the valley broadens out.

★★Cahors. *Description p 59.*

Leave Cahors by ① on the D 911 which overlooks the Lot.

Mercuès. – Facilities. Once the property of the count-bishops of Cahors, the château is now a hotel. Occupying a remarkable site overlooking the north bank of the Lot, the château was a fortified castle in 1212, enlarged in the 14C, besieged several times during the Hundred Years' War and the Wars of Religion, altered in the 15C and became in the 16C a château with terraces and gardens. It was only entirely restored last century. There is an outstanding **view★** of the valley from the château.

From Mercuès continue along the D 911 and then turn right on the D 6.

Catus. – Pop 775. The **chapter house**, which adjoins the church and was once part of a former priory, contains fragments of carvings and beautiful Romanesque capitals, one of which represents the Apparition of Christ before the Apostles.

West of Mercuès the road leaves the valley for a short distance to cross a flourishing countryside of vineyards and orchards; then the road returns to the river, following it closely.

Luzech. – *Description p 102.*

Follow the south bank, there are good views along the valley.

Albas. – Pop 545. This village has narrow streets lined with old houses.

Anglars. – Pop 182. A Crucifixion adorns the church's Renaissance main doorway.

Bélaye. – Pop 204. Bélaye, once the fief of the bishops of Cahors, stands on top of a hill. An extensive **view★** of the Lot Valley may be gained from the top of the spur and from the upper square of this little village.

Grézels. – Pop 263. Overlooking the village is the **feudal castle of La Coste**, several times razed and rebuilt. The bishops of Cahors possessed a fief which extended over the Lot Valley from Cahors to Puy-l'Évêque and Grézels marked the limits of their territory; therefore, a stronghold was built to defend the entrance into their fief.

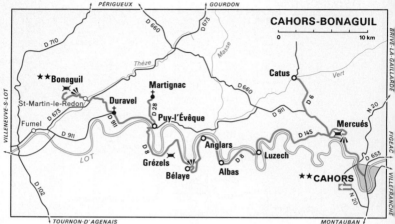

During the Hundred Years' War, it was transformed into a fortress, severely damaged during the different wars and restored in the 14 and 16C, it was abandoned after the Revolution.

The curtain wall and crenellated corner towers are the castle's oldest part.

Puy-l'Évêque. – *Description p 123.*

To get to Martignac from Puy-l'Évêque, first take the D 28, which rises rapidly above the valley, then a local road.

Martignac. – This tiny village has a rustic church built in a beautiful yellow stone and crowned by a tall, asymmetrical half-timbered bell tower. The nave and chancel are decorated with 15C **frescoes** (in poor condition). Yellow and ochre tones predominate. Although the drawing is stilted, the facial expressions and the composition of the frescoes make them interesting. In the nave: a nobleman sitting on a man's back illustrates sloth, another carrying a ham in his arms is gluttony, while a woman riding a goat signifies lust. Facing this fresco is another showing the Coronation of the Virgin and the Elect being guided to Paradise by St Michael and received at the Gates by St Peter. A Laying in the Tomb, angels, and on the vault, a Christ in Majesty, hand raised in benediction, may be seen in the chancel.

Return to Puy-l'Évêque and take the D 911.

The terraces and hillsides are covered with vines, while the wide alluvial valley is carpeted with fields.

Duravel. – Pop 875. The 11C church has historiated capitals decorating the chancel. There is an archaic crypt supported by columns with rough-hewn capitals. The bodies of Saints Hilarion, Poémon and Agathon lie buried at the back of the apse.

The *ostension*, or solemn exhibition of relics to the faithful, is held every five years.

From Duravel take a small road towards St-Martin-le-Redon, then the tourist road to Bonaguil (Route touristique de Bonaguil).

★★Bonaguil Castle. – *Description p 49.*

LUZECH
Pop 1 690

Michelin map 🏷79 fold 7 or 🏷235 fold 14 — Local map p 102

Luzech has grown up on the narrowest part of a tongue of land almost completely encircled by a loop in the Lot River. The isthmus at this point is some 100yds wide. The town is crowned by the old castle keep. It is bordered to the north by the former Roman city of Impernal and to the south by the Pistoule Promontory, washed by the waters of the river as it describes the bend. Thanks to a reservoir, which has been created by the construction of a dam upstream from the peninsula, a watersports centre has been set up.

Impernal Hill. – Impernal Hill was a natural defence which has been inhabited since prehistoric times; recognising its potential, the Gauls transformed the plateau into a powerful stronghold. A citadel, of which the square keep can still be seen, was built below it in the Middle Ages. In 1118, Richard Lionheart was master of the citadel. Luzech became the seat of one of the four baronies of Quercy and was sought as a prize by the English in the Hundred Years' War. Nevertheless, the town resisted all their attacks and became an important strongpoint. During the Wars of Religion, it remained a faithful bastion of Catholicism under the bishops of Cahors.

Excavations of the Impernal site have revealed walls and traces of buildings dating from the Roman and Gaulish periods.

★Viewpoint (Point de vue). – From the top of Impernal Hill, the view encompasses Luzech clustered at its foot, Pistoule Promontary, like a ship's prow slicing through the wide alluvial plain, and the Lot winding between luxuriant crops.

Old town. – Grouped in the old Barry Quarter, picturesque alleyways link Rue du Barry-del-Valat to the quays.

Around Place des Consuls, on the other side of Place du Canal, several examples of medieval architecture have been preserved: Penitents Chapel (12C), Capsol Gateway with its brick pointed arch, Consuls' House with its elegant paired windows.

⊙ **Armand Viré Archaeological Museum** (Musée archéologique Armand-Viré). – *In the Consuls' House*. Set up in the fine vaulted cellar, the museum retraces the history (from the Palaeolithic Age to the Gallo-Roman times) of the site of Luzech. Among the items displayed (excavated at the Impernal site and the cave found on the hillside) is the exceptional **reduced model of Trajan's column★**, diffused throughout the Roman Empire in the early 2C AD, and the unusual Gallo-Roman **hinged spoon**, of bronze and iron.

Keep (Donjon). – *Entrance via Place des Consuls*. The entrance used to be by the small pointed-arched doorway opening onto the first floor. From the 13C keep's terrace the view plunges into the brown-tiled roofs of the town, nestled amidst meadows and crops with hills along the horizon.

Notre-Dame-de-l'Ile. – The chapel, set in a calm landscape of vines and orchards backed by hills, hemming the Lot, stands at the isthmus's furthest point. This Flamboyant Gothic sanctuary is a pilgrimage centre, which dates back to the 13C.

EXCURSION

Cambayrac. – Pop 99. *8km – 5 miles to the south*. The hamlet possesses an odd-looking church identified from afar by its wall belfry. Inside, the Romanesque apse and the side chapels were covered, in the 17C, by an unusual marble and stucco decor in the classical style.

★ LA MADELEINE SITE

Michelin map **75** north of fold 16 or **235** fold 1 – Local map 84

The location of La Madeleine Site *(access via Tursac and the bridge to l'Espinasse)* is remarkably contrasted with the wooded plateau and the Vézère's alluvial plain below. The terrain is formed by the river's most distinctly shaped and narrowest meander (100m –109yds at its source expanding to 2.2km – 1 mile). On the rock above stand the remains of a medieval castle.

⊙ Midway up the hill, and protected by a rock overhang, lies an old **troglodyte village**, which may have been occupied from the 10 to the 18C. The village is made up of some 20 dwellings carved out of the rock, near a spring and protected by a narrow fortified entrance; about 100 people could live there during troubled times. A chapel, transformed in the 15C, (enlarged, pointed vaulting added), consecrated to St Mary Magdalene, gave the site its name.

At the foot of the cliff, under the village, lies the prehistoric deposit which established the characteristics of the Magdalenian Culture *(qv)*, preponderant during the last 60 centuries of the Upper Palaeolithic Age. The richness and quality of the items discovered by Lartet and Christy in 1863 (for example the ivory plaque of an engraved mammoth) enabled Mortillet, 6 years later, to propose a classification of the diverse epochs of prehistory based on the products (bone, flint) of human industry *(photograph p 21)*. The majority of the objects are exhibited in the museums at Les Eyzies *(p 83)* and St-Germain-en-Laye *(see Michelin Green Guide to Ile de France)*.

MARCILHAC-SUR-CÉLÉ   Pop 240

Michelin map **79** fold 9 or **235** fold 11 — Local map p 69

Marcilhac is picturesquely built in the centre of an amphitheatre of cliffs in the smiling Célé Valley.

Interesting old houses surround the ruins of a Benedictine abbey.

The legal jungle. – In the 11C Marcilhac Abbey controlled but let fall into ruins the modest sanctuary of Rocamadour; noticing this negligence some monks from Tulle installed themselves in the sanctuary; but in 1166 the discovery of the body of St Amadour *(qv)* turned the sanctuary into a rich and famous pilgrimage place. Marcilhac recalled its rights and expelled the monks from Tulle. Soon afterwards the Abbot of Tulle threw out the Marcilhac monks and again occupied Rocamadour; then the lawsuits began.

The case was acrimonious and the Bishop of Cahors, the papal legate, the Archbishop of Bourges, the pope himself, were all called on to give judgment, but they avoided pronouncing a decision; finally, after a hundred years of squabbling, Marcilhac accepted an indemnity of 3 000 sols and gave up its claim to Rocamadour. Marchilhac Abbey enjoyed remarkable prosperity until the 14C, but during the Hundred Years' War it was virtually destroyed by marauding bands of Englishmen and French mercenary troops. After the Reformation, the abbey, now only a ghost of its former self, fell into the hands of the Hébrards of St-Sulpice *(p 68)*. It finally disappeared during the Revolution.

SIGHTS

⊙ **Former Abbey**. – The ensemble is made up of two very distinct parts.

Romanesque part. – The west porch and the first three bays of the nave are open to the sky. They are flanked by a tall square tower, which was probably fortified in the 14C. A round-arched door on the south side is topped by sculpture forming a **tympanum** and depicting the Last Judgment: Christ in Majesty, with figures on either side representing, it is believed, the sun and the moon, appears above two thick-set angels with open wings, St Peter and St Paul. These carvings are archaic in style and would appear to date from the 10C. Go through this doorway and enter the church to the right.

Gothic part. – This part of the church, closed to the west from the fourth bay on, dates back to the 15C and is built in the Flamboyant style. The chancel has stellar vaulting and is circled by an ambulatory. The chapel on the right is adorned with wood carvings of episodes in the life of Christ; the one on the left has 15C frescoes: Christ in Benediction with the twelve Apostles; under each Apostle is his name and a phrase which characterises him. The coat of arms in the centre is that of the Hébrards of St-Sulpice.

On leaving the church, bear right (in the second Romanesque bay) onto the path to the former chapter house, which has delicately carved Romanesque capitals decorating the bays.

Make for an esplanade shaded by plane trees; a round tower marks the site of the abbot's house. Turn right and walk beside the Célé, following the ruins of the abbey ramparts, across from the cliff which looms above the river. Go through the postern and round the church to return to the starting point.

★**Bellevue Cave (Grotte de Bellevue)**. – *1.5km – 1 mile to the northwest.* The route leading up to the cave is a *corniche* road overlooking the Célé Valley and giving fine **glimpses** of the village and abbey. After a series of four steeply rising hairpin bends, branch off to the left in the direction of the hamlet of Pailhès. *Car park beyond and on the left.*

Discovered in 1964, this cave was opened to the public two years later. The cave contains a remarkable variety of concretions: stalactites, stalagmites, frozen falls, columns of different widths and vast flows of white calcite striped with ochre or dark red. Its large chamber is wonderful; the variety of eccentrics seem to flower like coral, forming different shapes in every direction.

The particularly delicate stalagmites resemble slim church candles. Hercules' Column (Colonne d'Hercule), reaching from the floor to the ceiling, is striking for its regularity. It is 4m — 13ft high with a circumference of 3.50m — 11 ft and the upper part is made up of a disc at an angle of 45° to the top of the column.

MAREUIL   Pop 1 215

Michelin map 🔢 southeast of fold 14 or 🔢 southeast of fold 30 — Local map p 105

Set between the vast open plains of Ribéracois and a more rugged landscape in the north, Mareuil-sur-Belle is a former barony, one of the four (the others being Beynac, Bourdeilles and Biron) in Périgord. It has kept its 15C castle.

From the castle, walk up the main street and note on the right through the openings in the wall an unusual neo-classical-style building. Two austere, protruding wings flank a portico held up by six Tuscan columns. Completed *c*1811, the building is most likely the work of Mathurin Blanchard, the architect of Rastignac *(qv)*.

Castle. – After having been the domain of the Mareuil family, the castle belonged to the Talleyrand-Périgords and then to the Montebellos, who own the castle to this day.

Built on the open plain, this fortress was protected by an impressive defensive system; remaining are the curtain wall and towers and a small section of the moat, fed by Belle River. From the entrance fort, a fortified postern, a ramp leads to the castle entrance which included a drawbridge defended by two round towers, topped by a machicolated watchpath. In the left tower is a Late Gothic chapel, damaged during the Revolution, with attractive ribbed vaulting. The restored main part of the castle, its buildings at a right angle, roofed with pink tile, opened with mullioned windows and linked together by an asymmetrical keep, overlooks a rampart-enclosed garden.

The visit includes the underground prisons and living quarters. The drawing room contains fine Louis XV furnishings and paintings by Nattier, Rigaud, Horace Vernet and Carolus Duran.

One room, entirely furnished in the Empire Style, is devoted to Marshal Lannes, duke of Montebello (1769-1809) and one of Napoleon's greatest generals. He took part in the *coup d'état* bringing Napoleon to power (1799), fought in the battles of Ulm, Austerlitz and Iéna (1805-06), and captured Saragossa (1809). Exhibited in the room is Lannes' memorabilia (letters, sword, bust of Napoleon by Canova, portraits...).

ROUND TOUR FROM MAREUIL *61km – 38 miles – about 2 hours*
Michelin map 🔢 folds 14 and 15 and 🔢 folds 4 and 5 or 🔢 folds 30 and 31

   Leave Mareuil on the D 708 northeast.

St-Sulpice-de-Mareuil. – Pop 128. The 12C Romanesque church has a lovely door. The porch, with three recessed arches held up by slender columns, is decorated with intriguing animals, people and scrolls. Inside, a dome on pendentives rests on historiated capitals.

   Take the D 93 south.

Vieux-Mareuil. – Pop 395. Facilities. The church, although built in the 13C, has all the characteristics of the Périgord Romanesque style; the nave is covered with three domes on pendentives, the two bay-long chancel is roofed with pointed-barrel vaulting and closed by a flat east end. The crenellations (16C) give the church a military aspect.

   Continue on the D 93 south.

Léguillac-de-Cercles. – Pop 319. The church is Romanesque, its nave is covered by two domes.

   Take the D 100 and the D 84 left. At a wayside cross bear left again.

Cercles. – Pop 137. All that remains of a Roman-esque priory is the church, the nave of which is 13C. The doorway presents six finely carved capitals.

La Tour-Blanche. – Pop 441. Coming from Cercles the visitor arrives at the foot of a mound overlooked by a 13C keep and the ruins of a stronghold which had been the fief of the Counts of Angoulême before being that of La Tours and Bourdeilles. The castle overlooks the village, which has preserved several lovely old houses and the Renaissance mansion of Nanchapt.

Take the D 84 towards Verteillac.

The itinerary passes at the foot of **Jovelle Castle's** (Château de Jovelle) ruins, the *lauze*-roofed chapel of which is still standing. Quite close to the castle a shelter, deco-rated with engravings (dating back *c*25 000 years), was discovered in 1983.

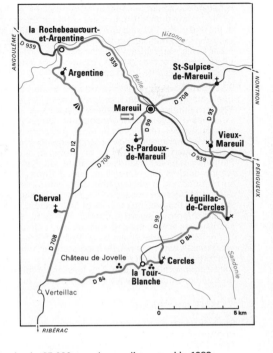

At Verteillac, turn right into the D 708 and left to Cherval.

Cherval. – Pop 295. This village has one of the loveliest domed churches of the region (restored by the Historic Buildings Commission). Four domes follow one right after another: three over the nave and one over the chancel, all held up by large pointed arches which assume the shape of the pendentives. The chancel vaulting is adorned with diamond-pointed rustication.

Return to the D 708 towards Mareuil then the D 12.

The road passes through a very wooded countryside, offering good views of Périgord Blanc *(qv)*.

2km – 1 mile before La Rochebeaucourt-et-Argentine bear right.

Argentine. – This unusual village perched on a limestone plateau, carved full of quarries and caves and looking like a Swiss cheese, has a charming 12C Romanesque chapel.

La Rochebeaucourt-et-Argentine. – Pop 408. La Rochebeaucourt has kept a 13C church built by monks of the Cluny order. Constructed in grey stone, its otherwise austere façade is enhanced by a rose window divided into seven parts. To the right of the façade stands a square two-storey bell tower.

The memory of Pauline de Tourzel (imprisoned with Louis XVI and his family at the Templar Prison) and her mother (governess to the royal children) is recalled in the former **castle park** of the Counts of Béarn (castle burned down in 1941), and in the Rochebeaucourt cemetery chapel.

Take the D 939 to Mareuil, bear right on the D 708 and left on the D 99.

St-Pardoux-de-Mareuil. – Lying on the valley slope, this hamlet's houses are grouped around a charming Romanesque church with its Saintonge-style façade and its superposed arches and arcades.

Return to Mareuil via the D 99 and the D 708.

★ MARTEL   Pop 1 441

Michelin map **75** fold 18 or **235** fold 2 — Facilities

Martel, built on the Haut-Quercy *causse* to which it has given its name (Martel Causse *qv*), is known as the "town of the seven towers". It still possesses many medieval buildings. Today it is a busy centre for the nut trade and the canning of local products.

The three hammers. – After stopping the Saracens at Poitiers in 732, **Charles Martel** pursued them into Aquitaine. Several years later he struck again and wiped them out. To commemorate this victory over the infidels and to give thanks to God, Charles Martel had a church built on the spot; soon a town grew up around the church. It was given the name of Martel in memory of its founder taking as its crest three hammers which were the favourite weapon of the saviour of Christianity.

Martel and the viscounty of Turenne. – The founding of Martel by the conqueror of the infidels is probably more fiction than fact. However, it is known that the viscounts of Turenne *(qv)* made Martel an important urban community as early as the 12C. In 1219, the Viscount Raymond IV granted a charter establishing Martel as a free town – exempt from the king's taxes, and with permission to mint money; yet the town stayed faithful to the king. Very quickly Martel established a town council and consulate and became the seat of the royal bailiwick and of the seneschalship.

It became a veritable court of appeal where all the region's judicial matters were treated; more than fifty magistrates, judges and lawyers were employed. Its peak was at the end of the 13 and beginning of the 14C; however, as in other parts of the region, the town suffered during the Hundred Years' War – tossed between English and French rule – and during the Wars of Religion – pillaged by the Huguenots. In 1738, when the sale of the rights of Turenne to the king occurred *(p 144)*, Martel lost its privileges and became just a castellany.

The rebellious son. – Martel was the scene, at the end of the 12C, of a tragic series of events which brought into conflict **Henry Plantagenet**, king of England and lord of all Western France, his wife Eleanor of Aquitaine and their four sons. The royal household was a royal hell. Henry could no longer stand the sight of Eleanor, who had previously been repudiated by the king of France, Lous VII, and shut her up in a tower. The sons, thereupon, took up arms against their father, and the eldest, **Henry Short Coat**, pillaged the viscounty of Turenne and Quercy. To punish him, Henry Plantagenet gave his lands to his third son, Richard Lionheart, and stopped the allowance paid to his eldest son. Henry Short Coat found himself without riches, surrounded and in an altogether desperate situation: to pay his foot-soldiers he plundered the treasure houses of the provincial abbeys. He took from Rocamadour the shrine and the precious stones of St Amadour, whose body was profaned; he sold Roland's famous sword Durandal. But as he was leaving Rocamadour, after this sacrilegious action, the bell miraculously began to toll: it was a sign from God. Henry fled to Martel, where he arrived with a fever; he felt death to be upon him and was stricken with remorse. He confessed his crimes while Henry II was sought to come and forgive his son on his death bed; Henry II was at the siege of Limoges and sent a messenger with his pardon. The messenger found Henry Short Coat lying in agony on a bed of cinders, a heavy wooden cross at his breast. Soon afterwards he died.

TOUR *time: 1 hour*

Former perimeter walls. – Boulevards – the Fossé des Cordeliers and the Fossé des Capitany – have been built on the site of the old ramparts (12 and 13C). The **Tournemire Tower (B)**, the former prison tower, crowned with machicolations and the Souillac and Brive Gateways (found at the end of Route de Souillac and Rue de Brive; *not on town plan*) recall the time when Martel was a fortified town, well protected by double perimeter walls. The second perimeter wall, built in the 18C, included the suburbs.

Leave the car in the car park along the north wall. Pass between the post office and the Tournemire Tower to enter the old town.

St-Maur. – This Gothic church has interesting defensive features: two battlemented towers rise from the ends of the flat east end and the main bay is surmounted by a line of machicolations. The bell tower, which is 48m – 157ft high and is flanked at its base by powerful buttresses, looks like a veritable castle keep with its narrow loopholes. Beneath the porch is a fine historiated Romanesque **tympanum** depicting the Last Judgment. It shows Christ seated, His head adorned with a cruciform halo, His arms stretched wide to show His wounds; two angels hold the instruments of the Passion while two others sound the trumpets of the Resurrection. The nave is wide and the chancel with its flat east end and stellar vaulting is lit by a large 16C **stained-glass window** showing God the Father, the four Evangelists and scenes from the Passion.

Rue Droite. – It is lined with old hôtels, one of which, Hôtel Vergres-de-Ferron (**D**), is adorned with a lovely Renaissance door.

★**Place des Consuls**. – In the centre of the square is the 18C **covered market**. On one side may be seen the town's former measures.

★**Hôtel de la Raymondie**. – This fine building was begun in *c*1280 by the viscount of Turenne and was completed in 1330. A crenellated belfry dominates the mansion which is flanked by a turret at each corner. In the 14C, this medieval fortress was transformed into a Gothic mansion. The court of honour is adorned with elegant four-lobed rose windows. The mansion, the former law courts, is now the town hall.

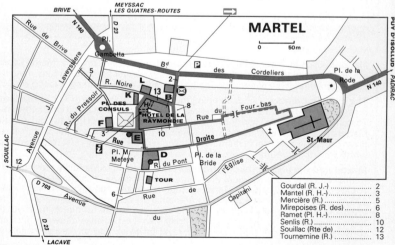

In the first floor rooms note the two carved wooden chimneypieces and the
ⓘ Renaissance low relief. In the keep's upper room a small **museum** contains items
found at the Puy d'Issolud excavations *(see below)*.

Fabri Mansion (Maison Fabri) (**E**). – This was where the young Henry died in 1183.

Hôtel de Chauffour (**F**). – On the west side of the square stands this 16-17C mansion.

Rue Tournemire (**13**). – This picturesque small street to the left of the Hôtel de la
Raymondie runs along the 13C Hôtel de la Monnaie (**K**) and other old houses such as
the unusual 16C grey mansion (**L**) which bears on one of its coat of arms the three
hammers, the arms of the town.

EXCURSION

★**Puy d'Issolud**. – *14km – 9 miles. Leave Martel to the east.*
The plateau near Vayrac, of which the highest point is Puy d'Issolud with an altitude
of 311m – 1 020ft, is bordered by steep cliffs overlooking little streams flowing into
the Dordogne.
Puy d'Issolud was surrounded, at the time of the Gauls, by such solid earthworks and
dry-stone defences that it was one of the most redoubtable oppidums of Quercy, and
is said to have been the former Uxellodunum, site of the last Gaulish resistance to
Caesar after Alesia. Some historians place Uxellodunum at Capdenac *(qv)*. The
battle, led by the Roman legionaries, was waged with unbelievable ferocity and, after
a stream had been diverted through underground caverns, ended with another
defeat for the Gauls. Caesar, angered at the resistance put up by the besieged Gauls
ordered, so it is said, each prisoner's right hand to be cut off.
Items discovered during excavations are on display in the museum of the Hôtel de
la Raymondie in Martel *(p 106)*.
From the plateau there is an extensive, although interrupted **view**★ of the Dordogne.

★ Château de MONBAZILLAC

Michelin map **75** folds 14 and 15 or **234** fold 8 – Local map p 46

ⓘ The Château de Monbazillac rises proudly amidst a sea of vines *(p 16)* on the edge
of a limestone plateau overlooking the valley of the Dordogne. It is owned by the
Monbazillac Wine Cooperative, which restored and refurbished it.
Built in 1550 this château, surrounded by a dry moat, attracts the eye with its elegant
silhouette in an architectural style half-way between the military and the Renaissance.
A crenallated watchpath and machicolations surmount the main building, which is
flanked at each corner by a massive round tower. The façade is pierced by a double
row of mullioned windows and a doorway ornamented in the Renaissance style. Two
tiers of dormer windows rise above the machicolations. The grey patina of the stone
tones in well with the brown tiled roofs of the turrets and the pavilions.
The north terrace affords a good view of the vineyard and beyond, of Bergerac
sprawled out in the Dordogne Valley.

Interior. – The **Great Hall**, its painted ceiling decorated with gilt foliated scrolls, has a
monumental Renaissance chimneypiece, 17C furnishings and two fine Flemish
tapestries of the same period. In an adjoining room are displayed rustic furniture
from the Périgord region. There are also interesting documents tracing the history of
Protestantism in France in another room.
Several rooms are open on the first floor; note in particular the Viscountess of
Monbazillac's **bedroom** furnished in Louis XIII style.
The former castle cellars house a small **wine museum** displaying harvesting and wine-
making equipment used in the past.

★ MONPAZIER   Pop 533

Michelin map **75** fold 16 or **235** north of fold 9 – Facilities

Monpazier was one of the *bastides (qv)* built to command the roads going from
Agenais to the banks of the Dordogne. The square, surrounded by arcades, the *carreyrous (qv)*, the old houses, the church and the ruined fortifications make it the best
preserved of the Périgord *bastides*.

A difficult start. – The *bastide*
of Monpazier was founded on
7 January 1285 by **Edward I**, king of
England and duke of Aquitaine. This
bastide was designed to complete
the defences and control of Périgord
begun in 1267 with the founding of
Lalinde, Beaumont, Molières and
Roquépine. To this end Edward I
allied himself with Pierre de
Gontaut, Lord of Biron. But difficul-
ties soon arose: delays occurred in
the building, there were disagree-
ments between the lord of Biron and
the people of Monpazier and hostilities broke out between the king of
England and Philip the Fair.

Place du 19-mars-1962

The situation soon became complicated with the result that during the Hundred Years' War the *bastide* was assaulted and pillaged as often by the English as by the French.

Monpazier receives royalty. – The Reformation, in which the Marshal of Biron took a prominent part, marked the start of a violent epoch. On 21 June 1574, the town was betrayed and fell into the hands of the well-known Huguenot leader, Geoffroi de Vivans, who later won fame with the capture of Domme *(p 72)*.

Jeanne d'Albret, who was going to the wedding of her son Henri of Navarre to Margaret of Valois, stayed at Monpazier. In her honour "the streets and squares were scrubbed and the dunghills were taken away". Such homage to the most militant Calvinist did not prevent the town from spending freely, soon afterwards, to receive the Duke of Anjou – the future Henry III of France – leader of the Catholics.

Buffarot the Croquant. – After the Wars of Religion were over, the peasants rose in a new revolt. The rebels, who were known as the *croquants (qv)*, held a great gathering at Monpazier in 1594. The revolt flared up again in 1637. Led by Buffarot, a weaver from the neighbouring town of Capdrot, 8 000 peasants tore through the countryside plundering the castles.

The soldiers of the Duke of Épernon pursued them and after some difficulty, captured Buffarot. He was brought back to Monpazier, and as leader of the revolt, was broken on the wheel in the main square.

SIGHTS

The general layout of the *bastide* can still be seen together with three of its original six fortified gateways; several houses have kept their ancient appearance.

The town is in the shape of a quadrilateral 400mx220m – 1312ft x 722ft, the main axe orientated north-south. Streets run from one end to the other, parallel with the longer sides, four cross-roads running east to west dividing the town into rectangular blocks. Originally all the houses had the unique characteristic of being of equal size and separated from each other by narrow spaces or *androns*, to prevent the spread of fire.

★**Place du 19-mars-1962.** – The picturesque main square is rectangular like the *bastide* itself. On the south side stands a covered market containing the old measures. Round the perimeter, the arcades or covered galleries, supported on arches, which are sometimes pointed, have kept their *cornières*.

St-Dominique. – The church façade has been restored at different times: the doorway was adorned with archivolts, the rose window and the gable rebuilt in *c*1550. The single aisle is wide, has pointed vaulting and is extended to form a polygonal east end.

Chapter house (Maison du Chapitre). – This 13C house stands near the church Place du 19-mars-1962 and was used as a tithe barn. It is lit by paired windows on the upper floor.

MONPAZIER

Admission times and charges to the sights described are listed at the end of the Guide.

Every sight for which there are times and charges is indicated by the symbol ⓥ in the margin in the main part of the Guide.

★★ MONTAL CASTLE

Michelin map 75 fold 19 or 235 fold 7 or 239 fold 39 – 3km – 2 miles west of St-Céré – Local map p 133

Montal Castle groups the harmonious mass of its buildings with their pepper-pot roofs on a wooded mound on a hillside near the smiling Bave Valley.

The miracle of mother love. – **Jeanne de Balsac d'Entraygues,** widow of Amaury de Montal, Governor of Haute-Auvergne, built in 1523 a country mansion on the site of a feudal stronghold for her eldest son, Robert, who was away warring in Italy for François I. The chatelaine had the best artists and workmen brought from the banks of the Loire to Quercy and by 1534, there could be seen the masterpiece begotten of a mother's tender pride.

"Hope no more". – Everything was ready to receive the proud knight. But days, years passed; Marignano, Pavia, Madrid are far away; the mother waited daily for her eldest son's arrival. Alas, only Robert's body returned to the castle. The dream crumbled. Jeanne had the high window from which she had watched for her son blocked up and beneath it she had carved the despairing cry "Hope No More" *(plus d'espoir)*. Jeanne's second son, Dordé de Montal, a church dignitary, was absolved by the pope from his ecclesiastical duties in order that he might continue the line; he subsequently married and had nine children.

Death and resurrection. – Montal was declared a national asset but became uninhabitable as a result of the depredations made during the Revolution: finally in 1879 it fell into the hands of a certain Macaire. This adventurer, permanently short of cash, made a bargain with a demolition group and divided the palace into lots: 120 tons of carved stone were parcelled up and sent to Paris. The masterpieces of Montal were then auctioned and dispersed throughout the museums and private collections of Europe and the United States. In 1908 Montal rose from the ruins: the new and devoted owner set about finding and buying back at ransom prices all the Montal treasures, until he had refurnished the castle. He donated it to the nation in 1913.

⏱ TOUR *time: about 3/4 hour*

Exterior. – Steeply pitched *lauzes* roofs and massive round towers with loopholes give the castle its fortress-like appearence. But this fierce exterior makes the contrast all the greater with the inner courtyard, designed with all the graceful charm of the Renaissance.
Montal consists of two main wings set at right angles linked at the corner by a square tower containing the staircase. A two-storey gallery, also set at a right angle to complete the square, was planned for the other two sides of the courtyard but was never erected. The façade of the main building, in all its rich decoration, is one of the castle's chief glories.

The frieze. – Above the ground floor windows and doors runs a frieze 32m – 105ft long. It is a marvel of decorative diversity: cupids, birds, fantasies appear beside shields and a huge human head. There are also initials of the founder and her sons: I (Jeanne), R (Robert) and D (Dordé).

The busts. – On the first floor the mullioned windows alternate with false bays with intricately carved pediments, which contain seven busts in high relief, all masterpieces of realism and taste. Each statue is a likeness of a member of the Montal family; from left to right they are: Amaury with a haughty air, wearing a hat; Jeanne, his wife and the founder of the castle, who has an almost conventual cast of countenance in which sorrow seems perpetual; Robert, the eldest son killed in Italy, wears a François I-style plumed hat; Dordé, the second son is shown as a young page; Jeanne's parents, Robert de Balsac with a Louis XII-style hat and Antoinette de Castelnau, and Dordé de Béduer, last member in the line, who was abbot of Vézelay.

The windows. – There are four and they recall, in their decoration, those of Chambord: the dormer gables have small supporting figures on either side and the niches contain statues.

Interior. – The entrance is at the corner, where the wings meet, by a door flanked by pilasters and topped by a lintel supporting several niches.

★★Renaissance staircase. – The staircase is built in the fine gold-coloured stone from Carennac, magnificently proportioned and decorated. Admire the fine carving beneath the stairs: ornamented foliage, shells, fantastic birds, initials and little figures go in to make a ceiling, the decoration of which completes that of the lierne and tierceron vaulting of the vestibules. This masterpiece of sculpture combines grace and imagination.

The apartments. – The guard room, vaulted with basket-handled arches, has a lovely chimneypiece, the Stag Room (Salle du Cerf) and the other rooms in which are to be found old pieces of furniture (mainly in the Renaissance and Louis XIII styles), retables, paintings and plates attributed to Bernard Palissy *(qv)*, and tapestries from Flanders and Tours form an admirable group.

★ MONTFORT

Michelin map 75 fold 17 or 235 fold 37 – Local map pp 76-77

Occupying a privileged site on the Dordogne River, Montfort has given its name to one of Périgord's most famous meanders.
The tiny *lauze*-roofed village nestles at the foot of its castle, perched on a rock pitted with holes.

★Montfort Meander (Cingle de Montfort). – A bend *(car park)* in the road (D 703), built into the rock, offers a lovely view★ below of a meander of the Dordogne: the course of the river is outlined by a row of poplars, while the castle clings to its promontory.

Montfort Castle. – The castle stands in a picturesque **setting★**. Its exceptional site roused the envy of those who wished to rule Périgord; its history consisted of a long series of sieges and battles. Belonging to the lord of Cazenac, the castle was siezed by the redoubtable **Simon de Montfort** *(qv)* in 1214, who razed it to the ground. It was rebuilt for the first time and then later destroyed three times – during the Hundred Years' War (1337-1453), under Louis XI (1461-83), and again by order of Henri IV (1562-1610) – only to be rebuilt. The left wing was restored at the end of the 19C and the other buildings date from the 15 and 16C.

MONTIGNAC — Pop 3 165

Michelin map **75** south of fold 7 or **233** fold 44 – Local map pp 116 and 146 – Facilities

Lying along the banks of the Vézère River, Montignac presents a group of houses around a tower, a last reminder of the fortress which once belonged to the counts of Périgord. In only a few years, this pleasant town became an important tourist centre due to the discovery of Lascaux Cave *(p 96)*.
Eugène Le Roy *(qv)*, the well-known Périgord writer, lived in Montignac.

Eugène Le Roy Museum (Musée Eugène-Le-Roy). – Housed in the tourist information centre, this museum is in part devoted to the author of *Jacquou le Croquant*; the room where Le Roy wrote the story of a peasant revolt has been reconstructed.
Other rooms are devoted to ancient crafts no longer practiced and reconstructions of scenes from local history.
There is also a small prehistoric collection.

EXCURSIONS

★Tour of Périgord Noir. – *56km – 35 miles from Montignac to Sarlat. Description p 115.*

★St-Amand-de-Coly. – *9km – 5 1/2 miles on the D 704 and a small road to the left. Description p 129.*

★Ans Country. – *Round tour 101km – 62 1/2 miles. Description p 38.*

La Grande Filolie. – *4km – 2 1/2 miles on the D 704 and a small road to the right. Description p 115.*

*Book well in advance as you may have difficulty
in finding a room for the night during the summer season.*

★ MONTPEZAT-DE-QUERCY — Pop 1 412

Michelin map **79** fold 18 or **235** fold 18 – Facilities

On the edge of Limogne Causse, this picturesque small Bas-Quercy town, which still displays its covered arcades and old half-timbered or stone houses, owes its fame and its artistic treasures to the munificence of the Des Prés family.

The Des Prés family. – Five members of this family, which came from Montpezat, became eminent prelates.
Pierre Des Prés, Cardinal of Préneste (now Palestrina in Italy), founded the Collegiate Church of St Martin, which he consecrated in 1344; his nephew, Jean Des Prés, who died in 1351, was Bishop of Coïmbra in Portugal and then of Castres in France. Three other members of the family were consecrated bishops of Montauban: Jean Des Prés (1517-39), who gave his famous Flemish tapestries to the collegiate church at Montpezat, Jean de Lettes (1539-56) and Jacques Des Prés (1556-89). Jacques was a warrior-bishop, an inveterate pursuer of the Huguenots. He fought on for 25 years, his diocese being one of the most ardent Protestant strongholds, and was killed in an ambush at Lalbenque, some 15km – 10 miles from Montpezat.

COLLEGIATE CHURCH OF ST MARTIN
(COLLÉGIALE ST-MARTIN) *time: 1/2 hour*

This church, which is dedicated to St Martin of Tours, was built in 1337 by an architect from the papal court at Avignon. Comparatively small in size, it has many of the characteristics of a Languedoc building: a single nave with no side aisles and chapels separated by the nave's interior buttresses.

Church vessel. – Unity, simplicity and harmony are brought to mind upon entering the church vessel. Its pointed vaulting has hanging keystones painted with the founder's coat of arms. The side chapels hold religious objects worth noting: a 15C Our Lady of Pity in multicoloured sandstone (1st chapel on the south side), three 15-16C Nottingham alabaster altarpiece panels (2nd chapel on the south side), 14C alabaster Virgin and Doves (2nd chapel on the north side), and two 15C wooden caskets (4th chapel on the north side).

★★Tapestries. – These 16C tapestries, which were especially made to fit the sanctuary and are nearly 25m – 82ft in length and 3m – 6ft in height, were woven in workshops in the north of France and consist of five panels, each divided into three scenes. They are of outstanding interest for they are in excellent condition, have brilliance and richness of colouring and they still hang in the exact spot for which they were designed.

Tapestry representing St Martin dividing his cloak

Sixteen scenes depict the best-known historic and legendary events in the life of St Martin and include the dividing of his cloak, many of the cures performed by the saint and his victorious struggle with the devil.

Each scene is accompanied by a quatrain in old French woven at the top of the panel.

★Recumbent figures. – Although the body of Cardinal Pierre Des Prés lies beneath the paving before the chancel, his statue and tomb carved in Carrara marble are at the right of the chancel entrance where they were placed in 1778. Opposite, making the pair, lies the recumbent figure of his nephew Jean Des Prés, a masterpiece of funerary statuary.

EXCURSION

Saux – *4km – 2 1/2 miles. Leave Montpezat to the west.*
This **church**, once the centre of a large parish, now stands isolated in the middle of the woods. The plain interior consists of three domed bays decorated with fine 14 and 15C **frescoes**. The best preserved are in the chancel and show Christ in Majesty with the symbols of the four Evangelists, the Crucifixion and scenes from the Childhood of Jesus. In the south chapel may be seen the legend of St Catherine; and in the north chapel, the legend of St George.

MUSSIDAN   Pop 3 236

Michelin map 🔢 south of fold 4 or 🔢 fold 41 – Local map p 80

Set on the banks of Isle River, this ancient Huguenot city is an industrial town.

Périgord's André Voulgre Museum of Popular Arts and Traditions (Musée des Arts et Traditions Populaires du Périgord André-Voulgre). – Located in the lovely Périgord mansion where Doctor Voulgre lived, this collection is rich and varied; it includes furniture, objects and tools assembled by the doctor during his lifetime.

A 19C handsomely furnished bourgeois interior – kitchen, dining room, drawing room, bedrooms – has been reproduced in several of the museum's rooms.

Workshops (cooper's shop, sabot maker, blacksmith) have also been reconstituted. A collection of agricultural machinery and tools is set up in the barn: a 1927 steam engine, a still, a tractor (1920) built with the tracks of tanks used in World War I, and a reaper-binder.

In a large exhibition hall, brass, pewter, glazed earthenware and stuffed animals are displayed.

EXCURSIONS

Round tour of 43km – 26 1/2 miles. *About 1 1/2 hours from Mussidan; the road skirts Crempse Valley.*
Château de Montréal. – This half-feudal, half-Renaissance building, surrounded by fine outbuildings, stands at the top of a hill overlooking the Crempse. In the 18C drawing room, Louis XVI medallion-backed chairs upholstered with the Fables of La Fontaine can be seen.

In the outbuildings is a 12C staircase roofed with a row of barrel vaults, forming steps and leading to the cellars; this proceeds into a natural cave adorned with small concretions.

According to the legend, the town of Montreal on the St. Lawrence owes its name to the lord of Montréal, Claude de Pontbriand, one of Jacques Cartier's companions on his second voyage to Canada.

A chapel was built in the 16C to shelter the reliquary of the Holy Thorn found on Talbot's body at the Battle of Castillon *(p 22)*.

Return to the D 38 and bear left on the D4.

Villamblard. – Pop 824. In the village stand the ruins of a 15C fortress. It still possesses fine moulded mullioned windows and an interesting ogee-arched portal.

Continue on the D4 and bear left on the D 107.

Grignols Castle. – This fortress, which belonged to the Grignols and Talleyrands, defended the road between Périgueux and Bordeaux. Perched on a rocky crest overlooking Vern Valley, the fortress is set on a triangular terrace between two moats. The buildings (built between 13 and 17C) overlap one another and are dominated by a square keep. Most of them were taken down during the Fronde (1648-52) *(qv)*. The 13C lords' room, although partly in ruins, contains lovely chimneypieces adorned with rosettes. Other furnished rooms in the castle can be visited.

Cross the Vern River and take the D 44 towards Neuvic-sur-l'Isle.

The road borders the poplar-lined river on its way to Neuvic-sur-l'Isle, an industrial town (large shoe factory).

The N 89 returns of Mussidan.

St-Martin-l'Astier – Pop 140. *4km – 2 1/2 miles northwest.* The unusual silhouette of this Romanesque church marks the limits of the Double *(qv)*. The large octagonal bell tower is held up by buttress-columns at each of the eight sides. Housed in the bell tower's lower section is a chapel vaulted with a dome, which is used as the chancel and communicates via a narrow door in one of the sides with the plain timber-roofed nave added not long after; the nave opens onto the exterior by a Romanesque door with five recessed arches.

★★★ PADIRAC CHASM (GOUFFRE DE PADIRAC)

Michelin map ▨▨ fold 19 or ▨▨▨ northeast of fold 7 or ▨▨▨ folds 38 and 39 – Facilities

The Padirac Chasm provides access to wonderful galleries hollowed out of the limestone mass of Gramat Causse *(qv)* by a subterranean river. A visit into the vertiginous well and a tour of the mysterious river and the vast caves adorned with limestone concretions give the tourist a striking impression of this fascinating underground world.

From legend to scientific exploration. – The Padirac Chasm terrorised the local inhabitants right up to the 19C, as the origin of this great hole was believed to be due to the devil.

St Martin, so the tale went, was returning from an expedition on the *causse* where he had been looking unsuccessfully for souls to save. Suddenly his mule refused to advance: Satan, bearing a great sack full of souls which he was taking to hell, stood before the saint. Satan mocked the poor saint and made him a proposition: he would give him the souls he had in his sack on condition that St Martin would make his mule cross an obstacle that he, the devil, would create on the spot. He hit the ground hard with his foot and the chasm gaped open. The saint coaxed his mule forward and the beast jumped clear, leaving hoofprints which are still visible, so that the beaten devil retreated to hell by way of the hole he had created.

The chasm served as a refuge for the people living on the *causse* during the Hundred Years' War and the Wars of Religion, but it would appear that it was towards the end of the 19C, following a violent flooding of the river, that a practicable line of communication opened between the bottom of the well and the underground galleries. The speleologist, **Édouard A. Martel**, was the first to discover the passage in 1889. Between 1889 and 1900 he undertook nine expeditions and in 1890 reached the Hall of the Great Dome.

Padirac was opened for the first time to tourists in 1898. Since then, numerous speleological expeditions have uncovered 22km – 13 1/2 miles of underground galleries.

The 1947 expedition proved by fluorescein colouring of the water that the Padirac River reappears above ground 11km – 7 miles away where the Lombard rises and at the St George's spring in the **Montvalent Amphitheatre** *(qv)* near the Dordogne.

During the expeditions of 1984 and 1985, a team of speleologists, paleontologists, prehistorians and geologists discovered a prehistoric site, 9km – 5 1/2 miles from the mouth of the hole, on an affluent of the Joly, with bones of mammoths, rhinoceroses, bisons, bears, cave-dwelling lions and deer, all of which were found to date from 150 to 200 000 years ago. Amidst the bones found were chipped flints dating from 30 to 50 000 years ago. Copies of some of the bones are exhibited in the chasm's entrance hall.

TOUR *time: about 1 1/2 hours*

Two lifts and staircases lead into the chasm, which is 99m – 325ft in circumference and to the pyramid of rubble, debris of the original falling-in of the roof. From the bottom of the lift (75m – 247ft), there is a striking view of walls covered by the overflow from stalagmites, vegetation and a little corner of the sky at the mouth of the hole. Stairs lead down to the underground river, 103m – 338ft below ground level. At the bottom, the 2 000m – 1 1/4 mile underground journey begins, 700m – 1/2 mile of which is by boat.

PADIRAC CHASM AND UNDERGROUND RIVER

Gallery of the Spring (Galerie de la Source). – This chamber is at the end of an underground canyon, the roof of which rises gradually; it is 300m – 984ft long and follows the upper course of the river that hollowed it out. At the far end is the landing-stage.

Smooth River (Rivière Plane). – A flotilla of flat-bottomed boats offers an enchanted journey over the smooth and astonishingly translucent waters of the river. The depth of the river varies from 50cm to 4m (20in to 13ft), but the water temperature remains constant at 10.5°C (51 °F). The height of the roof rises progressively to reach a maximum of 78m – 256ft; from the boat the different levels of erosion corresponding to the successive courses of the river may be seen.

At the end of the boat trip admire the **Great Pendant** (Grande Pendeloque) of **Rainfall Lake** (Lac de la Pluie). This giant stalactite, the point of which nearly touches the water, is the ultimate pendant in a chaplet of concretions 78m – 256ft in height.

Crocodile Path (Pas du Crocodile). – A narrow passage between high walls links the underground lake and the chambers to be visited next. Look to the left at the **Great Pillar** (Grand Pilier), 40m – 131ft high.

The Hall of the Great Natural Dams (Salle des Grands Gours). – A series of pools separated by *gours,* natural limestone dams, divides the river and the lake into superb basins, beyond which can be seen a 6m – 20ft waterfall. This is the end of the area open to tourists.

Upper Lake (Lac Supérieur). – This lake is fed only by water infiltrating the soil and falling from the roof; the level is 20m – 66ft above that of the Smooth River. *Gours* ring the lake's emerald waters.

Hall of the Great Dome (Salle du Grand Dôme). – The great height of the roof is most impressive – 91m – 295ft up – in this, the largest and most beautiful of the Padirac caverns. The belvedere, built half-way up, enables the rock formations and the flows of calcite decorating certain parts of the walls to be seen. The return trip (to the landing-stage) offers you interesting views of the Great Pillar and the Great Pendant. From the end of the Gallery of the Spring, four lifts (to avoid the walk up 455 steps) lead back to the entrance.

ADDITIONAL SIGHT

Tropicorama Zoo (Zoo le Tropicorama). – Located in a verdant site, admire the Bonzaï garden, cacti, rare tropical plants and the zoo, housing a large collection of exotic birds (parrots, horn bills, toucans, birds of prey etc) and an interesting selection of mammals (rare monkeys, lemurs, ocelots etc). Some of the animals roam freely.

PARCOUL   Pop 377

Michelin map 75 fold 3 or 233 fold 40 – 9.5km – 6 miles west of Ste-Aulaye

Located on the border of Périgord and Angoumois, this small village has an interesting church. Note its very ornate Romanesque apse in the Charente style.

Le Paradou Recreational Park (Parc de Loisirs du Paradou). – *2km – 1 mile south on the D 674 towards La Roche-Chalais.*
Spread over 15ha – 38 acres this recreational park, with its lake, offers enjoyment for one and all. Among the activities found in the park are miniature golf, tennis, a Far West train and the spectacular waterslides.

PAUNAT   Pop 217

Michelin map 75 fold 16 or 235 north of fold 5 – 7km – 4 miles northeast of Trémolat

Paunat lies snugly in a small valley near the confluence of the Dordogne and the Vézère. It possesses an impressive Romanesque church which formed part of a monastery once attached to the powerful Abbey of St-Martial at Limoges.

St-Martial. – Built in fine ochre-coloured stone in the 12C, this church was altered in the 15C. The exterior is austere with bare walls and high flat buttresses rising right to the roof eaves, which is covered in small tiles. The massive belfry porch, with an upper storey chamber vaulted with a dome on pendentives, seen rarely in the Périgord, leads to the church's vast main body. The long nave with its soaring pointed vaulting extends to the transept crossing, which is capped by a dome resting on pointed arches. A restoration program was launched in 1977. The ground excavations have uncovered, at the north pillar, parts of the lower wall (12C) and other earlier parts which may date from the 9 and 10C.

Michelin map 🎫 fold 9 or 🎫🎫🎫 northeast of fold 14 – Local map p 69

Prehistoric man performed religious rites in this cave *(p 149)* lost to history, and only rediscovered thousands of years later in 1922. Interesting for its natural decoration, there are also wall paintings and carvings which are of great documentary value to prehistorians.

The underground explorers. – Two boys of fourteen were the heroes of the Pech Merle Cave rediscovery.

Inspired by the expeditions and discoveries made in all the region by Abbé **Lemozi**, the priest from Cabrerets, who was a prehistorian and speleologist, the boys explored a small fault known only as having served as a refuge during the Revolution. The two friends pushed ahead, creeping along a narrow, slimy trench cut by wells and blocked by limestone concretions. After several hours their efforts were rewarded by the sight of wonderful paintings.

Abbé Lemozi, who soon afterwards explored the cave scientifically, recognised the importance of the underground sanctuary; it was decided to open it to tourists. In 1949 the discovery of a new chamber led to the finding of the original opening through which men had entered the cave about 10 to 20 000 years ago.

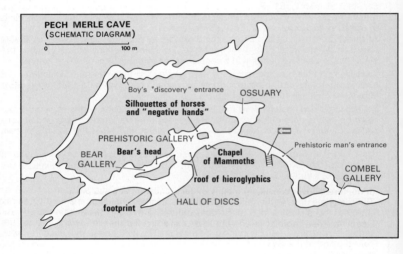

PECH MERLE CAVE
(SCHEMATIC DIAGRAM)
0   100 m

Boy's "discovery" entrance
OSSUARY
Silhouettes of horses and "negative hands"
PREHISTORIC GALLERY
Prehistoric man's entrance
Bear's head
BEAR GALLERY
Chapel of Mammoths
COMBEL GALLERY
roof of hieroglyphics
footprint
HALL OF DISCS

Ⓥ **TOUR** *time: about 1 3/4 hours*

In addition to the interest that there is for lovers of speleology in seeing caverns of vast size communicating with each other through wide openings and decorated with beautiful concretions, the Pech Merle Cave offers prehistorians the sight of highly advanced paintings and engravings and material traces of prehistoric man's sojourn there.

Visitors may, at present, walk through 1 200m – 1 mile of chambers and galleries. The upper level of the Prehistoric Gallery (Salle Préhistorique) is called the **Chapel of Mammoths** (Chapelle des Mammouths) or the black frieze; it is decorated with drawings of bison and mammoths outlined in black and forming a frieze 7m – 23ft long by 3m – 10ft high.

The Hall of Discs (Salle des Disques) is ornamented with many strange concretions that look like discs; the origin of their formation remains unsolved. The footprints made by a prehistoric man may be seen petrified for ever, in the once wet clay of a *gour* (natural dam).

Farther on are huge, impressive columns, eccentrics with fine protuberances that defy the laws of gravity and cave pearls, whose colours range from the shining white of pure calcite to red-ochre caused by the presence in the limestone of clay and iron oxide.

Go down a narrow passageway, where a bear's head has been engraved, to the lower level of the Prehistoric Gallery, where one wall is decorated with the **silhouettes of two horses**, covered and surrounded by dots, mysterious symbols and outlined hand prints, known as "negative hands" *(illustration p 21)*. These prints were made by stencilling in different pigments around the hands placed flat against the rock. The horses are depicted with deformed silhouettes (similar to those at Lascaux): a huge body and a tiny head. These prints and the roof of hieroglyphics decorated a sanctuary older than that of the Chapel of Mammoths.

In the last cave to be visited, Combel Gallery (Salle de Combel) are the bones of cave bears and the roots of an oak tree that bored down into the cave in search of moisture.

Ⓥ **Amédée Lemozi Museum** (Musée Amédée-Lémozi). – This is a research and information centre on the prehistory in Quercy. On the lower floor, which is open to the public, there is an attractive and informative display of bones, tools, arms, ustensils and works of art from 160 different prehistoric sites, ranging from the Lower Palaeolithic to the Iron Age. In an adjoining room are exhibited photographs of the decorated caves in the region (in particular Pech Merle and Cougnac). The museum visit ends with a film on palaeolothic art in Quercy.

Michelin map 🔲 fold 19 or 🔲 northeast of fold 22 – Local map p 130

The old village, overlooked by its castle ruins, is perched in a remarkable **setting★**, clinging to a rock spike which rises sheer above the left bank of the Aveyron in the prettiest part of its course *(p 127)*. There is a good view from the D 33 to the north of the village and from the D 133 to the south.

The complicated outline of the powerful medieval fortress with its jagged walls, in some cases poised on the very edge of the rock and seeming to defy all the laws of gravity, rises above the flat roofs of the village houses.

Village. – *Leave the car on the D 9, at the entrance to the village*. A narrow street leads to the church, whose bell tower, pierced by a pointed arch, marks the entrance to the fortified village. The chancel lost its bastion-like appearance in the 17C, when the church's main entrance was opened.

From the bell tower, a picturesque street lined with old houses climbs to the castle, then descends to Peyrière Gate on the village's opposite side.

The 17C plague cross, which brings to mind the scourge that hit Penne several times, indicates the path to climb to the tower ruins.

Castle. – The castle's location made it a key factor in the history of Quercy. At the time of the Albigensian Crusade, it became the stake in the bloody wars fought by the lord of Penne, supporting the revolt, and the followers of Simon de Montfort *(qv)*. Later, during the Hundred Years' War, the English and the local troops seized it from each other time after time. It only fell into ruins last century.

From the tip of the promontory, enjoy a good **view★** of the towers and jagged walls of the castle, of Penne and the Aveyron Valley.

The towns and sights described in this Guide are shown in black on the maps.

★ PÉRIGORD NOIR

Michelin map 🔲 folds 7 and 17 or 🔲 fold 2 and 6

A vast cretaceous plateau, carved by the Vézère River to the west and the Dordogne River to the south, overruns into Sarladais.

Périgord Noir means Black Périgord and the word "black" refers to the dark colour of the forest cover consisting mainly of oaks, chestnut and sea pines.

The materials used in the building of houses, castles, châteaux, manor-houses and churches consist of: walls of golden-coloured limestone (from the region) and steeply-pitched roofs covered with *lauzes* or small flat tiles in a warm brown hue. These architectural elements, combined with the rolling, wooded countryside, compose a lovely picture.

Part of Périgord Noir is described in the itinerary of the Dordogne Valley from Souillac to Limeuil *(pp 76-78)*, the other part in the Vézère Valley itinerary from Montignac to Limeuil *(pp 146-147)*, while the itinerary described below journeys along the triangle formed by the Vézère and Dordogne Rivers.

FROM MONTIGNAC TO SARLAT

56km – 35 miles – about 3 hours – local map p 116

Montignac. – *Description p 110.*

> *Leave Montignac on the D 704 towards Sarlat. After 4km — 2 1/2 miles bear right towards La Grande Filolie.*

La Grande Filolie. – Set in the hollow of a small valley, this charming castle *(photograph below)*, dating from the 14 and 15C, presents a group of overlapping buildings and towers linked together. This part-castle, part-farm is built in golden-coloured limestone and covered with a superb roof of *lauzes*. The castle includes, the nobles' residence, a 15C quadrangular building, flanked at each end by a square machicolated tower, a Renaissance wing, a gatehouse, with its bartizan, and a chapel, which at one end has a round tower with a very pointed roof.

La Grande Filolie

Return to the D 704 and take the first road on the left towards St-Amand-de-Coly.

★St-Amand-de-Coly. – *Description p 129.*

From St-Amant take the D 64 and go south.

★St-Geniès. – Pop 710. With its church, manor-house and numerous *lauzes*-roofed houses, this village is one of the loveliest of Périgord Noir.

Located at the top of a mound, the **Cheylard Chapel** (Chapelle du Cheylard), a small Gothic edifice, is adorned with lovely 14C frescoes depicting medievally dressed figures (horseman, craftsman).

The road, on the left after a wayside cross, descends into a cool valley to St-Crépin-et-Carlucet.

St-Crépin-et-Carlucet. – The charming **Cipières Manor-House** (Manoir de Cipières) was built at the end of the 16C at the spot where a fortified building had once stood. Entirely roofed in

lauzes, the square main building is framed by turrets.

The Romanesque **church**, farther down, was altered during the Gothic period.

Continue winding along this narrow country road through the valley to Carlucet.

Carlucet. – Pop 310. St-Crépin and Carlucet form one *commune*. The church of Carlucet has an unusual 17C cemetery. Some of the tombs have been set in carved recesses in the curtain wall.

Join up with the D 60 and turn right.

Salignac-Eyvigues. – *Description p 137.*

Eyrignac Manor-House (Manoir d'Eyrignac). – Lovely 18C **gardens★** (avenues of greenery, with parterres of yew, boxwood and hornbeam) surround an elegant 17C manorhouse of the Sarlat region.

The chapel, located in a square pavilion near the entrance, is decorated with a tiny balustraded gallery.

At Simeyrols take the D 47 towards Sarlat.

The road, to the south, crosses **Ste-Nathalène**, which has an austere Romanesque church.

Temniac. – The chapel of Notre-Dame, set on a hill overlooking Sarlat, offers a good **view★**, of that city.

A pilgrimage centre, this 12C structure presents certain Romanesque Périgord School characteristics *(qv)*: nave vaulted with two domes and a pentagonal chancel. Near the chapel stands the curtain wall of a castle (now in ruins), which had been a commandery of the Knights Templars before it became the residence of the bishops of Sarlat.

★★Sarlat. – *Description p 138*

THE WARS OF RELIGION IN PÉRIGORD

Religious strife still exists, and yet it is hard to imagine Périgord during the Wars of Religion. This lovely, harmonious region became a battlefield due to religious ideals.

Imagine this region ravaged for some thirty years (1562-94) by eight military campaigns. Towns and cities were constantly changing hands (Sarlat, Périgueux, Mussidan, Cahors, Domme, Villefranche-du-Périgord) and people massacred, most often at the fall of a town (Mussidan, Sarlat) or in revenge (La Chapelle-Faucher).

Those mighty castles, some of which had been used diring the Hundred Years' War were once again ideal strongholds for their cause (Catholic: Bourdeilles, Puymartin, Hautefort, Mareuil; Protestant: Les Bories, Montfort, Cardaillac).

Military men made a reputation defending their beliefs: Montluc for the Catholics and De Coligny and Vivans for the Protestants.

Today as you drive through the region, there are still a few reminders of the Huguenots. Often a cluster of trees and a tombstone will indicate a Protestant family tomb; most towns have a temple, the Protestant place of worship.

Michelin map 75 fold 5 or 233 fold 42 – Local map p 81

Périgueux is an ancient town built in the fertile valley of the Isle River. Its history can be read through its urban architecture and its two distinctive quarters where each is marked by the domes of its sanctuary: the Cité Quarter *(p 122)*, dominated by St-Etienne's tiled roof and Puy St-Front Quarter *(p 119)* with the Byzantine silhouette of the present cathedral bristling with pinnacles. There is a good overall view of the town from the bridge beyond Cours Fénelon to the southeast.

The splendid Vésone. – The town of Périgueux derives from the sacred spring known as the Vésone. It was near the stream, on the Isle's south bank, that the Gaulish **Petrocorii** (Petrocorii, which meant the "four tribes" in Celtic, gave its name both to Périgueux and Périgord) built their chief defensive town. After siding with Vercingetorix against Caesar, the Petrocorii finally had to accept Roman domination but benefited greatly from the *pax romana*, which enabled the city to become one of the finest of all Aquitaine. Vesunna, as the town was then called, spread beyond the bend in the Isle; temples, a forum, basilicas, an arena were built and an aqueduct over 7km – 4 miles long was constructed to carry water to the baths. But in 3C AD the city's prosperity was destroyed by the Alemans, who sacked this town as well as seventy other towns and villages throughout Gaul.

The unfortunate town. – To avoid further disaster the Vesunnians enclosed themselves within a narrow fortified enclosure; stones from the temples were used to build powerful ramparts, the arena was transformed into a keep. In spite of all these precautions, the town suffered the depredations alternately of pillage and fire by such barbaric invaders as the Visigoths, Franks and Norsemen. Such misfortune reduced Vesunna to the status of a humble village and finally even its name died; it was known as "the town of the Petrocorii" or more simply still as the "Cité".
St Front later established the town as an episcopal seat and, in the 10C, it became the unassuming capital of the County of Périgord.

The ambition of Puy St-Front. – A little sanctuary containing the tomb of St Front, apostle of Périgord, was built not far from the Cité. Beginning as the object of a pilgrimage, the sanctuary became a monastic centre. A busy market town, Puy St-Front grew up round the monastery, soon eclipsing the Cité in size.
The townspeople of Puy St-Front joined the feudal alliances against the English kings, established an emancipated consular regime and then sided with Philip Augustus against King John of England.
Little by little, the all-invading St-Front annexed the Cité's prerogatives; fights between the rivals increased. The Cité, unable to win against a neighbour who was under the protection of the king of France, had to accept union. On 16 Septembre 1240, an act of union established that the Cité and Puy St-Front would now form one community governed by a mayor and 12 consuls.
The municipal constitution was established in 1251 and the two towns united under the name of Périgueux. Nevertheless, each town kept its distinctive characteristics; the Cité belonged to the clerics and aristocrats while Puy St-Front belonged to the merchants and artisans.

Loyal Périgueux. – "My strength lies in the trust of my fellow citizens" such is the proud motto of Périgueux. The town, separated from France under the *Treaty of Brétigny* in 1360, was the first to answer the call of Charles V to take up arms against the English. It was in Périgueux that Du Guesclin planned the famous campaigns which enabled him to chase the English from the land.
Soon afterwards, Count Archambaud V, bribed by the English, openly betrayed the king and ill-treated the consuls. Protracted warfare began between the loyal townsfolk and their wicked overlord; when the royal troops arrived, Archambaud V fled and parliament claimed Périgord on behalf of the crown.
During the Fronde (1648-52) the loyalty of Périgueux was questioned unexpectedly by Condé. The Fronde supporters laid siege to the town; the churches of St-Front and St-Étienne were badly damaged. Their patience exhausted, the leaders forced the people to revolt; the garrison was rendered useless and soon afterwards the king's men entered the town in triumph.

Périgueux becomes Préfecture. – In 1790, when the Dordogne *département* was created, Périgueux was chosen over Bergerac *(qv)* as *Préfecture*. The town, which had slowly become dormant, encountering no changes in the 18C but the construction of the Allées de Tourny (by the administrator of the same name), was suddenly the object of a building boom. The old quarters were enhanced with avenues and new squares.

Périgueux today. – A small regional capital in the centre of an agricultural region, Périgueux is especially a market town. Its gastronomic specialities, with truffle and *foie gras* occupying first place, have become known around the world.
Its functions are essentially administrative and commercial.

★**DOMED CHURCHES** *time: 1 hour*

★**St-Étienne-de-la-Cité** (BZ). – Built in the 12C on the site of the ancient temple of
⊘ Mars, this church, the town's first Christian sanctuary, was consecrated by St Front to the martyr Stephen and was the cathedral church until 1669.
It included four bays lined up, one right after another, roofed with four domes and preceded by an imposing belfry porch. When the town was occupied in 1577, the Huguenots took down all but the two east bays. The episcopal palace, nearby, was also destroyed. Restored in the 17C, mutilated again during the Fronde, secularised during the Revolution, St-Étienne was reconsecrated at the time of the First Empire. The church as it now stands is a good example of the pure Périgord-Romanesque style. Still visible outside are the beginning of a ruined bay and the torn foundations of a dome that was demolished.

Inside, it is interesting to compare the architecture of the two bays built within a fifty-year interval. The first, built in the early 12C, is archaic, primitive, short and dark. The arches serve as wall ribs and the dome is illuminated by small windows which open onto the top of the dome. The second is less massive, more elongated and luminous. Its dome rests on pointed arches held up by square pillars, made less heavy in appearance by twinned columns. Moulded small columned windows illuminate an elegant columned blind arcade which supports an open passage.

This part was greatly damaged by the Huguenots; when it was rebuilt in the 17C, scrupulous attention was paid to recopying what had once existed.

Against the south wall of the first bay is an elegant 17C **altarpiece★** in oak and walnut built for the seminary. Facing it is a carved arcade, part of the tomb of Jean d'Astide, bishop of Périgueux (1160-69), which now frames the 12C baptismal font.

★St-Front Cathedral (Cathédrale St-Front) (DZ). – This cathedral, dedicated to St Front, first bishop of Périgueux, is one of the largest in southwest France and one of the most curious. It would have been a magnificent example of the Périgord-Romanesque style if it had not been remodelled so often and practically rebuilt in the 19C by Abadie, who was so influenced by this restoration that it helped him design the Sacré Cœur Basilica in Paris *(see Michelin Green Guide to Paris)*.

A chapel first stood on the site of the saint's tomb in the 6C. An abbey, the origin of which Augustinian or Benedictine, is uncertain, was established around the sanctuary. In 1047 a larger church was consecrated. This second building was almost completely destroyed by fire in 1120, whereupon it was decided to construct an even bigger church by extending the damaged building.

This third basilica, completed about 1173, was Byzantine in style, domed and with a ground plan in the form of a Greek cross. This architecture, which is uncommon in France, recalls St Mark's in Venice and the church of the Apostles in Constantinople. This was the first domed church to be built on the Roman road, which was still used in the Middle Ages by many travellers going from Rodez to Cahors and on to Saintes. In 1575, during the Wars of Religion, St-Front was pillaged by the Huguenots, the treasure was scattered and the saint's tomb destroyed. Successive restorations, conducted without any respect for the original plan, removed its initial appearance. The complete reconstruction, undertaken 1852-1901 under the supervision of the architects Abadie and Boeswillwald, included the destruction, pure and simple, of the conventual buildings, only the cloisters remain standing.

The domes of St-Front

Exterior. – *Stand in Place de la Clautre to have an overall view*. Before the restoration, the domes were covered with stones and tiles and the pinnacles did not exist. Only the 12C bell tower — which was at the point where the two churches (which make up the actual church) meet — has been more or less preserved. There is the 11C church to the west with two domed bays and 12C church remodelled by Abadie. The façade of the 11C church overlooks Place de la Clautre.

Interior. – Enter the cathedral by the north door. In order to respect the chronological order of the building's construction, the remains of the 11C church (on the west side) should be seen first. Steps, emphasising the two axes and different levels of the two churches, lead to two 11C bays roofed with octagonal domes placed on high drums. From its prestigeous Romanesque model, the "new" church appropriated the dimensions, the boldness of its domes on pendentives and the strength of the odd-looking pillars carved in places in the shape of a cross.

Adorning the back of the apse is a monumental **altarpiece★★** in walnut; this masterpiece of baroque sculpture, from the Jesuit College, recounts the Dormition and the Assumption of the Virgin. The 17C stalls are from the old Benedictine abbey of Ligueux. Admire the **pulpit★**, a fine example of 17C craftsmanship, where Hercules is holding up the stand while two atlantes carry the sounding board.

The five monumental brass candelabra, hanging at each of the bays, were designed by Abadie.

Ⓥ **Cloisters**. – The cloisters date from the 12, 13 and 16C and present a half-Romanesque, half-Gothic architectural style. The chapter house is covered with groined vaulting resting on columns. The enormous pine-cone-like mass in the centre of the cloisters had once been on the top of the bell tower; during the Revolution it was replaced by a weathercock which was later replaced by Abadie's angel. Presented in the cloisters' galleries are architectural elements (columns, capitals, statues, tombs...) of St-Front before its restoration.

★**PUY ST-FRONT QUARTER** *time: 2 hours*

The old quarter of artisans and merchants has recovered its old aspect. A conservation program for safeguarding this historic area has been established and it has been undergoing major restoration. Its Renaissance façades, courtyards, staircases, noble town houses and shops have been brought back to life; the pedestrian streets have rediscovered their function of avenues.

Place du Coderc and Place de l'Hôtel de Ville are colourfully animated mornings with their fruit and vegetable market, while Place de la Clautre is where the larger Wednesday and Saturday market is held. During the winter, the prestigeous truffle and *foie gras* market attract hordes of connaisseurs. While in the summer, the restaurants, overflowing onto the sidewalks, serve that reputable Périgord cuisine *(p 35)* in an atmosphere of days past...

Start at the Mataguerre Tower.

Ⓥ **Mataguerre Tower (Tour Mataguerre)** (CZ B). – This round tower (late 15C) crowned by a machicolated parapet is pierced by arrowslits. It was part of the defensive system which protected Puy St-Front in the Middle Ages. On Rue de la Bride side part of the ramparts can be seen. The name Mataguerre is believed to have come from an Englishman who was imprisoned in the tower.

From the top is a view of the old quarter with its tiled roofs and towers of the noblemen's town houses, domes of St-Front and the neighbouring hills, one of which is the well-known Écornebœuf Hill (*écorner*: to break the horns of an animal; *bœuf*: ox) so named because the hill was so steep that the oxen broke their necks... and lost their horns.

Go up Rue de la Bride and Rue des Farges.

Rue des Farges (CZ). – At no 4 stands the **House of the Women of Faith**, whose medieval (13C) layout is still visible inspite of its damaged state: pointed arches on the ground floor and rounded arches on the upper storey. A small bell turret set in one corner brings to mind the fact that in the 17C the building was a convent, whose congregation gave the house its name.

It is said that the building housed Du Guesclin during the Hundred Years' War.

Rue Aubergerie (CZ 9). – At no 16, the **Hôtel d'Abzac de Ladouze** is made up of a main building, an octagonal tower and a corbelled turret, characteristics of 15C architecture. At nos 4 and 8 the **Hôtel de Sallegourde**, also 15C, presents a polygonal tower and a machicolated watchpath.

Rue St-Roch (CDZ 49). – At no 4 an elegant arcaded window is decorated with diamond-work.

Rue du Calvaire (DZ 16). – The condemned, on their way to be executed on Place de la Clautre, came up this street, their *calvaire* (meaning tribulation). Lining it are several doors ornamented with nailheads. At no 3 is a Renaissance door.

Place de la Clautre (DZ 26). – An interesting view of the imposing St-Front Cathedral can be had from here. Underneath the square are tombs.

Place du Thouin (DZ 54). – The two bronze cannons with the inscription "Périgueux 1588" were excavated at Place du Coderc in 1979 on the site of the armoury, the old consulate *(see below)*.

Daumesnil's Birthplace (Maison Natale de Daumesnil) (DYZ D). – *7 Rue de la Clarté*. In this house with its 18C façade, **General Pierre Daumesnil** was born on 27 July 1776. This military man followed Napoleon to Arcola, to Egypt, and to Wagram, where he lost a leg. In 1814, while governor of the Vincennes fortress, he retorted to the enemy, who laid siege and demanded him to leave: "I'll surrender Vincennes, when you give me back my leg" *(see Michelin Green Guide to Paris)*.

Place de l'Hôtel-de-Ville (CZ 37). – The town hall is located in the 17 and 18C **Hôtel de Lagrange-Chancel** (CZ H). At no 7 stands a 15C house with a polygonal staircase tower characteristic of the period. Its machicolations, as well as the shop giving onto the street, are neo-Gothic.

Place du Coderc (DY 27). – This was the geographic and administrative centre of the Puy St-Front Quarter. In the early 19C the old consulate *(see above)*, the heart of municipal and legislative life, still had its old square belfry, some 600 hundred years old. The covered market was built at its place in *c*1830.

Ⓥ **Rue de la Sagesse** (CDY 50). – At no 1, the **Lajoubertie House** (CDY E) contains an elegant **Renaissance staircase★**, square in plan and decorated with a coffered ceiling depicting mythological scenes, one of which recounts Venus putting down her weapons. The intertwined H and S represent the initials of the Hauteforts and Solminihacs.

Place St-Louis (CDY). – This square is known locally as Foie Gras Square, as it is here that the *foies gras (qv)* are sold in late fall.

It is enhanced by a modern fountain, adorned with a bronze sculpture by Ramon.

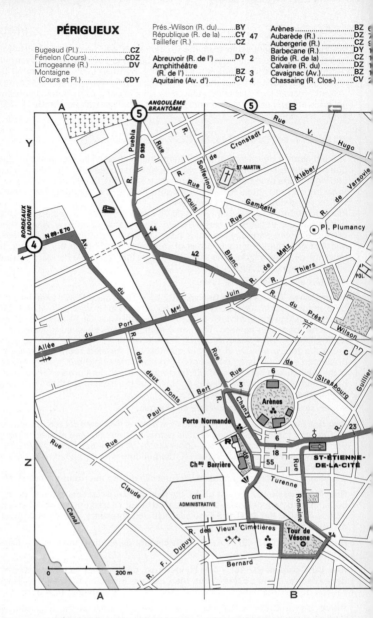

Tenant House (Maison Tenant) or **Pastrycook's House (Maison du Pâtissier)** (DY F).
This former *hôtel*, belonging to the Talleyrand family, is made up of two wings at a right angle. The façade looking onto Rue Eguillerie possesses a Gothic window. The door on the corner, which leads to a small courtyard, has a tympanum with, oddly enough, a squinch above it.

★Rue Limogeanne (DY). – In the past, this street led to Limogeanne Gate (Porte Limogeanne), which opened onto the Limoges road. A large pedestrian street, it is lined by numerous stores and several elegant Renaissance *hôtels*.
In the courtyard of the **Hôtel de Mérédieu** (no 12) is a 15C carved doorway adorned with a coat of arms, added in the 17C.
At no 7, in the centre of the wrought-iron imposte appear the initials A.C.; they belong to Antoine Courtois, the famous 18C caterer, whose sublime partridge pâtés were discussed at the Court of Prussia; his headquarters were in the cellars of this *hôtel*.
The elegant Renaissance façade of the **Estignard Mansion** (no 5) is embellished with dormers, pediments, mullioned windows and pilaster capitals decorated with heads of men, animals and other motifs.
In the courtyard of no 3 is a lovely doorway with a lintel decorated with grotesques and a tympanum, Gothic in style, bearing a salamander, François I's crest.
Lapeyre House (no 1), which is at the corner of Place du Coderc, has a corbelled corner turret.

Passage Daumesnil (DYZ 30). – Enter on Rue Limogeanne, across from no 3. The passageway consists of courtyards and small squares linked together by alleyways. The buildings, leaning against each other which sprung up through the centuries, were demolished, creating open spaces, revealing the fine 15, 16 and 17C façades. The passage ends on Rue de la Miséricorde.
While crossing Rue St-Front, made in the 19C, look to the left to see the unusual Masonic Lodge (Loge Maçonnique).

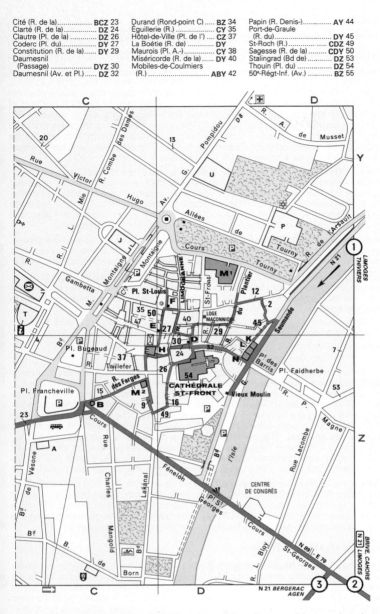

Rue de la Constitution (DY 29). – At no 3 is a **doorway** with a crocketed arch. At no 7, the **Hôtel de Gamançon** also known as the Logis St-Front, is the seat of the Historical Buildings Commission. There are two 15C wings set at right angles, linked by a staircase tower, flanked by a corbelled turret and pierced by mullioned windows. Wrought iron embellishes the well.

Rue du Plantier (DY). – The houses on the right of the street have lovely terraced gardens unfurling down to the Isle River. Walk beyond Rue Barbecane to the Mint (no 24) with its very steep crocketed gable, which dates the building to the 16C.

Rue Barbecane (DY 12). – **Hôtel de Fayrolle** (no 14) is opened by an early 17C doorway.

Rue de l'Abreuvoir (DY 2). — In this tiny stepped street, there is a fine view of the Isle with St-Georges's (19C) bell tower in the distance.

Rue du Port-de-Graule (DY 45). – A medieval atmosphere still pervades this paved street lined with low doorways.

The quays (Boulevard Georges-Saumande) (DYZ). – Along the river, several fine houses stand side by side.

The **Lambert House** (DZ K), called the House with Columns, because of its gallery, is a fine Renaissance *hôtel* with two wings set at a right angle and illuminated by mullioned windows. Next to it, the **Cayla House** (DZ L), also called the Consul's House, was built on the ramparts in the 15C. The roof is decorated with Flamboyant-style dormers. At the corner of Avenue Daumesnil, the **House of Lur** (DZ N) dates from the 16C.

Continue along the quays, and on the other side of Avenue Daumesnil is the **old mill** (Vieux Moulin), all that remains of the granary of the St-Front chapter which used to perch right over the river.

CITÉ QUARTER: ANCIENT WAY *time: 1 hour*

On the site of ancient Vesunna, this quarter possesses numerous Gallo-Roman ruins.

Arena (Arènes) (BZ). – A pleasant public garden occupies the space where the arena once stood. Built in the 1C, this elliptical amphitheatre, one of the largest in Gaul, (153m x 125m – 502 x 410ft) had a capacity for 20 000 people. Great blocks of stone still mark the stairwells, the vomitoria and the vaulting, but the whole lower part of the building remains buried below ground. Demolition of the arena began in 3C, when the amphitheatre was turned into a bastion and became part of the city ramparts. In the 11C, a count of Périgord built a fortress in the arena, only to be dismantled after Archambaud V's betrayal in 1391. The arena was next transformed into a quarry, its stone being used to build houses in the town.

Norman Gate (Porte Normande) (BZ). – It made up part of the ramparts, or more precisely, a defence wall 5m – 16 1/2ft thick which had rapidly been built in the 3C to protect the town from barbarian invasions. It was made of parts of the temples and monuments of Vesunna. This concentration of capitals, column shafts, cornices and other carved items are an eloquent archaeological testimony. It was here that the altar used for the sacrifice of bulls, exposed in the Périgord Museum, was discovered.

Romanesque House (Maison Romane) (BZ R). – Located at the entrance to the garden, set on the ramparts, this 12C rectangular building has a cradle-vaulted crypt in its lower part. Next to the house stands a tower, part of the Gallo-Roman curtain wall.

Barrière Castle (BZ). – Also built on the ramparts, the 12C keep surmounts one of the rampart towers. Remodelled during the Renaissance, the castle has kept its fine door and its Flamboyant-style staircase tower. Its pinnacles and crockets bring to mind the staircase tower at L'Herm Castle *(p 93)*.

> *Turn around and bear right on Rue de Turenne, bear right on it, and cross the railway bridge which enters into Rue des Vieux-Cimetières.*

From the bridge there is an interesting view of the ancient wall.

> *Turn left into Rue des Vieux-Cimetières.*

⊘ **"Villa" of Pompeïus (Villa de Pompeïus) (BZ S).** – The ruins of this *domus* (incorrectly called villa) were discovered in 1959 during the early stages of a building project.
The excavations uncovered the base of this wealthy Gallo-Roman residence. Its rooms give onto a square court lined with a peristyle. Built in the 1C, it was remodelled and raised the following century due to flooding. The lower part of the walls of the first *domus* were decorated with frescoes with different motifs (geometric, vegetal, sea animals). The *domus* had all the comforts: a hypocaust (a heating system: hot air circulated through brick pipes), baths with a warm room *(tepidarium)*, a steam room *(sudatorium)* a hot room *(caldarium)* and a cold plunge *(piscina)* as well as individual baths. There were also workshops for the smith and potter.

⊘ **Vesunna's Tower (Tour de Vésone) (BZ).** – This tower, 20m – 65 1/2ft high and 17m – 56ft in diameter, is all that remains of the temple dedicated to the titular goddess of the city. The temple, which was built in the heart of the forum in the old Cité when the Antonines were in power in the 2C AD, originally had a peristyle, was surrounded by porticoes and framed by two basilicas. The tower is still impressive.

ADDITIONAL SIGHTS

★**Perigord Museum (Musée du Périgord) (DY M¹).** – The museum, located on the Allées ⊘ de Tourny, on the site of the former Augustinian convent, was created to house the Gallo-Roman finds of ancient Vesunna, upon which were added the wealth of objects uncovered in the numerous prehistoric sites in the region. It is today one of the most important museums of prehistory in France. An ethnography collection completes the museum's presentation. The collections are described in order of the tour.

Ethnography Section. – Concerned mainly with Oceanian and African art, the weapons, jewellery, masks and statuettes evoke customs and civilisations which at times recall certain aspects of the prehistoric era. Note the adze (a type of ax) from the Cook Islands, the wooden handle of which was carved with a stone chisel and tools from Australia.

Prehistoric Section. – Corridor C presents an introduction to prehistory, initiating the visitor to the technique of making tools.
The Maurice Féaux Gallery is devoted to the Lower Palaeolithic Era and presents especially flint bifaces and stone tools. To be seen in a display case is the Neanderthaloid skeleton from Régourdou (c 70 000 BC) found near Montignac *(qv)*. The Michel Hardy Gallery is concerned with the Middle and Lower Palaeolithic Age as shown through the massive carved blocks from Castel-Merle, the painted flat stones from Mas d'Azil and especially the skeleton of the Chancelade man (15 000 years old) which was found in the Raymonden shelter, among his furnishings. Remarkable small objects, engraved in stone or bone, from the Magdalenian Period *(qv)* are worth looking at closely.
The Henri Breuil Gallery illustrates the evolution from the Neolithic Era to the Iron Age, using as examples the sandstone used to polish the flint, polished axes, earthenware, bronze axes and jewellery.

Gallo-Roman Archaeological Section. – For the most part, this collection (mosaics, steles, funerary cippius, glassware and earthenware) has been formed with the finds from the excavations of the ancient town of Vesunna.
Note the **altar**, found near the Norman Gate *(see above)*, dedicated to Cybele (a goddess who personified Earth), which was used for the sacrifice of animals. Carved on one of its sides note a bull's head wreathed with a fillet on which was hung the sacrificial knife, hook (to rip out the animal's entrails), pitcher and libatory cup.
In another room, a panel of reconstituted mural frescoes reveals the Pompeiian decoration during the reign of Augustus.

Popular Arts and Traditions Section. – Assembled in the former Augustinian convent's chapel are several Limousin enamels, statues, recumbent figures and enameled terracotta figures from Thiviers used as ornamental finials on roof cresting; note the one representing an man at arms.

Painting Department. – Note the **diptych from Rabastens**, 13C illuminated manuscripts on large parchment, as well as a portrait of Fénelon by F. Bailleul, a Canaletto and among the regional works, caricatures by the humourist Sem (1863-1934).

Cloisters. – These galleries house the lapidary collection which covers all periods: Gallo-Roman inscriptions, funerary steles, Renaissance sculptures, architectural elements from St-Front including an altarpiece representing the Death of the Virgin (12C)

⊙ **Périgord Military Museum (Musée Militaire du Périgord) (CZ M²)**. – Arms and weapons of all sports, standards and uniforms evoke the military history of Périgord from the Middle Ages to today. The great military men of the region are also honoured: Bugeaud, Deputy of the Dordogne and General Daumesnil (qv).

Terracotta figures (16C) used as finials on roof cresting from the Château de la Borde at Festalemps

Particularly honoured, is the 50th Infantry Regiment stationed in Périgueux since 1876; note one of the regiment's flags, which the Colonel Ardouin wrapped around his body after the surrender of Sedan to prevent it from falling into enemy hands.

EXCURSIONS

★**Chancelade Abbey**. – *3km – 2 miles west. Description p 70.*

★**Dronne Valley**. – *Round tour of 110km – 68 miles. Description p 80.*

Caussade Castle (Château de Caussade). – *10km – 6 miles northeast.*
Standing in a clearing of the Lanmary Forest, this noble fortress has reproduced, on a smaller scale, all the characteristics of a 15C stronghold. Its polygonal curtain wall, surrounded by a moat (half-filled), is flanked by square towers.

★ Château de PUYGUILHEM

Michelin map **75** northeast of fold 5 or **233** fold 31 – 10km – 6 miles west of St-Jean de-Côle – Local map p 81

⊙ The Château de Puyguilhem was built at the beginning of the 16C by Mondot de la Marthonie, first President of the Parliaments of Bordeaux and Paris, and resembles many of the Loire Valley châteaux, which were built during the reign of François I. It was bought by the Fine Arts Department in 1939.
The main building is flanked on one side by a massive round tower joined to an octagonal turret, on the other side by an asymmetrical tower with cant walls, containing the main staircase. The decoration is uniform, overall, and has considerable harmony of style. The pierced balustrade at the base of the main building's roof, dormer windows, finely carved chimneys, mullioned windows, and the decorated machicolations on the great round tower all contribute to the building's elegance.
Inside note the carved **chimneys**★ especially the one in the guard room, with its mantelpiece ornamented with foliage and medallions. On the first floor note the partly modern chimney illustrating Hercules' Labours. Its uprights are adorned with shell-shaped niches and on the entablature are depicted six of the Labours.
Also of interest are the chestnut timber-work of the ceiling, in the great hall on the second floor and the carved main staircase.

PUY-L'ÉVÊQUE   Pop 2 333

Michelin map **79** south of fold 7 or **235** fold 14 – Local map p 102 – Facilities

This small town, which took its present name (*évêque* = bishop) when it came under the overlordship of the bishops of Cahors, occupies one of the most picturesque sites in the valley downstream from Cahors. The old houses in golden stone are overshadowed by the church and the castle keep. From the opposite bank, at the entrance to the suspension bridge, the best **view** of the whole town can be had.

⊙ **Church (Église)**. – The church was built on the northeast side of the town at the furthest point in the defence system, of which it was part. Before the church, stands a massive belfry porch flanked by a turret and buttresses. The doorway, surmounted by an ogee-arched pediment, is adorned with statues including figures of the Virgin and St John at the feet of Christ on the Cross. The nave was built in the 14 and 15C and ends in a polygonal apse. In the churchyard there are many old tombs and on the left of the church a wayside cross ornamented with sculpture in the archaic style.

Keep (Donjon). – The keep, all that remains of the episcopal castle, dates back to the 13C. Enjoy an extensive view of the Lot Valley from the Truffière esplanade adjoining the keep and the town hall.

PUYMARTIN CASTLE

Michelin map 🔢 fold 17 or 🔢 southeast of fold 2 – 7km – 4 miles northwest of Sarlat

⊘Built in golden stone and roofed with *lauzes*, the castle stands on a steep hill in the heart of Périgord Noir. Constructed in the 15 and 16C (restored in 19C), it comprises several main buildings, linked by round towers and girt by curtain walls. During the Wars of Religion it was a Catholic stronghold against the Protestants of Sarlat.

Inside, the **decoration**★ and **furnishings**★ are remarkable. The state room is hung with 18C Aubusson *verdures* in fresh green tones. The next room is adorned with interesting *grisaille* mural paintings on mythological themes. The main hall has a chimney decorated in *trompe l'œil* and a ceiling with beams painted in the 17C; note in particular a set of six Flemish tapestries illustrating the Trojan War, a table and chairs in Louis XIII style, a Regency chest of drawers and a Louis XV writing desk.

The tour proceeds to a hexagonal defence chamber, with stellar vaulting, then on to the attic rooms before ending on the ground floor in the old guard room adorned with furnishings, tapestries and paintings.

★★★ ROCAMADOUR   Pop 795

Michelin map 🔢 folds 18 and 19 or 🔢 fold 6 or 🔢 fold 38 – Local map p 91 – Facilities

Rocamadour *(photograph p 37)*, towered over by its slender castle keep, groups a mass of old dwellings, oratories, towers and precipitous rocks on the rugged face of a *causse* cliff rising 150m — 492ft above the Alzou Canyon.

★★★**The site**. – One should arrive in Rocamadour by the L'Hospitalet road *(p 127)*. From a belvedere terrace there is a remakable **view** of Rocamadour: the Alzou winds its way between fields at the bottom of a gorge, while some 500m – 1 640ft up, pinioned to the cliff face, can be seen the extraordinary outline of this village, the unbelievably bold construction of which appears to defy the force of gravity. The religious buildings rise above the village centre the whole crowned by castle ramparts.

The morning, when the sun shines fully on the rock, is the best time of all for looking at the view. There is another striking view of Rocamadour to be had from the D 32, the Couzou road, as descending from the plateau, you pass a road going off to the left.

HISTORICAL NOTES

The enigmatic St Amadour. – The identity of St Amadour, who gave his name to the sanctuary village, has never been firmly established. A 12C chronicler reported that in 1166 "a local inhabitant having expressed the wish to be buried beneath the threshold of the Chapel of the Virgin, men began to dig a grave only to find the body of a man. The corpse was placed near the altar so that it might be venerated by the faithful and from that time onwards miracles occured".

Who was this mysterious personage whose tomb appeared to be so old? The most contradictory theories have been advanced: some contend that he was an Egyptian hermit, others that it was St Silvanus.

The most accepted theory, since the 15C, is that the body was that of the publican Zaccheus, a disciple of Jesus and husband of St Veronica, who, meeting Christ on His way to Calvary, wiped His face, which was covered in blood and sweat, with her kerchief. Both Zaccheus and Veronica were obliged to flee Palestine. They took a boat and were guided on their journey by an angel. They established themselves in Limousin. On the death of Veronica, Zaccheus retired to the deserted and wild Alzou Valley where he preached. It is pure legend but one thing is certain; there was a hermit and he knew the rock well as is often sheltered him.

The *Langue d'Oc* expression – *roc amator* – he who likes the rock – established the name of this village sanctuary, which became Roc Amadour and finally Rocamadour.

The fame of Rocamadour. – From the time that the miracles began until the Reformation, the pilgrimage to Rocamadour was one of the most famous in Christendom. Great crowds gathered; 30 000 people came on days of major pardon and plenary indulgence. Since the village was too small to house all the pilgrims, the Alzou Valley was transformed into a vast camp. Henry Plantagenet, king of England, was miraculously cured and was among the first to kneel before the Virgin; his example was followed during the Middle Ages by the most illustrious personages including St Dominic, St Bernard, St Louis and Blanche of Castile, Philip IV the Fair, Philip VI and Louis XI. Veneration of Our Lady of Rocamadour was established at Lisbon, Oporto, Seville and even in Sicily; the Rocamadour standard, flown at the Battle of Las Navas at Tolosa, put the Mohammedans to flight and gave victory to the Catholic kings of Spain.

Pilgrimage and penitents. – Ecclesiastical, and in some cases, lay tribunals used to often impose the pilgrimage on sinners. It was a considerable penance, employed especially towards Albigensian heretics, who were said to hate the Mother of God. On the day of his departure, the penitent attended mass and then set forth dressed in clothes covered with large crosses, a big hat upon his head, a staff in his hand and a knapsack on his back. On reaching the end of his journey, the pilgrim stripped himself of his clothes, climbing the famous steps on his knees in his shirt and chains were bound round his arms and neck. On being brought before the altar to the Black Virgin in this humiliating condition he pronounced his *amende honorable*. A priest recited prayers of purification and removed the chains from the penitent, who, now forgiven, received from the priest a certificate and a kind of lead medal bearing the image of the miraculous Virgin, called a **sportelle** *(p 126)*.

But the pilgrimages were not always conducted for pious ends: lords and town consuls sought the protection of Our Lady when making a treaty or signing a charter. Others came to Rocamadour to see the crowds and indeed to do business.

Decline and renaissance. – Rocamadour reached its zenith in the 13C. Favours not even given to Jerusalem were granted to it; money poured in, but riches brought the covetous.

For a hundred years the Abbeys of Marcilhac *(qv)* and Tulle disputed who should own the church at Rocamadour; Tulle was finally awarded the honour by arbitration. During the Middle Ages, the town was sacked several times: Henry Short Coat *(qv)*, in revolt against his father Henry Plantagenet, pillaged the oratory in 1183; during the Hundred Years' War, bands of English and the local soldiery plundered the treasure in turn; during the Wars of Religion, the Protestant, Captain Bessonies seized Rocamadour to desecrate it and lay it to waste; only the Virgin and the miraculous bell escaped. The body of St Amadour, still whole, was thrown to the flames, but would not burn! Furious Bessonies hacked it with his axe and broke it. Rocamadour did not rise from its ruins; the abbey remained idle until it was finally extinguished by the Revolution. In the 19C, the bishops of Cahors tried to revive the pilgrimage and the churches were rebuilt. Though much of its splendour has vanished, Rocamadour has once again found the fervour of its pilgrims and is today a very respected pilgrimage centre.

THE VILLAGE *time: 1/2 hour*

The village is a pedestrian precinct offering three possible accesses: on foot starting from l'Hospitalet (2km – 1 mile north), by lift from the plateau, near the castle or by the little train starting at Alzou Valley.

Once a fortified town, Rocamadour still retains much that bears witness to its past. Go through **Figuier Gateway** (Porte du Figuier) **(AZ)**, which was already a gateway to the town in the 13C, and enter the main street which is now cluttered with souvenir shops. The narrow street, clinging to the living rock, is vertically overlooked by a peculiar tiered arrangement of houses, churches and the castle.

Beyond the Salmon Gate (Porte Salmon), which is crowned by a two-storey tower, the town hall can be seen to the right.

Town Hall (Hôtel de Ville) **(BZ H)**. – The town hall is located in a 15C house (restored), known as the Couronnerie or the House of the Brothers. In the council chamber there are two fine **tapestries★** by Jean Lurçat which portray the flora and fauna of the *causse*.

Rue de la Couronnerie, passes under the 13C Hugon Gate (Porte Hugon) and continues, until it reaches the Low Gate (Porte Basse) and a picturesque quarter where small houses descend the slope to the banks of the Alzou. Nearby stands the old fortified mill, known as the Mill of Roquefrège (Moulin de Roquefrège).

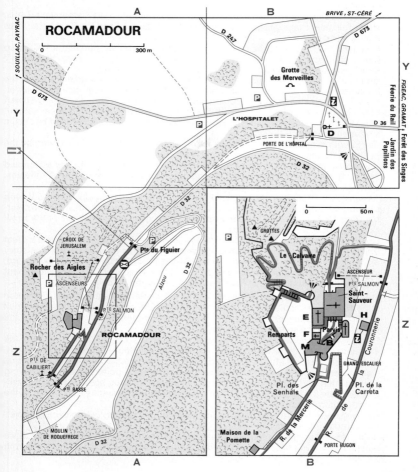

THE ECCLESIASTICAL CITY *time: 1 1/2 hours*

Climb the 223 steps of the Great Stairway *(Via Sancta)*. Pilgrims often make this ascent, kneeling at every step.
The first 141 steps lead, in five flights, to terraces on which once stood buildings for the canons to live in. These have now been converted into shops and hotels.

The fort (BZ B). – This vast building of military appearance, formerly the palace of the bishops of Tulle, stands at the base of the huge cliff face. It was here that important pilgrims lodged. Built in the 14C, it was greatly restored in the 19C.
This terrace is called Place des Senhals because of the pilgrims' insignia called *senhals* or *sportelles (p 124)* that were made there; coming out on to the square is the small Rue de la Mercerie.

Rue de la Mercerie (BZ). – In this, the oldest street in Rocamadour, lined with terraced gardens, can be seen the 14C **House of the Pomette** (Maison de la Pomette). It ends at the 13C Cabiliert Gate (Porte de Cabiliert), once flanked by a defensive tower. The **Fort Gateway** (Porte du Fort) which opens under the palace perimeter wall leads to the sacred perimeter wall. Seventy-five steps climb up to the square surrounded by its churches.

Churches' parvis (BZ). – The parvis, which is also known as Place St-Amadour, is fairly small and has seven churches: Basilica of St-Sauveur opposite the stairway, St-Amadour's Crypt below the basilica, the Chapel of Notre-Dame or Miraculous Chapel on the left, the three chapels of St-Jean-Baptiste, St-Blaise and Ste-Anne on the right and the Chapel of St-Michel standing on a terrace to the left.

Basilica of St-Sauveur (Basilique St-Sauveur). – This 11-13C Romanesque-Gothic sanctuary dedicated to St Saviour has two naves of equal size, each of which has three bays divided by massive columns. One of the basilica walls is made out of the cliff's living rock, upon which the arches of the third bay seek support. The mezzanine was added in the last century to enlargen the basilica during the great pilgrimages.
Above the altar stands a fine 16C **Christ**, in polychrome wood, the cross of which represents a lopped off tree.

St-Amadour's Crypt (Crypte St-Amadour). – It is a sanctuary which lies below the basilica. It is made up of a flat chevet and two bays with quadripartite vaulting. It used to be a place of worship: the body of St Amadour was venerated here.

Chapel of Notre-Dame (Chapelle Notre-Dame) (BZ E). – From the parvis, 25 steps lead to the Miraculous Chapel or Chapel of Our Lady, considered the "Holy of Holies of Rocamadour". It is there that the hermit is believed to have hollowed out an oratory in the rock.
In 1476 the chapel was crushed by a rock-fall; it was rebuilt in the Flamboyant Gothic style. This new chapel, sacked during the Wars of Religion and the Revolution, was restored last century.
On the exterior façade, to the right of the Flamboyant doorway, part of the 13C fresco remains, illustrating the dance of death of the "three living and three dead men": three menacing skeletons are ready to bury or kill their victims.
On the altar, in the semi-darkness of the chapel, blackened by candle smoke, is the miraculous Virgin, also called **Black Madonna★**. This reliquary statue, carved in walnut, rustic in style, dates from the 12C. It is small in size (69cm – 27in), the rigidly-seated Virgin holding the Infant Jesus, with the face of an adult, on Her left knee, without touching Him. It was covered with silver plating; several pieces, blackened by candle smoke and oxidation remain.
The interior is adorned with many votive offerings: ex-votos and chains worn by the penitents during certain ceremonies of repentance.
Suspended from the roof, hangs the miraculous **bell**, made of iron plates assembled and most likely dating from the 9C. It rang out of its own accord to foretell miracles, as when sailors lost at sea invoked Our Lady of Rocamadour.
As early as the 11C the pilgrimage to Rocamadour was very popular with the Breton sailors; and a chapel dedicated to Our Lady of Rocamadour was built at Camaret-sur-Mer *(see Michelin Green Guide to Brittany)*. This explains the presence of the small sailor figures among the ex-votos.
On leaving the chapel, stuck in the cliff face above the doorway, one can see a great iron sword, which legend identifies as **Durandal**, Roland's famous sword. The story recounts that Roland, surrounded by the Saracens and unable to break his sword, implored the Archangel Michael and threw him his sword, which in one movement implanted itself in the rock of Rocamadour, far from the Infidels.

St-Michel's Chapel (Chapelle St-Michel) (BZ F). – This Romanesque chapel, dedicated to St Michael, is sheltered by a rock overhang. The apse, which houses a small oratory, juts out towards the square. It was used for services by the monks of the priory, who had also installed a library.
On the wall outside are two frescoes representing the Annunciation and the Visitation: the skill of the composition, the richness of colour – ochre, yellow, reddish-brown, and the royal blue background, protected from condensation and, therefore, well preserved – and the grace of movement all seem to point to the works having been painted in the 12C. They may well have been inspired both by Limousin reliquaries (note the figures in relief in the background) and Byzantine mosaics (note the swarthy complexions).
Below them, a 14C fresco depicts an immense St Christopher, patron saint of travellers and thus of pilgrims.
Inside, the chancel is adorned with paintings (not as well conserved as those outside): Christ in Majesty is surrounded by the Evangelists; further down a seraph and the Archangel Michael weigh souls.

⊘ **Museum of Sacred Art (Francis-Poulenc)** (BZ M²). – It is dedicated to the famous composer Francis Poulenc (1899-1963), who having received a revelation during a visit to Rocamadour in 1936, composed *Litanies à la Vierge Noire de Rocamadour*. The museum presents an important collection of sacred art which came from the churches' treasuries, donations and from several churches in the Lot. In the hallway various documents recount the history of Rocamadour and its pilgrimage, with the help of maps and a statue of St James as a pilgrim (Rocamadour was a pilgrims' stop on the way to Santiago de Compostela).

The vestibule displays objects from the sanctuary: 13C stained glass (the only remaining stained glass from the basilica) showing the death of St Martin and the 17C reliquary casket of St Amadour, which contained the relics of the saint's body destroyed during the Wars of Religion.

The first gallery contains objects (ex-votos, paintings and items in carved wood) dating for the most part from the 17C. A naive panel (1648) shows St Amadour hailing the Virgin with the *Ave Maria*, next to it, a baroque statue of Flemish origin represents the prophet Jonas as an old man writing.

The treasury has assembled fine items which came from the once fabulous treasure of the sanctuary. **Limoges reliquary caskets** from Lunegarde and Laverhne (both 12C) and Soulomès (13C), ornamented with enamelwork, demonstrate the craftsmanship of the Limousin artist. Among the other works displayed note the reliquary of St Agapit, in the form of a head, the reliquary monstrance in silver surmounted by a Crucifixion with the Virgin and St John on either side, a 15C silver processional cross and a 12C seated Virgin in wood. The next gallery contains 17, 18 and 19C religious paintings.

> *On leaving the museum take the gallery, known as the tunnel, which passes beneath the Basilica of St-Sauveur and comes out on a terrace overlooking Alzou Canyon.*

THE PLATEAU *time: 3/4 hour*

Calvary (Calvaire) (BZ). – A shaded Stations of the Cross winds up towards the ramparts. After passing the caves (grottes) of the Nativity and the Holy Sepulchre, the great Cross of Jerusalem (Croix de Jérusalem), brought from the Holy Land by the Penitential Pilgrims, can be seen.

⊘ **Ramparts (Remparts)** (BZ). – These are the remains of a 14C fort which was built to block the rocky spur and protect the sanctuary. Leaning against the fortress, the residence of the chaplains of Roc-Amadour was built in the 19C. From the ramparts, which rise above a sheer drop, there is an unforgettable **panorama★★★** of the *causse*, the site of Rocamadour and the rock amphitheatre surrounding it.

⊘ **Eagles' Rock (Rocher des Aigles)** (AZ). – There is a breeding centre for birds of prey.

> *To return to the village, go back to an esplanade which is on the same level as the Ecclesiastical City and take the lift to the main street near Salmon Gate (Porte Salmon).*

L'HOSPITALET

The name of this village, clinging to Rocamadour's cliff face, comes from the small hospital founded in the 11C by Hélène de Castelnau to nurse the pilgrims on the pilgrim road from Le Puy (Auvergne) to Santiago de Compostela. There remain but few ruins of this hospital; the Romanesque **chapel** (BY D), which is set in the middle of the churchyard, was remodelled in the 15C.

L'Hospitalet is very much visited for its viewpoint which gives onto the site of Rocamadour. There is a large tourist information centre.

⊘ **Merveilles Cave (Grotte des Merveilles)** (BY). – Discovered in 1920, this small cave, only 8m – 24ft deep, has some lovely formations: stalagtites, stalagmites and natural limestone dams *(gours)* into which are reflected the cave roof and its concretions.

On the walls are cave paintings dating back, most likely, from the Solutrean Period (*c*18 000 years ago), representing outlined hands, black spots, a few horses, a cat and the outline of a deer.

⊘ **Model Railway Exhibit (Féerie du rail)**. – Sixty model trains wind about a giant **model★** (70sq meters – 754sq feet) with scenes of city, mountain and country life composed with accessories, lights and sound.

⊘ **Butterfly Garden (Jardin des papillons)**. – In a vast greenhouse (climatic control) butterflies of all sizes and colours live in complete liberty. These ephemeral beauties, whose life span lasts about 2 weeks, come from the world over (Malaysia, Madagascar, United States, South America...).

⊘ **Monkey Forest (Forêt des Singes)**. – Living in liberty, on 10ha – 25 acres of woodland, are 150 monkeys in an environment similar to the upper plateaux of North Africa from where they originated. These monkeys are Barbary apes *(see Gibraltar in Michelin Green Guide to Spain)* and macaques, a species which is becoming extinct.

*Join us in our never ending task
of keeping up to date.
Send us your comments and suggestions, please.*

**Michelin Tyre PLC
Tourism Department
Davy House, Lyon Road - HARROW - Middlesex HA1 2DQ.**

Michelin map 🔲 fold 17 or 🔲 west of fold 6 – Local map p 76-77 – Facilities

The village of La Roque-Gageac, huddled against the cliff which drops vertically to the Dordogne Valley, occupies a wonderful **site**★★ – one of the finest in this part of the valley, which within a few miles includes Domme, Castelnaud and Beynac-et-Cazenac.

This village has picturesque alleyways, lined with simple farmers' and artisans' dwellings and the more noble residences, leading to the church built into the rock face. From here the view carries out over the Dordogne, hemming in fields and meadows cut by lines of poplars.

★★**View**. – The best view of La Roque-Gageac is from the west: the late afternoon sun highlights the tall grey cliff face covered with holm-oaks, while the houses, with their stone slab *(lauzes)* or tile roofs, stand reflected in the calm waters of the river below. In the foreground can be seen the outline of the Château de la Malartrie; at the other end of the village, standing at the foot of the sheer rock-face, is the charming Tarde Manor-house.

Tarde Manor-house (Manoir de Tarde). – Two pointed gabled buildings, opened by mullioned windows, are flanked by a round tower. This charming manor-house is associated with the Tarde family, the most famous members of which are the canon Jean Tarde, 16C Sarlat humorist, historian, cartographer, astronomer, mathematician, etc. and Gabriel Tarde, a 19C sociologist.

Château de la Malartrie. – A building built in the early 20C, greatly influenced by the 15C style.

*The **Michelin Sectional Map Series** at a scale of 1:200 000 (1cm: 2km) covers the whole of France.*
For the maps to use with this Guide see p 3.
You may pick out at a glance
 - the motorways and major roads for a quick journey
 - the secondary or alternative roads for a traffic-free run
 - the country lanes for a leasurely drive
These maps are a must for your holidays.

Michelin map 🔲 southeast of fold 6 or 🔲 east of fold 1

The church alone escaped when the Germans set about burning the town in March 1944 as a reprisal; the town has been rebuilt.

Church (Église). – The entrance is by an interesting belfry porch containing a doorway built in the style of the First Renaissance. It was constructed about 1530 and is ornamented with Corinthian capitals and surmounted by a finely carved lintel; the decoration is profane and somewhat surprising, under the circumstances, since it consists of mermaids and women.

The church's main vessel has three aisles of equal height built in the Flamboyant style; the pointed vaulting is supported by round pillars reinforced by remarkable engaged twisted columns.

EXCURSIONS

★**Rouffignac Cave (Grotte de Rouffignac)**. – *5km – 3 miles to the south.*
This dry cave, which is also called the Cro de Granville, was known as early as the 15C. The galleries and chambers extend for more than 8km – 5miles. The tour (4km – 2 1/2 miles), which is made by electric railway, takes in all the principal galleries. In 1956 Professor L.R. Nougier called attention to the remarkable group of paintings marked with black lines and **engravings**★ produced during the Middle or Upper Magdalenian Period (some 10 - 13 000 years ago). These engravings are of horses, ibexes, rhinoceroses, bison and a great number of mammoths, among which may be seen the "Patriarch" and an amazing frieze depicting two herds locked in combat. There is an outstanding group of drawings on the ceiling of the last chamber (unfortunately disfigured with graffiti).

L'Herm Castle. – *6km – 3 1/2 miles northwest. Description p 93.*

La Douze. – *Pop 700. 14km – 8 1/2 miles to the west.* The small La Douze **church** was built in the Gothic style in the 14 and 15C. A massive belfry porch leads to a low nave with pointed vaulting.

The interior has preserved carvings of local popular inspiration; they figure among the rare religious examples of Renaissance furnishings in Périgord.

The tall **altarpiece** has a large slab of stone illustrating a Crucifixion, with a background thick with trees and castles. Kneeling on either side are Pierre d'Abzac, baron of Ladouze, and his wife Jeanne de Bourdeille, both accompanied by their patron saints.

The **pulpit** is adorned with three carved panels framed by small columns and arches appearing in perspective. On either side of the central panel depicting St Peter, patron saint of the church, is a crown of vegetation and the coat of arms of Pierre d'Abzac and Jeanne de Bourdeille.

On the left of the entrance a baptismal font has been placed on the shaft of a Gallo-Roman column decorated with rosettes and figures in Archaic style.

Michelin map 🔢 south of fold 7 or 🔢🔢🔢 south of fold 25 – Local map p 116

Tucked away in the fold of a small valley off of the Vézère Valley, is St-Amand-de-Coly, its old *lauze*-roofed houses clustering round the impressive abbey church.

The village and its church

★★Church (Église). – This church, of fine yellow limestone, is one of Périgord's most amazing fortified churches. A considerable defence system, now almost entirely uncovered, protected the buildings of the abbey, which was established in this spot by Augustinian canons in the 12C.

Exterior. – The huge pointed arch of the doorway supports the **porch-keep** and gives an impression of great strength. Once the keep was pierced by loopholes; in its upper part corbels, still visible, supported watch-turrets; within the porch are a round arched clerestory window with, below, a doorway surrounded by motifs carved in archaic style. Bear left to look at the east end. Here the apsidal chapels, protected by a defensive structure, contrast in their graceful design with the severe lines of the upper parts of the walls of the nave and transept roofed with *lauzes*.

Interior. – Pure lines and decorative simplicity combine to increase the beauty of the lofty interior. Above the transept crossing is an archaic dome on pendentives. The chancel, raised eight steps above the nave, ends in a flat east end and is roofed with quadripartite vaulting. There was once a passage running right round the eaves of the building which formed part of its defence system: there remain a cornice, supported by consoles, which extends round the chancel and part of the transept, traces of the square pillars that once stood in the transept crossing; and the door leading to the upper chamber in the keep.

◎ Opposite the church, in the **former presbytery** an audio-visual show on the church and its history is presented.

Michelin map 🔢 fold 19 or 🔢🔢🔢 southwest of fold 19

St-Antonin, an old city on the borders of Quercy and Rouergue, faces a vertical cliff of rocks known as the Anglars Rocks (Roc d'Anglars) on the far side of the Aveyron Valley. The houses, with nearly flat roofs covered in round tiles faded by the sun, rise above the north bank of the river.

So delightful was the setting of this Gallo-Roman resort, forerunner of the present town, that it was given the name of Noble-Val. An oratory founded by St Antonin, who came to convert this part of Rouergue, was replaced in the 8C by an abbey.

The town developed rapidly during the Middle Ages, as can be seen by the 13, 14 and 15C houses which were once the residences of rich merchants.

SIGHTS

★Former Town Hall (Ancien Hôtel de Ville). – This mansion was built in 1125 for a lord named Archambault, and is one of the oldest examples of civil architecture in France. In the 14C it was the consuls' residence; Viollet-le-Duc restored it in the 19C, adding on top of it a square machicolated belfry in the Italian Tuscan style, after a project he presented in 1845. It now houses a museum.

The façade consists of two storeys. The gallery of small columns on the first floor is adorned with two pillars bearing statues of King Solomon and Adam and Eve; the second storey is divided into three sets of twin bays.

◎ **Museum (Musée)**. – The museum contains a collection on prehistory which is particularly rich in artifacts from the Magdalenian Period. One room covers local traditions and folklore.

Covered market (Halle). – In front of the covered market, the solid pillars of which hold up the timber framework, stands an unusual 14C Calvary.

Town Hall (Mairie). – It is located in a former convent built in the 18C.

Old houses. – In the old town hall quarter, narrow streets are lined with medieval houses, their tall façades dressed with pointed arches and mullioned windows.

Anglars Rocks Viewpoint (Belvédère du Roc d'Anglars). – *4.5km – 2 1/2 miles; cross the river to Anglars Rocks*. From the viewpoint there is a wide view of a stark landscape of plateaux traversed by the wooded valleys of the Aveyron and the Bonnette; at the foot of the rock face lies the village of St-Antonin.

EXCURSIONS

★⬚1 **Aveyron Gorges (Gorges de l'Aveyron)**. – *Round tour of 49km – 30 miles – about 3 hours – local map below. Leave St-Antonin by the south, cross the Aveyron and take the road on the right, built along a disused railway track.*
After 2.5km – 1 1/2 miles turn left into a fine **corniche road**★★ which rises rapidly. Pass through the hamlet of Vieilfour with its round tiled roofs. Shortly after passing through a tunnel, there is a belvedere, above a sheer drop, from which there is a good view of the Aveyron, enclosed by tall rock walls. When descending towards the river, Brousses comes into view.

At Cazals cross the river.

The road begins to climb immediately and passes between vineyards, affording views of the meanders in the Aveyron River and the valley floor covered with peach and apple orchards and meadows cut by lines of poplars.

Penne. – *Description p 115.*

Leave Penne to the south by the D 9, which affords lovely **views**★ of the village. The road drops down over the edge of the plateau before crossing this region of sparse vegetation with stunted bushes and the occasional vine. The road then descends again into the valley where the high, wooded hillsides are often strewn with rocks.

★**Bruniquel**. – *Description p 57.*

Follow the road built along the right bank of the Aveyron from Bruniquel to Montricoux.

Montricoux. – *Description p 57.*

Return to St-Antonin by the D 958.

This road running through the Garrigue Forest (Forêt de la Garrigue) affords glimpses of the Aveyron Gorges below and to the right. Then take a *corniche* road overlooking the Aveyron.

⬚2 **Upper Aveyron Valley**. – *Round tour of 42km – 26 miles – about 2 hours – local map below. Leave St-Antonin to the northeast.*

⊘ **Bosc Cave (Grotte du Bosc)**. – The galleries, once the bed of an underground river now dry, go back some 220yds underneath the plateau between the Aveyron and Bonnette Valleys. Stalactites and eccentrics decorate the cave *(for more details on caves and chasms see p 17)*.
A mineralogical and prehistoric museum has been set up in the reception hall.

Continue along the D 75, then take the D 20 to the right and the D 33 to the left.

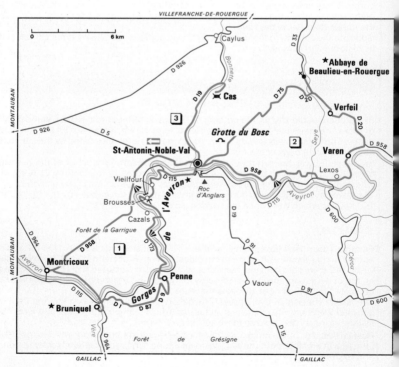

★**Abbey of Beaulieu-en-Rouergue**. – *Description p 42.*

Turn around and follow the D 33.

Verfeil. – Pop 425. This small but charming bastion lies in the Seye Valley. Its old houses with their flower-decked façades, surround a covered market rebuilt of stone. In the church, both the high altar in historiated gilt wood and the 17C wood figure of Christ came from the former Abbey of Beaulieu-en-Rouergue.

Take the D 20 and then the D 958 to the right.

The road follows the Aveyron, which flows at this point along the wide valley floor carpeted with meadows and crops.

Varen. – *Description p 145.*

At the entrance to Lexos, the road passes near a large cement works. 2km – 1 mile after Lexos bear right on the D 33, then left on the road signposted "St-Antonin par le coteau".

The road climbs rapidly along the hillside, affording more and more glimpses of the Aveyron Valley to which it returns after a winding descent. The river, outlined with a string of poplars, flows at the foot of tall cliffs covered with sparse vegetation. A little before St-Antonin, the road and river run closely together along the narrow valley bounded by steep rocky sides.

③ **Cas Castle (Château de Cas)**. – *6km – 3 1/2 miles north – local map p 130.*
⊙ Built in the 12C, Cas Castle was rearranged in the 14 and 16C. In the 13C it was a Templar commandery; it then became the property of the powerful Cardaillac family and then that of the Lastic Saint-Jals'.
This solid white limestone edifice contains furnished rooms.

ST-AVIT-SÉNIEUR   Pop 385

Michelin map 🖽 fold 16 or 🖾🖽 fold 5

This small village is dominated by a massive church and conventual buildings which are the remains of an old Benedictine abbey built in the 11C to the memory of St Avitus, the soldier turned hermit.

⊙ **Church (Église)**. – The church exterior is austere and rugged: in the 14C the building was fortified, as can be seen from the crenellations crowning the porch, the tall and nearly blind walls of the nave and east end, and the towers, linked by a watchpath on either side of the façade.
The nave is very spacious and has fine Angevin vaulting adorned with ribs, or liernes, and finely carved keystones. The building ends in a chancel with a flat east end. The size of the transverse arches leads one to believe that it was originally intended that the church be roofed with domes. A watchpath runs beneath the springing of the vaulting.

Conventual buildings (Bâtiments monastiques). – The only traces of the former abbey to be seen are a few arches of the former cloisters and the chapter house. In the
⊙ monks' former dormitory, above the chapter house, a **Geology Museum** (Musée de Géologie) has been set up. It is concerned, for the most part, with the Dordogne Basin.
Excavations have revealed the foundations of the conventual buildings and of a primitive Romanesque church.
From the inner court there is a good overall view of the upper part of the church's nave.

★ ST-CÉRÉ   Pop 4 207

Michelin map 🖽 folds 19 and 20 or 🖾🖽 fold 7 or 🖾🖽🖽 fold 39 – Local map p 133 – Facilities

The picturesque old houses of St-Céré cluster in the smiling Bave Valley, below the tall St-Laurent Towers. St-Céré stands at the junction of the roads from Limousin, Auvergne and Quercy, and has become a place to stay in its own right because of its pleasant **site**★. It is also an excellent starting-point for walks and excursions in Haut-Quercy.

A prosperous town. – The viscounts of Turenne, overlords of St-Céré, granted a charter, in the 13C, with franchises and many advantages to the town. Other charters enriched the town because of their right to hold fairs and establish trading houses. Consuls and officials administered the town, the defence of which was assured by St-Laurent Castle and a formidable line of ramparts. Even the Hundred Years' War left the town practically unscathed. With the 16C dawned a new period of prosperity.

An early Academician. – St-Céré had the honour to be the birthplace of Marshal **Canrobert**, who won glory as a soldier in Algeria, was commander-in-chief in the Crimea and distinguished himself at St-Privat in the Franco-Prussian War of 1870.
The town can also count the poet **François Maynard** *(qv)* among her most famous citizens. The poet, son of a member of Parliament, though born in Toulouse in 1582, spent many years of his life in St-Céré. While still young, he managed to obtain the post of secretary to Marguerite of Valois, at one time the wife of Henri IV.
He soon became known as one of the most skilful court poets of the period. Malherbe noticed him, as did also Cardinal Richelieu, who honoured him by nominating him a member of the Academy he had just founded. The story goes that Maynard, who enjoyed receiving honours but was not above receiving money, asked the Cardinal for a tangible expression of the latter's confidence.

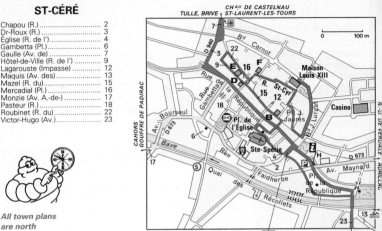

ST-CÉRÉ

All town plans are north oriented.

Blatantly he asked: "But if I'm asked what you have asked me to do and what in return I've received from you what would you have me say?" "Nothing" the Cardinal was said to have replied dryly.

Dismissed by Parisian society, the poet came to live in St-Céré. He devoted himself to versification, frequented literary circles and society and went to the fabulous receptions given at Castelnau-Bretenoux. When he died in 1646, he was buried beneath the chancel of the Church of Ste-Spérie in St-Céré.

Jean Lurçat and St-Céré. – Born in 1892 in the Vosges, Jean Lurçat who was destined to be a doctor, oriented himself to painting, decoration of theatrical scenery, mosaics and ceramics. He soon became interested in the tapestry as a medium and it is as a painter-cartoonist that he achieved world renown.

After a period spent in Aubusson, he participated in the Resistance movement and discovered the Lot. He established himself in St-Céré in 1945. It was in the St-Laurent Towers that he set up his studio and where he lived until his death in 1966.

Lurçat had the Aubusson tapestry factory weave most of the tapestries for which he had drawn cartoons.

OLD TOWN

The 15, 16 and 17C houses give St-Céré a picturesque character all its own. Some houses still have their half-timbered corbelled façades and fine roofs of brown tiles.

Place de l'Église. – Ste-Spérie, a very old place of worship, was rebuilt in the 17 and 18C in the Gothic style.

In the square near the east end, the **Hôtel de Puymule** (15C) is a turretted edifice pierced with doors and windows, decorated with ogee arches.

Cross Rue de la République, a busy shopping street, bearing left in Rue du Mazel.

Rue du Mazel (15). – This street and the surrounding area form one of the most charming districts in the old town, with old houses and fine doorways. At the corner of Rue St-Cyr, note the 15C **Hôtel Ambert (B)** with its two corbelled turrets and Renaissance doorway.

Further on the right, the narrow cobblestoned **Impasse Lagarouste (12)**, a stream in the middle, is overshadowed by tall corbelled houses.

Place du Mercadial (16). – This was the market square where fishermen brought their catch which was displayed on the *taoulié*, a stone bench beside the 15C **Jean de Séguier's House (D)** at the corner of Rue Pasteur. From this spot, there is a lovely view of the square lined with half-timbered houses standing out against the St-Laurent Towers. The **Consuls' House (E)** has an interesting Renaissance façade giving onto Rue de l'Hôtel-de-Ville.

Rue St-Cyr. – At the beginning of the street stands a lovely medieval house with three corbelled façades. Further on, to the right, is the 15C **Hôtel de Miramon (F)** flanked with a corner turret. The street, which extends in a semicircle and is lined with old houses, ends in Rue du Mazel.

On leaving Rue du Mazel take Boulevard Jean-Lurçat to the left.

Louis XIII Mansion (Maison Louis XIII). – This fine mansion has an elegant façade adorned with a loggia.

ADDITIONAL SIGHTS

Casino Gallery (Galerie du Casino). – In addition to temporary exhibitions, there is a large collection of **Jean Lurçat's tapestries**★ on permanent display. The tapestries combine matter, form and colour and depict fabulous animals and cosmic visions.

St-Laurent Towers (Tours de St-Laurent). – *2km – 1 mile to the north*. Perched on a steep hill which overlooks the town, the two tall medieval towers and curtain wall are a familiar local landmark.

Although the road to the right is private, the restriction is not strictly enforced. A track *(1 hour on foot Rtn)* skirts the ramparts and offers pleasant **views**★ of the town, the Bave and Dordogne Valleys and the surrounding plateaux.

★**Studio-Museum Jean Lurçat** (Atelier-musée Jean-Lurçat). – In the ground floor rooms
⊘ (studio, drawing room, dining room) of this *c*1900 house Lurçat's works (tapestries,
cartoons – one of which is still where the artist had left it when struck by death –
ceramics, lithographs, watercolours, wall paper) are exhibited. Note the copies of the
thrones ordered by Haile Selassie, emperor of Ethiopia in 1956.

⊘ **Haut-Quercy Automobile Museum (Musée automobile du Haut-Quercy).** – Some thirty
vehicles in working order are exhibited here. Several models have become proto-
types: the Citroën P 17 Caterpillar (1930), which took part in the Trans-Asian
Expedition known as the *Croisière Jaune*, the Volkswagen cross-country vehicle, the
amphibian Schwimmwagen (1942), the Citroën ID 19 (1962) and the Citroën 2 CV
Sahara (1965), 4-wheel drive and two engines.

EXCURSIONS

★**1 Bave Valley: from St-Céré to Castelnau-Bretenoux.** – *25km – 15 1/2 miles –
about 3 hours – local map p 133. Leave St-Céré westwards.*

The towers of Montal Castle soon come into view on the left, rising above fertile
fields and meadows lined with poplars.

★★**Montal Castle.** – *Description p 109.*

The road towards Gramat rises above the Bave Valley, offering views of St-Laurent
Towers.

★**Presque Cave** (Grotte de Presque). – The cave consists of a series of chambers and
⊘ galleries that go back 350m – 380yds into the rocks. Concretions, especially stalag-
mite piles in curious shapes and frozen falls along the walls with a thousand facets,
have accumulated in the Drapery Chamber (Salle des Draperies), the High Chamber
(Salle Haute), the Chamber of the Great Basin (Salle de la Grande Cuve) and the Red
Marble Hall (Salle de Marbre Rouge). Slender columns of astonishing whiteness
stand at the entrance to the Hall of Wonder (Salle des Merveilles).

At Le Boutel turn right to Autoire.

★**Autoire Amphitheatre** (Cirque d'Autoire). – Leave the car in a parking area. Take, on the
left of the road, the path that overlooks the Autoire River, which here forms a series
of waterfalls (belvedere).
Cross the little bridge and go up the steep stony path cut in the rocks. Very soon a wonderful **view**★★ of the amphitheatre, the valley and the village of Autoire can be seen.

★**Autoire.** – Pop 233. Autoire in its picturesque **setting**★ is completely Quercynois in character. Wandering through the streets, the visitor may see enchanting vignettes: a
fountain at the centre of a group of half-timbered houses, old corbelled houses with
brown-tiled roofs, elegant turreted manors and mansions.
From the terrace near the church, with its fine Romanesque east end, there is a good
view of the Limargue Mill and the rocky amphitheatre that lies to the southwest.

★**Loubressac.** – Pop 405. This old fortified town stands on a rocky spur overlooking the
south bank of the Bave River. From near the church, there is a good **view** of the valley
and of St-Céré, identified by its towers. Walk through the enchanting narrow alleys
as they wind between brown-tiled houses to the castle's postern.
This 15C manor-house, which was rebuilt in the 17C, stands on a remarkable **site**★ at
the very end of the spur on which the village was built. Several buildings with pointed
brown-tiled roofs line the main courtyard.
The D 118 and the D 14, taken at the hamlet of La Poujade, descend towards the
Bave Valley, offering fine **views**★ of the Dordogne Valley dominated by the impressive outline of Castelnau-Bretenoux Castle.

★★**Castelnau-Bretenoux Castle.** – *Description p 66.*

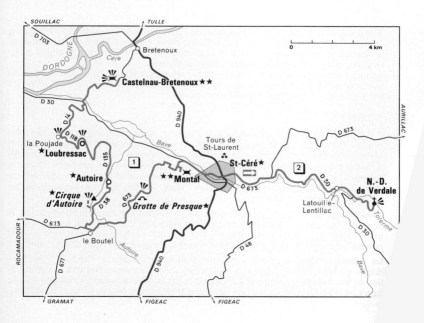

② **Chapel of Notre-Dame de Verdale**. – *10km – 6 miles east plus 1 hour on foot Rtn – local map p 133.*

The road passes wooded hills and meadows at it goes up the Bave Valley.

Beyond Latouille-Lentillac a narrow road branches off to the left from the D 30; follow this to a hamlet where you will leave the car.

Walk up a path, which runs beside the Tolerme, where it falls in cascades over the rocks. One crosses the stream twice on primitive wooden bridges before the path starts to climb steeply, in a hilly setting, and finally leads to the pilgrimage chapel of Our Lady of Verdale which stands perched on a rocky crag. From the crag there is a wide **view**★ of the Tolerme Gorges and the chestnut-covered hills.

★★ ST-CIRQ-LAPOPIE   Pop 179

Michelin map 📖 fold 9 or 📖 northeast of fold 14 – Local map pp 100-101 – Facilities

St-Cirq-Lapopie (pronounced St-Sear), facing a semicircle of white cliffs and itself standing perched (80m – 262ft) on a rocky escarpment that drops vertically to the left bank of the Lot, occupies a remarkable **setting**★★

HISTORICAL NOTES

The village

A contested stronghold. – It seems probable that men have been tempted to occupy this rock commanding the valley since Gallo-Roman times. The present name of the site commemorates the martyrdom of the young St Cyr, killed with his mother in Asia Minor during the reign of Diocletian; his relics were brought back, it is said, by St Amadour *(qv)*. The La Popies, local lords in the Middle Ages, gave their name to the castle built on the cliff's highest point and, by extension, to the village that grew up at its foot.

The history of the fortress is a long series of sieges. In the struggle against Pepin the Short in the 8C, Waïfre, Duke of Aquitaine, placed his last hopes in this bastion. In 1198 Richard Lionheart tried in vain to seize the stronghold.

During the Hundred Years' War, the English fought bitterly to take St-Cirq from the garrison, commanded by the lord of Cardaillac, who remained loyal to the king of France. In 1471, Louis XI ordered the castle to be demolished but the ruins were still of sufficient strategic importance for the Huguenots to fight for them during the Wars of Religion. In 1580, Henri de Navarre, the future Henri IV, ordered such walls of the valiant fortress as were still standing, to be knocked down.

The end of a craft. – St-Cirq-Lapopie had a strong guild of wood-turners dating back to the Middle Ages. Even last century, there were a considerable number of craftsmen still to be seen working their primitive lathes; their industry added a picturesque note to the old-fashioned village alleyways.

Today, a number of artisans (potters, leather workers, silk screeners...) have replaced them, occupying the same houses, opened by a pointed arch and in front of which the wood-turner used to set up his work-bench.

SIGHTS

It is a perennial pleasure to wander along narrow, steeply sloping streets lined with houses with lovely brown-tiled roofs. The corbelled façades and exposed beams of some of the houses are further ornamented with Gothic windows, or bays with mullioned windows, in the Renaissance style. Most of the houses have been diligently restored by artists, particularly painters and craftsmen who have been attracted by the beauty of St-Cirq-Lapopie and the Lot Valley. Among the most famous are the writer André Breton and the painter Pierre Daura.

ırch (Église). – This 15C sanctuary stands on a rock terrace overlooking the Lot. A ˙ belfry-tower, flanked by a round turret, stands at the front end.
the main body of the church has pointed vaulting and contains several ⁊ statues. There is a good view from the terrace to the right of the church.

ɔtte Castle. – Seat of the tourist information centre. The two main buil- ɩ flanked by a battlemented turret, house a **museum** containing the dona- Rignault (painter and collector) to the Lot *département*. Exhibited are old ɲaissance cabinet and sideboard, 14C dowry chest), 14 and 15C statues, from China and frescoes dating from the Ming Dynasty.

La Popie. – Take the path that starts on the right of the town hall *(mairie)*, to reach the castle ruins and the highest part of the cliff. From the cliff top (telescope), on which once stood the keep of La Popie fortress, there is a remarkable **view**★★ right over the village of St-Cirq, with the church clinging to the cliff face, of a bend of the Lot River, encircling a chequerboard of arable fields and meadows outlined with poplars, and to the north, of the wooded foothills that border the Gramat Causse.

Le Bancourel. – Follow the D 40 towards Bouziès for 300m – 330yds to reach this rock promontory overlooking the Lot. A lay-by esplanade *(car park)* has been built where the D 8 branches off to the left from the tourist road that has been cut *corniche*-fashion in the cliff *(pp 100-101)*.
There is a **view**★ from Le Bancourel of the valley of the Lot and St-Cirq, with the rock of La Popie rising up out of the village.

ST-CYPRIEN Pop 1 730

Michelin map 75 fold 16 or 235 east of fold 5 – Local map pp 76-77 – Facilities

St-Cyprien clings to the side of a hill near the north bank of the Dordogne, in a setting of hills and woodlands characteristic of the Périgord Noir *(qv)*. It is dominated by the massive outline of its church around which cluster old houses.

Church (Église). – The church, belonging to an abbey for Augustinian canons, was built in the 12C and restored in the Gothic period. Its size is impressive; it still has a Romanesque belfry keep. Inside, the main body of the church, which is enormous, has pointed vaulting. A wealth of 17C furnishings include altarpieces, pulpit, stalls, organ loft and a wrought iron balustrade.

EXCURSIONS

Berbiguières. – Pop 185. *5km – 3 miles to the south by the D 48 and then the D 50 to the left*. The village is dominated by a 17C château with ramparts flanked by battlemented turrets.

Redon l'Espi Chapel (Chapelle de Redon l'Espi). – *7.5km – 4 1/2km east*.
Lost in the middle of a remote valley, this sober Romanesque chapel is flanked to the south by the ruins of a small monastery; the buildings were ransacked during the Wars of Religion in the 16C. The name of the chapel, Redon Espi, is said to come from the Latin *rotondo spino*, possibly the evocation of a reliquary of the Holy Thorn, preserved for centuries at the nearby St-Cyprien Abbey.

★ ST-JEAN-DE-CÔLE Pop 343

Michelin map 75 north of fold 6 or 233 south of fold 32

The old houses and Gothic bridge give the village, with its unusual church and castle, an antique charm. This charming picture is enhanced by the golden stones which blend nicely with the brown of the small roof tiles. An old, narrow humpbacked bridge with cutwaters spans the Côle, a tributary of the Dronne.

Church (Église). – This former priory chapel was started in the 11C. It is outstanding for the curious shape of the bell tower pierced by windows, the nave which is high in proportion to its length, the capitals which divide the south chapel and the chancel, the sculpture found at roof level and the old covered markets built onto the east end. Inside, note the 17C oak woodwork in the chancel. The nave is covered by a wooden ceiling replacing the collapsed dome, the pendentives of which may still be seen; on the south side, in a chapel, note the recumbent figure in a niche.

⊘ **Marthonie Castle**. – A gallery houses a collection of old publicity posters and handmade paper. All that remains of the 12C castle is the tower and its foundations (on the square); several mullioned windows are preserved from the 15 and 16C, when the castle was rebuilt. The basket-arched gallery and the staircase, with straight ramps, also with eccentric or basket arches inside, date from the 17C.

EXCURSIONS

★**Round tour of 24km – 15miles**. – *Leave St-Jean-de-Côle to the west.*
★**Château de Puyguilhem**. – *Description p 123.*
　　Once in Villars turn left onto the D 82. After 3km — 2 miles bear right.
★**Villars Caves** (Grottes de Villars). – A winding corridor leads to chambers ornamented
⊘ with beautiful concretions, among which you will see yellow ochre draperies, two small natural limestone dams *(gours)*, and particularly fine white stalactites hanging from the cave ceiling.
The amazingly white concretions in the first galleries to be passed through are formed from almost pure and very brilliant calcite. Some of the chamber walls are decorated with prehistoric paintings done with manganese oxide and go back 17000 years dating most likely from the period when Lascaux was painted. The calcite deposit covering some of the paintings proves their authenticity.
　　Return to St-Jean-de-Côle.

Thiviers. – Pop 4 215. *7.5km – 4 1/2 miles to the east*. This small, busy town is famous throughout the region for its markets and fairs *(foies gras*, fattened poultry and truffles)*.
Château de Vaucocour, which is Renaissance-Gothic in style and has been frequently restored, looks down from its towers and turrets on the Isle Valley.

Built in a picturesque loop of the Vézère River, this charming village, overrun by greenery, possesses two castles and one of the finest Romanesque churches of Périgord.

★**Church (Église).** – The church was part of a Benedictine priory which was founded in the 12C and depended upon the Sarlat abbey. The edifice was built on the ruins of a Gallo-Roman villa. The remains of one of its walls can be seen on the river side.

From the square, the apse, the perfectly smooth radiating chapels and the fine square two storey arcaded bell tower form a harmonious unit. The church is roofed with the heavy limestone slabs *(lauzes)* of Périgord Noir.

Inside, the transept crossing is vaulted with a dome, whereas the arms of the transept communicate with the nave via narrow passageways.

The apse and south radiating chapel are decorated with parts of Romanesque frescoes, where red is the predominant colour.

La Salle Castle. – Standing on the square, this small castle built of dry-stone has a fine 14C square keep crowned with machicolations.

Château de Clérans. – This elegant 15 and 16C building, flanked with machicolated towers and turrets, borders the river.

Cemetery Chapel (Chapelle du cimetière). – This small 14C chapel is covered, like the church, with *lauzes*.

Church

ST-MARTIN-DE-GURÇON   Pop 526

Located in Gurçon Country on the boundary line of Périgord and Guyenne, St-Martin possesses an interesting church.

ⓥ**Church (Église).** – Its fine façade in the Saintonge style dates from the 12C. The doorway, without tympanum, opens onto five smooth recessed arches held up by ten columns, with capitals carved with birds and monsters. Above the doorway, an arcade of seven rounded arches resting on small columns, is edged with a moulding decorated with heads, on top of which is a fine cornice with carved modillions. Inside, the third bay is roofed with an ovoid-shaped dome.

EXCURSIONS

Montpeyroux. – *10km – 6 miles to the southwest.*
This excursion goes through Gurçon Country: a flat countryside dominated by mounds, crowned by limestone tables, and where vineyards grow.

Carsac-de-Gurson. – In this village, surrounded by vineyards, stands a church, the Romanesque façade of which presents all the characteristics of the Saintonge style.

Continue towards Villefranche-de-Lonchat, turn left onto the D 32 and left again onto a small road which passes below Gurson Castle.

Gurson Castle. – Set on a mound, the castle has preserved some of its fortifications. The castle was given by Henry III of England, Duke of Aquitaine, to his seneschal Jean de Grailly. It was rebuilt in the 14C.
At the foot of the castle is a lake.

After the castle, turn right, then left into the D 10.

Montpeyroux. – Pop 318. The Montpeyroux mound is crowned by a group of buildings which includes the church and château. At the far end of the mound is a lovely view of the region: low squat houses scattered among the vines.
The Romanesque **church**, surrounded by its churchyard, possesses a Saintonge style façade similar to the one at St-Martin-de-Gurçon. Note the lovely cornice with carved modillions running round the apse, which is covered with a blind arcade made of nine arches.
Near the church stands an elegant 17 and 18C château. It is composed of a main building flanked by two pavilions at right angles, cantoned by round towers. Each opening is surmounted by an *œil-de-bœuf* window.

*The **Michelin Green Guide France** aims to make touring more enjoyable by outlining a variety of touring programmes, easily adapted to personal taste.*

ST-PRIVAT

Michelin map **75** west of fold 4 or **233** norhtwest of fold 41 – Local map p 80

Called also St-Privat-des-Prés, this village located on the border of Périgord and Charentes has a lovely Romanesque church which used to belong to a 12C Benedictine priory, which was dependent of Aurillac Abbey.

★Church (Église). – Its main façade was very much influenced by the Romanesque Saintonge style. Its fine doorway includes nine rounded recessed arches forming an archivolt carved with geometric designs. Above it is blind arcading. A shelter for the village, the church has preserved some evidence of its role as a fortress: on the eastern side the raising of the chevet as a defence tower, on the western side the thickness of the façade wall into which a defence corridor was built and on the upper walls traces of merlons. The inside is attractive with its very narrow pointed-barrel vaulted aisles; the dome of the transept crossing was added after the church was built. On either side of the semicircular oven-vaulted apse, both tiny chapels (very restored) contain a 17C wood **altarpiece**. At the entrance is a fine Romanesque baptistry.

Museum of Popular Arts and Traditions of the Dronne and Double Regions (Centre d'art et traditions populaires du pays de Dronne et de Double). – Located near the church, the museum has assembled a variety of objects recalling traditional life of this region. A grocer's shop, artisans' workshops and a hairdresser's has been reconstituted. Also exhibited are different items relevant to the 19C school room (maps, benches...), clothes, tools, etc. An annexe exhibits wooden **models★** of castles, châteaux and cathedrals found in France.

ST-ROBERT

Michelin map **75** east of fold 7 or **239** fold 25 – 5km – 3 miles northwest of Ayen

St-Robert is pleasantly situated amid hills facing a typical Dordogne landscape of poplars and walnut trees. It was used as the setting for the television series *Des Grives aux Loups*, taken from local author Claude Michelet's *(qv)* novel of the same name. From the terrace of the town hall, there is a good **view** of the church's east end and of the surrounding countryside.

★Church (Église). – Only the transept, supporting an octagonal bell tower at the crossing, and the well-proportioned chancel remain from the original 12C building. The turret and square tower which flank the east end are evidence of the defences in the 14C. The chancel is lit by a clerestory and is divided from the ambulatory by six columns topped by interesting historiated capitals; the capitals attached to the ambulatory wall, were carved in a more archaic manner — note the two old men pulling at their beards. On the left stands a figure of **Christ** in wood (13C) from the Spanish School.

STE-FOY-LA-GRANDE

Michelin map **75** folds 13 and 14 or **234** north of fold 8

Alphonse de Poitiers, brother of Saint Louis, founded this bastide *(qv)* in 1255 on the south bank of the Dordogne. It is an animated market town selling regional products (fruit, flowers, tobacco) as well as a wine centre.
St-Foy is also the home town of the surgeons **Jean-Louis Faure** (1863-1944), **Paul Broca** (1824-80) founder of the school of anthropology, **Élie Faure** (1873-1937) art critic and historian whose writings were important in the study of art history and the Reclus brothers.

Reclus brothers. – Among the famous family of five brothers – four writers and one surgeon – there was **Élisée** (1830-1905) who wrote the monumental work *Géographie Universelle* and was obliged to leave France in 1851 for his republican ideas; **Élie** (1827-1904), **Onésime** (1837-1914), **Armand** (1843-1927); and the youngest, **Paul** (1847-1914) not a writer but a surgeon, whose name has been given to Reclus disease.

Town. – An atmosphere of days past permeates Place de la Mairie (Place Gambetta), surrounded by covered arcades and old houses (medieval, Renaissance, 17C); the tall spire (62m – 203ft) of its neo-Gothic church overlooks the town.
In Rue de la République note no 53, a house flanked by a corner turret, no 94, a carved half-timbered 15C house and no 102, a house with a corner turret.
A lovely stroll along the river, flowing below the ramparts, is recommended.

SALIGNAC-EYVIGUES

Michelin map **75** folds 17 and 18 or **235** fold 2 – Local map p 116

The village is perched on the hillside, not far from the Dordogne Valley and dominated by its imposing castle.

Castle. – There is a good overall view from the D 60, east of the village, of this medieval fortress still belonging to the family of Archbishop of Cambrai, François de Salignac de la Mothe-Fénelon *(qv)*.
The castle, which was built between the 12 and 17C, is still encircled by ramparts. Mullioned windows lighten the façade of the main building, which is flanked by round and square towers. The whole building is enhanced by the warm colour of the stone and the lovely stone slab *(lauzes)* roofs.
Go up a Renaissance spiral staircase to visit several rooms with interesting furnishings, mainly in the Renaissance and Louis XIII styles.

In the heart of Périgord Noir, Sarlat-la-Canéda was built in a hollow surrounded by wooded hills. Its charm lies in its preservation of the past; it still "feels" like a small market town – the home of merchants and clerks during the Ancien Régime (period before the Revolution) – with narrow medieval streets, Gothic and Renaissance *hôtels* (restored) and the famous **Saturday market**.

HISTORICAL NOTES

From abbey to bishopric. – Sarlat grew up around a Benedictine abbey founded in the 9C and to which, under Charlemagne, had been entrusted the relics of St Sacerdos, Bishop of Limoges and of his mother, St Mondane.

The abbots were all powerful, until the 13C when internal strife and corruption caused their downfall. In 1299, the *Book of Peace*, an act of emancipation, signed by the community, the abbey and the king, stated that the abbot preserved his role of lord but that the consuls were given all administrative power concerning the town itself. In 1317, however, Pope John XXII divided the Périgueux diocese and proclaimed the Sarlat episcopal see, which extended far beyond the Sarladais. The abbey church, therefore, became a cathedral and the monks formed a chapter.

Sarlat's golden age. – The 13 and early 14C had been a prosperous time for this active market town, but the Hundred Years' War left it weakened and depopulated. Therefore, when Charles VII, in order to thank Sarlat and its population for its loyalty and strong resistance against the English (and yet Sarlat was ceded to them with the *Treaty of Bretigny* in 1360) bestowed upon them numerous privileges (new revenues and certain tax exemptions), the people of Sarlat began reconstruction. Most of the *hôtels* now seen were built between 1450-1500. This has created an architectural unity which is appreciated by the townspeople and tourists alike.

The magistrates, clerks, bishops, canons and merchants formed a comfortable class of society which included such men of letters as Étienne de La Boétie.

The completely faithful friend. – Étienne de La Boétie, who was born in Sarlat in 1530 in a house that can still be seen *(p 135)*, became famous on many counts. He proved himself to be a brilliant magistrate in the Bordeaux Parliament and an impassioned writer – he was only eighteen when he wrote the compelling appeal for liberty, *Discourse on Voluntary Subjection* or *Contr'un – Against One*, which inspired Jean-Jacques Rousseau when he came to write the *Social Contract*. He formed a friendship with **Michel de Montaigne** that was to last until he died and which has been immortalized by posterity. Montaigne was at La Boétie's bedside when the young man died all too early in 1563; thinking of his friend, Montaigne wrote his famous *Essay on Friendship* in which he propounded the maxim: "If I am pressed to explain why I was fond of him, I feel I can only reply: because he was himself and I am myself..."

Sarlat's secular architecture. Sarlat's old quarter was cut into two in the 19C by the "Traverse" (or Rue de la République) separating it into a more populated western section and a more refined eastern section.

The *hôtels* are quite unique: built with ashlar-work selected from a fine golden-hued limestone, with an interior courtyard; the roofing, made of heavy limestone slabs *(lauzes)*, demanded a steeply pitched framework so that the enormous weight (500kg/m²) could rest on thick walls; and as the years passed floors were added: a medieval ground floor, a Gothic Rayonnant or Renaissance upper floor and classical roof cresting and lantern turrets.

This architectural unit escaped modern building developments in the 19 and 20C because of its distance from the main road network. It was chosen in 1962 as one of the new experimental restoration projects, the goal of which was to preserve the old quarters of France's towns and cities. The project, begun in 1964, has allowed the charm of this small medieval town to be recreated.

La Boétie's House

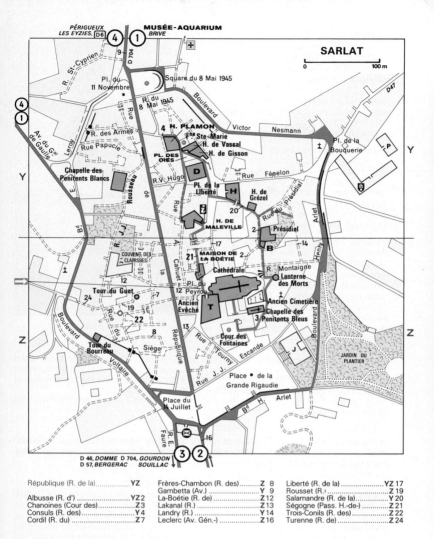

★★ OLD SARLAT *time: 1 1/2 hours*

Start from Place du Peyrou.

★La Boétie's House (Maison de la Boétie) (Z). – This house, built in 1525 by Antoine de La Boétie, a criminal magistrate in the seneschal's court at Sarlat, was the birthplace of Étienne de La Boétie *(qv)*.

Small shops on the ground floor were identified by a large arch; the two upper floors of Italian Renaissance style have large single mullioned windows, framed by pilasters carved with medallions and lozenges. The steeply pitched gabled roof is decorated with crockets; and the left side is opened by a heavily ornamented dormer window *(photograph p 33)*.

On the house's left side is Passage Henri-de-Ségogne *(p 141)*.

Former bishopric (Ancien Évêché) (Z T). – To the right of St-Sacerdos Cathedral, is the former bishopric. Its façade is opened by windows in the Gothic style on the 1st floor, Renaissance on the 2nd floor and above an Italian Renaissance loggia, added by the Italian bishop Nicolo Goddi, friend of Catherine de' Medici. The interior has been transformed into a theatre.

St-Sacerdos Cathedral (Cathédrale St-Sacerdos) (Z). – St-Sacerdos Church was built here in the 12C. In 1504 the Bishop Armand de Gontaut-Biron had the church razed, in order to build a cathedral.

However, when the bishop left Sarlat in 1519, the construction work ceased for more than a century. Although the present church was built during the 16 and 17C, the base of the west façade's tower is Romanesque. Of its three storeys, the lowest is formed of blind arcading, the second has open bays, while the third is a 17C addition.

Inside, the most striking features are the elevation and harmonious proportions of the vessel. Among the furnishings are an 18C organ loft and an organ by Lépine (a well-known family of organ makers).

Leave by the south door.

The first courtyard is bordered by the **Chapel of the Blue Penitents** (Chapelle des Pénitents Bleus), a pure Romanesque building (12C), a vestige of the Benedictine abbey *(p 138)*. From here notice the south side of the cathedral supported by flying buttresses, the side chapels built between the buttresses and the bulbous-shaped lantern crowning the bell tower.

Continue into the **Cour des Fontaines** and then turn left into the second courtyard, the **Cour des Chanoines (3)**, which is enclosed on its north side by the Chapel of the Blue Penitents. Go round the chapel, by the right, to reach the east end of the cathedral, which is adjoined by buildings with *lauzes* roofs.

Former cemetery (Ancien Cimetière) (Z). – Excavations around the east end have enhanced the funerary niches carved out of the retaining wall and have permitted the creation of a terraced cemetery garden using 12-15C tombstones found in the earth recovered from the site.

Lantern of the dead (Lanterne des Morts) (Z). – Built at the end of the 12C, this curious cylindrical tower topped by a cone and divided by four bands contains two rooms. The room on the ground floor has domical vaulting held up by six pointed arches; the other room is in the cone part of the tower and is inaccessible to man.

Lantern of the dead

A number of hypotheses have been raised concerning the lantern's function: it could have been a tower built when St Bernard (he had blessed bread which miraculously cured the sick) visited the town in 1147; or a lantern of the dead (but it is difficult to imagine how the lantern was lit because the top room was inaccessible); or a funerary chapel.

From the garden near the lantern, there is a fine **view** of the cathedral's east end and its different courtyards.

Take the alley across from the garden.

At the corner of the dead end (where the old rest-stop for post-horses can be seen) and Rue d'Albusse stands the **Hôtel de Génis (Z B)**, a massive, plain 15C building where the overhanging upper storey is supported by seven stone corbels.

Go down Rue d'Albusse and turn into Rue du Présidial.

Presidial (Présidial) (Y). – This building was the seat of the royal court of justice created in 1552 by Henri II.

Peer through the gate to get a glimpse of the 16C façade with its two large openings, one above the other, and the heavy stone slab *(lauzes)* roof. Note the odd octagonal lantern turret (added in the 17C), with a roof in the form of a bell and propped up by supports.

Turn around and go along Rue de la Salamandre.

Hôtel de Grézel (Y). – Built at the end of the 15C, the town house straight ahead has a half-timbered façade with a tower and a lovely Flamboyant Gothic ogee-arched doorway.

The skill and artistry of the carpenter and roofer can be admired by looking further down onto several of the roofs: the fine layout of the *lauze*, following perfectly the roof line down to where the roof widens and levels out (this is achieved by furring: thin strips of board are nailed under the roof line); this technique was used to compensate for the thickness of the walls.

Place de la Liberté (Y). – Animated by cafés, Sarlat's main square has on its east side the 17C **town hall** (Hôtel de Ville – **Y H**) and on its north side the old, secularised church of **Ste-Marie (Y D)**, the chancel of which has been destroyed and, therefore, has made a space which is used today as the stage set for the summer Sarlat Theatre Festival. Note the *lauze* roof of Ste-Marie and several of the nearby roofs which have small dormer-like windows; these small triangular openings were used for the airing of the attic. Behind the "set" and used as a backdrop is the **Hôtel de Gisson** (16C), made up of two buildings joined by a hexagonal staircaise tower with a remarkable pointed *lauze* roof.

★Place des Oies (Y). – Rightfully called Goose Square, this is the place where on Saturdays people from far and wide come to haggle over prices of geese and, of course, the delicious goose liver *(foie gras)*.

It is an elegant architectural ensemble of turrets, pinnacles and corner staircases.

★Rue des Consuls (Y 4). – The *hôtels* in this street exemplify beautifully Sarlat architecture from the 14-17C.

Hôtel de Vassal (Y). – Located on a corner of Place des Oies, this 15C *hôtel* has two buildings on a right angle flanked by a twin battlemented turret.

★Hôtel Plamon (Y). – As identified by the shield on the pediment above the doorway, this *hôtel* belonged to the Selves de Plamon family, members of the cloth merchants' guild. Because it is made up of a group of buildings built at different epochs, it is particularly interesting to observe the evolution of the different architectural styles used in Sarlat construction.

The 14C ground floor is opened by two large pointed arches, the first floor by three Gothic bays ornamented with Gothic Rayonnant tracery, and the second floor by 15C mullioned windows.

Left of the *hôtel* is the very narrow Plamon Tower with windows which as they go up in storey, recede in size; this architectural ruse tends to make the tower seem much longer than it is.

On the corner of the street is a rounded overhanging balcony supported by a squinch. Go into the courtyard to admire the elegant 17C wooden **staircase★**.

Turn around.

Ste-Marie Fountain (Fontaine Ste-Marie) (Y). – Standing opposite the Hôtel de Plamon, the fountain plays in a grotto.

Follow Rue Albéric-Cahuet. In a small square, take the vaulted passage on the left, which cuts through the Hôtel de Maleville.

★Hôtel de Maleville (Y). – This mansion is also known as the Hôtel de Vienne after the man who built it, Jean de Vienne. Born of humble parents in Sarlat in 1557, he successfully climbed the social ladder to become Financial Secretary under Henri IV. Later, the town house was bought by the Maleville family; a member of this same family, Jacques de Maleville *(p 72)*, helped write the *Code Civil.*

Three already existing and older houses were combined in the mid-16C to form a seignorial dwelling. The tall, narrow central pavilion, like a noble tower, is preceded by a terrace under which opens the arched main doorway surmounted by medallions depicting Henri IV and Marie de' Medici. It is flanked by a corbelled turret which joins it to the left wing.

The right wing, overlooking Place de la Liberté, has a gable which very much resembles one at La Boétie's House *(p 139)*, although it is in a later Renaissance style with its bays surrounded by small columns supporting entablature and pediment.

Passage Henri-de-Segogne (Z 21). – Between Hôtel de Maleville and La Boétie's House, this alleyway permits the visitor to amble under an arch, and passageways. Picturesque half-timbered buildings have been restored and, in summer, artisans can be seen selling their crafts.

ADDITIONAL SIGHTS

Western Section. – The area west of the "Traverse" is a maze of narrow, twisting, sloping alleys where certain houses are being restored, whereas in other cases demolition is the only solution.

Rue des Trois-Conils (des Trois Lapins) (Z 22). – This street turns sharply left at the foot of a house flanked by a tower, which once belonged to consuls.

Executioner's Tower (Tour du Bourreau) (Z). – This tower, which was part of the ramparts, was built in 1580.

Watch Tower (Tour du Guet) (Z). – Overlapping the buildings, the watch tower is crowned by 15C machicolations and flanked by a corbelled turret.

Rue Jean-Jacques Rousseau (Y). – In this mysterious quarter of convents and walled gardens, the battlemented turret at the corner of Rue de La Boétie marks the site of **Ste-Clare's Convent**, a vast 17C building at right angles.

Chapel of the White Penitents (Chapelle des Pénitents Blancs) (Y). – This 17C building, a former chapel, has a classical doorway surrounded by columns.

It now houses a **Museum of Sacred Art** (Musée d'Art Sacré). Most of the exhibits date from the 16 to 18C. There are several *Pietà* (a 17C one in the glass case), a 16C tabernacle in multicoloured wood, sections of magnificent wooden baroque retables and, in particular, a lovely statue of an Angel in Adoration.

★Museum-Aquarium (Musée-Aquarium). – *Access via Avenue Gambetta and ① on the town plan, then follow the signposts.*

This museum's aim is to explain the Dordogne River and everything related to it: fishing, fishing vessels, navigation, construction of dams, etc.

About thirty freshwater species from the region swim about in vast aquariums. Anadromous fish (Atlantic salmon, lamprey, shad) and freshwater species (pike, perch, barbel, bleak) can be seen side by side.

Fishing techniques are explained on panels and they are illustrated with displays of nets and a *gabare (qv)* (flat-bottomed boat). The most original of fishing techniques used was seining. An immense net was dropped; extending from one bank of the river to the other, catching a large quantity of migrating fish swimming up river to spawn. This type of fishing has practically disappeared due to the damming up of rivers.

A film shows the large-scale management measures used to attract the migrating fish in spite of the dams: collecting the fish, fishing ladders. Other audio-visual methods complete this fluvial display.

EXCURSIONS

Temniac. – *3km – 2 miles north. Description p 116.*

Puymartin Castle. – *9km – 5 1/2 miles northwest. Leave Sarlat by ④. Description p 124.*

The **Michelin Green Guide France**
presents a selection of the most interesting
and distinctive sights along the main tourist routes.

SORGES

Michelin map 📖 fold 6 or 📖 fold 43 – Facilities

Sorges, a pleasant town famous as a truffle market in the early 19C, is situated on the road from Périgueux to Limoges, near the valley of the Isle, as the plateaux rise gently from Périgord Blanc to Nontronnais.

Church (Église). – This Romanesque-domed building has a massive square bell tower with paired windows and a fine Renaissance doorway.

Truffle Centre (Maison de la Truffe). – Truffles are an important Périgord speciality. A museum, housed in the tourist information centre, features this product with the help of tables, maps, photographs, films and literary passages. *For more on truffles see pp 15 and 35.*
A walk to the truffle beds marked "A la découverte des Truffières" has been mapped out 2km – 1 mile from Sorges.

The practical information chapter,
at the end of the Guide, regroups
 - a list of the local or national organisations supplying additional information
 - a section on admission times and charges.

★ SOUILLAC

Michelin map 📖 fold 18 or 📖 fold 6 – Local maps pp 75, 76 and 91 – Facilities

Souillac, at the confluence of the Corrèze and the Dordogne, in the centre of a fertile region, the abundance of which contrasts with the poverty of the *causses (qv)* or limestone plateaux of Martel and Gramat, is a small town bustling with trade and tourists. It developed in the 13C, growing up around the abbey which was a dependency of the Benedictine Monastery at Aurillac; today, the town is crossed by the N 20.
When the Benedictines settled in the plain of Souillès – so-called after the local word *souilh*, meaning bog or marshland where wild boar wallow – they replaced the community established there previously by St Eligius. The monks drained the land continuously, transforming the marsh into a rich estate. Souillac Abbey was plundered and sacked several times by the English during the Hundred Years' War, but rose from its ruins each time through the tenacity of its abbots. Greater disasters, however, befell it during the Wars of Religion: in 1562 Protestant bands pillaged the monastery; ten years later the monastery buildings were set on fire and only the abbey church, protected by its domes, escaped the flames. The abbey was rebuilt in the 17C and attached to the Maurist Congregation, but is ceased to exist during the Revolution.

Former abbey church (Ancienne église abbatiale). – *Time: 1/2 hour.* Start from the Place de l'Abbaye, from where one can admire the beautiful Romanesque east end decorated with blind arcades and round arched bays.
Originally the abbey was dedicated to St Mary; now it takes the place of the former parish church destroyed during the Wars of Religion. Of the old parish church all that remains is a large damaged bell tower known as the Beffroi — The Belfry. The church was built at the end of the 12C and bears a resemblance to the Romanesque-Byzantine cathedrals of Périgueux, Angoulême and Cahors, but it is more advanced by the weightlessness of its pillars and the height of its large arches than the cathedral of Cahors, from which it was inspired.
The building has a wide main body surmounted by three deep domes resting on pendentives. To the left, in the first bay, stands a 16C polyptych painted on wood: the Mysteries of the Rosary; and in the second bay hangs a large canvas by Chassériau: *Christ on the Mount of Olives.*

★The back of the doorway. – There is mastery in the composition of this doorway made up of the remains of the old doorway, which was mutilated by the Protestants and was placed inside the nave of the new church, when it was erected in the 17C.
Above the door, framed by the statues of St Peter on the right and St Benedict on the left, is a low relief relating episodes in the life of the Monk
Theophilus, Deacon of Adana in Cilicia: a new abbot, misled by false reports, removes Theophilus from his office of treasurer of the monastery of Adana; Theophilus, out of resentment, signs a pact with the devil to regain his office (left). Repenting his sins, Theophilus implores forgiveness and prays to the Virgin Mary (right) who appears before him in his sleep, accompanied by St Michael and two angels who guard her; they bring him the pact he made with the devil and she shows how she has had his signature annulled and has obtained his pardon. The right engaged pillar, which was originally the central pillar of the doorway, is richly decorated. The right side depicts concupiscence during the various stages of one's life; on the main facet monstrous animals grip and devour one another. The left side announces the remission of sin by the sacrifice of Isaac. The hand of Abraham is held back by the messenger of God.
On either side of the door are fine low reliefs, in boldly decorative stances of the prophet Isaiah★★ (right), striking in its expression and the patriarch Joseph (left). Beneath the narthex is a crypt containing primitive sarcophagi.

Prophet Isaiah

★**Museum of Automata** (Musée de l'automate). – *Enter by the parvis of St-Pierre Abbey.*

⊙ The museum consists of some 3 000 objects, including 1 000 automata donated by the **Roullet-Decamps** family, who for four generations were leaders in the field. In 1865 Jean Roullet created his first mechanical toy: a small gardener pushing a wheel barrow. In 1909 he created the first Christmas window display for the Bon Marché department store.

The collection illustrates the evolution of this art from Antiquity to the present-day. These mechanical objects were considered precious enough to offer to nobility; they were also offered as sophisticated toys and used as publicity items...

Note especially the **Jazzband** (1920), an electric automata with black musicians performing a concert; or the lovely fairy-like **Snow Queen** (1956), after the tale by Hans-Christian Andersen. The large robot switches on and regulates the animation, light and sound of the automata.

★ LE THOT

Michelin map **75** south of fold 7 or **235** fold 2 – 7km – 4 miles south of Montignac – Local map p 146

⊙ Created in 1972, this **Centre of Research and of Prehistoric Art**, in a modern building of vast galleries, is set on Le Thot hill overlooking the Vézère Valley.

A film shows animals of the Palaeolithic era in their natural environment; and audio-visual presentation explains prehistoric art with examples from the caves of Niaux in Ariège, Altamira in Spain *(see Michelin Green Guide to Spain)*, Pech Merle in Lot *(qv)* and Lascaux *(qv)*.

Huge photographs and casts illustrate the diverse aspects of cave painting. A model situates the prehistoric period in the history of civilisations.

Panels explain the realisation of the Lascaux facsimilie *(p 106)* and a moulding reproduces the curious scene, in the small Well Gallery, of a bison charging a man, represented schematically, while a rhinoceros moves away.

From the terrace, which is a continuation of the centre, a lovely **view** can be had of the cultivated Vézère Valley countryside and the wooded Lascaux hill.

In the **park** live the animals – deer, wild sheep, horses similar to tarpans, European bison and Przewalski's horses – most often represented by prehistoric man.

TOURTOIRAC   Pop 756

Michelin map **75** fold 7 or **233** northwest of fold 44

This small market town, nestled in the greenery on the banks of the Auvézère, was the seat of a royal abbey in the 12C. The cemetery contains the tomb of an extraordinary character.

Orélie-Antoine I, King of Araucania and Patagonia. – Antoine Orélie de Tounens was born in Périgord in 1825. By 1858 he was practising as a lawyer in Périgueux, but was largely unknown. Suddenly he was seized by the ambition to live on a scale larger than life. He had become convinced that a bold man could subdue the backward tribes of South America and establish a powerful kingdom on the borders of Chile and Argentina. He borrowed a large sum of money and set sail for Chile, where he was greeted by the Indians as a liberator and in 1860 proclaimed himself King of Araucania under the title of Orélie-Antoine I. He raised an army and promulgated a constitution. Chile became distrustful of what was going on and caught and imprisoned the *Libertador*. The king, repatriated to France, did not lose heart but gathered funds for a second expedition. In 1869 he landed secretly in Patagonia. After fantastic adventures, he was once more repatriated. Two further attempts were equally unsuccessful and in 1878, at Tourtoirac, where he had retired, this comic opera character, who nearly gave France a kingdom, died.

⊙ **Abbey** (Abbaye). – These remains of this former Benedictine abbey, founded in the 11C, stand in the gardens of the presbytery. To the right, a small priory chapel with barrel vaulting and amphora-like objects set in the wall for the purpose of improving the acoustics, stands side by side with the monk's bread oven and the watchpath. Of the former trefoil-shaped abbey church, only the transept, surmounted by a powerful square bell tower, remains. The apse was destroyed during the Revolution. Note the fine capitals, carved at the beginning of the 12C, and the dome on pendentives. The much altered nave is now used for worship. The chapter house under the presbytery has been restored, revealing remarkable Romanesque twin capitals. It gives access to the cloisters' ruins.

Michelin Guides

The Red Guides (hotels and restaurants)

**Benelux - Deutschland - España Portugal - main cities EUROPE - France
Great Britain and Ireland - Italia**

The Green Guides (picturesque scenery, beautiful buildings and scenic routes)

**Austria - Canada - England: The West Country - France - Germany - Great Britain -
Greece - Italy - London - Mexico - Netherlands - New England - New York City -
Portugal - Rome - Scotland - Spain - Switzerland - Washington DC
and 10 Guides on France**

An old dictum stated that of Pompadour, Ventadour and Turenne, it was Turenne that reigned – such was the pride of this capital of the old viscounty, the houses of which form a picturesque crescent round the castle ruins.

HISTORICAL NOTES

The small town with a great past. – As early as the 11C, a fortress was set on the outlier of the Martel Causse. In the 15C, Turenne held sway over a third of Bas-Limousin, Haut-Quercy and the Sarladais or 1 200 villages and a number of abbeys. The viscounty, in its heyday, enjoyed enviable privileges: like the king of France, the viscounts ruled absolutely, ennobling subjects, creating offices and consulates, minting money and levying taxes.

The La Tour d'Auvergne-Turenne families. – The name Turenne became famous through the family of La Tour d'Auvergne. In the 16C, Henri de la Tour d'Auvergne was leader of the Limousin Huguenots and the most valiant supporter of the Reformation. As a reward for his zeal, Henri IV had him marry the heiress to the Duchy of Bouillon, Charlotte de la Marck; the Turennes then went to live in Sedan and administered their viscountcy, which remained sovereign, from afar. Charlotte died three years after her marriage, leaving the titles of Duke de Bouillon and Prince of Sedan to her husband Henri, who remarried Elizabeth of Nassau. His youngest son, also a Henri, will become the Great Turenne. His eldest son, who inherited the viscounty and title of Duke de Bouillon, participated in the Fronde (an aristocratic rebellion against Mazarin to which Turenne had associated himself in its beginnings – 1648); and in 1650 he set up a meeting between two supporters of the Fronde, the Princess of Condé and his son the Duke of Enghien. The meeting, celebrated with such pomp and magnificence, was baptised "Turenne's wild week" and in consequence the people of Turenne were taxed for two years to refill the impoverished accounts. This meeting helped bring the young Turenne back into favour with the Queen-Regent in 1652.

Henri de Turenne (1611-75), France's marshal-general was a brilliant military man who helped end the Thirty Years War due to his great skill during his campaign in Germany (1643-48) and who also played an important role (1652-53) in the suppression of the Fronde, preventing the young Louis XIV from being captured by the rebels. Louis XIV ordained that the Great Turenne be buried beside the French kings and Du Guesclin at St-Denis. Napoleon considered him the greatest soldier of modern times and had him moved to the Invalides in Paris in 1800 *(see Michelin Green Guide to Paris)*.

Happy were the people of the viscounty. – The inhabitants living in the reflected glory of their lord's prowess in battle, passed their days quietly within their small state and were envied since they suffered none of the tithes, which fell too heavily on other French peasants. This golden age had to end. In 1738, the last member of the La Tour d'Auvergne dynasty, the ninth viscount, sold the viscounty to Louis XV for 4 200 000 livres, ending the quasi-complete independence of this French state. Once united to the French kingdom, the taxes of the former viscounty were multiplied by ten!

TOUR *time: 1 1/2 hours*

Lower town. – At the foot of the hill is the Barry-bas Quarter, the old part of town. On **Place du Foirail**, the Hôtel Sclafer (**B**), with its loggia, was the notaries' residence in the 17C. Facing it is a small shop (15C) (**D**) pierced by a large arcade.

Rue du Commandant-Charollais goes into **Place de la Halle (8)**.

The town houses along this square show the wealth of its inhabitants, especially the **Vachon House**, the residence of the consuls of Turenne in the 16 and 17C.

Between two town houses, the narrow **Rue Droite** climbs towards the castle.

The street is lined with old houses with overhanging upper storeys and small shops.

Bear right on Rue Joseph-Rouveyrol and note the **House of the Old Chapter House**, the tower of which is ornamented with a lovely Flamboyant-Gothic-style doorway.

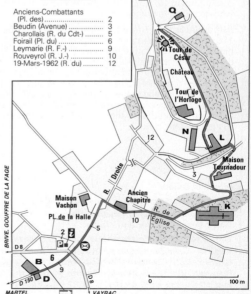

TURENNE

Church (Église) (K). – The construction of the church was decided upon by Charlotte de La Marck in 1593, the year Henri IV converted to Catholicism. After Charlotte's death, Elizabeth of Nassau took over the project; and yet it was consecrated only in 1668. In the form of a Greek cross, the church has an unusual ornamentation – a yellow and white mosaic forming a chevron pattern.

The 17 and 18C furnishings include stalls and a high altar surmounted by a carved and gilded wood altarpiece depicting the Passion of Christ. Later on, the *trompe l'œil* decoration between the twisted columns was added.

Just above the church, a vast building, the **Tournadour Mansion** was the town's former salt storehouse.

Upper town. – Access is through the **fortified gateway** of the second of the three curtain walls which protected the castle. On the right the Seneschal's House (**L**) has an elegant tower. On the left the **Capuchin's Chapel** (Chapelle des Capucins) (**N**) (1644) houses exhibitions.

Go round the castle from the right. A series of manor-houses, roofed with slate and flanked by squat towers have names which evoke their past purpose – the Gold Foundry (**Q**), for example.

Castle. – The castle was dismantled by the king once the viscounty was sold to the crown. Only the Clock and Caesar's Towers, at each end of the promontory, were spared. The **site★** is remarkable. Imagine this promontory covered by the castle, its outbuildings and chapel (behind the Clock Tower).

Clock Tower (Tour de l'Horloge). – The former keep's (13C) guard room with pointed barrel vaulting can be visited. Objects recalling Turenne's past are on display. Above it is the mint or treasury.

Caesar's Tower (Tour de César). – This round tower with irregular stone bonding seems to date from the 11C. A staircase goes up to the top, from where there is a great **panorama★★** of the region. In the foreground one looks down onto the village's slate roofs, in the distance, beyond a green and valleyed landscape appear the Monts du Cantal to the east and the Dordogne Valley directly southwards (viewing table).

Return to Place du Foirail by the fortified gateway and Rue Droite.

EXCURSION

★La Fage Chasm (Gouffre de la Fage). – *7km – 4 miles northwest. Local map p 56.*
The underground galleries form two separate groups, which can be visited successively. A staircase leads into the chasm which was created by the collapse of the roof section. The first group of chambers, to the left, have fine draperies in the form of jellyfish and display a great richness of colour. In the Organ Hall (Salle des Orgues), the concretions are played like a xylophone.

The second group, with many stalagmites and stalactites, also has a forest of needle-like forms hanging from the roof. In the last chamber excavations are underway to uncover bones from prehistoric times.

VAREN
Pop 909

Michelin map 🎟🎟 fold 19 or 🎟🎟🎟 southwest of fold 19 – 16km – 10 miles east of St-Antonin-Noble-Val – Local map p 130

The charming and picturesque old town of Varen stands on the north bank of the Aveyron, its houses clustered round the Romanesque church, which is protected by large-scale defences.

Enter the old part of town from the south.

The old fortified gateway, the Porte El-Faoure, leads to narrow streets lined by half-timbered and clay houses with overhanging upper storeys and flat roofs covered with round tiles.

Castle. – This is a massive keep topped by a machicolated watchpath and flanked by a corbelled turret. In this castle, the Lord-Prior of Varen shut himself up when he challenged the decisions of the Bishop of Rodez and wished to prove his complete independence. In 1553 the Council of Trent replaced the monks in the Benedictine priory by a more tractable college of 12 canons.

★St-Pierre. – The church, part of the town's defence, was built at the end of the 11C. Its west face was included in the perimeter wall – the side door was opened in 1758 and the present doorway was opened in 1802, when the moats were done away with. The former doorway, walled-up in the 16C, led to the old town via the east end; two archaic capitals still remain, representing St Michael slaying the dragon (left) and Samson opening the lion's jaws (right). A plain square bell tower rises above the flat chancel and two semicircular apsidal chapels. The north aisle supported by huge flying buttresses includes several bays.

The main part of the building is pure Romanesque in style and consists of a long nave of nine bays separated from the aisles by square pillars. The chancel and apsidal chapels are adorned with 17C stalls and interesting capitals with plant motifs, tracery, animals and cherubs surrounding the Tree of Life.

Looking for a pleasant hotel or camping site in peaceful surroundings?
*You couldn't do better than look in the current **Michelin Guides***
FRANCE *(Red Guide hotels and restaurants)*
and
CAMPING CARAVANING FRANCE

Michelin map 🆅🆃 folds 7 and 8 and 16 and 17 or 🅰🅱🅶 folds 215 and 26 and 🅱🅷🅶 folds 1, 2 and 5

This valley is a tourist route remarkable both for the beauty of the countryside it passes through and for its fascinating prehistoric sites, particularly around Montignac and Les Eyzies-de-Tayac, a region inhabited for approximately the past 100 000 years *(see notes on prehistory pp 18-21)*.

THE PÉRIGORD STRETCH OF THE VÉZÈRE

From Brive to Limeuil
108km – 67 miles – allow 1 day – local map below

Increased by the waters of the Corrèze, the Vézère, which came from the north, suddenly changes course and flows westwards to run through a typically Périgord countryside where willows, poplars and strangely hewn cliffs form a harmonious landscape.

Brive-la-Gaillarde. – *Description p 54.*

Leave Brive westwards.

The N 89 crosses the Brive Basin, the centre of market gardening and fruit growing, and joins the Vézère near St-Pantaléon.
Between Larche and Terrasson the road leaves the valley on the D 60, which climbs onto the plateau.

Chavagnac. – At the limit of the Corrèze *causse (qv)* and Périgord, this village is dominated by a powerful keep topped with corbels, the remains of a 13C castle. The 12C church has kept its dome.

The picturesque D 63 winds through walnut tree plantations. On the way down to Terrasson, notice vineyard-laden slopes.

Terrasson-la-Villedieu. – Pop 6 309. Terrasson, built beside the Vézère, has its old quarters rising in tiers up the side of a hill overlooking the left bank of the river, across from La Villedieu. It is a busy little town with a prosperous trade in truffles and walnuts.

The **church** was built in the upper part of the old town in the 15C and has undergone repeated restoration. The single aisle, transept and chancel have pointed vaulting.

From the terrace, on the north side of the church, one sees the site of Terrasson: on the left, the slate roofs of the houses of the upper town spill down the hillside to the Vézère, spanned by two bridges; in the distance beyond the part of the town built on the right bank, is the Périgord countryside with its characteristic lines of poplars, walnut plantations and rich arable land, slowly making room for houses.

The old bridge, Pont Vieux, was built in the 12C and is complete with cutwaters.

Between Terrasson-la-Villedieu and Condat, the road follows the valley floor before crossing to the right bank of the river. 3km – 2 miles after Condat, the river cuts through wooded slopes.

Montignac. – *Description p 110.*

★★**Lascaux II; Régourdou.** – *Description p 97.*

From Montignac to Les Eyzies, the road follows closely the course of the river, which is lined by magnificent poplars. This is the most attractive part of the valley.
From D 65, shortly after Montignac, the elegant outline of the Château de Losse towering above the Vézère can be seen between the trees.

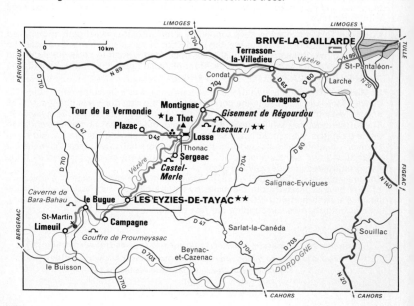

⊘**Château de Losse.** – This elegant 16C building stands in a verdant setting perched high on a rock above the right bank of the Vézère River. A terrace adorned with a balustrade, supported by a fine basket-handled arch, stands before the main building, which is flanked by a round tower at one corner. Inside, there are splendid furnishings (16C Italian cupboards and coffers, Louis XIII furniture) and especially **tapestries.** Note the fresh colours of the Flemish tapestry in the tower room and the Florentine tapestry depicting the *Return of the Courtesan* in the main chamber; both are 17C.

Sergeac. – Pop 138. This village is pleasantly situated beside the Vézère at a spot where tall cliffs line the valley.

The village of Sergeac, which has an interesting and delicately carved 15C cross standing at its entrance, also possesses old houses roofed with *lauzes* and a turreted manor-house, the remains of a commandery, which once belonged to the Order of St John of Jerusalem. The restored Romanesque **church**, despite its porch of fine ochre-coloured stone and recessed arches, still retains a fortified appearance with its loopholes, machicolations and bell tower. A rounded triumphal arch supported by twinned columns opens onto the chancel with a flat east end, which is adorned with archaically carved capitals.

Castel-Merle. – This site, which is well-known to the specialists, was for a long time closed to the public. Some of the finds – bones, flints, head-dresses – discovered are exhibited in the museums of Les Eyzies, St-Germain-en-Laye and Périgueux.

⊘Near the site, a small local **museum** exhibits a number of interesting artefacts from the Mousterian Age to the Gallo-Roman era. Note the handsome necklaces, found during the excavations, made of stone and bone beads, teeth and shells.

⊘Several **shelters** *(abris)* are visited, one of which contains wall sculptures (bison, horses) of the Magdalenian Age. In the Souquette shelter a section of strata is shown with the different levels from the Aurignacian Age to the modern era.

The said **Fort of the English**, upstream, is a fine shelter under rock, rearranged in the Middle Ages, entered by a staircase carved into the rock. This is an astounding example of a troglodyte dwelling with living quarters, stables... Its location enabled its inhabitants, who occupied it during troubled times, to watch the Vézère.

★**Le Thot.** – *Description p 143.*

La Vermondie Tower (Tour de la Vermondie). – This curious leaning tower, which, it is said, was demolished by the Saracens in 732, stands near a 15C manor-house, on a hillside overlooking the Vézère. A delightful legend tells how, long ago, a young prince was held prisoner in the tower; every day his fiancée passed below; moved by the young people's misfortune, the tower leaned so low one day that the couple was able to exchange kisses.

Plazac. – Pop 502. The Romanesque church, in the centre of a churchyard planted with cypress trees, stands on a hillock overlooking the village. The 12C belfry-keep is roofed with *lauzes* and embellished with blind arcades resting on Lombard bands.

> *Return to Thonac. For this section of the itinerary between Thonac and Les Eyzies-de-Tayac see pp 83 and 84 respectively the local map and text.*

After Thonac, the road affords repeated and most pleasant views of typical Périgord landscapes: a background of meadows, a line of poplars or willows mirrored in smooth waters and tall, eroded white and grey cliffs, spattered with scrub and evergreen oaks. These caves, in some cases hanging over the road, served as shelters for prehistoric man. Such scenery is often to be found south of St-Léon-sur-Vézère, as for instance at La Roque-St-Christophe, at Rusac and near Les Eyzies-de-Tayac, with castles and manor-houses adding a touch of elegance.

★**St-Léon-sur-Vézère.** – *Description p 136.*

★**St-Christophe Cliff.** – *Description p 86.*

Le Moustier. – *Description p 85.*

Tursac. – *Description p 86.*

★★**Les Eyzies-de-Tayac.** – *Description p 83.*

Beyond Les Eyzies, the valley widens, the slopes flatten, the crops interspersed with plantations of walnut trees become more frequent.

Campagne. – Pop 220. Facilities. At the opening of a small valley, stands the small Romanesque church preceded by a belfry.

The **castle** of the lords of Campagne, built in the 15C, was very much restored in the 19C. The towers, with their crenellations and machicolations flanking the living quarters and the Neo-Gothic elements, give the castle the appearance of an English manor-house. The last Marquis de Campagne gave the castle to the state in 1970.

Le Bugue. – *Description p 58.*

The D 703 in the direction of Bergerac and the D 31 towards Trémolat leads to the delightful country **Chapel of St-Martin** (Chapelle St-Martin), built at the end of the 12C.

Limeuil. – *Description p 78.*

---

*Drive through French towns using the plans in the **Michelin Red Guide France**.*
Features indicated include:
  - throughroutes and by-passes
  - new roads
  - car parks and one-way systems
All this information is revised annually.

Puy d'YSSANDON

Michelin map 75 west of fold 8 or 239 fold 25

The Puy d'Yssandon commands an extensive panorama since it stands in the centre of an undulating region where fertile fields and plantations of maize, tobacco, fruit and walnut trees alternate with pastures divided by quickset hedges and lines of poplars.

Access. – From the D 151 in the hamlet of La Prodelie take a steep road, the D 151ᴱ. After 2 km – 1 mile there is a first viewing table.

The remarkable **panorama★** includes, beyond the characteristic Dordogne landscape, the Limousin heights to the north, the Périgord hills to the west, the Brignac plain to the south with the Yssandon Tower in the foreground and, to the east, the mountains of Auvergne. Pass the ruined tower, that was once part of a massive 14C castle, which came under the control of the viscounts of Limoges, on the way to the top of the hill (alt 355m – 1 165ft) where many remains of the Gallo-Roman period have been found.

Leave the car in front of the church.

A wide path leads round the churchyard to a second viewing table, which gives details of the semicircular view over the Brive region.

Dordogne Valley at Belcastel

Practical
Information

BEFORE LEAVING

The **French Government Tourist Office** at 178 Piccadilly, London WIV OAL, ☎ (071) 499 69 11 (24-hour answering service with recorded message) and 610 Fifth Avenue, New York 10020-2452, ☎ (212) 757-1125 will provide information.

In the USA "France-On-Call" has been set up by the French Government Tourist Office; information on hotels, restaurants, transportation, etc can be obtained by dialling: 900-420-2003.

How to get there. – You can go directly by scheduled national airlines, by commercial and package-tour flights, possibly with a rail or coach link-up or you can go by cross-Channel ferry or hovercraft and on by car or train.

For railway information enquire at the French Railways, 179 Piccadilly, London WIV OBA; ☎ (071) 409 35 18.

Enquire at any good travel agent and remember, if you are going in the holiday season or at Christmas, Easter or Whitsun, to book well in advance.

CUSTOMS AND OTHER FORMALITIES

Papers and other documents. – A valid national **passport** (or in the case of the British a Visitor's Passport) is all that is required.

For the car you need a valid **driving licence, international driving permit, car registration papers** (logbook) and a **nationality plate** of the approved size. Insurance cover is compulsory and, although the International Insurance Certificate (Green Card) is no longer a legal requirement in France, it is the most effective proof of insurance cover and is internationally recognised by the police and other authorities.

There are no customs formalities for tourists bringing their caravans into France for a stay of less than 6 months. No customs document is necessary for pleasure boats or outboard motors for a stay of less than 6 months but the registration certificate should be kept on board.

Motoring regulations. – The minimum driving age is 18 years old. Certain motoring organisations run accident insurance and breakdown service schemes for their members. Enquire before leaving. A **red warning triangle** or hazard warning lights are obligatory in case of a breakdown.

It is compulsory for the front and back seat passengers to wear **seat belts**. Children under ten must be on the back seat.

The **speed limits**, although liable to modification are: motorways 130kph – 80mph (110kph – 68mph when raining); national trunk roads 110kph – 68mph; other roads 90kph – 56mph (80kph – 50mph when raining) and in towns of 50kph – 31mph. The regulation on speeding and drinking while driving are strictly interpreted – usually by an on-the-spot fine and/or confiscation of the vehicle. Remember to **cede priority** to vehicles entering from the right. There are tolls on the motorways.

Medical treatment. – For **British visitors** it is necessary to have Form E 111 which testifies to your entitlement to medical benefits in EEC countries from the Department of Health and Social Security. With this, medical treatment may be obtained in an emergency and after the necessary steps, a refund of part of the costs of treatment from the local social security offices (Caisse Primaire de l'Assurance Maladie). It is, however, still advisable to take out comprehensive insurance cover.

Nationals of non-EEC countries should make enquiries before leaving with your insurance company regarding policy limitations.

The bill for treatment in French hospitals or clinics must be settled by the person concerned. Reimbursement can then be negotiated with the insurance company according to the policy held. First aid, medical advice and night service rota are available from chemists (*pharmacie:* identified by a green cross).

Currency. – There are no currency restrictions on what you can take into France in the way of currency. To facilitate export of currency in foreign bank notes in excess of the given allocation, visitors are advised to complete a currency declaration form on arrival.

Your passport is necessary as identification when cashing cheques in banks. Commission charges vary, with hotels charging more than banks when "obliging" non-residents on holidays or at weekends.

Banks are open Mondays to Fridays from 9am to 4pm; some bank branches are open on Saturday mornings. Cash distributors, found near most banks, accept international credit cards.

Credit cards. – American Express, Carte Bleue (Visa/Barclaycard), Diners Club and Eurocard (Mastercard/Access) are widely accepted in shops, hotels and restaurants and petrol stations. In case of theft or loss report to affiliated bank and call collect to appropriate card company.

Customs. – Apply to the Customs Office for a leaflet on customs regulations and the full range of "duty free" allowances.

Make up your own itineraries
- *The map on pp 6-7 gives a general view of tourist regions,*
  the main towns, individual sights and recommended routes in the Guide.
- *The above are described under their own name in alphabetical order*
  (p 37) or are incorporated in the excursions radiating from a nearby town
  or tourist centre.
- *In addition the layout diagram on page 3 shows the **Michelin Maps** covering*
  the region.

DULY ARRIVED

Consulates. – **British** – 353 Boulevard du Président-Wilson, 33073 Bordeaux Cedex; ☎ 56 42 34 13.

American – 22 Cours du Maréchal Foch, Bordeaux, 33080; ☎ 56 52 65 95.

Embassies. – **British** – 35 Rue du Faubourg-St-Honoré, 75008 Paris; ☎ 42 66 91 42.

American – 2 Avenue Gabriel, 75008 Paris; ☎ 42 96 12 02.

Tourist Information Centres. – The **Michelin Red Guide France** gives the addresses and telephone numbers of the tourist information centres (*syndicats d'initiative*) identified by an 🛈 to be found in most large towns and many tourist resorts. They can supply large scale town plans, timetables and information on local entertainment facilities, sports and sightseeing.

The Regional Tourist Office — Comité Régional de Tourisme — publishes brochures for the various regions (*see below*).

Postal information. – **Poste Restante**: Name, Poste Restante, Poste Centrale, *département's* postal number followed by the town's name, France. The Michelin Red Guide France gives local postal code numbers.

Postal rates. – UK: letter – 2.30F; postcard – 2.10F

USA: aerogramme – 4.20F; letter (20g) – 3.80; postcard – 3.50F.

Telephone. – Public phones using pre-paid phone cards (50 or 120 units; *télécarte*) are in operation in many areas. Cards available from post offices, tobacconists and newsagents.

Electric current. – Mostly 220 volts. European circular two pin plugs are the rule so an adaptor may be necessary.

Public holidays. – National museums and art galleries are closed on Tuesdays.

The following are days when museums and other monuments may be closed or may vary their hours of admission:

New Year's Day	France's National Day **(14 July)**
Easter Sunday and Monday	Assumption **(15 August)**
May Day **(1 May)**	All Saint's Day **(1 November)**
V.E. Day **(8 May)**	Armistice Day **(11 November)**
Ascension Day	Christmas Day
Whit Sunday and Monday	

School holidays (two weeks) at Christmas, in winter (late February to mid-March) and spring; in summer from early July to early September; there is also a week long break in late October to early November.

USEFUL ADDRESSES

Dordogne Telegraph, a quarterly publication in English with articles on the area, can be bought locally.

Tourist information. – Listed below are the local, regional, *département...* tourist information centres and the Loisirs-Accueil (officially-backed booking service):

– **Maison du Périgord**: 30 Rue Louis-le-Grand, 75002 Paris; ☎ 47 42 01 78.
– **Comité Départemental du Tourisme de Corrèze**: Maison du Tourisme, Quai Baluze, 19000 Tulle; ☎ 55 26 46 88.
– **Loisirs-Accueil**: for address and telephone number see Comité Départemental above.
– **Office Départemental du Tourisme de la Dordogne**: 16 Rue Wilson, 24000 Périgueux; ☎ 53 53 44 35.
– **Loisirs-Accueil**: for address and telephone number see Comité Départemental above.
– **Comité Départemental du Tourisme du Lot**: Chambre de Commerce et d'Industrie, 107 Quai Cavaignac, BP 71, 46001 Cahors Cedex; ☎ 65 35 07 09.
– **Loisirs-Accueil**: 430 Avenue Jean-Jaurès, 46004 Cahors Cedex; ☎ 65 22 19 20.
– **Comité Départemental du Tourisme de Tarn-et-Garonne**: Hôtel des Intendants, Place du Maréchal-Foch, 82000 Montauban.
– **Loisirs-Accueil**: Place du Maréchal-Foch, 82000 Montauban; ☎ 63 63 31 40.

Accomodation. – **Michelin Red Guide France** (hotels and restaurants) and **Michelin Guide Camping Caravaning France** see p 10.

Country Houses and Châteaux. – Bed and breakfast offered in country houses and châteaux. For information and reservations: Agence E.T.I. — Engineering de Tourisme International, 15 Rue Foch, 46000 Cahors ☎ 65 22 22 32.

Rural accommodation. – Enquire at the Fédération Nationale des Gîtes de France, 35 Rue Godot-de-Mauroy, 75009 Paris; ☎ 47 42 20 20 which will give their local headquarters' address or 47 42 25 43 (answering machine).

In London: Gîtes de France, 178 Piccadilly, London WIV OAL; ☎ (071) 493-3480.

For **ramblers and trekkers** consult the guide: Gîtes et refuges en France by A. and S. Mouraret, Editions La Cadole, BP 303, 75723 Paris Cedex 15; ☎ 45 75 45 36.

Tourism for the handicapped. – Some of the sights described in this guide are accessible to handicapped people. They are listed in the publication "Touristes quand même! Promenades en France pour les voyageurs handicapés" produced by the Comité National Français de Liaison pour la Réadaptation des Handicapés (38 Boulevard Raspail, 75007 Paris). This booklet covers nearly 90 towns in France and provides a wealth of practical information for people who suffer from reduced mobility or visual impairment or are hard of hearing.

The **Michelin Red Guide France** and the **Michelin Camping Caravaning France** indicate rooms and facilities suitable for physically handicapped people.

OUTDOOR ACTIVITIES

Rambling. – The long-distance footpaths Topo Guides are edited by the Fédération française de la Randonnée pédestre: Comité national des sentiers de Grande Randonnée. To buy them enquire at the information centre, 64 Rue de Gergovie, 75014 Paris; ☎ 45 45 31 02. They give detailed maps of the paths and offer valuable information to the rambler. For local short-distance footpaths, enquire at the tourist information centres.

Canoe-kayak. – Canoes and kayaks may be hired along the rivers, in camping sites or sports clubs.
Apply to Fédération Française de Canoe-Kayak, 87 Quai de la Marne, 94340 Joinville-le-Pont; ☎ 48 89 39 86.
The larger organisations (listed below) offer excursions of several days:
– Excursions on the Dordogne and Lot Rivers: Safaraid, Albas, 46140 Luzech; ☎ 65 36 23 54; in season (15 June to 15 September) enquire at Camping Echo du Malpas, 19400 Argentat; ☎ 55 28 80 70.
– Excursion on the Vézère River ☎ 53 50 72 64.

Cruising. – Two publishers *(listed below)* produce guides to cruising on French canals. Both series include numerous maps and useful information and are provided with English translations:
– Navicarte, Éditions Cartographiques Maritimes; 7 Quai Gabriel-Péri, 94340 Joinville-le-Pont; ☎ 48 85 77 00.
– Guides Vagnon, Les éditions du plaisancier, 100 Avenue Général-Leclerc, 69641 Caluire-et-Cuire; ☎ 78 23 31 14.
Information is also available from the Loisirs-Accueil Lot *(see tourist information p 151)*.

Riding holidays. – For addresses of a **riding centre** near you apply to the Association départementale du tourisme équestre du Lot, BP 103, 46002 Cahors; ☎ 65 35 07 09. This organisation sells a map of the *département* at a scale 1: 200 000 on which the long-distance footpaths and riding paths are indicated.
Association de tourisme équestre de la Dordogne: Chambre d'agriculture, 4-6 Place Francheville, 24000 Périgueux; ☎ 53 09 26 26.

Horse-drawn caravans (roulotte). – Apply to the Office Départemental du Tourisme de la Dordogne; see tourist information above for address and telephone number.
Departure points are Issigeac (southeast of Bergerac) and Quinsac (north of Périgueux).
In the Lot apply to the Attelages de la Vallée du Lot, Domaine de la Taillade, Duravel, 46700 Puy-l'Évêque; ☎ 65 36 53 53.

Carriage rides (calèches). – Apply to the Office Départemental du Tourisme de la Dordogne; see tourist information above for address and telephone number.
– Attelages de la Vallée du Lot *(see horse-drawn caravans above)*
– Attelages de Bellemare, 46200 Lacave; ☎ 65 37 05 85.

Cycling holidays. – Bicycles may be hired in most towns at the railway station (Gare SNCF) — Bergerac, Le Bugue, Cahors, Gourdon, Gramat, Rocamadour-Padirac, Sarlat, Souillac; or apply to Safaraid, Albas, 46140 Luzech; ☎ 65 36 23 54.

Speleology. – In the Lot apply to the Comité Départemental de Spéléologie, M. Jean Robert Broqua, 46230 Bach; ☎ 65 31 70 81.

Angling. – Obey national and local laws; become a member (for the year in progress) of an affiliated fishing association in the *département* of your choice, pay the annual fishing tax. Map-brochure "Fishing France" (Pêche en France) published and distributed by the Conseil Supérieur de la Pêche 134 Avenue de Malakoff, 75016, Paris; ☎ 45 01 20 20.
For information apply:
– for Lot: Fédération départementale des associations agréées de pêche et de pisciculture, 182 Quai Cavaignac, 46000 Cahors; ☎ 65 35 50 22.
– for Dordogne: Fédération départementale de pêche, 2 Rue Antoine-Gadaud, 24000 Périgueux; ☎ 53 53 44 21.
– for Corrèze: Fédération départementale des associations agrées de pêche et de pisciculture, 1 Avenue Winston-Churchill, 19000 Tulle; ☎ 55 26 11 55.

Golfing. – For information on golfing enquire at the Fédération Française de Golf, 69 Avenue Victor-Hugo, 75016 Paris; ☎ 45 02 13 55; they have edited a map with France's golf courses (number of holes, addresses and telephone numbers).

Cooking holidays. – For information on the various holidays offered enquire at the local or departmental Loisirs Accueil *(see tourist information p 151)*.

Hunting. – For information on the various holidays offered enquire at the local or departmental Loisirs Accueil *(see tourist information p 151)*.

PRINCIPAL FESTIVALS

Early January

Brive-la-Gaillarde .... Fair of Kings (Truffle Fair)

Mid-June to mid-September

Beaulieu-en-Rouergue .... Contemporary Art Exhibit

July

Cahors .... Blues Festival
Rocamadour .... Art Festival (theatre, poetry)
Souillac .... Jazz Festival
A town in Dordogne .... *Félibrée (qv)* in Périgord

July and August

Aubazine .... Classical music concerts in abbey church
Bonaguil .... Music Festival
Brantôme .... Classical music concerts
Collonges-la-Rouge .... Town illuminated
Gourdon .... Summer Festival (concerts, theatre)
St-Amand-de-Coly .... Périgord Noir Music Festival
St-Léon-sur-Vézère .... Périgord Noir Music Festival
Turenne .... Classical music concerts

Mid-July to mid-August

Beaulieu-en-Rouergue .... Contemporary Music Festival
St-Céré .... Music Festival

3rd week in July

Montignac .... International folklore meetings

Weekend after 14 July

Brive-la-Gaillarde .... Festival of the *bourrée* Limousin (Limousin local dance)

End of July

Rouffignac .... Goose Fair (odd years)

End of July to early August

St-Robert .... Classical music concerts
Sarlat .... Drama Festival

August

Périgueux .... Pantomime Festival
In Quercy .... Quercy Blanc Festival
Rocamadour .... *Son et lumière*

1st weekend in August

Gourdon .... Medieval Fair

Mid-August

St-Amand-de-Coly .... Concert of hunting horns and mass held in honour of St Hubert

Week of 8 September

Rocamadour .... Pilgrimage

Early November

Brive-la-Gaillarde .... Book Fair

Winter

**Throughout Lot
and Périgord** .... *Foie Gras* market

ADMISSION TIMES AND CHARGES

Admission times and charges are liable to alteration without prior notice. Due to the fluctuations in the cost of living and the constant change in opening times, the information below is given only as general indication.

The information applies to individual adults and, whenever possible, children. However, special conditions regarding times and charges for parties are common and arrangements should be made in advance. In some cases admission is free on certain days, e.g. Wednesdays, Sundays or public holidays.

Churches, chapels, abbeys... do not admit visitors during services. Tourists should, therefore, refrain from visits when services are being held. Times are indicated if the interior is of special interest and the church, chapel... has unusual opening times. Visitors to chapels are often accompanied by the person who keeps the key. A donation is welcome.

Lecture tours are given regularly during the tourist season in Bergerac, Cahors, Domme, Périgueux, Rocamadour, St-Jean-de-Côle and Sarlat. Apply to the tourist information centre.

When guided tours are indicated, the departure time of the last tour of the morning or afternoon will be up to an hour before the actual closing time. Most tours are conducted by French-speaking guides but in some cases the term "guided tours" may cover group-visiting with recorded commentaries. Some of the larger and more frequented sights may offer guided tours in other languages. Enquire at the ticket office or book stall. Other aids for the foreign tourist are notes, pamphlets or audioguides.

When parking your car in unattended car parks or isolated sites please make sure to leave no valuables in your car.

Enquire at the tourist information centre for local religious holidays, market days, etc.

Every sight for which there are admission times and charges is indicated by the symbol ⊘ in the margin in the main part of the guide.

A

AGONAC

St-Martin. – Open July and August Tuesdays, Wednesdays, Thursdays and Fridays; the rest of the year apply to the parish priest.

LES ARQUES

Zadkine Museum. – Open 1 July to 30 September and during Easter and Christmas holidays 10.30am to 6pm; the rest of the year Saturdays and Sundays 2 to 6pm; 15F; ☎ 65 22 84 81 (caretaker).

St-André-des-Arques. – Apply at the Zadkine Museum *(see above)*.

ASSIER   🗓 Place de l'Église, 46320 ☎ 65 40 50 60

Castle. – Guided tours (time: 1/2 hour) 1 June to 30 September 10am to noon and 2.30 to 6.30pm; the rest of the year by appointment only; closed Tuesdays; ☎ 65 40 57 31.

AUBAZINE   🗓 19190 ☎ 55 27 25 25

Former Abbey. – Guided tours (time: 3/4 hour) 1 July to 30 September 3.15 and 4.30pm; Easter to 30 June 4pm; the rest of the year 4pm on Sundays and Mondays to Saturdays apply in advance 12F, children (under 10) free; ☎ 55 84 61 29.

B

BEAULIEU-EN-ROUERGUE

Abbey. – Guided tours (time: 1/2 hour) Easter to late September 10am to noon and 2 to 6pm; for an appointment out of season apply in writing two weeks in advance; closed Tuesdays and 1 May; 15F, children 5F; ☎ 63 67 06 84.

BERGERAC   🗓 97 Rue Neuve-d'Argenson, 24100 ☎ 53 57 03 11

Tobacco Museum. – Open 10am to noon and 2 to 6pm (5pm Saturdays); Sundays 2.30 to 6.30pm; closed Mondays and holidays; 10F; ☎ 53 63 04 13.

Museum of Urban History. – Open 10am to noon and 2 to 5.30pm; Sundays 2 to 6.30pm; closed all day Monday, Saturday afternoons and holidays; 13F; ☎ 53 57 80 92.

Recollects' Cloisters. – Guided tours (time: 1/2 hour) July and August 10.30 to 11.30am and 1.30 to 5.30pm; the rest of the year by appointment only; closed Saturdays, Sundays and holidays; 4F; ☎ 53 57 12 57.

Museum of Wine, River Boating and Cooperage. – Open 10am to noon and 2 to 5.30pm; Saturdays 10am to noon; Sundays 2.30 to 6.30pm; closed Mondays and holidays; 10F; ☎ 53 57 80 92.

Museum of Sacred Art. – Open daily during spring and summer holidays Tuesdays to Sundays 3.30 to 6pm; the rest of the year Wednesdays and Sundays 3.30 to 6pm; 7F; ☎ 53 57 33 21.

BEYNAC-ET-CAZENAC
🛈 24220 ☎ 53 29 50 75

Castle. – Guided tours (time: 1 hour) 1 April to 30 September 10am to noon and 2.30 to 6.30pm; 1 October to 15 November and March 10am to noon and 2.30 to dusk (tour given during daylight hours as there is no electricity); 24F, children 11F; ☎ 53 29 50 40.

Museum of Proto-History. – Open 15 June to 15 September 10am to 7pm; 15F; combined ticket to museum and park 25F, children 5F; ☎ 53 29 33 08.

Archaeological Park. – Same admission times and charges as the Museum of Proto-History *(see above)*.

BIRON CASTLE

Guided tours (time: 1 hour) 1 July to 7 September 9am to noon and 2 to 7pm; 8 September to 15 October 9.30am to noon and 2.30 to 6pm; 16 October to 15 December and 1 February to 31 March 10am to noon and 2 to 5pm; 1 April to 30 June 9.30am to noon and 2 to 6pm; closed Tuesdays and 16 December to 31 January; admission charge; ☎ 53 22 62 01.

BONAGUIL CASTLE

Guided tours (time: 1 1/2 hours) June to August 10 and 11am and 12 noon, 2, 3, 4 and 5pm; Palm Sunday to May and September 10.30am and 2.30, 3.30 and 4.30pm; 20F; ☎ 53 71 39 75.

LES BORIES CASTLE

Guided tours (time 1/2 hour) 1 July to 30 September 10am to noon and 2 to 7pm; the rest of the year by appointment only (1 week in advance); ☎ 53 06 00 01.

BOURDEILLES
🛈 Town Hall (Mairie), 24310 ☎ 53 05 73 13

Castle. – Guided tours (time: 3/4 hour) 1 July to 7 September 9am to noon and 2 to 7pm; 8 September to 15 October 9.30am to noon and 2 to 6pm; 16 October to 15 December and 1 February to 31 March 10am to noon and 2 to 5pm; 1 April to 30 June 9.30am to noon and 2 to 6pm; closed Tuesdays except 1 July to 7 September; 22F (18F out of season), children 8F (4F out of season); ☎ 53 03 73 36.

BRANTÔME
🛈 Pavillon Renaissance, 24310 ☎ 53 05 70 87

Bell Tower. – Guided tours (time: 1/2 hour) July and August only 9.30am to 12.30pm and 2 to 7pm; 10F; ☎ 53 05 80 63.

Conventual Building. – Guided tours (time: 35min) 1 July to 7 September 9am to noon and 2 to 7pm; 1 April to 30 June and 8 September to 15 October 9.30am to noon and 2 to 6pm; 16 October to 31 March 10am to noon and 2 to 5pm; closed Tuesdays except in July and August; 10F; ☎ 53 05 80 63.

Caves. – Same admission times as the conventual buildings *(see above)*; 5F.

Fernand Desmoulin Museum. – Same admission times as the conventual buildings *(see above)*; 5F.

Excursion

Château de Richemont. – Guided tours (time: 1/2 hour) 15 July to 31 August 10am to noon and 3 to 6pm; closed Sunday mornings and all day Friday; 10F, children 5F.

BRIVE-LA-GAILLARDE
🛈 Place du 14-Juillet, 19100 ☎ 55 24 08 80

St Martin Collegiate Church. – Open 9am to noon and 2 to 7pm; closed Sunday afternoons; ☎ 55 85 90 56.

Hôtel de Labenche. – Open 10am to 6.30pm (6pm 1 November to 31 March); closed Tuesdays; 20F; ☎ 55 24 57 54.

Edmond Michelet Centre. – Open 10am to noon and 2 to 6pm; closed Sundays and holidays; ☎ 55 74 06 08.

Excursion

Noailles: Church. — Apply to Mme. Grammond or M. Delmas for the key.

BRUNIQUEL
🛈 Town Hall (Mairie), 82800 ☎ 63 67 24 91

Castle. – Open July and August 10am to 12.30pm and 2 to 7pm; April, May and October Sundays, weekends and holiday weekends 10am to 12.30pm and 2 to 6pm; June and September Sundays and holidays 10am to 12.30pm and 2 to 6pm, Mondays to Saturdays 2 to 6pm; 7F, children 3F; ☎ 63 67 27 67.

LE BUGUE

Aquarium. – Open 1 July to 15 September 10am to 7pm; the rest of the year 10am to noon and 2 to 6pm; closed all day Monday and Tuesday mornings; 30F, children 20F.

Fossil Site. – Open July and August 10am to 7pm; mid-March to late June and early to mid-September 10am to noon and 2 to 7pm; the rest of the year 2 to 6pm; closed Sundays and Mondays; 15F, children 13F; ☎ 53 07 16 79.

Bara-Bahau Cave. – Guided tours (time: 35min) 14 July to 25 August 9.30am to 7pm; the rest of the year 10.30 to 11.30am and 3 to 5pm; closed 2 November to Palm Sunday; 20F, children (5-12 years) 10F; ☎ 53 07 27 47.

Excursion

Proumeyssac Chasm. – Guided tours (time: 3/4 hour) 14 July to 25 August 9.30am to 7pm; the rest of the year 9.30 to 11.30am and 3 to 5.30pm; closed 2 November to Palm Sunday; 26F, children (5-12years) 14F; ☎ 53 07 27 47.

The **Michelin Red Guide France** *revises annually its 550 town plans showing:*
 - throughroutes and by-passes,
 - new roads, car parks and one-way systems
 - the exact location of hotels, restaurants and public buildings.
With the help of all this updated information, take the harassment out of town driving.

C

CADOUIN

Cloisters. – Guided tours (time: 1/2 hour) 1 July to 7 September 9am to noon and 2 to 7pm; 8 September to 15 October 9.30am to noon and 2 to 6pm; 16 October to 15 December and 1 February to 31 March 10am to noon and 2 to 5pm; 1 April to 30 June 9.30am to noon and 2 to 6pm; closed Tuesdays (except 1 July to 7 September); 18F, children 8F; ☎ 53 22 06 53.

Pilgrimage Museum. – Same admission times and charges as the Cloisters *(see above)*.

CAHORS   🖪 Place Aristide-Briand, 46000 ☎ 65 35 09 56

Valentré Bridge. – Guided tours (time: 1/2 hour, including audio-visual presentation) July and August 10am to 12.30pm and 2.30 to 7pm; 10F, children (to 12 years) 5F; ☎ 65 35 09 56.

St Stephen's Cathedral. – Open Easter to 1 November 8.30am (10am Sundays) to 7pm (6pm the rest of the year); closed Sunday afternoons 1 November to Easter.

Chapel of St-Gausbert. – Open 1 July to 15 September 10am to 7pm.

Roaldès Mansion. – Open 15 June to 30 September, the week preceeding Easter and that of 1 May 10am to noon and 2 to 6pm; 15F, children (under 7) 5F.

St-Barthélemy. – Apply to the presbytery.

CAPDENAC   🖪 Town Hall (Mairie), 46100 ☎ 65 34 17 23

Keep: Museum. – Guided tours (time: 1/2 hour) 1 June to 30 September 9am to noon and 2.30 to 6.30pm; 7F; ☎ 65 34 17 23.

Roman Fountain. – Guided tours (time: 1/2 hour) 1 June to 30 September 8.30am to noon and 2.30 to 6.30pm; 7F; ☎ 65 34 17 23.

CARENNAC   🖪 Town Hall (Mairie), 46110 ☎ 65 38 48 36

Cloisters. – Open 1 July to 31 October 9am to 7pm; 6F.

CASTELNAU-BRETENOUX CASTLE

Castle. – Guided tours (time: 3/4 hour) 1 April to 30 September 9am to noon and 2 to 6pm; the rest of the year 10am to noon and 2 to 5pm; closed Tuesdays, 1 January, 1 May, 1 and 11 November and 25 December; 15F, children 5F; ☎ 65 38 52 04.

St Louis Collegiate Church. – Open July and August 9.30am to 7pm; September to October and April to June 10am to 6pm.

CASTELNAUD CASTLE

Open 1 May to 15 September 10am to 7pm (6pm 16 September to 15 November and Palm Sunday to 30 April); 20F, children (10-18 years) 10F; ☎ 53 29 57 08.

CÉLÉ VALLEY

Cuzals: Quercy Open-Air Museum. – Guided tours (time: 1 1/2 hours) June to September 10am (9.30am in June) to 7pm; April, May and October 10.30am and 3pm; closed Saturdays; 38F, children (9-16 years) 19F; ☎ 65 22 58 63.

CÉNEVIÈRES CASTLE

Guided tours (time: 1 hour) Easter to 1 November 10am to noon and 2 to 6pm; 17F, children 8F; ☎ 65 31 27 33.

CHANCELADE ABBEY

Conventual Buildings. – Open July and August 2 to 7pm; 10F; ☎ 53 04 86 87.

COUGNAC CAVES

Guided tours (time: 1 hour) July and August 9am to 6pm; September and October and Palm Sunday to 30 June 9.30 to 11am and 2.30 to 5pm; 20F, children (5-12 years) 10F; ☎ 65 41 18 02.

D

DOMME
🖪 Place de la Halle, 24250 ☎ 53 28 37 09

Towers' Gateway. – Guided tours (time: 20min) 15 June to 15 September 2 to 4pm; 20F, children 15F; ☎ 53 28 37 09.

Caves. – Guided tours (time: 1/2 hour) 16 June to 15 September 9.30am to noon and 2 to 7pm (6pm 1 April to 15 June and 16 September to 31 October); 18F, children (5-12 years) 9F; ☎ 53 28 37 09.

Museum of Popular Arts and Traditions. – Open July and August 10am to 12.30pm and 2 to 7pm; April, May, June and September 10am to noon and 3 to 6pm; 10F, children 5F; ☎ 53 28 37 09.

DORDOGNE VALLEY

Belcastel Castle. – To visit apply to the owners.

Château de la Treyne. – Guided tours (time: 1/2 hour) of the park, gardens and chapel June to September 10am to noon and 2 to 6pm; closed Mondays; 10F, children 5F; ☎ 65 32 66 66.

Cénac: Church. – Open Easter to 1 November 9am to 6.30pm; the rest of the year apply at the presbytery; ☎ 53 28 32 73.

Les Milandes Castle. – Guided tours (time: 40min) July and August 9.30 to 11.30am and 1 to 6.30pm; Palm Sunday to June and September 10 to 11.30am and 1 to 6pm; 20F, children 15F; ☎ 53 29 50 73.

Couze-et-St-Front: Larroque Mill. – Workshops open 9am to noon and 2 to 5pm; closed Saturdays, Sundays and holidays; 5F; ☎ 53 61 01 75.

DOUBLE

Vanxains: Church. – To visit apply to the town hall, which is open Mondays, Tuesdays, Thursdays and Fridays and Saturday mornings; closed Saturday afternoons and all day Sundays and August.

DRONNE VALLEY

Grand-Brassac: Fortified Church. – Apply to Mme. Lacour, in the house opposite the church.

La Chapelle-Faucher: Castle. – Guided tours (time: 3/4 hour) 15 June to 15 September 10am to noon and 2 to 7pm; 15F; ☎ 53 54 81 48.

E

ESPAGNAC-STE-EULALIE

Church. – Guided tours 10am to noon and 3 to 6pm; ☎ 65 40 00 69.

EXCIDEUIL
🖪 Place du Château, 24160 ☎ 53 62 95 56

Church. – Apply to Mme. de Genouillac, 2 rue Jean-Chanoix.

EYMET
🖪 Place de l'Église, 24500 ☎ 53 23 74 95

Keep: Museum. – Guided tours (time: 40min) mid-June to mid-September 3 to 6.30pm; 8F, children 4F; guided tours possible during Easter holidays, 1 and 8 May etc enquire in advance; ☎ 53 23 92 33 (during meal time).

LES EYZIES-DE-TAYAC

National Museum of Prehistory. – Open 15 March to 30 November 9.30am to noon and 2 to 6pm (5pm the rest of the year); closed Tuesdays, 25 December and 1 January; 10F, children 5F; ☎ 53 06 97 03.

Font-de-Gaume Cave. – Guided tours (time: 3/4 hour) 1 April to 30 September 9am to noon and 2 to 6pm; the rest of the year 10am to noon and 2 to 4pm (5pm October); closed Tuesdays, 1 January, 1 May, 1 and 11 November and 25 December; 24F, children 5F; ☎ 53 06 97 48.
In season number of visitors are limited: tickets ar sold only at 9am for the day.

ADMISSION TIMES AND CHARGES

Tayac Church. – Apply at the presbytery; ☎ 53 06 97 59.

Museum of Speleology. – Open 15 June to 15 September 10am to 6pm; closed Saturdays and 14 July; 10F, children 5F; ☎ 53 59 45 74.

Lower Laugerie Deposit. – Guided tours (time: 1 hour) 1 June to 30 September 10am to 6pm; closed Saturdays; 20F, children 18F; ☎ 53 06 97 12.

Upper Laugerie Deposit. – Guided tours (time: 3/4 hour) May to October at 5pm, closed Tuesdays; November to April at 3pm, closed Tuesdays and Fridays; closed 1 January, 1 May, 1 and 11 November and 25 December; 18F; ☎ 53 06 97 48.

Grand Roc Cave. – Guided tours (time: 1/2 hour) 1 July to 15 September 9am to 7pm; the rest of the year 9am to noon and 2 to 6pm; closed mid-November to mid-March; 27F; ☎ 53 06 96 76.

Carpe-Diem Cave. – Guided tours (time: 1/2 hour) July and August 9.30am to 6pm; the rest of the year 10am to noon and 2 to 6pm; closed mid-November to mid-March; 18F, children 9F; ☎ 53 06 91 07.

St-Cirq Cave. – Guided tours (time: 1/2 hour) July and August 10am to 6pm (3pm the rest of the year); 15F, children 5F; ☎ 53 07 14 37.

Le Moustier: Prehistoric Shelter. – Guided tours (time: 1/2 hour); apply to Mme. Roy, Auberge de Vimont, 24620 Peyzac-Le-Moustier (near the site).

St-Christophe Cliff. – Open 1 June to 15 September 9.30am to 6.30pm; the rest of the year 10am to noon and 2 to 6pm; closed mid-November to early March; 21F, children 11F; ☎ 53 50 70 45.

Prehistory Park. – Open 1 May to 30 September 9am to 7pm; the rest of the year 9am to noon and 2 to 6pm; closed 11 November to Palm Sunday; 20F, children 11F; ☎ 53 50 73 19.

Les Combarelles Cave. – Guided tours (time: 3/4 hour); same times and charges as the Font-de-Gaume Cave; closed Wednesdays, 1 January, 1 May, 1 and 11 November and 25 December; 24F, children 5F; ☎ 53 06 97 72.
In season number of visitors are limited: tickets are sold only at 9am and 2pm.

Bernifal Cave. – Open July and August 9.30am to 6pm; 1 April to June and September and October 9.30am to noon and 2 to 6pm; the rest of the year by appointment only; 20F; ☎ 53 29 66 39.

Cap-Blanc Shelter. – Guided tours (time: 1/2 hour) July and August 9.30am to 7pm; the rest of the year 10am to noon and 2 to 6pm; closed November to Easter; 17F, children 9F; ☎ 53 59 21 74.

La Grèze Cave. – Guided tours June to September; apply to Mme. Veyret at Marquay; ☎ 53 29 68 91.

Information in this Guide is based on tourist data provided at the time of going to press.
Improved facilities and changes in the cost of living make alterations inevitable: we hope our readers will bear with us.

F

FIGEAC 🛈 Mint (Hôtel de la Monnaie), Place Vival, 46100 ☎ 65 34 06 25

Mint: Museum. – Open 15 June to 15 September 10am to noon and 3 to 6pm; the rest of the year 2.30 to 5.30pm; closed Sundays and holidays except 14 July and 15 August; 6F, children 3F; ☎ 65 34 06 25.

Champollion Museum. – Open 2 May to 30 September 10 am to noon and 2.30 to 6.30pm; closed Mondays (except in July and August); 15F; ☎ 65 34 66 18.

FOISSAC CAVES

Guided tours (time: 1 hour) July and August 10 am to 6.30pm; 1-15 September and June 10 to 11.30am and 2 to 6pm; Easter to 31 May and 16 September to October Sundays and holidays 2 to 6pm; 23F, children 12F; ☎ 65 64 77 04.

G

GAVAUDUN

Keep. – Open March to December 9am to noon; 2F; guided tours (time: 1 to 1 1/2 hours) 3 to 6pm; 8F; ☎ 53 40 82 29.

Excursions

St-Sardos-de-Laurenque: Church. – For the key apply to the house near the church; ☎ 53 40 82 29.

Sauveterre-la-Lémance: Fortress. – Open in the summer; ☎ 53 40 67 17.

GOURDON
🅸 Allée de la République, 46300 ☎ 65 41 06 40

St-Pierre. – Apply at the presbytery.

Franciscan Church. – Apply at the tourist information centre; ☎ 65 41 06 40.

Excursions

Notre-Dame-des-Neiges Chapel. – Apply at the presbytery.

Le Vigan: Church. – Open July and August 10am to 12.30pm and 5 to 7.30pm; the rest of the year enquire at the town hall (☎ 65 41 12 46) or at the presbytery.

GRAMAT CAUSSE

Gramat Safari Park. – Open Easter to 1 November 9am to 7pm; the rest of the year 2 to 6pm; 26F, children 16F; ☎ 65 38 81 22.

Gramat: French Police Training Centre for Handlers and Dogs. – Open 2nd Thursday in June to 2nd Thursday in September and during school holidays (refer to Zone B: Toulouse Academy) Thursdays (except holiday Thursdays) 3.30 to 5pm; ☎ 65 38 71 59 extension 102.

Cougnaguet Mill. – Guided tours (time: 1/4 hour) 1 July to 31 August 9am to noon and 2 to 7pm; September and 1 April to 30 June (10am to noon and 2 to 6pm; 10F, children (6-12 years) 7F; ☎ 65 32 63 09.

Roussillon Castle. – Guided tours (time: 1 hour) 1 July to 25 August Wednesdays and Thursdays 2 to 5pm; the rest of the year by appointment only; 15F, children 10F; ☎ 65 36 87 05.

H

HAUTEFORT, CHÂTEAU DE
🅸 24390 ☎ 53 50 40 27

Guided tours (time: 3/4 hour) Palm Sunday to 20 November 9am to noon and 2 to 7pm (5pm November); 20F, children 10F; ☎ 53 50 51 23.

L'HERM CASTLE

Open 15 June to 30 September 10am to 7pm; closed Sunday mornings; 12F, children 6F; ☎ 53 05 46 61; out of season apply by telephoning (during meal time) 75 31 75 93.

L

LABASTIDE-MURAT

Murat Museum. – Guided tours (time: 1/2 hour) 10am to noon and 2.30 to 6.30pm; closed Tuesdays; 10F, children 7F.

Excursions

Soulomès: Church. – Open in summer 9am to 7pm.

LACAVES CAVES

Guided tours (time: 1 1/4 hours) 14 July to 25 August 9am to 7pm; the rest of the year 9am to noon and 2 to 6pm (5.30pm in October, 6.30pm June to 13 July); closed 16 October to spring term (around Easter) holidays; 26F, children 15F; ☎ 65 37 87 03.

LANQUAIS, CHÂTEAU DE

Open 1 April to 31 October 10am to noon and 2.30 to 6pm; closed Thursdays except holiday Thursdays; 20F, children 15F; ☎ 53 61 24 24.

LARAMIÈRE

Laramière Priory. – Guided tours (time: 1/2 hour) 1 May to 30 September 2.15 to 5.30pm; closed Tuesdays; 10F; out of season apply by telephoning; ☎ 65 45 36 91.

LARROQUE-TOIRAC CASTLE

Guided tours (time: 1/2 hour) 9 July to 9 September 10am to noon and 2 to 6pm; 15F, children (under 12 years) 7.50F.

LASCAUX CAVE
🅸 Place Bertran-de-Born, 24290 Montignac ☎ 53 51 82 60

Lascaux II. – Guided tours (time: 3/4 hour) July and August 9.30am to 7pm; the rest of the year 10am to noon and 2 to 5.30pm; closed Mondays (except in July and August) and January; 42F, children (5-12 years) 20F combined ticket with the Le Thot Centre of Research and of Prehistoric Art; ☎ 53 51 95 03.
In July and August it is recommended that you arrive at 9am under the arcades of the Montignac tourist information centre to obtain a ticket for the day because visitors are limited to 2 000 a day; the rest of the year tickets are sold on the site itself.

Régourdou. – Open 1 June to 31 August 9am to 6pm; 1 September to 11 November 9am to noon and 2 to 6pm; 12 November to 30 May 9.30am to noon and 2 to 6pm; 20F, children (under 12) free; ☎ 53 51 81 23.

LIZONNE VALLEY

Lusignac: Church. – For the key apply to Mme. Pervallet; ☎ 53 91 61 17.

Nanteuil-Auriac: Church. – If closed apply to the town hall; ☎ 53 91 05 04.

St-Paul-Lizonne: Church. – For the key apply at one of the houses near the church.

LOC DIEU ABBEY

Guided tours (time: 3/4 hour) 1 July to 10 September 10am to noon and 2 to 6.15pm; closed Tuesdays; 16F ☎ 65 29 51 18.

LOWER LOT VALLEY

St-Pierre-Toirac: Church. – Open Easter Sunday to 1 November 9am to 8pm.

Catus: Chapter House. – Open 8.30am to 8pm.

Grézels: Feudal Castle of La Coste. – Open 15 June to 30 September 2 to 7pm; guided tours (time: 1 1/2 hours) of the castle 5pm; exhibit: 15F, castle: 10F, combined ticket 20F; ☎ 65 21 34 18.

LUZECH
🚩 Town Hall (Mairie), 46140 ☎ 65 30 72 32

Armand Viré Archaeological Museum. – Open 15 May to 15 September 9.30am to noon and 3 to 7pm; ☎ 65 20 17 27.

*The **Michelin Green Guide France**,
an informative travel guide,
aims to make touring more enjoyable
by highlighting the country's
natural features, historic sites
and other outstanding attractions.*

M

LA MADELEINE SITE

Troglodyte Village. – Open 1 July to 7 September 9am to noon and 2 to 6.30pm; 8 September to 15 October 9.30am to noon and 2 to 6pm; 16 October to 30 November and March 10am to noon and 2 to 5pm; 1 April to 30 June 9.30am to noon and 2 to 5.30pm; closed Tuesdays (except 1 July to 7 September); ☎ 53 53 85 50.

MARCILHAC-SUR-CÉLÉ

Former Abbey. – Guided tours (time: 1/2 hour) 9am to noon and 2 to 7pm.

Bellevue Cave. – Guided tours (time: 40 min) July and August 9am to noon and 2 to 7pm; early September to late October and after spring school holidays Saturdays, Sundays and holidays 10am to noon and 2 to 6pm; during spring school holidays 10am to noon and 2 to 6pm; 20F, children 10F; ☎ 65 40 65 57.

MAREUIL
🚩 24340 ☎ 53 60 99 85

Castle. – Guided tours (time: 3/4 hour) 2.30 to 6.30pm; closed Saturdays and 2 November to 31 March; 16F, children (7-17 years) 9F; ☎ 53 60 91 35.

Excursion

La Rochebeaucourt-et-Argentine: Castle Park. – To visit apply to the pisciculture.

MARTEL
🚩 Palais de la Raymondie, 46600 ☎ 65 37 30 03

Hôtel de la Raymondie: Museum. – Open July and August; 4F; apply at the town hall; ☎ 65 37 30 03.

MONBAZILLAC, CHÂTEAU DE

Guided tours (time: 3/4 hour) 1 June to 30 September 10am to 12.30pm and 2 to 7.30pm; the rest of the year 10am to noon and 2 to 5pm (6pm in May); 16F, children 9F; ☎ 53 57 06 38.

MONTAL CASTLE

Guided tours (time: 3/4 hour) July and August 9.30am to noon and 2.30 to 7pm (6pm the rest of the year); closed Saturdays and 1 November to Friday before Palm Sunday; 17F, children (5-14 years) 8F; ☎ 65 38 13 72.

MONTIGNAC   🖪 Place Bertran-de-Born, 24290 ☎ 53 51 82 60

Eugène Le Roy Museum. – Guided tours (time: 3/4 hour) July to October and April to June 9.30am to noon and 2.30 to 6.30pm; the rest of the year 10am to noon and 2.30 to 5.30pm; closed Sundays (except in July and August) and holidays (except 14 July and 15 August); 7F, children 4F; ☎ 53 51 82 60.

MONTPEZAT-DE-QUERCY   🖪 Town Hall (Mairie), 82270 ☎ 63 02 07 04

Excursion

Saux: Church. – For the key apply at Montpezat-de-Quercy's town hall.

MUSSIDAN   🖪 9 Rue de la Libération, 24400 ☎ 53 81 04 77

Périgord's André Voulgre Museum of Popular Arts and Traditions. – Guided tours (time: 1 to 1 1/2 hours) 1 June to 15 September 9.30am to noon and 2 to 6pm; the rest of the year Saturdays, Sundays and holidays 2 to 6pm; closed 16 to 30 September and 1 December to 28 February; 10F; ☎ 53 81 23 55.

Excursions

Château de Montréal. – Guided tours (time: 35 min) 1 July to 30 September 10am to noon and 2.30 to 6.30pm; 20F, children 10F; ☎ 53 81 11 03.

Grignols Castle. – Guided tours (time: 3/4 hour) 15 June to 15 September 2 to 6.30pm; closed Wednesdays; 15F, children 10F.

P

PADIRAC CHASM

Chasm. – Guided tours (time: 1 1/2 hours) July 8.30am to noon and 2 to 6.30pm; August 8am to 7pm; April, May, June, September and October 9am to noon and 2 to 6pm; 30.50F; ☎ 65 33 64 56.

Tropicorama Zoo. – Open 15 May to 25 September 9am to 8pm; 25F, children 10F.

PARCOUL

Le Paradou Recreational Park. – Open 1 May to 30 September 9am to 11pm; ☎ 53 91 42 78.

PECH MERLE CAVE   🖪 46330 Cabrerets ☎ 65 31 27 12

Cave. – Guided tours (time: 1 hour) Palm Sunday to 1 November 9.30am to noon and 1.30 to 5.30pm (4.45pm October); combined ticket for the museum and cave 35F, children 19F; ☎ 65 31 27 05.
Arrive early number of visitors per day is limited.

Amédée Lemozi Museum. – Open Palm Sunday to 1 November 9.30am to noon and 1.30 to 5.30pm; 18F, combined ticket for the museum and cave 33F, children 17F; ☎ 65 31 27 05.

PÉRIGORD NOIR

Eyrignac Manor-House. – Guided tours (time: 3/4 hour) 1 July to 30 September 2.30 to 6.30pm; the rest of the year Sundays only 2.30 to 6.30pm or by applying in advance; closed 2 November to Easter; 25F, children 20F; ☎ 47 66 51 21 (Paris number).

PÉRIGUEUX   🖪 1 Avenue d'Aquitaine, 24000 ☎ 53 53 10 63

St-Étienne-de-la-Cité. – Open 8am to 7pm; 7am to 1pm Sundays.

St-Front Cathedral: Cloisters. – Apply to the priest Abbé Beaupuy; ☎ 53 53 23 62.

Mataguerre Tower. – Guided tours (time: 1/2 hour) July and August Tuesdays to Fridays at 10am as part of the Gallo-Roman Tour or 2.30pm as part of the Medieval-Renaissance Tour; 18F, children (6-12 years) 8F; for information enquire at the tourist information centre *(see 🖪 above)*.

Rue de la Sagesse: Lajoubertie House. – Same admission times as the Mataguerre Tower *(see 🖪 above)*.

Rue de la Constitution: Hôtel de Gamançon. – Not open to the public; only exterior visible.

"Villa" of Pompeïus. – Guided tours (time: 1 1/2 hours) July and August Tuesdays to Fridays at 2pm as part of the Gallo-Roman Tour; 14F; closed holidays; for information enquire at the tourist information centre *(see 🖪 above)*.

Vesunna's Tower. – Included in the Gallo-Roman Tour *(see above)*.

Périgord Museum. – Open 1 July to 30 September 10am to noon and 2 to 6pm (5pm the rest of the year); closed Tuesdays and holidays; 5F; ☎ 53 53 16 42.

Périgord Military Museum. – Open 1 June to 30 September 10am to noon and 2 to 6pm; the rest of the year 2 to 6pm; closed Sundays and holidays; 10F; ☎ 53 53 47 36.

PUYGUILHEM, CHÂTEAU DE

Open 1 July to 7 September 9am to noon and 2 to 7pm; 8 September to 15 October and 1 April to 30 June 9.30am to noon and 2 to 6pm; 16 October to 15 December and 1 February to 31 March 10am to noon and 2 to 5pm; closed 16 December to 31 January and Tuesdays (except 1 July to 7 September); 18F, children 8F; ☎ 53 54 82 18.

PUY-L'ÉVÊQUE
🚹 Rue Saint-Sauveur, 46700   ☎ 65 21 35 54

Church. – Open July and August 10am to noon and 4 to 6pm.

PUYMARTIN CASTLE

Guided tours (time: 3/4 hour) 1 April to 30 September 10am to noon and 2 to 6.30pm; 20F; ☎ 53 59 29 97.

R

ROCAMADOUR
🚹 Town Hall (Hôtel de Ville), 46500   ☎ 65 33 62 59

Town Hall. – Open 1 July to 31 August 10am to 8pm; 1 April to June and September to 15 November 10am to noon and 3 to 7pm, closed Wednesdays. 5F; ☎ 65 33 62 59.

Churches' Parvis. – Guided tours (time: 1 hour) June to September 9am to noon and 2 to 6pm; closed Sundays; 6F; ☎ 65 33 63 29.

Museum of Sacred Art (Francis-Poulenc). – Open Easter to 1 November 9am to noon and 2 to 5pm; 12F, children 8F; ☎ 65 33 63 29.

Ramparts. – Open 1 July to 31 August 9am to 7pm; the rest of the year 9am to 12.30pm and 2 to 6pm; closed 2 November to Saturday before Palm Sunday; 5.50F; ☎ 65 33 63 29.

Eagles' Rock. – Guided tours (time: 1 hour) Palm Sunday to 1 November 10am to noon and 2 to 7pm; 25F, children 12F; ☎ 65 33 65 45.

L'Hospitalet

Merveilles Cave. – Guided tours (time: 1/2 hour) 1 July to 31 August 9am to 12.30pm and 1.30 to 7pm; the rest of the year 10am to noon and 2 to 6pm; closed 3 November to the Saturday before Palm Sunday; 15F, children (6-12 years) 8F; ☎ 65 33 67 92.

Model Railway Exhibit. – Open July and August 9am to noon and 2 to 7pm, evenings 8.30 to 11pm; Palm Sunday to June and September and October 10am to noon and 2 to 6pm; 20F, children 10F; ☎ 65 33 71 06.

Butterfly Garden. – Open July and August 9am to 6.30pm; the rest of the year 10am to noon and 2 to 5.30pm; closed 15 October to 30 March; 22F, children 12F; ☎ 65 33 71 72.

Monkey Forest. – Open mid-June to August 9am to 7pm; the rest of the year 10am to noon and 2 to 6pm; closed 12 November to 31 March; 22F, children 11F; ☎ 65 33 62 72.

ROUFFIGNAC
🚹 24580   ☎ 53 05 41 71

Excursions

Rouffignac Cave. – Guided tours (time: 1 hour) 1 July to 15 September 9 to 11.30am and 2 to 6pm; the rest of the year 10 to 11.30am and 2 to 5pm; closed 1 November to Saturday before Palm Sunday; 21F, children 10F; ☎ 53 05 41 71.

La Douze: Church. – Apply at Épicerie Claude in the village or at the town hall in the morning.

S

ST-AMAND-DE-COLY

Church: Former Presbytery. – Slide show (time: 35min) July and August 10am to noon and 3 to 6pm; 10F.

ST-ANTONIN-NOBLE-VAL
🚹 Town Hall (Mairie), 82140   ☎ 63 30 63 47

Former Town Hall: Museum. – Open July and August 3 to 6.30pm; September, October, April and June Saturdays, Sundays and holidays 3 to 4pm; November to March Saturdays 3 to 4pm; closed Tuesdays and 1 January, 1 May and 25 December; 7.20F, Children (under 16 years) 2.10F; ☎ 63 30 63 47.

Excursions

Bosc Cave. – Open 14 July to 15 August 10am to 7pm; 1 to 13 July and 16 August to 31 August 10am to noon and 2 to 7pm; the rest of the year Sundays and holidays 2 to 6pm; closed last Sunday in September before Easter Sunday; 20F; ☎ 63 30 60 03.

Cas Castle. – Guided tours (time: 1 hour) July and August 10am to noon and 2 to 6pm; the rest of the year Saturdays and Sundays 10am to noon and 2 to 6pm; closed Mondays and late October to Easter; 18F, children 10F; ☎ 63 67 07 40.

ST-AVIT-SÉNIEUR

Church. – Temporarily closed for restoration.

Conventual Buildings: Geology Museum. – Guided tours (time: 1 hour) 1 July to 31 August 2 to 6pm; closed Mondays; 18F; ☎ 53 22 41 51.

ST-CÉRÉ
🖪 Place de la République, 46400 ☎ 65 38 11 85

Casino Gallery. – Open 9.30am to noon and 2 to 6.30pm; Sundays and holidays 11.30am to 12.30pm and 2.30 to 7pm; closed Tuesdays October to late June and 31 December and 1 January; ☎ 65 38 19 60.

St-Laurent Towers: Studio-Museum Jean Lurçat. – Open Easter holidays and 14 July to 30 September 9.30am to 12.30pm and 2.30 to 6.30pm; 15F; ☎ 65 38 28 21.

Haut-Quercy Automobile Museum. – Open Easter to September 10am to noon and 2 to 6pm; closed Tuesdays Easter to May; 20F, children 15F; ☎ 65 38 15 72.

Excursion

Presque Cave. – Guided tours (time: 1/2 hour) 1 July to 31 August 9am to noon and 2 to 7pm (6pm the rest of the year); closed 1st Sunday in October to school spring holidays; admission charge; ☎ 65 38 07 44.

ST-CIRQ-LAPOPIE

La Gardette Castle: Museum. – Open 1 July to 31 August 10am to noon and 2 to 7pm (6pm the rest of the year); closed November to March and Tuesdays April to June and September and October; 10F; ☎ 65 31 23 22.

ST-JEAN-DE-COLE
🖪 Town Hall (Mairie), 24800 ☎ 53 62 30 21

Marthonie Castle. – Guided tours (time: 1 hour) 1 July to 31 August 10am to noon and 2 to 7pm; 10F.

Excursion

Villars Caves. – Guided tours (time: 1/2 hour) 15 June to 15 September 10 to 11.30am and 2 to 6.30pm; 16F, children 10F; ☎ 53 54 82 36.

ST-MARTIN-DE-GURÇON

Church. – Open Sundays 9am to noon; ☎ 53 80 77 23.

ST-PRIVAT

Museum of Popular Arts and Traditions of the Dronne and Double Regions. – Open 1 June to 30 September 3 to 6pm; the rest of the year apply to the town hall; 10F, children 5F; ☎ 53 91 22 87.

SALIGNAC-EYVIGUES

Castle. – Guided tours (time: 1/2 hour) 15 June to 30 September 10am to noon and 2 to 6pm; closed Tuesdays; 20F.

SARLAT
🖪 Place de la Liberté, B.P. 114, 24203 Cedex ☎ 53 59 27 67

Chapel of the White Penitents: Museum of Sacred Art. – Open Easter to 15 October 10am to noon and 3 to 6pm; closed Sunday mornings; 10F.

Museum-Aquarium. – Open 15 June to 15 September 10am to 7pm; the rest ot the year 10am to noon and 2 to 6pm; 19F, children (under 12) 12F; ☎ 53 59 44 58.

SORGES
🖪 Truffle Centre (Maison de la Truffe), 24420 ☎ 53 05 90 11

Truffle Centre. – Open July and August 10am to noon and 2 to 6pm; the rest of the year 2 to 5pm; closed Tuesdays except July and August; 14F, children 7F; ☎ 53 05 90 11.

SOUILLAC
🖪 B.P. 99, 46200 ☎ 65 37 81 56

Museum of Automata. – Open July and August 10am to noon and 3 to 7pm; September, October, April, May and June 10am to noon and 3 to 6pm; the rest of the year 2 to 5pm; closed Mondays except in July and August, Tuesdays from November to March and holidays; 25F; ☎ 65 37 07 07.

T

LE THOT

🖪 Place Bertran-de-Born, 24290 Montignac ☎ 53 51 82 60

Centre of Research and of Prehistoric Art. – Open July and August 9.30am to 7.30pm; the rest of the year 10am to noon and 2 to 5pm; closed Mondays except in July and August and January; 18F, children 8F, combined ticket with the Lascaux Cave; ☎ 53 53 44 35.

In July and August it is recommended that you arrive at 9am under the arcades of the Montignac tourist information centre to obtain a ticket for the day because visitors are limited; the rest of the year tickets are sold on the site itself.

TOURTOIRAC

Abbey. – Open in summer 9am to 6pm; the rest of the year apply at the town hall.

TURENNE

🖪 19500 ☎ 55 85 94 38

Castle. – Open 1 April to 30 October 9am to noon and 2 to 7pm; 7F.

Excursion

La Fage Chasm. – Guided tours (time: 50min) 16 June to 15 September 9am to 7pm; the rest of the year 2 to 6.30pm; Sundays and holidays 10am to 6.30pm; closed 1 November to Palm Sunday; 18F, children 12F; ☎ 55 85 80 35.

V

VÉZÈRE VALLEY

Château de Losse. – Guided tours (time: 35min) 14 July to 23 August 10am to 6.30pm; the rest of the year 10am to 12.30pm and 2 to 6.30pm; closed the 3rd Monday in September to 29 June; 20F, children 9F; ☎ 53 50 70 38.

Castel-Merle: Museum. – Guided tours (time: 3/4 hour) 15 July to 30 August 10am to noon and 2 to 6pm; the rest of the year 2 to 6pm; closed Mondays and 16 September to 14 June; 10F; ☎ 53 50 77 45.

Shelters: guided tours (time 3/4 hour) 1 July to 31 August 10am to 6.30pm; the rest of the year 10am to noon and 2 to 5.30pm; closed Wednesdays except in July and August and 1 October to Easter; 16F, children 7F; ☎ 53 50 79 70.

INDEX

Cahors Lot......................... Towns, sights and tourist regions followed by the name of the *département* (for abbreviations see below).

Le Roy, Eugène................ People, historical events and subjects.

Isolated sights (caves, castles, château, abbeys, dams...) are listed under their proper name.

L.-et-G. **Lot-et-Garonne**..... *Départements* where abbreviations have been used.
T.-et-G. **Tarn-et-Garonne** .